Resistance to Love in Medieval English Romance

Studies in Medieval Romance

ISSN 1479-9308

General Editor
Corinne Saunders

This series aims to provide a forum for critical studies of the medieval romance, a genre which plays a crucial role in literary history, clearly reveals medieval secular concerns, and raises complex questions regarding social structures, human relationships, and the psyche. Its scope extends from the early middle ages into the Renaissance period, and although its main focus is on English literature, comparative studies are welcomed.

Proposals or queries should be sent in the first instance to one of the addresses given below; all submissions will receive prompt and informed consideration.

Professor Corinne Saunders, Department of English, University of Durham, Durham, DH1 3AY

Boydell & Brewer Limited, PO Box 9, Woodbridge, Suffolk, IP12 3DF

Resistance to Love in Medieval English Romance

Negotiating Consent, Gender, and Desire

HANNAH PIERCY

D. S. BREWER
Published with the support of the Swiss National Science Foundation

First published 2023
D. S. Brewer, Cambridge

ISBN 978 1 84384 672 7

D. S. Brewer is an imprint of Boydell & Brewer Ltd
PO Box 9, Woodbridge, Suffolk, IP12 3DF, UK
and of Boydell & Brewer Inc.
668 Mt Hope Avenue, Rochester, NY 14620–2731, USA
website: www.boydellandbrewer.com

A CIP catalogue record for this book is available
from the British Library

The publisher has no responsibility for the continued existence or accuracy
of URLs for external or third-party internet websites referred to in this book,
and does not guarantee that any content on such websites is, or will remain,
accurate or appropriate

Please note that some of the discussion in this book addresses
sensitive issues including sexual violence

This publication is printed on acid-free paper

For Mum and Dad

Contents

Acknowledgements

I am hugely grateful to everyone who has helped me complete this book by offering support in any way. Thanks to all those who generously read drafts of this material and provided helpful feedback, especially Corinne Saunders, Carolyne Larrington, Venetia Bridges, Annette Kern-Stähler, Kirsty Bolton, Jane Bonsall, Lucy Brookes, Olivia Colquitt, Hope Doherty-Harrison, Rachel Fennell, Curtis Runstedler, Tess Wingard, and the anonymous reviewers for Boydell & Brewer. My work has been greatly improved by your suggestions and any remaining errors are, of course, my own. Thanks to my patient and encouraging editors, Caroline Palmer and Elizabeth McDonald – working with you has been a pleasure and a privilege. I am especially thankful for Caroline's detailed attention to the manuscript in its final stages and dedicated work for the open access funding application. I am also grateful to everyone who offered help with book proposals, especially Mary Bateman, Daisy Black, Amy Burge, Amy Louise Morgan, and Laura Varnam. My sincere thanks to the Swiss National Science Foundation, which funded the Open Access publication of this book – I am delighted to have this opportunity to make my work freely available. Further open access funding was provided by the University of Bern and swissuniversities.

Conversations with Corinne Saunders and Elizabeth Archibald shaped this project at an early stage; I am very grateful for their support and encouragement. My colleagues at the University of Bern also offered helpful advice and feedback: particular thanks to Annette Kern-Stähler again for all of your support with this project, and to A. E. Brown, Matthias Berger, and Nicole Nyffenegger for useful discussions. I have been fortunate to work at two wonderful institutions during the course of this project, and I would like to thank everyone in the Department of English Studies at Durham University and the Department of English at the University of Bern, especially the Medieval Studies section. I would also like to thank my students at these institutions, for always keeping me motivated to ask new and exciting questions. Funding from the Northern Bridge Consortium (Arts and Humanities Research Council) enabled me to undertake a PhD; without this support, pursuing an academic career and writing this book would not have been possible.

I have presented work in progress for this project at various conferences. I am especially grateful to the organisers and attendees of the Gender and Medieval Studies conferences from 2017–22, the Medieval Insular Romance conferences in Cardiff 2018 and Durham 2022, and everyone involved with panels on romance at Leeds International Medieval Congress in 2018 and 2019. I have found a welcoming and supportive academic community at these events. In addition to those already mentioned, I would like to thank Lucy Allen-Goss, Anum Dada, Lucy Hinnie, Alicia Spencer-Hall, Lucy Stone, Usha Vishnuvajjala, and Maria Zygogianni for academic kindness, solidarity, and most importantly friendship. Thanks to the #RemoteRetreat community for their support and encouragement while I was writing this book. I am also grateful to the contributors to *Reconsidering Consent and Coercion in Medieval Literature*, and my wonderful co-editor, Jane Bonsall, for keeping me excited about the topic of medieval consent and for their collegiality and collaborative spirit.

Thanks for practical assistance go to Abbie Garrington and the team at Durham Research Office. Thanks for much-needed distractions from work go to the Psych group chat (AKA Grey College MCR), the Keswick girls' WhatsApp, and other friends around the world. You know who you are and I value your friendship dearly.

Finally, a huge thanks to the Piercys, Morris/Grange/Moores, and Nansons. To Mum and Dad: thank you for believing in me and cheering me on with whatever I decide to do, while also reminding me that it is okay if it doesn't work out. This book is dedicated to you in a small token of my gratitude, but I am more grateful than words (even all of these words!) can say. Thanks to my brother, Jon, for your friendship and encouragement. Thanks to Lyra, the best feline companion anyone could ask for. And finally to Ryan, who knows more about *Blanchardyn and Eglantine* than most people in medieval studies, and whose patience and encouragement I am forever grateful for. Thank you for helping me chase my dreams and for all of our adventures together.

Abbreviations

EEBO	Early English Books Online
EETS	Early English Text Society
e. s.	Extra Series
FRETS	French of England Translation Series
IAFOR	International Academic Forum
JIAS	*Journal of the International Arthurian Society*
n. s.	New Series
OED	*Oxford English Dictionary*
ÖNB	Österreichische Nationalbibliothek
o. s.	Original Series
PC	Pillet and Carstens: bibliographic numbers assigned by Alfred Pillet and Henry Carstens to identify troubadour poems
PMLA	*Publications of the Modern Language Association of America*
s. s.	Supplementary Series
TEAMS	Teaching Association for Medieval Studies

A note on citation practices:

French prose romances that are divided into chapters are cited by page numbers, with chapter numbers given in parentheses immediately after.

Introduction

A t the beginning of the romance of *Amadas et Ydoine*, the hero is mocking-ly nicknamed 'le fin amoureus' ['the Perfect Lover'] for his lack of inter-est in love.[1] The eponymous protagonist of *Sir Degrevant* initially lives 'as an anker' [anchorite], refusing to consider taking a wife or lover.[2] Felice in *Guy of Warwick* rejects all suitors, no matter their status, while Eglantine in William Caxton's *Blanchardyn and Eglantine* is referred to as 'the proude lady in loue' for her refusal to consider marriage.[3] While these romance protagonists reject love and marriage in general, others resist particular relationships because of concerns about differences of status, race, and/or faith. Horn tells Rymenhild that she ought not to love him because of their apparent status disparity, Bevis initially rejects Josian because of her Muslim faith, and Custance is unwilling to marry the Sultan of Syria despite his conversion to Christianity. Moments like these recur throughout the corpus of medieval English romance, but they have not previously received extensive consideration. This book asks: what happens if we take these moments seriously as expressions of resistance to love? Though individual examples are often briefly represented and swiftly overcome, they have a greater cumulative effect, forming a motif that threads through the wider romance corpus. Resistance to love can work in opposition to other romances' emphasis on ideal, freely given love, on social mobility through marriage, and on romantic attraction as the motivator of religious conversion. This motif recurs across the chronology and variety of medie-val English romance, from twelfth-century Anglo-Norman *lais* to fifteenth-century prose works, from romances written for courtly and royal readers to

---

[1] *Amadas et Ydoine: roman du XIIIe siècle*, ed. by John R. Reinhard, Classiques français du moyen âge, 51 (Paris: Champion, 1926), line 98; *Amadas and Ydoine*, ed. & trans. by Ross G. Arthur, Garland Library of Medieval Literature, Series B, 95 (New York: Garland, 1993), p. 22.

[2] *The Romance of Sir Degrevant*, ed. by L. F. Casson, EETS, o. s., 221 (London: Oxford University Press, 1949; repr. 1970), Cambridge University Library, MS Ff.1.6 (the Fin-dern manuscript), line 63.

[3] William Caxton, *Blanchardyn and Eglantine, c. 1489*, ed. by Leon Kellner, EETS, e. s., 58 (Oxford: Oxford University Press, 1890), for example in the table of contents, p. 3, but this is also the most common name by which she is referred to within the romance.

gentry romances and works widely circulated in early print, and from Arthurian works to hagiographical romances. Its prevalence suggests that it was a useful device for romance writers and their readers and that we ought to attend to the uses it serves, including the ways in which it reinforces or subverts contemporary cultural constructions of consent, gender, and desire.[4]

I use 'resistance to love' as an umbrella term that encompasses active refusal to love or marry; indifference; resistance to loving or marrying a particular person because of factors like their social status, race, or religion; rejections of adultery; and also what we might identify today as asexuality, aromanticism, or sometimes other queer sexual orientations.[5] As this breadth indicates, 'resistance to love' encompasses rejections of romantic relationships, but also of marriage and sex. Middle English romances tend to conflate love, sex, and marriage, because they focus on love as a constitutive element in marriage and usually depict sexual relationships primarily within matrimony. There are, therefore, relatively few scenarios in which resistance to love does not also entail resistance to sex, though sex with one person can be rejected while romantic commitment to another is upheld. Chapter 5 deals specifically with situations in which adulterous sex is rejected in order to maintain fidelity to a prior romantic commitment, but even there the person who issues a proposition usually presents it as a request for love rather than sex. Sex, love, and marriage can and should be treated distinctly in some cases, but Middle English romance frequently collapses these categories and so 'resistance to love' often stands in for 'resistance to love, marriage, and sex' in this book.

My focus on 'resistance' is intended to align with other recent work attending to sexual and gendered violence in medieval literature; to point to the potentially subversive nature of resistance to love as a questioning of or challenge to romance's normative trajectory; and to anticipate the discussion of resistance as a reading practice.[6] I do also use other terms, including 'un-

---

[4] When I use the term 'reader(s)', I include people who came into contact with romance literature in any form, whether oral or written.

[5] In keeping with current usage, I deploy 'queer' as a general term encompassing a range of LGBTQ+ sexualities and genders, including asexuality and aromanticism, in line with Eve Kosofsky Sedgwick's now-classic definition of queer as referring to 'the open mesh of possibilities, gaps, overlaps, dissonances and resonances, lapses and excesses of meaning when the constituent elements of anyone's gender, of anyone's sexuality aren't made (or *can't* be made) to signify monolithically': *Tendencies* (London: Routledge, 1994), p. 7. I recognise, however, that individual preferences on terminology differ.

[6] For example, *Rape Culture and Female Resistance in Late Medieval Literature*, ed. by Sarah Baechle, Carissa M. Harris, and Elizaveta Strakhov (University Park: Pennsylvania State University Press, 2022); Sara V. Torres and Rebecca F. McNamara, 'Female Consent and Affective Resistance in Romance: Medieval Pedagogy and #MeToo', *New Chaucer Studies: Pedagogy and Profession*, 2.1 (2021), 34–49; Boyda Johnstone, '"Far semed her hart from obeysaunce": Strategies of Resistance in *The Isle of Ladies*',

willingness to love' where the will and wilfulness are particularly at issue. The will held an important place in scholastic discussions of consent and innocence, and takes on a prominent role in secular writing, such as the works of Geoffrey Chaucer.[7] But I also draw on modern work on the will, particularly Sara Ahmed's discussion of how 'the judgement of willfulness derives from a social scene: how some have their will judged as a problem by others', and how it is particularly 'parts that are not willing the preservation of the whole [that] are charged with willfulness, including nonproductive and nonreproductive parts'.[8] This resonates with the portrayal of resistance or unwillingness to love, which can involve a rejection of socially and sexually reproductive roles. However, 'resistance to love' remains the overarching term used throughout this book to bring together a variety of individual manifestations and explore the sum of their parts.

Because of the extensive and varied nature of this motif, this book cannot be comprehensive. I leave out resistance to love because of age difference; rejections of lesbian, gay, or other kinds of queer relationships; and resistance to incest.[9] While the latter would sit uneasily within the framework of resistance to love because of its associations with violence and abuse, I leave out resistance on the grounds of age or queerness because this tends to serve more

---

Studies in the Age of Chaucer, 41 (2019), 301–24. The term 'resisting reader' was coined by feminist literary critic Judith Fetterley in *The Resisting Reader: A Feminist Approach to American Fiction* (Bloomington: Indiana University Press, 1978). It has been applied to medieval romances: see Helen Cooper, *The English Romance in Time: Transforming motifs from Geoffrey of Monmouth to the death of Shakespeare* (Oxford: Oxford University Press, 2004), p. 226; Susan Crane, *Gender and Romance in Chaucer's 'Canterbury Tales'* (Princeton: Princeton University Press, 1994), p. 111; Roberta L. Krueger, *Women Readers and the Ideology of Gender in Old French Verse Romance* (Cambridge: Cambridge University Press, 1993).

[7] For example, in the works of St Augustine of Hippo, including *De civitate Dei. The City of God*, trans. by George E. McCracken, Loeb Classical Library, 411, 7 vols (Cambridge, MA: Harvard University Press, 1957), I, I. 16–19; *De libero arbitrio*, ed. by William Green, Corpus christianorum series latina, 29 (Turnhout: Brepols, 1970). For discussions of Chaucer's varied explorations of the will, see Jill Mann, 'Chance and Destiny in *Troilus and Criseyde* and the *Knight's Tale*', in *Life in Words: Essays on Chaucer, the Gawain-Poet, and Malory*, ed. by Mark David Rasmussen (Toronto: University of Toronto Press, 2014), pp. 42–61; Elizabeth Robertson, 'Apprehending the Divine and Choosing To Believe: Voluntarist Free Will in Chaucer's *Second Nun's Tale*', *Chaucer Review*, 46.1–2 (2011), 111–30; Mark Miller, *Philosophical Chaucer: Love, Sex, and Agency in the 'Canterbury Tales'* (Cambridge: Cambridge University Press, 2004).

[8] Sara Ahmed, *Willful Subjects* (Durham, NC: Duke University Press, 2014), pp. 19, 20.

[9] These forms of resistance do appear within romance writing. Resistance because of age occurs in *Le Bone Florence of Rome*, Chaucer's *Merchant's Tale*, and arguably *The Wife of Bath's Tale*; resistance to incest appears in *Emaré* and John Gower's 'Tale of Apollonius of Tyre'. An explicit rejection of a queer relationship features in the French *Roman de Silence*.

simplistic ideological functions. Age is not open to negotiation and debate (though of course attitudes to it are), unlike the social constructs of gender, status, race, and faith on which I focus. Explicit rejections of queer relationships are unusual in Middle English romance, perhaps because its focus on love and sexuality within marriage leads to queer desires being represented more rarely and subtly.[10] Where this does occur, it tends to serve homophobic and transphobic purposes: even in the *Roman de Silence*, a work that interrogates binary perceptions of gender through its portrayal of Silence, Silence's rejection of the Queen operates in a homophobic manner that also seems to re-impose binary gender. In addition, I do not discuss characters who simply do not fall in love in romance literature, of whom there are a good many, though they are not usually the central protagonist. Instead, I focus on active expressions of resistance or indifference to love. This departs from the broader romance trope of love as so overpowering that experiencing it is almost by definition against one's will.[11] This trope is clearly connected to what I call resistance to love and it offers valuable insights into how medieval people understood the emotions and psychology of love in their own terms; it also at times intersects with resistance to love when it is weaponised as a means to convince a reluctant partner of the suitor's helplessness. However, active resistance or absolute indifference hold different implications for understanding romance as a genre, because they offer an opportunity to either question or reinforce its normative trajectory towards love and marriage.

This book explores why romance characters resist love, both in terms of the reasons romances provide for such resistance and the functions this resistance serves on a narrative level. I attend to the implications for understanding medieval sexualities and how relationships were actively negotiated in romance writing and real life. This focus on negotiation aligns with contemporary reconsiderations of how we talk about sex and rape in the modern world,[12] connected to the recognition of the 'narrow parameters' and 'conceptual thinness' of consent as a term that has been collapsed into other, meaningful different, ways of talking about sexual practices.[13] I do frequently use the term consent

---

[10] For discussion of the subtle ways in which lesbian desires may be represented in Middle English romances, see Lucy M. Allen-Goss, *Female Desire in Chaucer's 'Legend of Good Women' and Middle English Romance* (Cambridge: D. S. Brewer, 2020).

[11] Cooper describes the sense of loss of agency as fundamental to romance's heroic conception of love: *The English Romance in Time*, pp. 230–1.

[12] Rebecca Kukla, 'That's What She Said: The Language of Sexual Negotiation', *Ethics*, 129.1 (2018), 70–97; Michelle J. Anderson, 'Negotiating Sex', *Southern California Law Review*, 78.6 (2005), 1401–38.

[13] Amia Srinivasan, *The Right to Sex* (London: Bloomsbury, 2021), p. xiii; Joseph J. Fischel, *Screw Consent: A Better Politics of Sexual Justice* (Oakland: University of California Press, 2019), p. 4. See further Katherine Angel, *Tomorrow Sex Will Be Good Again: Women and Desire in the Age of Consent* (London: Verso, 2021); Quill R. Kukla, 'A Nonideal Theory of Sexual Consent', *Ethics*, 131.2 (2021), 270–92.

(and coercion) in this book: while recognising that consent is an inadequate concept for ethical sexual conduct, its limitations reflect its use in the medieval period, where it was largely considered a granting of permission or assent by one person to another. Consent is, therefore, a useful framework for medieval scholarship, as 'the historical sources themselves speak to and about consent', but I supplement it with a focus on negotiation to highlight the active exchanges and influences that could affect the decision to consent (or not) to a particular relationship.[14]

Continuing this focus on exchange and influence, I investigate how resistance is received and interpreted by other characters and the narrator within a romance, revealing how these intradiegetic responses reflect contemporary social categories and perceptions of different kinds of relationships. I use an intersectional approach, attending to how romance not only makes love and marriage desirable goals but presents particular kinds of love and marriage as desirable and in doing so discriminates in overlapping ways along axes of race, status, and gender.[15] I also track the usual, though not inevitable, development of resistance into love. This pattern can be a consensual one, involving the immediate and unexpected experience of love at first sight, which indicates love's ability to overcome willed determination to avoid it. It can also involve a process of active negotiation, a deliberation of the terms on which a relationship might be acceptable or advantageous, particularly when social status or religious conversion is at stake. Such moments of negotiation are particularly valuable because they offer insights into medieval expectations as to how relationships might develop and the factors that influence this. As A. E. Brown notes, medieval representations of the borders between friendship and romantic love are rare, and the lack of distinction drawn between types of love can make it difficult to tell at precisely what point a friendship might moderate into the pull of romantic or sexual attraction.[16] As Brown also observes, this is not a problem exclusive to medieval literature, as we still struggle to find the terms with which to frame different kinds of affection today.[17] While the

---

[14] Lucia Akard and Alice Raw, 'Global Response: Futures of Medieval Consent', *Studies in the Age of Chaucer*, 44 (2022), 'Colloquium: Historicizing Consent: Bodies, Wills, Desires', ed. by Carissa M. Harris and Fiona Somerset, 363–7 (p. 364).

[15] Kimberlé Crenshaw first used the term intersectionality to explore how race and gender overlap as layers of discrimination in the experiences of Black women. Intersectional approaches respond to 'the need to account for multiple grounds of identity when considering how the social world is constructed', including those of race, gender, class, and sexuality. See Kimberlé Crenshaw, 'Mapping the Margins: Intersectionality, Identity Politics, and Violence against Women of Color', *Stanford Law Review*, 43.6 (1991), 1241–99 (p. 1245).

[16] A. E. Brown, 'Lancelot in the Friend Zone: Strategies for Offering and Limiting Affection in the *Stanzaic Morte Arthur*', in *Emotion and Medieval Textual Media*, ed. by Mary C. Flannery (Turnhout: Brepols, 2018), pp. 75–97 (p. 76).

[17] *Ibid.*, pp. 85–6.

5

examples I discuss are mostly positioned as potential romantic relationships within their generic contexts, points of negotiation may nonetheless provide insights into how relationships develop into new categories, offering different perspectives to portrayals of love at first sight. In contrast to the models of both negotiation and spontaneous desire, transformations from resistance to acceptance can also be coercive, at the extreme involving sexual violence, psychological manipulation, or even magic to enforce love. Rape itself is not usually a means by which unwillingness becomes acceptance, as romances tend to preserve an illusion of consent, combining portrayals of sexual violence with a focus on the affects of love, for example.[18] But the romances discussed in this book demonstrate that a certain level of force – sometimes moderating into pressure or persuasion – is acceptable within the genre, and at times even endorse this as a means of punishment or subjugation for someone who considered themselves above love and marriage.

Portrayals of resistance to love in romance literature, and the various ways in which it is or is not rewritten as desire, therefore offer an opportunity to reassess the genre's relationship to sexual violence, coercion, and consent. While previous discussions have focused most often on the contrasting extremes of representations of rape and *raptus* versus free consent to love, resistance to love illuminates more diverse and subtle coercive practices.[19] Amy Vines has argued that we need to consider coercion and sexual violence in medieval literature more broadly, 'reading all sexual misconduct, from the innocent yet unwanted kiss to the more overt acts of forced coitus' to reveal

---

[18] Corinne Saunders argues that 'the lady may be gained through force, but not force enacted against her person': 'A Matter of Consent: Middle English Romance and the Law of *Raptus*', in *Medieval Women and the Law*, ed. by Noël James Menuge (Woodbridge: Boydell Press, 2000), pp. 105–24 (p. 116).

[19] Kathryn Gravdal, 'The Poetics of Rape Law: Chrétien de Troyes's Arthurian Romance', in *Ravishing Maidens: Writing Rape in Medieval French Literature and Law* (Philadelphia: University of Pennsylvania Press, 1991), pp. 42–71; Saunders, 'A Matter of Consent'; Corinne Saunders, *Rape and Ravishment in the Literature of Medieval England* (Cambridge: D. S. Brewer, 2001), pp. 187–264, 283–310; Amy N. Vines, 'Invisible Woman: Rape as a Chivalric Necessity in Medieval Romance', in *Sexual Culture in the Literature of Medieval Britain*, ed. by Amanda Hopkins, Robert Allen Rouse, and Cory James Rushton (Cambridge: D. S. Brewer, 2014), pp. 161–80. For a focus on mutual consent, see Helen Cooper, 'Desirable desire: "I am wholly given over unto thee"', in *The English Romance in Time*, pp. 218–68. While not primarily focused on romance, see also Baechle, Harris, and Strakhov, *Rape Culture and Female Resistance*; Carissa M. Harris, *Obscene Pedagogies: Transgressive Talk and Sexual Education in Late Medieval Britain* (Ithaca: Cornell University Press, 2018); Suzanne M. Edwards, *The Afterlives of Rape in Medieval English Literature* (Basingstoke: Palgrave Macmillan, 2016); *Teaching Rape in the Medieval Literature Classroom: Approaches to Difficult Texts*, ed. by Alison Gulley (Leeds: Arc Humanities Press, 2018); *Representing Rape in Medieval and Early Modern Literature*, ed. by Elizabeth Robertson and Christine M. Rose (New York: Palgrave, 2001).

'the fundamental place of male sexual aggression in the implicit expectations of medieval chivalric behaviour'.[20] Coercive responses to resistance to love can uncover diverse manifestations of male sexual aggression, but can also go beyond the aims Vines outlines, exposing forms of coercion and pressure that are perpetrated upon, as well as by, men. Complementing and adding to previous work on rape and consent, I seek to uncover a wider and more nuanced picture of sexual violence, gendered constraints, and coercive practices, in keeping with the focus on 'the problems posed by consent' in the recent *Studies in the Age of Chaucer* colloquium 'Historicizing Consent'.[21] I argue in particular that imaginative literature enabled discussion of coercive practices that fall outside of the medieval legal category of *raptus*, facilitating recognition of such practices *as* coercive.

This book, then, uses the motif of resistance to love to expose how romance constructs normative models of consent, gender, and desire, as well as to probe the tensions and limitations of these constructions. On the simplest level, its aim is to uncover the widespread use of resistance to love as a motif within medieval English romance. Following Helen Cooper's field-changing book *The English Romance in Time*, motif studies have become a well-established approach to Middle English romance in particular, which is the primary focus of this book. Motif studies offer a means of acknowledging the disparate textual connections of Middle English romances, connections which have traditionally been difficult to account for because of the formulaic nature of romance, the sporadic survival of Middle English romances and uncertainties about their transmission, and the widespread medieval practice of borrowing without citation.[22] I do not argue for direct lines of influence between individual romances but pursue connections between different kinds of works by tracing the recurrence and adaptation of resistance to love through romance's generic diversity. Liz Herbert McAvoy's use of Nicholas Royle's and Hélène Cixous's writing on textual haunting, the idea of widespread but shadowy networks of influence, provides a helpful model here.[23] McAvoy

---

[20] Vines, 'Invisible Woman', p. 180.

[21] 'Colloquium: Historicizing Consent: Bodies, Wills, Desires', ed. by Carissa M. Harris and Fiona Somerset, *Studies in the Age of Chaucer*, 44 (2022), 267–367.

[22] Megan G. Leitch's discussion of romance intertextuality is helpful here: 'Introduction, Middle English Romance: The Motifs and the Critics', in *Romance Rewritten: The Evolution of Middle English Romance, A Tribute to Helen Cooper*, ed. by Elizabeth Archibald, Megan G. Leitch, and Corinne Saunders (Cambridge: D. S. Brewer, 2018), pp. 1–24.

[23] Liz Herbert McAvoy, 'Textual Phantoms and Spectral Presences: The Coming to Rest of Mechthild of Hackeborn's Writing in the Late Middle Ages', in *Women's Literary Cultures in the Global Middle Ages: Speaking Internationally*, ed. by Kathryn Loveridge, Liz Herbert McAvoy, Sue Niebrzydowski, and Vicki Kay Price (Cambridge: D. S. Brewer, 2023), pp. 209–24. McAvoy draws on Nicholas Royle, *The Uncanny* (Manchester: Manchester University Press, 2008) and Hélène Cixous, 'Fiction and Its

uses textual haunting to investigate the previously overlooked influence of medieval women's devotional writing; her work offers a suggestive proto-type for the way motifs recurring across apparently unconnected romances can reveal a broader nexus of generic relationships spanning canonical and non-canonical romances. As well as tracing the development and variation of this motif within romance, I examine its implications for understanding con-temporaneous views of consent, gender, and desire. To establish the particular functions of resistance to love in medieval English romance, and especially its subversive or conservative potential, the remainder of this Introduction first places it in the context of contemporary cultural and literary discourses.

Cultural Contexts

Consent: Marriage Practices and Raptus *Law*

Medieval concepts of consent were situated within two different discourses: the definition of marriage in canon law and the legal concept of *raptus*. In theory, marriage had been dependent on consent from the time of the Church fathers. However, this was not established in canon law until the 1130s, under the influence of Gratian, Peter Lombard, and Pope Alexander III.[24] By the end of the twelfth century, following the decretal Alexander III issued c. 1180, there was widespread understanding that marriage was formalised upon the exchange of words of mutual consent in the present tense. If consent was for-mulated in the future tense, a marriage became binding once consummated.[25] Marriage should, but did not have to, take place in a church; witnesses were necessary for a marriage to be upheld in a church court but not to sanctify marriage before God.[26] In theory, this gave priority solely to the consent of the individuals being married.[27] The use of 'force and fear' to coerce people into marriage was expressly forbidden, offering an important backdrop against which to consider romance depictions of coercion.[28] In practice, however, things were more complicated: familial interests, wealth, and political power probably continued to have as much, if not more, influence than individual

---

Phantoms: A Reading of Freud's *Das Unheimliche* (The "uncanny")', trans. by Robert Dennomé, *New Literary History*, 7.3 (1976), 525–48.

[24] For a good summary of medieval marital practices, see Elisabeth van Houts, *Married Life in the Middle Ages, 900–1300* (Oxford: Oxford University Press, 2019), pp. 1–25.

[25] See van Houts, *Married Life*, pp. 1–3, 7–9; Cathy Hume, *Chaucer and the Cultures of Love and Marriage* (Cambridge: D. S. Brewer, 2012), p. 7; Shannon McSheffrey, *Marriage, Sex, and Civic Culture in Late Medieval London* (Philadelphia: University of Pennsylvania Press, 2006), p. 22.

[26] McSheffrey, *Marriage, Sex, and Civic Culture*, pp. 21–2.

[27] See further Conor McCarthy, *Marriage in Medieval England: Law, Literature and Practice* (Woodbridge: Boydell Press, 2004), p. 19.

[28] *Ibid.*, pp. 24, 27–8.

consent upon the marriages of the middle and upper classes,[29] the primary audiences for the romances I discuss.[30] For these groups, consent, as many scholars have pointed out, may have been not so much a matter of free choice as a question of whether you accepted your family's will.[31] While canon law upheld the idea of individual, freely given consent, in practice marital arrangements were embedded in wider networks of human agency. At times this may have resulted in coerced marriages, but in other ways this focus on negotiating consent with regard for different concerns and agencies partially echoes contemporary work that challenges the association of consent with what it sees as the illusion of individual autonomy in the modern world.[32]

The establishment of consent as a principle within canon law affected contemporary marriage patterns and expectations. Marriages increasingly took

---

[29] See further Hume, *Chaucer and the Cultures of Love and Marriage*, pp. 12–16; Ruth Mazo Karras, *Sexuality in Medieval Europe: Doing Unto Others*, 2nd edn (London: Routledge, 2012), p. 146; McSheffrey, *Marriage, Sex, and Civic Culture*, pp. 17–18; McCarthy, *Marriage in Medieval England*, p. 44; *Women of the English Nobility and Gentry, 1066–1500*, ed. & trans. by Jennifer Ward (Manchester: Manchester University Press, 1995), p. 15.

[30] Middle English romances have been associated with gentry and urban middle-class readers (as well as some aristocrats, especially in connection with Arthurian romances), although they could have reached lower-class groups, including household servants, through reading aloud. See Michael Johnston, *Romance and the Gentry in Late Medieval England* (Oxford: Oxford University Press, 2014); Amy N. Vines, *Women's Power in Late Medieval Romance* (Cambridge: D. S. Brewer, 2011), pp. 8–10; Melissa Furrow, *Expectations of Romance: The Reception of a Genre in Medieval England* (Cambridge: D. S. Brewer, 2009); Felicity Riddy, 'Middle English romance: family, marriage, intimacy', in *The Cambridge Companion to Medieval Romance*, ed. by Roberta L. Krueger (Cambridge: Cambridge University Press, 2000), pp. 235–52 (pp. 235–9); Carol M. Meale, '"gode men / Wiues maydnes and alle men": Romance and Its Audiences', in *Readings in Medieval English Romance*, ed. by Carol M. Meale (Cambridge: D. S. Brewer, 1994), pp. 209–25; Susan Crane, *Insular Romance: Politics, Faith, and Culture in Anglo-Norman and Middle English Literature* (Berkeley: University of California Press, 1986); Bart Besamusca, 'Readership and Audience', in *Handbook of Arthurian Romance: King Arthur's Court in Medieval European Literature*, ed. by Leah Tether and Johnny McFadyen (Berlin: de Gruyter, 2017), pp. 117–32; Michael Johnston, 'New Evidence for the Social Reach of "Popular Romance": The Books of Household Servants', *Viator*, 43.2 (2012), 303–31; Ad Putter, 'Middle English Romances and the Oral Tradition', in *Medieval Oral Literature*, ed. by Karl Reichl (Berlin: de Gruyter, 2012), pp. 335–51; Karl Reichl, 'Orality and Performance', in *A Companion to Medieval Popular Romance*, ed. by Raluca L. Radulescu and Cory James Rushton (Cambridge: D. S. Brewer, 2009), pp. 132–49; Ad Putter, 'A Historical Introduction', in *The Spirit of Medieval English Popular Romance*, ed. by Ad Putter and Jane Gilbert (London: Routledge, 2013; first publ. 2000), pp. 1–15 (p. 8).

[31] Hume, *Chaucer and the Cultures of Love and Marriage*, p. 6; Saunders, *Rape and Ravishment*, p. 21. For a fuller discussion of the influence of family and friends on late medieval marriages, see McSheffrey, *Marriage, Sex, and Civic Culture*, pp. 74–109.

[32] See Kukla, 'A Nonideal Theory of Sexual Consent'.

place between people of a similar age, although amongst royalty there could still be a significant age gap, with young women (in their early to mid-teens) marrying much older men.[33] The age of consent was twelve for girls, fourteen for boys, though children could be betrothed before this.[34] In addition to age, broad parity in social standing was essential. There was room for intermarriage between the closest classes, such as the aristocracy and gentry, or the gentry and the urban elite later in the period,[35] but 'all levels of society adhered to the social (and ideal) norm that its young people were best married as "equals", that is of the same social rank'.[36] Age and status parity aligned with the increasing expectation that love would develop within marriage – that is, rather than marrying *for* love the emphasis was on the '*potential* for love', as Shannon McSheffrey puts it.[37] Late medieval secular society seems to have expected and accepted marriage as a social norm,[38] and to have encouraged and desired love within it, a development perhaps arising from the indissolubility of marriage.[39]

This is not to say that marriage was *the* dominant, celebrated pattern within medieval English society. Although marriage was a sacrament, the church still primarily viewed it as a compromise and not an ideal. Ruth Mazo Karras weighs up the secular and religious perspectives, suggesting:

> Perhaps it would be wrong to call marriage the norm for medieval people, since many ecclesiastical writers saw marital sex as a necessary evil, but it was certainly the expectation for most. That does not mean that heterosexual desire was a good thing, or even the default condition against which other desires were set; it was 'concupiscence,' the result of Eve's and Adam's disobedience.[40]

The church, secular practices, and literary representations had different but overlapping conceptions of love, marriage, and sexuality. While love and marriage were not always celebrated, secular society and its imaginative fiction tended to uphold their value.

---

[33]   van Houts, *Married Life*, p. 90.
[34]   For marriages that took place at a very young age consummation would be expected only after puberty. See van Houts, *Married Life*, pp. 88–9.
[35]   Hume, *Chaucer and the Cultures of Love and Marriage*, pp. 15–17.
[36]   van Houts, *Married Life*, p. 30.
[37]   McSheffrey, *Marriage, Sex, and Civic Culture*, p. 19.
[38]   Barbara J. Harris, *English Aristocratic Women, 1450–1550: Marriage and Family, Property and Careers* (Oxford: Oxford University Press, 2002), p. 88; Hume, *Chaucer and the Cultures of Love and Marriage*, pp. 18–19; Karras, *Sexuality in Medieval Europe*, pp. 75–6.
[39]   See John Gillingham, 'Love, Marriage, and Politics in the Twelfth Century', *Forum for Modern Language Studies*, 25.4 (1989), 292–303.
[40]   Karras, *Sexuality in Medieval Europe*, p. 8.

The other major cultural discourse of consent was the legal discussion of rape and *raptus*. By 1275, rape and abduction had begun to be amalgamated into the single crime of *raptus* in English law with the introduction of the First Statute of Westminster. This statute did focus on consent, describing *raptus* as a crime that occurred 'maugre seon [gre]' ['against her will'].[41] However, the Second Statute of Westminster, issued in 1285, changed this emphasis.[42] As Caroline Dunn notes, the broader focus of Westminster II is legislation against abduction rather than rape.[43] The French text of Chapter 34 is the only ambiguous case, where ravishment may refer to rape instead of or as well as abduction. This addresses cases both with and without the woman's consent:

> Purveu est que si homme ravist femme espouse, damoisele, ou autre femme desoremes, par la ou ele ne se est assentue ne avaunt ne apres, eit jugement de vie e de membre.
>
> E ensement par la ou homme ravist femme, dame espouse, damoisele, ou autre femme a force, tut seit ke ele se assente apres, eit tel jugement come avaunt est dit si il seit ateint a la suite le Rei, e la eit le Rei sa suite.[44]

Raptus could still be prosecuted as a crime that occurred without a woman's consent, but consensual *raptus* (elopement or consensual sex) could also be prosecuted. Dunn argues that this reflects 'an increasingly concerted effort to prohibit, and more stringently punish, elopements disguised as ravishment', though notes that there was still concern for the victim of ravishment and options for appealing rape remained.[45] The 1382 Statute of Rapes continues the marginalisation of individual consent, ruling that a family's or husband's right to sue for *raptus* was equivalent to that of the woman.[46] Corinne Saunders and Caroline Dunn have taken different approaches to the effects of these laws. While Saunders argues that they create 'a legal marginalisation of the raped

---

41 The text and translation of this statute are given in Caroline Dunn, *Stolen Women in Medieval England: Rape, Abduction, and Adultery, 1100–1500* (Cambridge: Cambridge University Press, 2012), pp. 196–7.

42 While Christopher Cannon argues that the first lines of Westminster II actually show renewed attention to consent, he agrees that a woman's (non-)consent is not what medieval lawyers are interested in: Cannon, 'Chaucer and Rape: Uncertainty's Certainties', in *Representing Rape*, pp. 255–79 (pp. 260–1; first publ. in *Studies in the Age of Chaucer*, 22 (2000), 67–92).

43 Dunn, *Stolen Women*, p. 31.

44 'It is provided, that if a man from henceforth do ravish a married woman, maid, or other, where she did not consent neither before nor after, he shall have judgment of life and member. And likewise where a man ravisheth a woman, married lady, maid, or other, with force, although she consent after, he shall have such judgment as before is said, if he be convicted at the king's suit, and there the king shall have the suit': Dunn, *Stolen Women*, p. 197.

45 *Ibid.*, p. 41.

46 The text of this statute is given in Dunn, *Stolen Women*, pp. 198–200.

woman', Dunn suggests that they rather 'fail[ed] a specific type of female victim – those women stolen and forced into marriages for profit', observing that fifteenth-century laws subsequently turn to this problem.[47] While *raptus* laws did seek to determine whether a woman had consented, they did so, as Christopher Cannon writes, 'to make the victim's consent *irrelevant*': consent was not the primary concern in legal assessments of *raptus*.[48]

Raptus, rape, and (non-)consent were also discussed in canon law, scholastic literature, and vernacular writing. As in secular law, consent was not the primary concern of medieval canon lawyers, although Saunders argues that there was 'a general sense that non-consensual sex was a graver crime than other forms of illicit intercourse'.[49] Consent was more central, however, to scholarly discussions of virginity, sin, and rape. St Augustine of Hippo was a key influence here, as his defence of rape victims' chastity (which accompanies his condemnation of Lucretia's suicide) crucially affirmed the power of the soul and the will to preserve chastity even if the body was forcibly violated.[50] As Elizabeth Robertson points out, Augustine acknowledges that 'consent is also a profoundly internal phenomenon, an act of the soul, governed by will and reason, and therefore interior, private, and ultimately indiscernible'.[51] This, as Robertson also notes, has been one of the key points of contention around consent in modern law, and indeed represents an epistemological challenge to attempts to determine non-consent, even as it 'grants that faculty of the soul its greatest freedom'.[52] While there were other perspectives focused upon the priority of the body in maintaining virginity, Augustine's words echoed through medieval scholastic and vernacular writing and provided a powerful affirmation of the importance – and unknowability – of consent.[53]

There were, then, multiple discourses of consent in the Middle Ages. While canon law in theory prioritised consent as *the* crucial factor in solemnising marriage, the marital practices of the middle and upper classes offered a more muted focus on consent as *assent* that took into account a variety of factors beyond individual preference. By 1285 individual consent was sidelined in English *raptus* law in favour of a focus on abduction or sex against the will of the family or husband – although this may have been against the woman's will

---

[47] Saunders, *Rape and Ravishment*, p. 62; Dunn, *Stolen Women*, pp. 50, 90–4.

[48] Cannon, 'Chaucer and Rape', p. 261.

[49] Saunders, *Rape and Ravishment*, pp. 84–5.

[50] Augustine, *De civitate Dei*, I, I. 16–19.

[51] Elizabeth Robertson, 'Response: A Telling Difference – Sexual Violence, Consent, and Literary Form', in *Rape Culture and Female Resistance*, pp. 167–80 (p. 171).

[52] *Ibid.*

[53] See *Ibid.*, pp. 169–73; Saunders, *Rape and Ravishment*, pp. 89–91. As examples of vernacular writings influenced by this Augustinian perspective, Saunders mentions the dialogue *Vices and Virtues (A Soul's Confession of its Sins with Reason's Description of the Virtues)* and Dan Michel of Inwit's *Ayenbite*: see *Rape and Ravishment*, pp. 114–16.

as well, and the option to appeal cases of rape remained. Outside of the legal system, scholastic and theological writers affirmed the importance of consent by suggesting that rape could not violate virginity. These ideas were carried over into vernacular religious writing and the hagiographical tradition.[54] Consent was a prominent and flexible concept in a range of medieval discourses, and romance portrayals engage with, add to, and in some cases recalibrate its significance and functions within these discourses.[55]

Raptus, *Coercion, and Rape Culture*

This book is not primarily about rape or *raptus*: 'resistance to love' would be an inadequate, insensitive, and unethical term in which to group victim-survivors of rape. However, resistance to love does intersect with portrayals of rape and *raptus* at times, particularly with regard to men's experiences. In the medieval period, *raptus* was considered a gendered crime (hence why I have been referring to rape victims as 'she' or 'her'). As Saunders writes,

> Ravishment was not a gender-specific crime, in that medieval laws addressing ravishment of ward apply to both male and female children; men as well as women could be abducted or sexually violated, but any such crime would have been considered assault rather than ravishment in legal terms. Ravishment takes on a special significance with regard to women: only women could bring a legal appeal of *raptus* (an appeal defined in terms of potential sexual violence and/or abduction). Thus although the issue of rape is associated with wider notions of abduction, the crime of *raptus* was understood as one against women and related to other gendered issues of marriage, virginity and consent. Whereas the issue of sexual violence against women is treated in detail and gains a symbolic resonance in various discourses, legal, theological and literary, for men there was no legal counterpart to the process of appeal of rape open to women.[56]

There are some isolated discussions of whether men could be victims of rape, but these are the exceptions to a gendered understanding of *raptus* and rape in the law.[57] This often remains the case in modern law: in the UK only people with a penis can commit rape, though people of any gender can be the victims

---

[54] For a discussion of rape, violation, and consent in hagiography, see Saunders, 'The Threat of Rape: Saintly Women', in *Rape and Ravishment*, pp. 120–51.

[55] Shannon McSheffrey and Julia Pope provide a helpful account of how 'law, chivalric culture, and social practice [...] formed a feedback loop, each playing into and reinforcing the others': McSheffrey and Pope, 'Ravishment, Legal Narratives, and Chivalric Culture in Fifteenth-Century England', *Journal of British Studies*, 48.4 (2009), 818–36 (p. 819).

[56] Saunders, *Rape and Ravishment*, p. 20.

[57] Dunn finds only one example in the legal record: *Stolen Women*, p. 55 n. 13. Saunders notes the references to men as victims and/or women as perpetrators in the works of Stephen of Tournai and Thomas Sanchez: *Rape and Ravishment*, pp. 83, 86. Katherine

of rape.[58] However, legal frameworks – medieval or modern – are not the sole criteria by which people recognise violating and harmful behaviour.[59] Literature offers a more flexible context in which additional forms of violation and unethical sexual behaviour can be explored. I argue that medieval litera-ture *does* attend to men's experiences of coercion and at times acknowledges the possibility of male rape. Because there is no clear medieval vocabulary to describe men as victim-survivors of rape, such portrayals intersect with those of resistance to love. On a wider scale, the romances I discuss depict varied forms of physical and psychological coercion, sexual violence, and assault, often with an awareness that they are violating and coercive practices. These features indicate that literature acknowledges experiences of violation and harm unrecognised in contemporary law and may have enabled people who had similar experiences to make sense of what happened to them. In this respect, my book responds to Lucia Akard and Alice Raw's call to 'look to understand the power of such an expression [of non-consent] for those who read or heard it', while also reflecting current understandings of literature as a vehicle through which trauma can be recognised and perhaps healed.[60] While this book is not about rape or *raptus*, my discussion intersects with these topics, as the motif of resistance to love illuminates the workings of medieval rape culture.

Rape culture can be defined as

> a complex of beliefs that encourages male sexual aggression and supports violence against women. It is a society where violence is seen as sexy and sexuality as violent. [...] Rape culture condones physical and emotional terrorism against women *as the norm*. [...] In a rape culture both men and women assume that sexual violence is a fact of life.[61]

Harvey uncovers cases that seem to be of male rape but were tried as sodomy: *The Fires of Lust: Sex in the Middle Ages* (London: Reakton, 2021), pp. 132–3, 197–8, 200–1.

[58] 'Sexual Offences Act 2003' (2003) <https://www.legislation.gov.uk/ukpga/2003/42/section/1> [accessed 6 January 2023].

[59] Lucia Akard makes a similar point, observing that 'the sources typically used to study rape do not offer many avenues for analyzing those sexual violations that fell outside the narrow legal definition of rape', when these experiences 'still could have been up-setting, traumatic, and harmful': 'Unequal Power and Sexual Consent: The Case of Cassotte la Joye', *Studies in the Age of Chaucer*, 44 (2022), 'Colloquium: Historicizing Consent', ed. by Harris and Somerset, 285–92 (pp. 286–7).

[60] Akard and Raw, 'Futures of Medieval Consent', p. 366. For a discussion focused on trauma and recovery in medieval literature, see Christina Lee, 'Healing Words: St Guth-lac and the Trauma of War', in *Trauma in Medieval Society*, ed. by Wendy J. Turner and Christina Lee (Leiden: Brill, 2018), pp. 259–73.

[61] Emilie Buchwald, Pamela R. Fletcher, and Martha Roth, 'Preamble', in *Transforming a Rape Culture*, ed. by Buchwald, Fletcher, and Roth, rev. edn (Minneapolis: Milkweed Editions, 2005), pp. i–xii (p. xi). Italics in original.

Sexual violence is often present 'on the margins of romance' and sometimes enters the foreground as part of the hero's chivalric development, as Vines has argued.[62] We need not necessarily agree that romance 'must *create* the threat of rape' to acknowledge that romances assume sexual violence to be a fact of life and thus reveal the workings of medieval rape culture.[63] Chaucer's *Wife of Bath's Tale* famously begins with a rape; in *Sir Gawain and the Green Knight* the lady tells Gawain that he could rape her if she refused his advances; in *Blanchardyn and Eglantine* the hero's adventures begin by rescuing a lady from rape. Aside from rape, there are a multitude of other instances involving sexual violence more broadly defined: Arthur and Alexander are conceived in acts that, at least in some versions of their stories, are deceptive if not actually rape itself, while other romance characters are pressured, coerced, tricked, and even blackmailed into sexual relationships against their will.[64] The almost inevitable conclusion of resistance to love in acceptance of a relationship, often through physical or psychological coercion, aligns with the operations of rape culture both in the emphasis on coercion and in the assumption that 'no' can eventually be transformed into 'yes' through persistence and pressure. Romance's nature as fictional, fantastic writing, and often even as wish-fulfilment, ought not to make us underestimate its investment in medieval rape culture.

Scholarship on medieval rape culture has recently received renewed impetus and redirection following the discovery of new records that unsettle previous understandings of Geoffrey Chaucer's implication in a charge of *raptus*.[65] These records suggest that *raptus* had an even broader remit than previously recognised, in this case apparently reflecting a context of procurement for employment rather than denoting abduction or sexual assault. Yet this discovery – as many have observed – does not detract from important feminist work on sexual violence and coercion in Chaucer's writing.[66] As Sarah Baechle argues, 'the real liberatory potential of Roger and Sobecki's discoveries' is that

---

[62] Quotation from Saunders, *Rape and Ravishment*, p. 187; Vines, 'Invisible Woman'.

[63] Gravdal, *Ravishing Maidens*, p. 43. Italics in original.

[64] I am indebted to Caitlin G. Watt's work on consent and deception in Alexander the Great narratives.

[65] For details, see Euan Roger and Sebastian Sobecki, 'Geoffrey Chaucer, Cecily Champaigne, and the Statute of Laborers: New Records and Old Evidence Reconsidered', *Chaucer Review*, 57.4 (2022), 407–37; Euan Roger, 'Appendix 2. Transcriptions and Translations', *Chaucer Review*, 57.4 (2022), 440–9.

[66] See, for example, Carissa M. Harris, 'On Servant Women, Rape Culture, and Endurance', *Chaucer Review*, 57.4 (2022), 475–83; Samantha Katz Seal, 'Whose Chaucer? On Cecily Chaumpaigne, Cancellation, and the English Literary Canon', *Chaucer Review*, 57.4 (2022), 484–97; Roger and Sobecki, 'Geoffrey Chaucer, Cecily Chaumpaigne, and the Statute of Laborers', pp. 436–7.

in effectively removing the question of a single man's guilt in a single moment of violence, they offer Chaucerians a moment to disengage – to remove at last the question of a specific moment of (ostensibly) true-or-false accusation from the reading of Chaucer's violated women, and instead to examine his narratives for the myths they embrace and the scripts they reproduce. In short, they free us to prioritize a *structural* approach to the sexual violence in the Chaucerian canon. […] We are freed to ask not what happened to one woman, but what discourses governed the lives of *all* women.[67]

Taking up Baechle's invitation, this book explores how romance discourses reflect, challenge, or reinforce contemporaneous forms of structural oppression and coercion (often, but not always, in gendered ways), while also focusing on individual examples.

I also extend Baechle's call for structural engagement to representations of consent, coercion, and violence in Sir Thomas Malory's *Morte Darthur*. As with Chaucerian studies (though to a lesser degree, perhaps because of the relative size of the field), feminist work on Malory has sought to address the two counts of the *raptus* of Joan Smith brought against Sir Thomas Malory of Newbold Revell in a 1451 inquisition at Nuneaton.[68] These accusations remain uncertain: while the language used indicates that *raptus* refers to rape rather than abduction, the charges were brought against Malory by Joan's husband, Hugh Smith, and Joan herself gave no evidence – which was 'in keeping with the procedure of bringing a charge of *raptus* by writ rather than appeal'.[69] Because the charges were brought in Hugh's name, some scholars have suggested that Malory may have had consensual but adulterous sex with Joan, arguing that the charges reflect Hugh's desire to punish Malory and his wife in keeping with the increasing use of *raptus* law to gain restitution for adultery.[70] It is also

---

[67] Sarah Baechle, 'Speaking Survival: Chaucer Studies and the Discourses of Sexual Assault', *Chaucer Review*, 57.4 (2022), 463–74 (p. 468). Italics in original.

[68] See Amy S. Kaufman, 'Malory and Gender', in *A New Companion to Malory*, ed. by Megan G. Leitch and Cory James Rushton (Cambridge: D. S. Brewer, 2019), pp. 164–76; Saunders, *Rape and Ravishment*, p. 234; Catherine Batt, 'Malory and Rape', *Arthuriana*, 7.3 (1997), 78–99. For a full record of the crimes of which Malory was accused, see Edward Hicks, *Sir Thomas Malory: His Turbulent Career* (Cambridge, MA: Harvard University Press, 1928; repr. 2014), pp. 33–6, 93–107; A. C. Baugh, 'Documenting Sir Thomas Malory', *Speculum*, 8.1 (1933), 3–29. In keeping with current scholarly consensus, I assume Sir Thomas Malory of Newbold Revell was the author of *Le Morte Darthur*.

[69] Saunders, *Rape and Ravishment*, p. 235.

[70] Christine Carpenter suggests that 'the fact that the offence allegedly took place on two separate occasions, that the woman was abducted on the second occasion and that the husband appealed Malory of rape […] suggests that this was one of those *raptus* pleas brought to bring to heel an errant wife or daughter': see 'Sir Thomas Malory and Fifteenth-Century Local Politics', *Bulletin of the Institute of Historical Research*, 53.127 (1980), 31–43 (pp. 37–8 n. 54); see further Saunders, *Rape and Ravishment*, p. 235. Batt takes a different view, arguing that 'the extant evidence also intimates that

possible that these charges and the other crimes Malory was accused of may have been politically motivated, either invented or exaggerated by Malory's enemies.[71] Rather than focusing restrictively on Malory's guilt or innocence of *raptus*, I address the portrayal of coercion within his work. The capacious nature of *Le Morte Darthur* lends itself to varied and at times contradictory perspectives, reminding us that, no less than today, 'alternative perspectives about rape […] existed concurrently, and a nuanced approach […] is required to understand how the same person might decry rape in certain cases and yet approve of, or engage in, the act in other contexts'.[72] At times it does feel necessary to acknowledge the accusations against Malory, as a reminder of the potential links between literary and real-life violence, but overall I am more interested in thinking about how the *Morte* – and romance more generally – is entangled with the values of medieval rape culture than in focusing on one case pertaining to its author.[73]

Sex, Sin, Gender, and Desire

Both medieval and modern societies facilitate the workings of rape culture through patriarchal and hierarchical systems, but their dominant cultural understandings of sex and sexuality differ greatly. The official view of the medieval church was that sex was permitted solely within marriage and for procreation, although sex to prevent oneself or one's partner committing adultery was also acceptable.[74] Indeed, following St Paul, the concept of the 'conjugal debt' made sex a duty within marriage if one partner desired it (chaste marriages had to be agreed by both parties).[75] This meant, of course, that there

---

Joan Smith, as a married woman who had suffered a rape, would not have had any other remedy in law but to allow her husband to bring the case on her behalf': 'Malory and Rape', p. 82.

[71] Saunders notes that Malory may have been 'if not "framed," then at least the victim of heightened pursuit', while Field argues that 'the number of people involved, the variety of the allegations, and […] their timing suggests that they were not wholly invented; but their comprehensiveness makes it plain that someone looked for people with grievances against Malory and organised them into court': Saunders, *Rape and Ravishment*, p. 236; P. J. C. Field, *The Life and Times of Sir Thomas Malory* (Cambridge: D. S. Brewer, 1993), p. 106.

[72] Dunn, *Stolen Women*, p. 54.

[73] I consider the *Morte Darthur* a romance, in line with its sources, dominant narrative motifs, and many other critical discussions by scholars of romance literature, though I acknowledge that there is ongoing debate about its genre: see, for example, K. S. Whetter, *Understanding Genre and Medieval Romance* (Abingdon: Routledge, 2016; first publ. Aldershot: Ashgate, 2008), 99–149.

[74] See further Karras, *Sexuality in Medieval Europe*, pp. 8, 37, 75–6; James A. Brundage, 'Sex and Canon Law', in *Handbook of Medieval Sexuality*, ed. by Vern L. Bullough and James A. Brundage (New York: Routledge, 1996), pp. 33–50 (pp. 33–6, 40–1).

[75] On the conjugal debt, see van Houts, *Married Life*, pp. 6, 8; McSheffrey, *Marriage, Sex, and Civic Culture*, p. 23. On chaste marriage, see Karras, *Sexuality in Medieval Europe*, p. 58.

was no concept of marital rape, but it also meant that consent to marriage effectively entailed consent to sex, which holds implications for understanding resistance to love, particularly where we might wish to compare this with modern conceptualisations of asexuality. Other ideas about sexual acts also differed greatly from our own: homosexual and other kinds of queer sex were considered sinful and strictly forbidden, but so too were adultery, non-procreative marital intercourse, and even marital intercourse in certain positions.[76] Instructions detailing how priests should deal with confessions of such acts suggest that they were practised, but the labelling of them as sinful may still have profoundly shaped lay perceptions.[77]

The wide variety of sexual acts deemed sinful by the church clearly foregrounds the limitations of our modern designations 'homosexual' and 'heterosexual', and even the more expansive term 'queer'.[78] Medieval sexualities were defined in drastically different terms to modern perceptions, predicated on an understanding of sexual *practice* rather than sexual *orientation*.[79] This does not mean that we should not use modern terms to discuss medieval sexualities, but it does mean that we should exercise caution and an awareness of the very different models of sexuality when doing so. Tracing LGBTQ+ histories is essential work that has unequivocally demonstrated queer identities to be an 'inextricable part of humanity or gender diversity'.[80] Using modern terms can carry intense affective and political value for people whose history has been hidden or erased. For this reason, I use the terms 'asexuality' or 'aromanticism' where resistance to love appears not to be willed but simply to be what we would recognise as a person's sexual or romantic orientation. I deploy these terms with attention to the similarities and differences between medieval and modern understandings, aiming not to judge the medieval according to modern ways of thinking but to draw upon modern language where this is the most concise, useful, and sensitive way to do justice to transhistorical resonances. I do not use 'asexuality' or 'aromanticism' as identifying terms throughout because most of the examples I discuss depart from modern understandings by presenting resistance to love as willed and even wilful. However, while resistance to love is more deliberate, temporary, and

---

[76] See Karras, *Sexuality in Medieval Europe*, pp. 92, 107, 172–3; Brundage, 'Sex and Canon Law', pp. 40–3.

[77] See Brundage, 'Sex and Canon Law', p. 41.

[78] See the discussion in Karras, *Sexuality in Medieval Europe*, pp. 7–10; James A. Schultz, 'Heterosexuality as a Threat to Medieval Studies', *Journal of the History of Sexuality*, 15.1 (2006), 14–29.

[79] See the extensive discussion in Karras, *Sexuality in Medieval Europe*.

[80] I take this quotation from the accessible overview of medieval trans lives, which sets out the value and stakes of such work, by Gabrielle Bychowski: 'Were There Transgender People in the Middle Ages?', *The Public Medievalist* (1 November 2018) <https://www.publicmedievalist.com/transgender-middle-ages/> [accessed 17 September 2022].

sometimes more specific than asexuality or aromanticism, there are resonances between these concepts. I draw particularly on Angela Chen's discussion of how asexual people can 'draw attention to sexual assumptions and sexual scripts – around definition, feeling, action – that are often hidden and interrogate the ways that these norms make our lives smaller'.[81] This is one of the main things I think resistance to love in romance does and is what I want this book, in turn, to do. Moments of resistance to romance's sexual and romantic scripts expose those scripts and the means by which they are upheld, while also offering brief glimpses of alternative possibilities for consent, gender, desire, and sexuality. In exploring these alternatives, as well as how they are usually closed down and normative scripts (re)asserted, I reveal how romance attempts to naturalise particular forms of love and desire.

I likewise make occasional use of 'heteronormativity', 'heteropatriarchy', and 'heterosexuality' – which have received particular criticism when deployed in relation to the medieval past – where they offer the most concise point of reference for the modern reader *and* reflect the specific context within the romance discussed.[82] While chastity and virginity were arguably 'the most fundamental' of the 'dominant sexualities organizing the self-definition and self-representation of medieval subjects in the world',[83] English romances place greater emphasis upon love and sexuality within marriage – and thus by necessity in this period love and sexuality between a man and a woman. Moreover, this book reveals the coercive lengths to which romances go to erase resistance to love and uphold desire and marriage. I therefore use modern terms where and because medieval romances deploy repressive strategies akin to those of modern heteronormativity, proceeding from the assumption that we cannot challenge a repressive framework if we do not recognise its history. In this respect, my argument aligns with Louise Sylvester's work on romance and heterosexuality, though I focus more on how points of tension illuminate romance's normative trajectory.[84]

As a social construct, understandings, representations, and expressions of gender have also differed throughout history. The church again offered a dominant framework, which argued that gender difference was God-given, with the subjection of women to men and the concurrent valorisation of masculine

---

[81] Angela Chen, *Ace: What Asexuality Reveals About Desire, Society, and the Meaning of Sex* (Boston: Beacon, 2020), pp. 6–7.

[82] See, for example, Karma Lochrie, *Heterosyncrasies: Female Sexuality When Normal Wasn't* (Minneapolis: University of Minnesota Press, 2005), p. xvi; Schultz, 'Heterosexuality', p. 20.

[83] Glenn D. Burger, *Conduct Becoming: Good Wives and Husbands in the Later Middle Ages* (Philadelphia: University of Pennsylvania Press, 2018), p. 24.

[84] Louise M. Sylvester, *Medieval Romance and the Construction of Heterosexuality* (New York: Palgrave Macmillan, 2008).

over feminine attributes part of the divine plan.[85] However, recent scholarship has uncovered more fluid, varied, and queer manifestations of gender, with key work exploring medieval trans lives.[86] While trans and non-binary people existed in the Middle Ages, concepts of masculinity and femininity were also varied in this period, shifting according to social status, relationship to the church, and age, pointing to the ways in which categories of difference intersected and exacerbated the effects of discrimination within medieval society.[87] As Susan Crane observes, another factor that influenced expressions of gender was genre.[88] Romance focused on displaying and performing gender: knightly masculinity is demonstrated by victories in battle and success in love, while femininity is upheld in part through romantic fidelity. Gender in romance thus requires repeated acts, resonating, as critics like Molly Martin have argued, with Judith Butler's argument that gender is 'performatively produced and compelled by the regulatory practices of gender coherence [...] constituting the identity it is purported to be'.[89] Butler's understanding of gender as a social construct created through repeated performance shapes my consideration of gender in this book. The first two chapters explore how resistance to love was understood and interpreted in gender-specific ways, but rather than perceiving this as a one-directional process in which resistance to love is influenced by gender, I argue that resistance to love forms one of the means by which romance defines and creates gendered norms.

Desire, too, was treated in different ways within individual literary frameworks and cultural contexts. For the church, desire was the result of the Fall and could be seen as innately sinful even within marriage, though this perspective became less common after the thirteenth century.[90] Medical models offered a different view. The understanding that conception 'could not take place unless both the man and the woman ejaculated [...] requir[ed] them

---

[85] Judith M. Bennett and Ruth Mazo Karras, 'Women, Gender, and Medieval Historians', in *The Oxford Handbook of Women and Gender in Medieval Europe*, ed. by Bennett and Karras (Oxford: Oxford University Press, 2013), pp. 1–18 (pp. 1–2, 5).

[86] See *Trans Historical: Gender Plurality before the Modern*, ed. by Greta LaFleur, Masha Raskolnikov, and Anna Kłosowska (Ithaca: Cornell University Press, 2021); *Trans and Genderqueer Subjects in Medieval Hagiography*, ed. by Alicia Spencer-Hall and Blake Gutt (Amsterdam: Amsterdam University Press, 2021); *Visions of Medieval Trans Feminism*, ed. by Dorothy Kim and M. W. Bychowski (= *Medieval Feminist Forum*, 55.1 (2019)).

[87] See Ruth Mazo Karras, *From Boys to Men: Formations of Masculinity in Late Medieval Europe* (Philadelphia: University of Pennsylvania Press, 2003).

[88] Crane, *Gender and Romance*, pp. 3–4, 6, 12.

[89] Molly Martin, *Vision and Gender in Malory's 'Morte Darthur'* (Cambridge: D. S. Brewer, 2010), pp. 12–13; Judith Butler, *Gender Trouble: Feminism and the Subversion of Identity* (New York: Routledge, 2002; first publ. 1990), p. 33.

[90] Karras, *Sexuality in Medieval Europe*, p. 92.

both to feel pleasure'.[91] In romance, as Cooper has persuasively argued, this develops into a broader acceptance and encouragement of women's 'desirable desire' – desire properly directed for and within marriage.[92] Resistance to love diverges from representations of desirable desire, offering a means by which we might probe to whom this desire was indeed desirable, but it also often transforms into this model, upholding the central place of desire, love, and marriage within romance.

These were the contexts from which romance representations of resistance to love and its related views of and insights into consent, coercion, gender, desire, marriage, sexuality, and rape culture emerged. Consent held a prominent yet ambiguous role in both marriage and accounts of *raptus*; legal definitions of *raptus* offered limited understandings of who could experience sexual violence and ravishment, upon which romances elaborated; while the church considered many kinds of sexual practices sinful, romance again offered a somewhat more flexible context, although one that in Middle English works tends to align with the celebration of love and marriage. The church, secular society, and literature offered varying ways of understanding these concepts in theory and in practice; in the literary sphere, attitudes also depended upon specific generic frameworks.

Literary Contexts

Genre

Recent work on genre has highlighted 'how the more immaterial aspects of narratives or texts shape our perception of them and their potential generic affiliations'; these aspects include the emotions represented in and evoked by a particular work, but also the implied attitude of a work towards certain emotions.[93] While this book is not about emotion *per se*, it contributes to scholarly work that emphasises how generic configurations shape perceptions of love, desire, and sex – all concepts with strong emotional components. Medieval literature offered a variety of generic contexts within which love, sex, and marriage were portrayed. While this book focuses exclusively on romance, attending to other genres only where romances display generic hybridity, it may be useful to survey briefly different generic approaches to romantic and sexual relationships to highlight the extent to which romance may be seen as distinct.

---

[91] *Ibid.*, p. 61.

[92] Cooper, 'Desirable desire'.

[93] Sif Ríkharðsdóttir, 'Hybridity', in *A Critical Companion to Old Norse Literary Genre*, ed. by Massimiliano Bampi, Carolyne Larrington, and Sif Ríkharðsdóttir (Cambridge: D. S. Brewer, 2020), pp. 31–45 (p. 41). See also her concept of the 'horizon of feeling': Sif Ríkharðsdóttir, *Emotion in Old Norse Literature: Translations, Voices, Contexts* (Cambridge: D. S. Brewer, 2017).

In literature with an explicit religious focus, whether hagiographical, mystical, or instructional, virginity was valued in and of itself (though marital chastity could also be praiseworthy), and desire and love were directed primarily towards God.[94] As the late twelfth- or early thirteenth-century *Hali Meiðhad* puts it (in one of its milder formulations), 'meithhad is Heovene cwen ant worldes alesendnesse, thurh hwam we beoth iborhen, mihte over alle mihtes ant cwemest Crist of alle' [maidenhood is the queen of Heaven and the world's redemption, through which we are saved, strength over all strengths and of all things most pleasing to Christ], while the fifteenth-century *Book of Margery Kempe* records Margery's vision of God telling her 'thu mayst boldly, whan thu art in thi bed, take me to the as for thi weddyd husbond'.[95] While religious works directed desire towards God, conduct literature tended to emphasise the importance of chastity and what Mary Flannery has described as shamefastness, a model of behaviour that involved constantly guarding oneself against sin and disgrace.[96] *Exempla* also condemn extra-marital sex, sometimes illustrating its eternal consequences in hell, as in 'The Adulterous Falmouth Squire'.[97] In contrast, fabliaux (a genre that is rare in Middle English outside the works of Chaucer) and other comic works often depicted lustful (and usually extra-marital) sexuality in explicit ways, sometimes to make a moral point rather than glorify such behaviour. The *pastourelle* also depict sexuality, desire, and rape explicitly, at times conflating desire and love not only with sex but also with rape, an uncomfortable combination for the modern reader.[98] Love lyrics often align with romance in positioning a woman's love as rightfully due to a worthy man, frequently dramatising moments where this obligation is disrupted and unrequited (as I will discuss in further detail, suggesting this may offer a source for resistance to love in romance). The generic terms I deploy here are often post-medieval, but the recognisable similarities of works now

[94] See further Sarah Salih, *Versions of Virginity in Late Medieval England* (Cambridge: D. S. Brewer, 2001).

[95] 'Hali Meithhad', in *The Katherine Group (MS Bodley 34)*, ed. & trans. by Emily Rebekah Huber and Elizabeth Robertson, TEAMS (Kalamazoo: Medieval Institute Publications, 2016), pp. 189–219 (8. 9); Margery Kempe, *The Book of Margery Kempe*, ed. by Barry Windeatt (Harlow: Pearson, 2000), 36 (lines 2951–2).

[96] See Mary C. Flannery, *Practising shame: Female honour in later medieval England* (Manchester: Manchester University Press, 2020).

[97] 'The Adulterous Falmouth Squire', in *Codex Ashmole 61: A Compilation of Popular Middle English Verse*, ed. by George Shuffelton, TEAMS (Kalamazoo: Medieval Institute Publications, 2008), pp. 351–6.

[98] See Sarah Baechle, Carissa M. Harris, and Elizaveta Strakhov, 'Introduction: Recovering the Pastourelle', in *Rape Culture and Female Resistance*, pp. 1–14; Baechle, Harris, and Strakhov, 'Reassessing the Pastourelle: Rape Culture, #MeToo, and the Literature of Survival', in *Rape Culture and Female Resistance*, pp. 17–28; Carissa M. Harris, 'Pastourelle Encounters: Rape, Consent, and Sexual Negotiation', in *Obscene Pedagogies*, pp. 103–49.

classified together suggest that medieval authors wrote with an awareness of other similar texts, regardless of whether they would have categorised them precisely as we do today.[99] Medieval literary works were thus situated within particular 'horizon[s] of expectations' (the set of generic and cultural conventions through which readers understand and writers construct their works) that shaped their portrayals of love, sex, and marriage.[100]

Romance, while a medieval term (albeit first a linguistic rather than generic designation), is a varied and capacious genre that sometimes intersects with those discussed above. Hagiographical romances place greater value upon virginity and often appear more uncomfortable with sexuality, as I suggest at various points in this book. Some romances seem to educate their readers about appropriate conduct, including marital fidelity but also perhaps ways of negotiating relationships. In the fabliaux-romances of Chaucer (such as *The Merchant's Tale*), desire can become more important than marital chastity, though this is not usually the case in the works I explore. Romances like *The Wife of Bath's Tale* also integrate *pastourelle* episodes and their violence into broader romance narratives. Romance's affinities with other genres leads to intra-generic variation, a diversity I hope to have conveyed in this book. However, most romances, and most Middle English romances in particular, value love, marriage, and sexuality within marriage.

In Middle English romance, virginity is not typically an absolute good in its own right: it is rather fidelity that matters. Romances often depict characters (especially women) trying to preserve their virginity for or chastity to their beloved, but not generally for its own sake: Ydoine and Josian, for example, remain virgins throughout their unwanted marriages, but do so primarily to save their virginity and sexual fidelity for their true love, Amadas or Bevis. The desire to remain a virgin does not often feature as a reason for resisting love in romance, outside of the Grail Knights' rejections of sex or Emelye's plea to retain her virginity in Chaucer's *Knight's Tale*. However much at odds this may seem with its wider valuation in medieval Christian culture, in most romances, as Peggy McCracken notes, 'the chaste body' – or, I would argue, the virginal body – 'is unusual' and can even be threatening.[101] In place of valuing virginity and devoting love primarily to God, one of romance's key 'horizon[s] of feeling' is the expectation that a worthy knight and a noble lady

---

[99] For discussion of how vernacular writers theorised their work, see *Vernacular Literary Theory from the French of Medieval England: Texts and Translations, c.1120–c.1450*, ed. & trans. by Jocelyn Wogan-Browne, Thelma Fenster, and Delbert W. Russell (Cambridge: D. S. Brewer, 2016).

[100] See Hans Robert Jauss, *Toward an Aesthetic of Reception*, trans. by Timothy Bahti (Minneapolis: University of Minnesota Press, 1982), pp. 20–32.

[101] Peggy McCracken, 'Chaste Subjects: Gender, Heroism, and Desire in the Grail Quest', in *Queering the Middle Ages*, ed. by Glenn Burger and Steven F. Kruger (Minneapolis: University of Minnesota Press, 2001), pp. 123–42 (p. 136).

will ultimately fall in love and marry.[102] This has often been acknowledged as a core trajectory within romance, though my application of this particular label is new.[103] While the balance does shift over time (from early works in which love may be found outside of marriage), in accordance with adherence to sources, and in relation to generic hybridity, the majority of Middle English romances anticipate love and marriage to be the correct fulfilment of a relationship between a knight and a lady. This normative trajectory positions resistance to love as a problem or disruption, highlighting the subversive potential of this motif. This may especially be the case in Middle English romance because of its prioritisation of marriage, but given the value placed upon *fin amor* in earlier French works, resistance to love may still have played a disruptive role in the earlier history of the genre.

Literary Precedents: Latin and French Sources

The primary focus of this book is Middle English romance, but the motif of resistance to love as it appears there builds on earlier precedents. Understanding its prior literary history, particularly its portrayal in the works of Ovid and in French romances, illuminates this motif's specific role and implications in Middle English romance.

Ovid's works were widely read as school texts in the Middle Ages and were known to some of the authors discussed in this book: there are clear allusions to Ovid in Marie de France's *Lais* and the works of Geoffrey Chaucer, while William Caxton was the first English translator of the *Metamorphoses* (from the French *Ovide moralisé*).[104] Ovidian literature offers a variety of different models

---

[102] The term is Ríkharðsdóttir's: see her definition in *Emotion in Old Norse Literature*, pp. 18–19.

[103] See, for example, Sara V. Torres, '*Sans merci*: Affect, Resistance, and Sociality in Courtly Lyric', *Studies in the Age of Chaucer*, 44 (2022), 'Colloquium: Historicizing Consent', ed. by Harris and Somerset, 325–34 (p. 333); Carolyne Larrington, *King Arthur's Enchantresses: Morgan and Her Sisters in Arthurian Tradition* (London: Tauris, 2006), p. 115; Cooper, 'Desirable desire'; Dhira Mahoney, '"Ar ye a knyght and ar no lovear?": The Chivalry Topos in Malory's *Book of Sir Tristram*', in *Conjunctures: Medieval Studies in Honor of Douglas Kelly*, ed. by Keith Busby and Norris J. Lacy (Amsterdam: Rodopi, 1994), pp. 311–24.

[104] On Ovid and Marie see, for example, Tracy Adams, '"Arte Regendus Amor": Suffering and Sexuality in Marie de France's *Lai de Guigemar*', *Exemplaria*, 17.2 (2005), 285–315; SunHee Kim Gertz, 'Transforming Lovers and Memorials in Ovid and Marie de France', *Florilegium*, 14 (1995), 99–122; R. W. Hanning, 'Courtly Contexts for Urban *Cultus*: Responses to Ovid in Chrétien's *Cligès* and Marie's *Guigemar*', *Symposium*, 35.1 (1981), 34–56. Much has been written about Ovid's influence on Chaucer: for a summary of some of the most important work in this field, see Jamie C. Fumo, 'Ovid: Artistic Identity and Intertextuality', in *The Oxford Handbook of Chaucer*, ed. by Suzanne Conklin Akbari and James Simpson (Oxford: Oxford University Press, 2020), pp. 219–37.

for resistance to love. The *Amores* portrays love as an experience that conquers the heart against one's will, advising that it is wise to yield to love because

> acrius invitos multoque ferocius urget
> quam qui servitium ferre fatentur Amor.[105]

This trope of love as warfare that besieges the resistant lover more stubbornly recurs in romance, particularly in works influenced by the *Roman de la Rose*. The *Ars Amatoria* offers a different, gendered model, portraying resistance as a tactic deployed by the female love-object. Ovid's *praeceptor* claims 'vir male dissimulat: tectius illa cupit' ['the man dissembles badly: she conceals desire better'],[106] suggesting

> Vim licet appelles: grata est vis ista puellis:
> Quod iuvat, invitae saepe dedisse volunt.[107]

While the *Ars Amatoria* justifies the use of force by claiming that women secretly enjoy it and only feign their resistance, the *Metamorphoses* perhaps more closely parallels the subtler explorations of coercion and resistance in Middle English romance. Within the *Metamorphoses*, Daphne, Syrinx, Caeneus-Caenis, and Pomona are all highly sought after but averse to suitors, perhaps providing a model for the proud lady in love discussed in Chapter 2. Atalanta imposes an impossible condition upon her suitors, prefiguring the recurrence of this strategy in romance, although the condition she sets differs from romance models: it is hard to imagine a romance heroine suggesting that her suitor must defeat her in a race. Anaxarete follows a different pattern, scorning Iphis's courtship until he despairs and commits suicide. In the *Metamorphoses*, these women often meet tragic endings involving rape, transformation to avoid rape, or, in Anaxarete's case, transformation as punishment for scorn. Such conclusions are very different to the most common outcome for resistant women in romance literature – marriage – although there are perhaps more similarities between these figures than is initially evident.

An Ovidian source that may have influenced portrayals of men's resistance to love also includes a tragic outcome that does not tend to recur in romance contexts. The myth of Narcissus is narrated in its earliest extant forms in Ovid's *Metamorphoses* and Konon's *Narratives*: Konon's is potentially earlier, but

---

[105] 'More bitterly far and fiercely are the unwilling assailed by Love than those who own their servitude': Ovid, *Heroides. Amores*, trans. by Grant Showerman, rev. by G. P. Goold, Loeb Classical Library, 41, 2nd edn (Cambridge, MA: Harvard University Press, 1977), I. 2. 17–18, trans. p. 323.

[106] Ovid, *The Art of Love and Other Poems*, trans. by J. H. Mozley, rev. by G. P. Goold, Loeb Classical Library, 232 (Cambridge, MA: Harvard University Press, 1929), I. 276, trans. p. 33.

[107] 'You may use force; women like you to use it; they often wish to give unwillingly what they like to give': *Ibid.*, I. 673–4, trans. p. 59.

the *Metamorphoses* was known and widely read in medieval Europe. Ovid describes how

> namque ter ad quinos unum Cephisius annum
> addiderat poteratque puer iuvenisque videri:
> multi illum iuvenes, multae cupiere puellae;
> sed fuit in tenera tam dura superbia forma,
> nulli illum iuvenes, nullae tetigere puellae.[108]

Narcissus' youth and desirability may offer a model for the men discussed in Chapter 1, while Narcissus' pride resurfaces but is particularly associated with women in romance. There were several medieval rewritings of the story of Narcissus, which may have offered additional points of influence. The *Roman de la Rose*, discussed below, incorporates the story of Narcissus, specifically describing him as proud and asserting that his self-love and resultant death are Love's just punishment for his earlier resistance. Other medieval rewritings include the twelfth-century French lay of *Narcisus et Dané*, which William Burgwinkle argues may have influenced Marie's *Lais*.[109] *Narcisus et Dané* is particularly interesting for its curious combination of what we would now recognise as heterosexual and queer desire. All Ovid's references to homosexual desire are removed, to the extent that Narcisus thinks his own reflection is a woman. This, coupled with the increased and active role of Dané in the poem, enacts a kind of heterosexualisation of the myth, though one that coexists with Narcisus' gender fluidity.[110] Other aspects of the *lai* focus on but also complicate gendered models for resistance to love: the prologue declares that women 'ne soit pas [...] trop fiere' ['should not be too haughty'] towards their lovers, although within the lay itself pride is associated with Narcisus.[111] John Gower's tale of Narcissus in his fourteenth-century *Confessio Amantis* also describes how Narcissus

> of his Pride a nyce wone
> Hath cawht, that worthi to his liche,

[108] 'Narcissus had reached his sixteenth year and might seem either boy or man. Many youths, and many maidens sought his love; but in that slender form was pride so cold that no youth, no maiden touched his heart': Ovid, *Metamorphoses, Books 1–8*, trans. by Frank Justus Miller, rev. by G. P. Goold, Loeb Classical Library, 42, 2 vols (Cambridge, MA: Harvard University Press, 1916), I, III. 351–5, trans. p. 149.

[109] William E. Burgwinkle, *Sodomy, Masculinity, and Law in Medieval Literature: France and England, 1050–1230* (Cambridge: Cambridge University Press, 2004), p. 142. See also Penny Eley, 'Introduction', in *Narcisus et Dané*, ed. & trans. by Penny Eley, Liverpool Online Series, Critical Editions of French Texts, 6 (Liverpool: University of Liverpool, 2002), pp. 7–30 (pp. 11, 20 n. 25).

[110] See further Eley, 'Introduction', p. 26.

[111] *Narcisus et Dané*, ed. & trans. by Eley, line 22. Eley argues the lay 'is designed first and foremost to serve as an exemplum of the potentially catastrophic consequences of pride in the arena of human relationships': Eley, 'Introduction', p. 27.

To sechen al the worldes riche,
Ther was no womman for to love.
So hihe he sette himselve above.[112]

This demonstrates the ideas about Narcissus and his relation to resistance to love that were circulating during the late fourteenth century, the time at which several of the romances discussed in this book were composed. The myth of Narcissus, both in its Ovidian form and through medieval rewritings, offers a suggestive source for resistance to love, even if this myth has a very different ending.

Ovid's works lie behind many of the other potential sources and analogues for resistance to love in medieval romance, pointing to the layers of intertextual connections that characterise romance writing. The Ovidian-influenced troubadour and *trouvère* poetry of medieval France may have offered another literary model, particularly for the proud lady in love discussed in Chapter 2.[113] Simon Gaunt notes that '*trouvères* [...] are best known for their *grands chants courtois*, songs of unrequited *fine amour* ("pure love"), modelled on the Occitan troubadour lyric, and addressed to a haughty noble lady'.[114] Women are often presented as undesiring, hard-hearted, or as delaying the fulfilment of desire, which recurs in some romances.[115] The trope of romance authors appealing to their indifferent ladies in narrative asides may also build upon troubadour models.[116] However, romance literature also gives the troubadours' and *trouvères*' lyric portrayals a narrative form, opening up different possibilities for exploring the development, experience, and effects of resistance to love. In romance, men's resistance to love, and resistance on the grounds of differing status, race, or faith, also become more prominent, expanding this motif in new directions.

---

[112] John Gower, 'Tale of Narcissus', in *Confessio Amantis*, ed. by Russell A. Peck, TEAMS, 2nd edn, 3 vols (Kalamazoo: Medieval Institute Publications, 2006), I, I. 2275–2398 (lines 2276–80).

[113] Judith A. Peraino notes Ovid's influence on the troubadours and *trouvères*: Peraino, *Giving Voice to Love: Song and Self-Expression from the Troubadours to Guillaume de Machaut* (Oxford: Oxford University Press, 2011), p. 12.

[114] Simon Gaunt, 'The Châtelain de Couci', in *The Cambridge Companion to Medieval French Literature*, ed. by Simon Gaunt and Sarah Kay (Cambridge: Cambridge University Press, 2008), pp. 95–108 (p. 95).

[115] For example, see *The Troubadour 'Tensos' and 'Partimens': A Critical Edition*, ed. by Ruth Harvey and Linda Paterson, 3 vols (Cambridge: D. S. Brewer, 2010), I, 160, trans. 161 (PC 77.1); 220–2, trans. 221–3 (PC 101.8a). For discussion, see Helen Dell, *Desire by Gender and Genre in Trouvère Song* (Cambridge: D. S. Brewer, 2008), pp. 80, 89, 93; Sarah Kay, *Subjectivity in Troubadour Poetry* (Cambridge: Cambridge University Press, 1990), p. 11; Sarah Spence, *Rhetorics of Reason and Desire: Vergil, Augustine, and the Troubadours* (Ithaca: Cornell University Press, 1988), p. 119.

[116] See, for example, *The Middle English Versions of Partonope of Blois*, ed. by A. Trampe Bödtker, EETS, e. s., 109 (London: Paul, Trench, and Trübner, 1912; repr. New York: Kraus, 1981), lines 2310–34.

The *Roman de la Rose*, itself shaped by Ovid's writings and troubadour and *trouvère* poetry, significantly influenced later romances and the works of Chaucer, including in its portrayals of *dangier*, violence, and resistance.[117] The *Rose*'s violent characterisation of love has often been commented upon; its imagery of love as a siege (recalling the Ovidian focus on love as warfare) may have influenced some of the more violent portrayals of subduing resistant lovers.[118] The *Rose* also comments on pride in love, not only through the Narcissus story, but in the God of Love's commandments, where he explains that

> Orgueilleus fet tot le contraire
> de ce que fins amant doit feire.[119]

This suggestively parallels the association of pride with transgression against love in later Middle English romances, where, as I will argue, this becomes a gendered model. The *Rose* also offers a striking example of the extent to which the consent of the beloved could become almost irrelevant in romance literature: although personifications such as Bel Acueil can consent to the lover, the rose itself, as an inanimate object, cannot.[120] Despite – or perhaps because of – the allegorical nature of Amant's quest, a form very different to the romances I discuss, the violence of non-consensual sex is clearly described in the graphic account of the plucking of the rose. The *Rose* fostered an awareness of, as well as a backlash against, the violence that could characterise romance narratives.[121] The *Rose*'s portrayal of Dangier, the personification of a strategy of rejection as a performance of modesty, positions

---

[117] Gaunt, 'The Châtelain de Couci', p. 104; Kay, *Subjectivity in Troubadour Poetry*, pp. 171–83; Sylvia Huot, *From Song to Book: The Poetics of Writing in Old French Lyric and Lyrical Narrative Poetry* (Ithaca: Cornell University Press, 1987), p. 304. Chaucer translated the *Rose* into Middle English, though only part of the fragmentary *Romaunt of the Rose* seems to reflect his translation. See the discussion in Philip Knox, *The 'Romance of the Rose' and the Making of Fourteenth-Century English Literature* (Oxford: Oxford University Press, 2022), pp. 27, 31, 189–93. Knox observes the wealth of evidence for medieval English readers of the *Rose*, p. 2.

[118] On the violence of love in the *Rose* see, for example, Marilynn Desmond, '*Tote Enclose*: The *Roman de la Rose* and the Heterophallic Ethic', in *Ovid's Art and the Wife of Bath: The Ethics of Erotic Violence* (Ithaca: Cornell University Press, 2006), pp. 73–115.

[119] Guillaume de Lorris and Jean de Meun, *Le Roman de la Rose*, ed. by Félix Lecoy, Classiques français du moyen âge, 92, 3 vols (Paris: Champion, 1965), I, lines 2119–20. 'The proud man does precisely the opposite of what the true lover should do': *The Romance of the Rose*, ed. & trans. by Frances Horgan (Oxford: Oxford University Press, 1994), p. 33.

[120] See further Noah D. Guynn, *Allegory and Sexual Ethics in the High Middle Ages* (Basingstoke: Palgrave Macmillan, 2007), p. 139.

[121] See, for example, the discussion of the *Querelle de la Rose* in Desmond, 'The *Querelle de la Rose*: Erotic Violence and the Ethics of Reading', in *Ovid's Art and the Wife of Bath*, pp. 144–64.

resistance to love as a stage within courtship; however, the romances I focus on portray such resistance as more subversive and problematic. The cultural prominence of the *Rose* may explain why resistance to love has most often been viewed as merely a stage in courtship and has not, until now, received serious consideration in its own right.[122]

Another work influenced by Ovid (perhaps indirectly) and potentially also by troubadour poetry, Andreas Capellanus's *De Amore*, may offer an additional source or analogue.[123] *De Amore* is a contentious work, with interpretations varying as to whether it is even about love at all; my reading here is limited to its surface discussions and the evidence they provide for contemporary perspectives on resistance to love.[124] *De Amore*'s dialogues, which recount attempted seductions, offer many instances of resistance. An episode within the dialogue between a noble man and woman suggestively anticipates romance representations of the proud lady in love, as the nobleman describes a vision of the God of Love's treatment of women in the afterlife according to their responses to love on earth. The third group of women he describes faces torments and punishments because 'omnes amoris postulantes deservire militiae abiecerunt' ['they repulsed all who asked to serve in the army of Love'].[125] Although they are not directly described as proud, a variation of this episode in the anonymous *Lai du Trot* claims

> Or lor fait molt chier comperer
> Lor grant orgoil et lor posnee.[126]

While it is uncertain whether the *Lai* or *De Amore* is the earlier work, and whether the reference to pride was omitted by Andreas or added in the *Lai*, either scenario could suggest a prominent association between pride and

---

[122] See, for example, Crane, *Gender and Romance*, p. 63, discussed below.

[123] P. G. Walsh, 'Introduction', in *Andreas Capellanus on Love*, ed. & trans. by P. G. Walsh (London: Duckworth, 1982), pp. 1–26 (pp. 3, 10, 12–16, 23); Kathleen Andersen-Wyman, *Andreas Capellanus on Love?: Desire, Seduction, and Subversion in a Twelfth-Century Latin Text* (Basingstoke: Palgrave Macmillan, 2007), p. 5. *De Amore* does not seem to have been known in Britain during the Middle Ages: see Cooper, *The English Romance in Time*, p. 310.

[124] On *De Amore* as a social critique of institutions, see Andersen-Wyman, *Andreas Capellanus on Love?* For a summary of critical approaches to *De Amore*, see Neil Cartlidge, *Medieval Marriage: Literary Approaches, 1100–1300* (Cambridge: D. S. Brewer, 1997), p. 25; Andersen-Wyman, *Andreas Capellanus on Love?*, pp. 18–25.

[125] *Andreas Capellanus on Love*, ed. & trans. by P. G. Walsh (London: Duckworth, 1982), p. 110, trans. p. 111.

[126] 'Now Love is making them pay dearly / For their great pride and their arrogance': 'Trot', in *Three Old French Narrative Lays: Trot, Lecheor, Nabaret*, ed. & trans. by Glyn S. Burgess and Leslie C. Brook, Liverpool Online Series, Critical Editions of French Texts, 1 (Liverpool: University of Liverpool, 1999), pp. 13–43 (lines 268–9).

rejecting love characteristic of medieval romances and *lais*, which is developed in greater detail in the motif of the proud lady in love.[127]

In addition to the *Lai du Trot* and the *Roman de la Rose*, other French and Anglo-Norman works are the direct sources for many of the Middle English romances upon which I focus; I discuss these sources at the relevant points throughout. I also directly attend to the representation of men who resist love in two Anglo-Norman works, *Guigemar* and *Amadas et Ydoine*, in Chapter 1, opening the book with a broader discussion before focusing on Middle English representations. Resistance to love clearly enters Middle English writing from the French tradition, but it is incorporated into and further developed within a variety of Middle English romances.

Reading Resistance: Subversive Possibilities

Resistance to love perhaps carries a greater sense of social transgression in the Middle English tradition compared with French works: because English romances focus more consistently upon the fulfilment of love within marriage, resistance takes on additional social and political functions here. In addition, the focus on love within marriage aligns Middle English romances more closely with the expectations governing their readers' own lives. By attending to the points of connection and disjunction between romance and real-life expectations, I am not suggesting that romance is mimetic, realistic, or naturalistic. Romances' reliance upon coincidental reunions, revelations of hidden identities, and super-human feats of prowess are fantastical, sometimes to the point of being ridiculous – though they are no less enjoyable or effective for this. Yet romances also engage with contemporary realities, not least in terms of their portrayal of marriage, love, gendered expectations, and dynastic concerns. My attention to points of contact between romance depictions and real-life models departs from, yet also builds upon, work on romance's 'radical fictionality'.[128] Katherine C. Little and Nicola McDonald argue that romance is distinguished by its conscious emphasis on make-believe, but that this difference from other contemporary genres allows it to 'imagine alternatives to and even deconstruct the values inherent in clerkly culture'.[129] In doing so, they suggest that fictionality does not prevent, but in fact facilitates, a certain – perhaps radical – relationship to the 'real' world.

---

[127] For the argument that *Trot* may be the earlier text, see Walsh, 'Introduction', p. 18. For the argument that *De Amore* influenced *Trot*, see *Les Lais anonymes des XIIe et XIIIe siècles: édition critique de quelques lais bretons*, ed. by Prudence Mary O'Hara Tobin (Geneva: Droz, 1976), p. 336.

[128] Katherine C. Little and Nicola McDonald, 'Introduction', in *Thinking Medieval Romance*, ed. by Little and McDonald (Oxford: Oxford University Press, 2018), pp. 1–10 (p. 4).

[129] *Ibid.*, p. 5.

Romances' expectation and celebration of love, desire, and marriage, and their relation to readers' own expectations, position resistance to love as a potentially subversive trope. Previous isolated discussions of resistance to love have not usually considered it in this light: Sylvester has argued that romances 'require a woman's (initial) refusal', but this book challenges such an argument by drawing attention to the anxieties that female resistance can provoke, as well as by exploring a much wider range of works in which resistance is not always gendered.[130] Crane too argues that 'no' becomes a gendered expectation in romance:

> Later romances, particularly under the influence of the *Romance of the Rose*, develop a strongly narrative impulse within courtship by relocating the difficulties that divide the knight and his beloved from external circumstances to the lady's own resistance. With this development, refusal becomes an integral part of courtship, an expected first response that the lover's efforts can overcome.[131]

In describing resistance as 'an expected first response', Crane conflates resistance to love with *dangier*, a gendered behavioural performance of rebuffing a lover as a gesture of modesty. *Dangier* does relate to resistance to love and I explore the points of connection where relevant, but resistance to love is not gendered in the same way, is not necessarily a deliberate strategy, and seems to provoke more anxiety within romances than the expected performance of *dangier*. Indeed, to conflate *dangier* and resistance to love, and to accept *dangier* as a pattern of behaviour rather than deconstructing it as a carefully crafted fiction, poses something of an ethical problem for the modern feminist reader. As Sara Torres notes, 'one of the most enduring fictions in amatory narrative is that women's refusal of consent is designed to advance, rather than terminate, courtship'.[132] To read *dangier* at face value is to accept the fiction that 'no' will inevitably become 'yes', which upholds the tenets of rape culture. I propose instead to take resistance to love seriously, valuing refusals for what they are rather than folding them into the structures of coercive courtship. Of course, there are other ways to read the examples I discuss: depictions of men resisting higher-status women could be seen as a disingenuous move, for example, but I choose to take their refusals seriously here. In honouring a romance protagonist's resistance *as* resistance, we can unpick coercive structures and their strategies for transforming resistance into acceptance.

Crane also positions resistance to love as a plot-generating device, which of course it is. As Samantha Katz Seal has argued, romance plots are 'often

---

[130] *Medieval Romance and the Construction of Heterosexuality*, p. 12.
[131] Crane, *Gender and Romance*, p. 63.
[132] Torres, '*Sans merci*', pp. 328–9.

precisely about the initial lack of female desire; it is when "women don't really want to" that the male lover is spurred to his most ardent pursuit'.[133] Yet while we might expect romances in which resistance to love motivates chivalric prowess to use this motif as a celebration of chivalric masculinity, such works often pose questions about and even critiques of masculine performance. Even where it ultimately advances the love-plot of a romance, the subversive potential of resistance to love can remain latent. The motif of resistance to love exemplifies romance's capacity to prompt questions about its assumed norms and gesture towards alternatives outside of those norms, even while arriving at a conventional ending. Such questioning is not a purely rhetorical exercise: as Laine E. Doggett points out, imaginative literature can function as 'indicators of social and cultural phenomena with the potential to shape and change attitudes, not merely [...] record[s] of attitudes'.[134] Romance does not just passively draw on the cultural and literary discourses described above but may have actively interrogated, challenged, and reconfigured these discourses, offering material for its readers to debate.[135]

Romance also has a more personal impact on its readers, encouraging them to want what it depicts as desirable. As I will argue throughout the course of this book, romance teaches its readers whom they ought and ought not to desire, and how they ought to behave in pursuit of their desires. In this respect, my book builds upon Nicola McDonald's work on romance as 'an enormously powerful cultural discourse', which 'both scripts our desires [...] and seeks to organize them into legible and socially acceptable forms'.[136] Romances achieve this not by offering an explicit didactic message but by consistently and repeatedly emphasising that love and marriage matter. Modern theorists of asexuality have pointed to the power literature has to shape its readers' understanding of their own sexuality:

> Many of us learn to desire by watching other people desire. [...] In theory, mimetic desire can be perfectly fine. In practice, the world is not a neutral place. [...] If you don't know who you are or what you want, the world will decide for you. It will show you a couple of options and tell you those are the only ones.[137]

[133] Samantha Katz Seal, 'Chasing the Consent of Alice Chaucer', *Studies in the Age of Chaucer*, 44 (2022), 'Colloquium: Historicizing Consent', ed. by Harris and Somerset, 273–83 (p. 275).

[134] Doggett, *Love Cures: Healing and Love Magic in Old French Romance* (University Park: Penn State University Press, 2009), p. 6.

[135] See Cooper on romance as 'a secular forum analogous to academic debate': *The English Romance in Time*, p. 13.

[136] Nicola McDonald, 'Desire Out of Order and *Undo Your Door*', *Studies in the Age of Chaucer*, 34 (2012), 247–75 (p. 247).

[137] Chen, *Ace*, p. 172.

Of course, I am not suggesting that the readers of romance thought their only options were to become chivalrous knights and wealthy heiresses, but I am suggesting that through its consistent celebration of love and marriage, romance 'delimit[s] a particular notion of what *is* right', of what is desirable.[138] It presents love and marriage as normal things to want; indeed, portrayals of resistance to love usually suggest that even if you do not want these things at first you will eventually come to do so. As Chen argues of the celebration of love in modern writing, 'the effect of these stories is powerful'. Yet she encourages us to 'look a little closer, and the authority can begin to crack'.[139] While transformations of resistance into desire portray marriage and love as normal and desirable, the initial presence of resistance may constitute a fault line through which romance's authority might start to crack. Expressions of resistance to love interrogate the genre's priorities and may be a means through which readers can question if they really share these priorities. In this way, this book seeks to contribute to queer readings of medieval literature: although I focus primarily on relationships between men and women, which often lead to marriage, I make such relationships the subject of critical inquiry, deconstructing how they are formed and presented as normative. By examining moments of resistance to sexual and gendered norms, particularly in the first two chapters, and by considering the extensive use of coercion in romance relationships, I aim to denaturalise their ubiquity, to examine the ideological forces that shape romance relationships, and to draw out instances of resistance to these ideologies. In keeping with the contemporary intersectional feminist turn to a political critique of desire, I both affirm that 'there is no entitlement to sex' – or love – and 'everyone is entitled to want what they want', while also taking account of how 'personal preferences [...] are rarely just personal'.[140] Deconstructing ideas of romantic or sexual obligation *and* the forces that shape what we do and do not desire form key threads throughout this book.

Resistance to Love in Medieval English Romance

This book is divided into two halves, which address different kinds of resistance to love. The first two chapters consider what I term 'romantic a(nti)pathy'. I coin this phrase to refer to romance representations of single characters who actively express indifference (apathy) or hostility (antipathy) towards love. The reception of romantic a(nti)pathy often differs according to gendered constructions: Chapter 1 therefore considers men who express

---

[138] McDonald, 'Desire Out of Order', p. 255. See further Sylvester, *Medieval Romance and the Construction of Heterosexuality*, p. 2.

[139] Chen, *Ace*, p. 135.

[140] Srinivasan, *The Right to Sex*, p. 88.

romantic a(nti)pathy, while Chapter 2 turns to a particular type of woman who resists love, whom I term 'the proud lady in love'. This gendered division is provisional and is not intended to be essentialising. It offers a practical means of focus and allows me to think about how gender is constructed by, as well as is an influence on, representations of romantic a(nti)pathy. The first two chapters demonstrate that women's resistance to love is usually presented as more transgressive than men's romantic a(nti)pathy.

Chapters 3, 4, and 5 take a different approach to resisting love, turning to characters who resist particular relationships because of social factors. This reveals how romance constructs not only love and marriage themselves as desirable but celebrates particular kinds of love and marriage that are defined by intersecting axes such as status, race, religion, and morality. Chapter 3 explores how resistance to *mésalliance*, relationships between people of different social status, illuminates anxieties about social mobility and the potential for coercion. Chapter 4 considers resistance on the grounds of race and/or faith to argue that constructions of racial and religious difference are entangled with and implicated in perceptions of desirability. Finally, Chapter 5 examines how resistance to adultery or infidelity offers opportunities to challenge the tenets of rape culture and the idea of love as obligatory. This might seem like quite a different kind of resistance to love, not least because it primarily takes the form of resistance to sex. However, it opens up perhaps surprising connections with, as well as differences from, the other forms of resistance I discuss, facilitating new perspectives on the romances discussed so far and thus providing a fitting conclusion to this book. A brief overall Conclusion draws together some of the key ideas traced throughout this work and reflects on the kinds of desire romance constructs as normative. Some of the chapters within this book offer a comprehensive discussion of the particular kind of resistance to love upon which they focus, while others focus on selective examples: resisting adultery, for instance, is a very popular motif and so I discuss only a few representative works. While broad lines of argument are advanced across each chapter, resistance to love serves different purposes in individual works and I therefore leave room for precise arguments about its particular function in each chapter's sub-sections. The combination of breadth of material and nuanced discussions of individual works in this book is crucial to allow me to make claims about the place of resistance to love in medieval English romance as a genre, while also preserving a sense of the diversity within both the motif and romance writing itself.

Just as resistance to love does not first appear in English romances, nor does it disappear from literature after the decline of medieval romance. Resistance to love is a common feature of the works of William Shakespeare[141] and recurs

---

[141] For example, in *The Taming of the Shrew, A Midsummer Night's Dream, Much Ado About Nothing, Troilus and Cressida,* and *Measure for Measure.*

in literature from Jane Austen's *Pride and Prejudice* to Louisa May Alcott's *Little Women*, Thomas Hardy's *Far from the Madding Crowd* to contemporary romance novels; the hit Netflix adaptation of Julia Quinn's Bridgerton novels also springs to mind. The ongoing popularity of this motif demonstrates the enduring relevance of this topic: while human understandings of and attitudes towards sexuality and love vary according to their cultural contexts, the resonance of resistance to love across literature and society over time provides evidence for queer orientations like asexuality and aromanticism as an innate part of the diversity of human sexualities. I do not argue, then, that resistance to love is an exclusive preoccupation of Middle English romance, but I do suggest that this motif had particular resonances within this tradition. It complicates the genre's normative celebration of love and marriage and offers new perspectives on its representation of consent, coercion, gender, and desire, revealing the subtlety and nuance with which romance writers approached these issues through the lens of imaginative fiction.

1

'Ar ye a knyght and ar no lovear?'
Men Who Resist Love

‘ **A** r ye a knyght and ar no lovear?’: the simple question Isode poses to
Dynadan in Thomas Malory's *Morte Darthur*, completed 1469–70,
is loaded with expectations about genre, gender, and desire.[1] Is it possible
to be a knight and not to be in love? The answer ought to be an obvious
yes – there are plenty of knights who are not specifically said to be in love,
and there are knights who define themselves by pledges of chastity and virginity, such as the Grail Knights. Yet Isode's question seems more specifically directed than this: is it possible to be a secular, worldly knight and to
avoid love? Abstracted from a religious context that celebrates chastity and
virginity, men's resistance to love starts to look more unusual. There are some
examples of men who express either hostility or active indifference to love
in romance, but there are not many such portrayals. This chapter focuses on
five examples, drawn from the Anglo-Norman and Middle English romances
of *Guigemar, Amadas et Ydoine, Troilus and Criseyde, Sir Degrevant*, and
Malory's *Morte Darthur*. This is not a large corpus, but it is a diverse one,
spanning the full chronological and formal range of insular romance writing.
The men who express resistance or indifference to love within these works
reflect this variation, at times being used for more subversive purposes and at
times functioning more conventionally. Some of these figures offer insights
into queer sexualities, particularly asexuality and homosexuality. Others
emphasise the normative function of romance literature, exemplifying the
eventual acceptance of love (and sometimes marriage). Some draw upon
religious models of chastity and virginity, but generally do so in a brief way –
the romance drive towards desire and love exerts a greater pull in these works
than in the more overtly religious narratives of the Grail. Because of the
diversity within these representations of men's romantic a(nti)pathy, I consider each narrative in turn. Men's reluctance might receive less consistent
and concentrated attention than the other kinds of resistance to love discussed

---

[1] Sir Thomas Malory, *Le Morte Darthur*, ed. by P. J. C. Field, 2 vols (Cambridge: D. S.
Brewer, 2013), I, 549. All primary quotations are from this edition and volume.

in this book, but it was nonetheless a subject of interest across the period of romance's greatest popularity. It allowed writers to reflect upon, explore, and question generic tropes and their relation to societal norms.

The chronological breadth of the romances discussed in this chapter also impacts the varied perspectives they offer on romantic a(nti)pathy, particularly the distinction between resistance to love and resistance to marriage. The development of ideas about love and marriage over the course of the medieval period, with the increasing prominence (at least in theory) of individual rather than familial consent, and the corresponding expectation that love will be located within marriage, shapes each work differently.[2] Marie de France's *Guigemar*, written in the twelfth century, is primarily concerned with reluctance to love. Marriage, as Glyn Burgess argues, is 'closely linked to the feudal and economic realities of life' at this time, and *Guigemar* – perhaps more than Marie's other works – attempts to liberate love from marriage, although it also interrogates the place of *fin amor* and its relationship to chivalric violence.[3] *Amadas et Ydoine* also indicates that elite marriages were usually arranged, depicting the political alliance between Ydoine and the Count of Nevers, but Amadas and Ydoine do marry eventually, signalling a shift towards uniting love and marriage. *Troilus and Criseyde* is unusual within Middle English romance for focusing primarily on love outside of marriage, but this reflects its classical setting rather than its contemporary context. It does still interact with and comment upon this context, however, particularly through the portrayal of Criseyde as a widow. Similarly, Malory's *Morte Darthur* replicates earlier expectations through its focus on love outside of marriage, characteristic of Arthurian tradition (although Malory also emphasises love leading to and culminating within marriage at times, such as in the 'Tale of Sir Gareth'). *Sir Degrevant* is more representative of the wider tradition of Middle English romances, adopting the later medieval perspective which saw love as ideally located within marriage and aligning resistance to love with resistance to marriage. However, even where men do specifically resist marriage, this is not generally considered to compromise their political, economic, or familial priorities. This contrasts to the portrayal of women's resistance to marriage, discussed in Chapter 2. Women's romantic a(nti)pathy is also directly juxtaposed to men's in some of the works discussed in this chapter, providing a particularly striking example of how resistance to love, and its transformation into desire, are impacted by and contribute to romance's construction of appropriate gender roles. This chapter considers how romantic a(nti)pathy expressed by men intersects with constructions of desire, gender, and consent.

---

[2] See the discussion in the Introduction.
[3] Glyn S. Burgess, 'Marie de France and the Anonymous Lays', in *A Companion to Marie de France*, ed. by Logan E. Whalen (Leiden: Brill, 2011), pp. 117–56 (p. 138).

Reconsidering *Guigemar*: Asexuality and Generic Dissonance

Guigemar, the hero of Marie's twelfth-century Breton *lai* of the same name,[4] has attracted significant scholarly attention for his a(nti)pathy towards love.[5] However, Guigemar has not received any extensive discussion in terms of asexuality or aromanticism, although the correlation here is clearer than perhaps any other example considered in this book.[6] Guigemar's attitude towards love is not prideful refusal but simply a lack of interest:

> De tant i out mespris nature
> Kë *unc de nul' amur n'out cure.*
> Suz ciel n'out dame ne pucele
> Ki tant par fust noble ne bele,
> Së il de amer la requeïst,
> Ke volentiers nel retenist.
> Plusurs le requistrent suvent,
> Mais il *n'aveit de ceo talent*;
> Nuls ne se pout aparceveir
> Kë il volsist amur aveir.

---

[4] I refer to the author of *Guigemar* as 'Marie' in accordance with the reference to 'Marie' as the writer of *Guigemar* in London, British Library, MS Harley 978. Although most editions and critical discussions refer to the author of the *Lais* as 'Marie de France', Jocelyn Wogan-Browne has argued that both the canon and the figure of 'Marie de France' are modern constructions: 'Recovery and Loss: Women's Writing around Marie de France', in *Women Intellectuals and Leaders in the Middle Ages*, ed. by Kathryn Kerby-Fulton, Katie Ann-Marie Bugyis, and John Van Engen (Cambridge: D. S. Brewer, 2020), pp. 169–89. For a more moderate view, see Keith Busby, 'The Manuscripts of Marie de France', in *A Companion to Marie de France*, pp. 303–17 (pp. 303–4).

[5] For example, see Logan E. Whalen, 'A Matter of Life and Death: Fecundity and Sterility in Marie de France's *Guigemar*', in *Shaping Courtliness in Medieval France: Essays in Honor of Matilda Tomaryn Bruckner*, ed. by Daniel E. O'Sullivan and Laurie Shepard (Cambridge: D. S. Brewer, 2013), pp. 139–50; Sharon Kinoshita and Peggy McCracken, *Marie de France: A Critical Companion* (Cambridge: D. S. Brewer, 2012), p. 119; Ruth Mazo Karras, *Sexuality in Medieval Europe: Doing Unto Others*, 2nd edn (London: Routledge, 2012), p. 188; Tracy Adams, '"Arte Regendus Amor": Suffering and Sexuality in Marie de France's *Lai de Guigemar*', *Exemplaria*, 17.2 (2005), 285–315; Rupert T. Pickens, '*En bien parler* and *mesparler*: Fecundity and Sterility in the Works of Marie de France', *Le Cygne*, n. s., 3 (2005), 7–22 (pp. 11–12).

[6] An exception – outside of medieval studies – is Gwendolyn Osterwald, 'Contradictions in the Representation of Asexuality: Fiction and Reality', *IAFOR Journal of Arts & Humanities*, 4.1 (2017), 36–44 (pp. 38–9). 'Asexual' is occasionally used casually with reference to *Guigemar*, but discussions are not expanded or interrogated beyond this: Sally A. Livingston, *Marriage, Property, and Women's Narratives* (New York: Palgrave Macmillan, 2012), p. 49; Adams, 'Suffering and Sexuality', p. 301; Sarah Spence, *Texts and the Self in the Twelfth Century* (Cambridge: Cambridge University Press, 1996), p. 129; Rupert T. Pickens, 'Thematic Structure in Marie de France's *Guigemar*', *Romania*, 95.2–3 (1974), 328–41 (p. 331).

Pur ceo le tienent a peri
E li estrange e si ami.[7]

The second line indicates that Guigemar is sexually and romantically attracted to no-one, though the passage subsequently emphasises his lack of interest in women specifically. Despite the particular focus on women, this passage, and the *lai* more broadly, can illuminate the history of asexuality. Although it is overtly love that Guigemar is said to be uninterested in, the passage seems to imply that this entails a rejection of sex, too; Guigemar could be considered both aromantic and asexual, and I employ 'asexual' in this section as a broader term denoting both possibilities.

That Guigemar is considered 'peri' [lost, or in danger] because of his apathy towards love suggests that this state is expected to endure, though it also presents asexuality negatively.[8] This negative assessment is also evident in the labelling of his lack of interest in love as a 'mespris' [wrong] and in the attempts to 'convert' Guigemar to (hetero)sexuality, illustrating the co-presence of asexuality and prejudice against it in the premodern era.[9] While virginity was celebrated in religious contexts, noblemen like Guigemar were expected to feel sexual and romantic desire. The focus seems to be on resistance to sex and love rather than marriage here, suggesting that Guigemar's transgression is not – initially – his refusal to marry but his disengagement from love and desire more generally. The concern with sexual and romantic rather than marital norms seems appropriate to the courtly context of this twelfth-century *lai*, written at a time when elite marriages were arranged for political rather than romantic reasons, and when romances often celebrated pre-, non-, or extra-marital love.[10] However, the focus does shift to marriage later in the *lai*,

---

[7] Marie de France, 'Guigemar', in *Marie de France: Lais*, ed. by Alfred Ewert (London: Bristol Classical Press, 1995), pp. 3–25 (lines 57–68, my emphasis). 'Nature had done him such a grievous wrong that he never displayed the slightest interest in love. There was no lady or maiden on earth, however noble or beautiful, who would not have been happy to accept him as her lover, if he had sought her love. Women frequently made advances to him, but he was indifferent to them. He showed no visible interest in love and was thus considered a lost cause by stranger and friend alike': Marie de France, 'Guigemar', in *The Lais of Marie de France*, ed. & trans. by Glyn S. Burgess and Keith Busby, 2nd edn (London: Penguin, 2003), pp. 43–55 (p. 44).

[8] On 'a peri' as 'in danger', see William E. Burgwinkle, *Sodomy, Masculinity, and Law in Medieval Literature: France and England, 1050–1230* (Cambridge: Cambridge University Press, 2004), p. 147.

[9] The 'mespris' Guigemar suffers may instead refer to a wrong or scorn he does to nature: see Burgwinkle, *Sodomy, Masculinity, and Law*, p. 141. Attempts to convert asexual people to heterosexuality remain an issue today: see Julie Sondra Decker, *The Invisible Orientation: An Introduction to Asexuality* (New York: Skyhorse, 2014), pp. 13, 102, 120–1.

[10] See Elisabeth van Houts, *Married Life in the Middle Ages, 900–1300* (Oxford: Oxford University Press, 2019), p. 218.

as Guigemar's friends 'femme voleient qu'il preisist' (645) ['wanted him to take a wife', p. 51], but

> Ja ne prendra femme a nul jur,
> Ne pur aveir ne pur amur.[11]

Guigemar's apathy towards love does affect his dynastic duty, but the fact that the lady he loves is (apparently) still married to someone else at the end of the *lai* is no barrier to its happy ending. This suggests that love and desire are the primary priorities, and Guigemar is seen as transgressive and unusual because he does not experience these feelings – because he is, or could today be considered, asexual.

The kinds of love and desire Guigemar does not experience are identified as love and desire for women, leaving open the possibility that he is uninterested in women specifically. Interpretations of Guigemar as gay, or queer where queer is used solely to mean gay (as it has been in some scholarship on *Guigemar*),[12] have served important purposes and may reflect contemporaneous associations between unmarried men and sodomy.[13] However, the assumption that a man must be gay if he is uninterested in women, a common myth in perceptions of asexuality today, rests upon a binary in which opposition to relationships with women suggests a desire for relationships with men.[14] This binary is (to state the obvious) not the sum total of human sexual orientations. Moreover, while 'queer' avoids the imposition of sexual binaries, it does not sufficiently express the specificity of Guigemar's sexuality. Guigemar certainly can be read as gay or queer, but to read Guigemar *solely* as gay is to contribute to the ongoing erasure of asexual identity. In this case, it is important to call an ace an ace.

While using the term asexuality holds political and affective value, given the lack of representation of ace experience even in modern media, reading Guigemar as asexual also impacts how we understand the subsequent

---

[11] 'Guigemar', lines 647–8. 'Never would he take a wife, for love or money': trans. by Burgess and Busby, p. 51. Although 'femme' could mean 'woman' as well as 'wife', the Anglo-Norman Dictionary translates 'prendre a femme' and 'aver a femme' as referring specifically to marriage; in *Guigemar*, the following lines seem to establish that the reference here is to marriage: 'Femme', *Anglo-Norman Dictionary (AND2 Online Edition)*, ed. by Geert De Wilde et al. (Aberystwyth University, 2021) <https://anglo-norman.net/entry/femme> [accessed 18 October 2021]. Modern translations of *Guigemar* agree fairly unanimously on the marital focus here.

[12] See, most prominently, William E. Burgwinkle, 'Queering the Celtic: Marie de France and the men who don't marry', in *Sodomy, Masculinity, and Law*, pp. 138–69.

[13] Katherine Harvey, *The Fires of Lust: Sex in the Middle Ages* (London: Reakton, 2021), p. 125.

[14] Angela Chen, *Ace: What Asexuality Reveals About Desire, Society, and the Meaning of Sex* (Boston: Beacon, 2020), p. 8; Decker, *The Invisible Orientation*, pp. 13, 102, 116–19.

development of the *lai*. So far, I have suggested that in *Guigemar* asexuality is co-present with prejudice against it. The narrative trajectory of the *lai* may seem to come down on the side of prejudice, reasserting norms as Guigemar eventually desires the lady whom he meets after boarding a mysterious un-manned ship. In this light, the *lai* endorses the overcoming of asexuality and the formation of romantic relationships, according with the early priorities of the romance genre. *Guigemar* may even be seen as erasing the possibility of asexuality by associating it with adolescence and implying that it is just a phase – a myth often levelled at LGBTQ+ people but which aces are perhaps particularly vulnerable to because asexuality 'is indistinguishable from "not yet" on the outside. It's impossible to prove a negative [i.e. a sexual orienta-tion to no-one]'.[15] Yet could we not also read *Guigemar* in the other direction: rather than Guigemar's acceptance of love effectively straightening his initial asexuality, couldn't his asexuality queer his acceptance of love?

Guigemar seems to function in a way comparable to Angela Chen's con-ception of asexual people as able to 'draw attention to sexual assumptions and sexual scripts [...] that are often hidden and interrogate the ways that these norms make our lives smaller'.[16] Marie may not be writing Guigemar as an asexual character, but she does seem to be using him to unpick the construction of love and desire in the romance genre, as sexual dissidence blends into generic dissonance. Although Donald Maddox suggests identi-fying 'instances of deliberate "ironic play" with convention' in the *Lais* is 'perceiv[ing] them anachronistically', this seems to me to underestimate the *Lais*.[17] As Andrew Taylor argues, the *Lais* 'encourage interpretation that is both attentive and daring [...] licensing us to read beyond the surface mean-ing'.[18] Marie's account of how Guigemar comes to accept love is a strange and disjointed one that may invite us to question romantic norms. Where oth-er romances depict a knight falling in love at the sight of 'the right woman', Marie introduces the antlered hind and its curse upon Guigemar to initiate his acceptance of love. Love is often externalised in medieval writing, but this more usually occurs through the image of Cupid's arrow striking the lover, emphasising the sudden, embodied quality of love and desire in response to the beloved.[19] This image is echoed but crucially differentiated when the antlered hind is struck by Guigemar's arrow. The antlered hind, as others

---

[15] Decker, *The Invisible Orientation*, p. 21. See further Chen, *Ace*, pp. 98–9.

[16] Chen, *Ace*, pp. 6–7.

[17] Donald Maddox, *Fictions of Identity in Medieval France* (Cambridge: Cambridge Uni-versity Press, 2000), p. 32.

[18] Andrew Taylor, *Textual Situations: Three Medieval Manuscripts and Their Readers* (Philadelphia: University of Pennsylvania Press, 2002), p. 104.

[19] See further Corinne Saunders, 'Love and the Making of the Self: *Troilus and Criseyde*', in *A Concise Companion to Chaucer*, ed. by Corinne Saunders (Oxford: Blackwell, 2006), pp. 134–55 (p. 140).

have argued, is itself a queer figure in terms of gender, and its queerness may impact our understanding of Guigemar.[20] It is the encounter with the antlered hind that causes Guigemar's attitude to love to change, which is portrayed as a deliberate decision rather than a shift in feeling over time. When it tells Guigemar of his fate, Guigemar is

> esmaiez.
> Començat sei a purpenser
> En quel tere purrat aler
> Pur sa plaie faire guarir;
> Kar ne se volt laissier murir.
> Il set assez e bien le dit
> Ke unke femme nule ne vit
> A ki il aturnast s'amur
> Ne kil guaresist de dolur.[21]

Because he does not intend to accept death, Guigemar wants to find a cure for his wound: in a sense, his lack of interest in love has already been overcome, as he now *wants* to find love, has acquired 'the desire for desire', to borrow R. Howard Bloch's words, without actually experiencing love or even being sure that he would be able to do so.[22] Guigemar's practical course of action demonstrates this wish to find love and save his life: he knows that he has never seen anyone whom he could love in his own country, and sends his squire away, for

> Ne volt ke nul des suens i vienge,
> Kil desturbast ne kil retienge.[23]

Through his desire to find a woman to love in order to heal his wound, Guigemar begins a quest for an objectless love that conforms to the antlered hind's imperative, perhaps reflecting on the drive to adhere to sexual norms even when they do not match internal desires.

The importance of the antlered hind also denaturalises the experience of love as a spontaneous response to another individual. In contrast to the usual

---

[20] See H. Marshall Leicester, Jr., 'The Voice of the Hind: The Emergence of Feminine Discontent in the *Lais* of Marie de France', in *Reading Medieval Culture: Essays in Honor of Robert W. Hanning*, ed. by Robert M. Stein and Sandra Pierson Prior (Notre Dame: University of Notre Dame Press, 2005), pp. 132–69 (p. 134); Burgwinkle, 'Queering the Celtic', pp. 154–6; Pickens, 'Thematic Structure', pp. 335–6.

[21] *Guigemar*, lines 124–32. 'Dismayed [...]. He wondered where he could go to find a cure for his wound, for he did not intend to allow himself to die. He knew full well, and said to himself, that he had never seen any woman whom he could love or who could cure him of his suffering': trans. by Burgess and Busby, pp. 44–5.

[22] R. Howard Bloch, 'The Medieval Text – "Guigemar" – as a Provocation to the Discipline of Medieval Studies', *Romanic Review*, 79.1 (1988), 63–73 (p. 70).

[23] 'Guigemar', lines 143–4. 'He did not want any of his followers to come and hinder him, or attempt to detain him': trans. by Burgess and Busby, p. 45.

point at which Cupid may strike down a lover, the antlered hind appears before the introduction of the beloved, unsettling her primacy. This denaturalisation of love is furthered by the inclusion of dissonant moments at the end of the *lai*, such as the scene in which Guigemar is unable to recognise the lady, declaring 'femmes se resemblent asez' ['women look very much alike'].[24] The lady's individuality and beauty are unmarked here: the important thing is that she is like other women. This may open up a reading in which she represents a means for Guigemar to conform to expectations rather than being an individual he desires, perhaps reflecting on the predictable and thus potentially unindividuated drive for a happy ending in romance.

Other aspects of the *lai*'s ending further develop Marie's subtle questioning of romantic and gendered norms, particularly through the violence it posits as necessary to romantic love and chivalric masculinity. When Meriaduc, who has taken the lady for himself after she escapes from her husband, refuses to 'rende' (842) ['restore', p. 54] the lady to Guigemar, Guigemar gathers all the men who have come to Meriaduc's aid in war and rides to his enemy, offering him their service. Then

> Guigemar ad la vile assise;
> [...]
>   tuz les affamat dedenz.
> Le chastel ad destruit e pris
> E le seignur dedenz ocis.
> A grant joie s'amie en meine.[25]

As Sharon Kinoshita and Peggy McCracken suggest, 'the lovers' reunion is bought at the cost of a scandalous breach of feudal honor', as 'Guigemar and Meriaduc are not mere acquaintances but "friends and companions"', and 'Guigemar is called upon to pay up an obligation [...] the *gueredun* owed in repayment of an unspecified debt of honor'.[26] Guigemar and his lady's 'joie' also seems 'astonishingly incongruous' with the devastation Guigemar unleashes upon Meriaduc's people.[27] Kinoshita and McCracken argue that this violence is 'occluded, first, by the intense compression of these events into a mere three lines and, secondly, by the exigencies of the love story, fulfilled in the narrator's quick cut to the long-deferred happy ending', suggesting that

24 'Guigemar', line 779; trans. by Burgess and Busby, p. 53. Burgwinkle also comments on this: *Sodomy, Masculinity, and Law*, p. 160.

25 *Guigemar*, lines 875–81. 'Guigemar besieged the town [...] he starved all those inside. He captured and destroyed the castle and killed the lord within. With great joy he took away his beloved': trans. by Burgess and Busby, pp. 54–5.

26 Kinoshita and McCracken, *Marie de France: A Critical Companion*, pp. 74, 75. Leicester briefly notes the 'more realistic political violence that start[s] to push through the surface of a happy ending': 'The Voice of the Hind', p. 139.

27 Kinoshita and McCracken, *Marie de France: A Critical Companion*, p. 75.

'all narrative threads are wrapped up with a rapidity that allows no second thoughts on Guigemar's course of action to surface'.[28] However, if we read Guigemar's initial apathy towards love as a disruption of romance's priorities, its presence at the start of the *lai* may encourage rather than silence interrogation and critique in the later episodes, enabling acknowledgement of the violence that can be associated with love in romance writing and indeed the violence of normative models of love and sexuality. Even at this early stage of romance writing, Marie is capable of interrogating the tropes upon which the genre depends.

Guigemar thus invites a double reading. On the surface, the *lai* conforms to generic expectations, restoring love and desire as norms. But dissonant moments, to which Guigemar's initial indifference to love may attune us, allow Marie to question these norms and to reflect on whom adherence to them serves. Both of these layers of reading have implications for understanding the history and role of asexuality: on the surface, *Guigemar* may imply that asexuality is a temporary state of sexual immaturity, but the hero's initial asexuality may also enable us to question his subsequent narrative trajectory. In this light, *Guigemar* aligns with the double potentiality of asexuality and adolescence that Simone Chess has identified in early modern drama, where 'staging disinterest in sex and romance through adolescent and child characters' allows playwrights to 'explore the limits and possibilities of asexuality without overtly suggesting it as a life-long option or orientation', offering possibilities for 'queer subversion and containment'.[29] Yet *Guigemar* may offer further potential here, not only depicting the way asexuality is contained but perhaps enabling us to dissect this containment and examine how norms are restored. Rather than endorsing the trajectory from romantic a(nti)pathy to love, the generic dissonance in *Guigemar* may enable us to register the effects of pressure to form romantic and sexual relationships. As Julie Sondra Decker points out, the association of asexuality with adolescence may hold some truth not because asexuality is exclusively an adolescent experience (it is not), but because this is the time at which many people realise they may be asexual, just as it is the time at which many people of any orientation start to understand whom and what they desire.[30] Marie's description of Guigemar's lack of interest in love certainly seems to suggest that he has reached a point where he is expected to feel love and desire rather than associating him with the childhood state of presexuality. There also seems to be some acknowledgement (albeit not of a positive kind) that this state may endure, so Marie

---

[28] *Ibid.*

[29] Simone Chess, 'Asexuality, Queer Chastity, and Adolescence in Early Modern Literature', in *Queering Childhood in Early Modern English Drama and Culture*, ed. by Jennifer Higginbotham and Mark Albert Johnston (Cham: Palgrave Macmillan, 2018), pp. 31–55 (p. 32).

[30] Decker, *The Invisible Orientation*, pp. 16, 77–8.

does not seem to suggest that it is something out of which Guigemar will eventually grow. That he does eventually fall in love thus perhaps not so much implies that this was inevitable but reveals the impact of consistent pressure to conform to sexual and romantic norms. Decker has written movingly of how 'the average asexual person spends too many of their formative years hearing explicit and implicit negative messages about lack of sexual attraction and interest. It doesn't take much to severely warp an impressionable, still-forming young mind': 'if everyone treats you like you're broken, you may eventually crack'.[31] We may be able to read Guigemar's normative ending as illustrating the power of this pressure to conform.

The internalisation of sexual norms may also be hinted at in the way the *lai* briefly doubles its portrayal of romantic a(nti)pathy, anticipating how this motif will develop in later romances. When Guigemar asks the lady for her love, she initially demurs, but Guigemar somewhat hypocritically tells her that

> la dame de bon purpens,
> Ki en sei eit valur ne sens,
> S'ele treve hume a sa manere,
> Ne se ferat vers lui trop fiere.[32]

No stranger himself to alienation from desire, Guigemar now appears to have internalised the compulsion towards love and sexuality and to ventriloquise it to others. This is also a gendered expression of norms, as Guigemar's warning to the lady not to be 'trop fiere' could refer to pride as well as harshness (as it is translated by Glyn Burgess and Keith Busby).[33] This may indicate that the association between pride and women's resistance to love, the subject of the next chapter, is extant even in early romances and *lais*, as Guigemar himself is never said to be proud. As the lady immediately accepts Guigemar's love in response, this aligns her resistance with the idea of *dangier*, where women are supposed to reject a lover as the first step in courtship. Her momentary reluctance is a stark contrast to Guigemar's, as well as to the more extreme, revealing, and enduring instances of resistance to love that are the subject of this book. However, this brief pairing together of men's and women's romantic a(nti)pathy offers a preview of a pattern discussed in the next few sections of this chapter. Marie seems to pick up on and influence generic norms, restoring expectations on the surface but allowing dissonant voices to continue to emerge throughout her work.

---

[31] *Ibid.*, pp. 16, 14.

[32] *Guigemar*, lines 519–22. 'The well-intentioned lady, who is worthy and wise, should not be too harsh towards a man, if she finds him to her liking': trans. by Burgess and Busby, p. 50.

[33] 'Fer²', *Anglo-Norman Dictionary* <https://anglo-norman.net/entry/fer_2> [accessed 7 March 2021].

Chastity or Pride? Gendering Resistance to Love in *Amadas et Ydoine*

The late twelfth- or early thirteenth-century Anglo-Norman romance of *Amadas et Ydoine* tells of two young people who fall in love but are separated by Ydoine's arranged marriage to the Count of Nevers, through which she nonetheless retains her virginity. They are eventually married after an episode of madness, the intrusion of a supernatural knight who attempts to abduct Ydoine, and Ydoine's apparent death. *Amadas et Ydoine* begins very similarly to *Guigemar*, as Amadas, the son of Ydoine's father's steward, is fifteen years old and is described as perfect but for his lack of interest in women. However, the way the plot develops highlights the more disruptive, questioning, and queer impact of Guigemar's asexuality compared to Amadas's romantic a(nti)pathy. Amadas falls in love when he admires Ydoine's beauty, and the romance endorses this development of love as normative and further offers insights into how romantic a(nti)pathy, love, and desire are shaped by and constitutive of gender in medieval romance.

Both Amadas and Ydoine resist love, a doubling that somewhat perversely associates them as a pair from the start. This may reduce the subversive potential of their resistance, as its resolution is anticipated from the beginning. This is particularly clear in the case of Amadas, who is mockingly nicknamed 'le fin amoureus' ['the Perfect Lover'] by his companions.[34] The poet's comment that 'ne savoient / Com il verai prophete estoient' (101–2) ['they didn't know what true prophets they were', p. 22] already anticipates that his romantic a(nti)pathy will be transformed not just into acceptance of love but the perfection of true love. This is exacerbated by the extent to which the couple's initial resistance is used to guarantee their virginity and fidelity to each other. Amadas's indifference is described first as a form of 'casteé' (94) ['chastity', p. 22], while Ydoine, pledging her love, declares

> C'onques n'amai jusqu'a cest jour,
> Ne n'amerai ja mais nul houme
> Autre que vous.[35]

While resistance to love is not generally a means of promoting virginity and religious chastity in romance literature, it can uphold the celebration of exclusive romantic commitment by insisting on a couple's absolute fidelity only to each other, serving a more conventional generic function.

---

[34] *Amadas et Ydoine: roman du XIIIe siècle*, ed. by John R. Reinhard, Classiques français du moyen âge, 51 (Paris: Champion, 1926), line 98; *Amadas and Ydoine*, ed. & trans. by Ross G. Arthur, Garland Library of Medieval Literature, Series B, 95 (New York: Garland, 1993), p. 22.

[35] *Amadas et Ydoine*, lines 1256–8. 'Until today I never have loved and I never will love any man but you': trans. by Arthur, p. 39.

However, while the alignment of Amadas's and Ydoine's initial romantic a(nti)pathy anticipates their subsequent connection, attitudes to their resistance are differentiated along gendered lines. When Amadas's lack of interest in love is described, we are told:

> Qu'il n'avoit teche, ne mais une,
> Qui pas n'estoit a gent commune:
> Qu'il n'avoit pas ou mont dansele
> Tant courtoise, france ne bele,
> Ne dame de nule devise,
> Ne pour biauté, ne pour frankise,
> Qu'il amast vaillant une alie.
> [...]
> Ne l'ont d'autre chose blasmé
> Fors que trop amoit casteé.[36]

His indifference is deemed unusual, but its interpretation as chastity does not just anticipate his later fidelity but also interprets it positively. In contrast, Ydoine's 'une teche' (171) ['one fault', p. 23] – a phrase directly linking her to Amadas – is condemned as pride:

> D'amour si sourquidie estoit
> Et si fiere et si orgilleuse,
> Vers tous houmes si desdaigneuse,
> Qu'el ne prisoit en son corage,
> [...]
> Nul houme u monde
> [...]
> Mult par estoit de grant orguel.[37]

Comparisons between Amadas's and Ydoine's resistance are encouraged by the structure of the opening sections: first Amadas's family situation, his nobility and talents, and his reluctance to love are described, then Ydoine's family situation, her beauty and nobility, and her romantic a(nti)pathy are presented.[38] This mirroring again anticipates the linking of the couple in love, but also draws attention to the gendered perception of romantic a(nti)pathy. Ydoine, like the women discussed in Chapter 2, is deemed arrogant for her

---

[36] *Amadas et Ydoine*, lines 81–94. 'They found only one flaw in him, one that is not common: there was no damsel in the world so courteous, noble or beautiful, no lady so renowned for beauty or for nobility that he would pay her any heed. [...] The knights blamed him only for loving chastity too much': trans. by Arthur, p. 22.

[37] *Amadas et Ydoine*, lines 176–84. 'She was so presumptuous toward love, so proud, so arrogant and disdainful toward all men that she would not give a place in her heart to any man [...] her pride was far too great': trans. by Arthur, p. 23.

[38] See *Amadas et Ydoine*, lines 35–120, 125–90; trans. by Arthur, pp. 21–2, 23.

refusal to love.[39] However, *Amadas et Ydoine* perhaps leaves open a means for the reader to question this gendered division: as 'chastity is the singular virtue of women', its association with Amadas's but not Ydoine's resistance seems surprising and may have enabled medieval readers to challenge this gendered portrayal.[40]

Within the romance, however, this contrast sets up the subsequent exploration of women's romantic a(nti)pathy as more extreme and problematic than men's resistance to love. Amadas immediately converts to love when he sees Ydoine and admires her beauty, offering an example of the overpowering nature of love at first sight that contrasts with the trajectory of *Guigemar* discussed above. There is some conventional emphasis on this overwhelming love being 'estre son voel' (235) ['against his will', p. 24], which is continued in his experience of lovesickness (333–4; trans. by Arthur, p. 26). However, Amadas's conversion to love is inspired or enacted entirely by his spontaneous desire for Ydoine, and not by any other consideration. Ydoine, on the other hand, rejects Amadas outright when he first approaches her, in terms very similar to those of Felice in *Guy of Warwick* (who is discussed in Chapter 2). Amadas petitions her again, and this time asserts that Ydoine

> Pechiet ferés et mult grant tort,
> Se me laissiés issi morir.[41]

He repeatedly insists that he will die if Ydoine does not save him: while pleading for mercy from the beloved is a common romance and lyric trope, it is also potentially coercive because it frames love as a moral obligation and exaggerates its stakes to those of life and death.[42] This technique of pressurising someone into love by claiming that a life is at stake is later used by Pandarus in *Troilus and Criseyde*. It also recurs in Alain Chartier's *Belle dame sans mercy*, where the lady attempts to refute it:

> Sy gracïeuse maladie
> Ne met gueres de gens a mort,

---

[39] *Amadas et Ydoine* is relatively early for an insular romance that includes a proud lady in love (c. 1190–1220), although *Ipomedon* (1180s) probably predates *Amadas*.

[40] Alcuin Blamires, *The Case for Women in Medieval Culture* (Oxford: Clarendon Press, 1997), p. 138. See further Mary C. Flannery, *Practising shame: Female honour in later medieval England* (Manchester: Manchester University Press, 2020), pp. 1, 15.

[41] *Amadas et Ydoine*, lines 695–6. 'Will be committing a great sin if you let me die like this': trans. by Arthur, p. 31.

[42] See further Sara V. Torres, 'Sans merci: Affect, Resistance, and Sociality in Courtly Lyric', *Studies in the Age of Chaucer*, 44 (2022), 'Colloquium: Historicizing Consent: Bodies, Wills, Desires', ed. by Carissa M. Harris and Fiona Somerset, 325–34 (especially pp. 325, 328).

> Mais il chiet bien que l'on le die
> Pour plus tost attraire confort.[43]

The *belle dame* recognises that this is a manipulative claim and disavows it, but she does so from the vantage point of later medieval writing, whereas Amadas's plea goes unchallenged within the romance.

To some extent it is this emotive appeal that awakens Ydoine's love, as it is only on his third attempt, when he faints before her, that

> Adont primes pités l'em prent;
> Ne quide avoir confession
> Ja mais a nul jor ne pardon
> Dou grant pechié que ele a fait,
> Se ele ensi morir le laist
> A grant angousse pour s'amour.
> Et d'autre part ra grant paour
> Qu'el n'en ait blasme et mauvais cri,
> S'en sa cambre muert devant li.[44]

While aspects of this description align Ydoine's emotional experience with Amadas's, only she is influenced by a fear of sin and public blame, indicating how 'the social risks involved in negotiating interpersonal emotions of love are understood as mainly borne by the lady'.[45] Ydoine later insists that the couple should 'sans pecié faire' (6727) ['commit no sin', p. 118], but wait until she can

> serai vostre espousee
> [...]
> Sans pecié a l'ouneur de Dé
> Par esgart de crestïenté.[46]

---

[43] 'Such a gracious malady / causes the death of no one, / but it serves well to say so, / to win consolation all the sooner': Alain Chartier, 'La belle dame sans mercy', trans. by Joan E. McRae et al., in *Alain Chartier, The Quarrel of the Belle dame sans mercy*, ed. by McRae (London: Routledge, 2014; first publ. Taylor & Francis, 2004), pp. 43–95 (xxxiv. 265–8). Thanks to Lucas Wood for conversations about the *belle dame* material.

[44] *Amadas et Ydoine*, lines 1075–83. 'Then, for the first time, she was seized by pity. She thought that she could never be absolved of her great sin if she let him die so painfully for love of her. She was terrified that she would be blamed and defamed if he died in her presence': trans. by Arthur, p. 37.

[45] Carolyne Larrington, '"This was a sodeyn love": Ladies Fall in Love in Medieval Romance', in *Medieval Romance, Arthurian Literature: Essays in Honour of Elizabeth Archibald*, ed. by A. S. G. Edwards (Cambridge: D. S. Brewer, 2021), pp. 93–110 (pp. 93–4).

[46] *Amadas et Ydoine*, lines 6747–50. 'Become your wife [...] with honor from God, with respect for Christianity and without sin': trans. by Arthur, p. 118.

This again illustrates how women attend, or were *supposed* to attend, more closely to societal expectations when considering their involvement in love. Amadas falls in love upon admiring Ydoine's beauty, responding only to his own feelings; Ydoine falls in love after Amadas exerts pressure on her and asks her to think about the social consequences of continuing to reject him.

While Amadas's romantic a(nti)pathy is short-lived, then, it contrasts significantly with Ydoine's resistance, facilitating the exploration of gendered norms and expectations. This pattern is continued in *Troilus and Criseyde* and *Sir Degrevant*. While there is no evidence that Geoffrey Chaucer knew *Amadas et Ydoine*, *Sir Degrevant* refers to Amadas and Ydoine, offering a possible direct line of influence. Recognising the significance of resistance to love in *Amadas et Ydoine* allows us to re-evaluate the prominence of this romance, which was widely known in medieval England at least in general terms, but which is not often discussed today.[47] *Amadas et Ydoine* sets a pattern of comparing and contrasting two reluctant lovers, which is continued by later romances, and which reveals the gendered stakes of love, consent, and coercion in romance literature.

Gender and Coercion in Geoffrey Chaucer's *Troilus and Criseyde*

Troilus and Criseyde also pairs together a man and a woman who are reluctant to love, and in doing so explores the different ways in which romantic a(nti) pathy can be transformed along gendered lines. This complex work – which draws upon a variety of genres, including romance, tragedy, history, and epic – is primarily known as the story of Troilus's 'double sorwe', his desperate passion for Criseyde and his subsequent betrayal by her.[48] Accordingly, Troilus is best known as a lover rather than a reluctant one, and indeed his romantic a(nti)pathy (like Amadas's) is short-lived, as he falls in love with Criseyde within the first three hundred lines of the poem. However, Troilus's resistance is significant, both for the way it is described early in the poem and for the way it impacts our reading of the narrative as a whole. Troilus's initial hostility towards love contributes to Chaucer's interrogation of the tropes of *fin amor*, while also developing a significant and sustained contrast to Criseyde. These topics have been discussed in previous criticism, but recognising the way that Chaucer deliberately aligns Troilus with literary portrayals of resistance to love can contribute not just to new understandings of how these features

---

[47] Helen Cooper notes that 'Tristan and Isolde may be more famous, but Amadas and Ydoine were celebrated in England as exemplary lovers alongside or even ahead of them': *The English Romance in Time: Transforming motifs from Geoffrey of Monmouth to the death of Shakespeare* (Oxford: Oxford University Press, 2004), p. 225.

[48] Geoffrey Chaucer, 'Troilus and Criseyde', in *The Riverside Chaucer*, ed. by Larry D. Benson, 3rd edn (Oxford: Oxford University Press, 2008), pp. 471–585 (I. 1).

operate within *Troilus and Criseyde* but also to recognising the significance and impact of resistance to love within romance writing more broadly.[49]

In the early sections of *Troilus and Criseyde*, Chaucer enhances and develops Troilus's romantic a(nti)pathy from Giovanni Boccaccio's *Il Filostrato*, associating it more closely with the romance and Ovidian trope of resistance to love. Unlike Boccaccio, Chaucer explicitly and repeatedly identifies Troilus's romantic a(nti)pathy as a form of pride: he is 'this fierse and proude knyght', 'as proud a pekok' as any Cupid has caught, while Boccaccio's description of 'how often follow effects all contrary to our intentions!' is extended by Chaucer to reflect specifically on

> How often falleth al the effect contraire
> Of surquidrie and foul presumpcioun;
> For kaught is proud, and kaught is debonaire.[50]

Troilus's pride is also directly contrasted with his sudden subjection to love, as 'he that now was moost in pride above, / Wax sodeynly moost subgit unto love' (I. 230–1). However, this emphasis on Troilus's pride seems to accord more with the representation of pride in early romances and the works of Ovid

---

[49] Barry Windeatt has written most extensively on Chaucer's approach to *fin amor* in *Troilus and Criseyde*: see '*Troilus and Criseyde*: Love in a Manner of Speaking', in *Writings on Love in the English Middle Ages*, ed. by Helen Cooney (New York: Palgrave Macmillan, 2006), pp. 81–97; *Troilus and Criseyde*, Oxford Guides to Chaucer (Oxford: Clarendon Press, 1992), pp. 212–44; 'Troilus and the Disenchantment of Romance', in *Studies in Medieval English Romances: Some New Approaches*, ed. by Derek Brewer (Cambridge: D. S. Brewer, 1988), pp. 129–47; '"Love that oughte ben secree" in Chaucer's *Troilus*', *Chaucer Review*, 14.2 (1979), 116–31; see also Richard Firth Green, 'Troilus and the Game of Love', *Chaucer Review*, 13.3 (1979), 201–20. On Criseyde's consent, see Louise M. Sylvester, *Medieval Romance and the Construction of Heterosexuality* (New York: Palgrave Macmillan, 2008), pp. 91–127; Elizabeth Robertson, 'Public Bodies and Psychic Domains: Rape, Consent, and Female Subjectivity in Geoffrey Chaucer's *Troilus and Criseyde*', in *Representing Rape in Medieval and Early Modern Literature*, ed. by Elizabeth Robertson and Christine M. Rose (New York: Palgrave, 2001), pp. 281–310; Louise O. Fradenburg, '"Our owen wo to drynke": Loss, Gender and Chivalry in *Troilus and Criseyde*', in *Chaucer's 'Troilus and Criseyde': 'Subgit to Alle Poesye': Essays in Criticism*, ed. by R. A. Shoaf (Binghamton, NY: Medieval and Renaissance Texts and Studies, 1992), pp. 88–106; Corinne Saunders, *Rape and Ravishment in the Literature of Medieval England* (Cambridge: D. S. Brewer, 2001), pp. 291–2; Jean E. Jost, 'Intersecting the Ideal and the Real, Chivalry and Rape, Respect and Dishonor: The Problematics of Sexual Relationships in *Troilus and Criseyde*, *Athelston*, and *Sir Tristrem*', in *Sexuality in the Middle Ages and Early Modern Times*, ed. by Albrecht Classen (Berlin: de Gruyter, 2008), pp. 599–632 (pp. 603–21).

[50] '*Troilus and Criseyde*', I. 225, 210, 212–14; Giovanni Boccaccio, *The Filostrato of Giovanni Boccaccio: A Translation with Parallel Text*, trans. by Nathaniel Edward Griffin and Arthur Beckwith Myrick (Philadelphia: University of Pennsylvania Press, 1929; repr. 2016), p. 145.

than with the insular tradition in which it becomes a gendered trope.[51] While other Middle English romances develop the motif of the proud lady in love, discussed in Chapter 2, Chaucer seems instead to build upon models like the *Roman de la Rose*, Ovid's Narcissus, and medieval rewritings of the Narcissus story, in which pride is not necessarily gendered. This is significant because while pride still frames resistance negatively, there may be slightly different implications for the representation of Troilus compared to the proud ladies here. While Troilus incites Cupid's anger and vengeance for his rejection of love, he does not provoke anxiety or attempts to challenge his resistance from the human characters within the poem. Indeed, his expression of romantic a(nti)pathy differs from those of the proud ladies and the other knights discussed in this chapter: while Troilus is determined not to fall in love with a particular woman, he does seem to participate in heterosexual cultural practices, such as the aesthetic appreciation and objectification of women. At the temple, he is to be found

> Byholding ay the ladies of the town,
> Now here, now there; for no devocioun
> Hadde he to non, [...]
> But gan to preise and lakken whom hym leste. (I. 186–9)

Aesthetic appreciation does not negate the possibility of asexuality or other queer orientations, but Troilus does seem to be positioned more as making a conscious choice to avoid loving any woman in particular than as being sexually uninterested in women generally.[52] This seems to be accepted by his own society as an expression of masculine detachment: Troilus leads a group of young knights with him, mocking any who show signs of devotion to one particular woman, in what could be seen as a variation on the 'felawe masculinity' Carissa Harris identifies in Chaucer's other works.[53] While Harris defines 'felawe masculinity' as predicated on membership of the mercantile–artisan class, its focus on homosocial bonds and dehumanising attitudes to women resonates with the portrayal of Troilus here. Troilus is condemned and punished by Cupid for his proud refusal to love, but not by his own society, in which it is accepted as masculine detachment.

---

[51] See the discussion in the Introduction.
[52] In this light, Troilus is similar to the knight in *Lai de l'Ombre*, whom Love determines to conquer because of his lack of commitment to one woman – though this knight, unlike Troilus, explicitly engages in sexual relationships without committing himself to love. See Jehan Renart, *Le Lai de l'Ombre*, ed. by Alan Hindley and Brian J. Levy, trans. by Adrian P. Tudor, Liverpool Online Series, Critical Editions of French Texts, 8 (Liverpool: University of Liverpool, 2004).
[53] Carissa M. Harris, *Obscene Pedagogies: Transgressive Talk and Sexual Education in Late Medieval Britain* (Ithaca: Cornell University Press, 2018), pp. 26–66.

Troilus being shot by Cupid's arrow is described in violent terms; as Cory James Rushton notes, 'the punishment aspect is obvious, given the eventual fate of Troilus'.[54] However, Chaucer also combines the violence of Troilus's subjection to love with an explicit focus on his consent. When Troilus has reflected on Criseyde's goodness, 'with good hope he gan fully assente / Criseyde for to love, and nought repente' (I. 391–2). Likewise, in Troilus's song, he asks love

> How may of the in me swich quantite,
> But if that I consente that it be?
>
> And if that I consente, I wrongfully
> Compleyne. (I. 412–15)

And again, when Pandarus urges Troilus to repent his pride towards the God of Love, Troilus proclaims 'a, lord! I me consente' (I. 936). The repeated use of 'consent' is striking and seems to be unusual in a romance context. The *Middle English Dictionary* and *Oxford English Dictionary* both list references to consent that come primarily from religious (and sometimes historical) sources, such as *Handlyng Synne*, the *South English Legendary*, and *Cursor Mundi*.[55] Only isolated examples from other romances are cited, such as *Kyng Alisaunder* (which is not referring to consent in the context of marriage or sex but in the context of political rule). In Chaucer's own work, forms of 'consent' appear most often in *The Parson's Tale* and *The Tale of Melibee*, suggesting that 'consent' did have religious and solemn connotations for Chaucer, too.[56] 'Assent' is more common in romance writing, although again seems somewhat over-represented in *Troilus and Criseyde*, along with *The Clerk's Tale*, amongst Chaucer's oeuvre.[57] While Fiona Somerset has argued that Troilus's thoughts reveal that 'his consent is irrelevant to the ways in which power is exercised', persuasively indicating how this reflection and the involvement of

---

54. Cory James Rushton, 'The Awful Passion of Pandarus', in *Sexual Culture in the Literature of Medieval Britain*, ed. by Amanda Hopkins, Robert Allen Rouse, and Cory James Rushton (Cambridge: D. S. Brewer, 2014), pp. 147–60 (p. 158).
55. 'Consenten v.', *Middle English Dictionary*, ed. by Frances McSparran et al., Middle English Compendium (Ann Arbor: University of Michigan Library, 2000–18) <https:// quod.lib.umich.edu/m/middle-english-dictionary/dictionary/MED9364> [accessed 4 February 2021]; 'Consent n.', *Middle English Dictionary* <https://quod.lib.umich. edu/m/middle-english-dictionary/dictionary/MED9361> [accessed 4 February 2021]; 'Consent, v.' and 'Consent, n.', *Oxford English Dictionary*, ed. by Michael Proffitt et al. (Oxford: Oxford University Press, 2020) <https://www.oed.com/view/Entry/39518> and <https://oed.com/view/Entry/39517> [accessed 1 October 2022].
56. See John S. P. Tatlock and Arthur G. Kennedy, *A Concordance to the Complete Works of Geoffrey Chaucer and to the Romaunt of the Rose* (Gloucester, MA: Peter Smith, 1963; first publ. 1927), p. 164.
57. *Ibid.*, p. 49.

Cupid problematises the idea of the bounded self, philosopher Quill Kukla's recent work on a non-ideal theory of sexual consent has explored how consent can be scaffolded and upheld while acknowledging the contingency of human agency.[58] Drawing upon Kukla's work, consent can be considered not irrelevant or relevant but relative: while Troilus's ability to consent is limited, his explicit narration of consent is unusual in the context of resistance to love and suggests that he, at least, feels that his consent *should* matter. Indeed, that Chaucer explicitly narrates his consent offers a significant and sustained contrast to Criseyde.

While Troilus explicitly proclaims his consent, even if this is compromised by Cupid's attack and his own initial resistance (which I have suggested can itself be seen as a choice), Criseyde's consent is more complex and uncertain. As Nicholas Perkins argues, 'Criseyde's constrained choices, and her movement towards loving Troilus, should not be diminished as acts of will or agency simply because they operate under constraint': Criseyde exemplifies the nuanced operation of agency by and through the figure of the reluctant lover, who is often constrained to love but also exerts a measure of choice and agency within the framework of constraint.[59] Criseyde does experience love for Troilus, asking 'who yaf me drynke?' (II. 651) in a clear allusion to the sudden passion of Tristan and Isolde's love.[60] Chaucer also gives Criseyde an extended monologue in which she debates whether she can love Troilus – a monologue that is similar to, if much more practical and measured than, Troilus's earlier musings on his love for her.[61] Yet this monologue consistently reveals Criseyde's indecision about love and her preoccupation with social concerns, recalling Ydoine's greater attention to social considerations in *Amadas et Ydoine*. Criseyde determines she may love, but fears the uncertainty of love, the loss of her liberty, and the potential for gossip. Switching between 'hope' and 'drede', 'hoot' and 'cold', Criseyde is still poised 'bitwixen tweye' (II. 810–11) when she abandons her musings to join her nieces. While Troilus commits to loving Criseyde, Criseyde's own feelings for Troilus and whether she desires to act on them remain uncertain. Criseyde's infamous 'slydynge'

---

58 Fiona Somerset, 'Consent/Assent', in *A New Companion to Critical Thinking on Chaucer*, ed. by Stephanie L. Batkie, Matthew W. Irvin, and Lynn Shutters (Leeds: Arc Humanities Press, 2021), pp. 27–41 (p. 39); Quill R. Kukla, 'A Nonideal Theory of Sexual Consent', *Ethics*, 131.2 (2021), 270–92.

59 Nicholas Perkins, *The gift of narrative in medieval England* (Manchester: Manchester University Press, 2021), p. 138.

60 See further Perkins, *The gift of narrative*, p. 139.

61 See further Saunders, 'Love and the Making of the Self', p. 144; Corinne Saunders, 'Affective Reading: Chaucer, Women, and Romance', in *Women's Literary Culture and Late Medieval English Writing*, ed. by Liz Herbert McAvoy and Diane Watt (= *Chaucer Review*, 51.1 (2016)), pp. 11–30 (p. 24).

(v. 825) is present from the outset of the poem, alongside her love, indecision, and experiences of coercion.[62]

The entanglement of Criseyde's consent with coercion is perhaps most evident in her response to Troilus's insistence that she 'yeldeth yow, for other bote is non!' (III. 1208), when she declares

> Ne hadde I er now, my swete herte deere,
> Ben yolde, ywis, I were now nought heere! (III. 1210–11)

Framing this as a response to a *demand* for consent (and thus consent given under duress) and obscuring its precise development by remaining unclear about when she had yielded, other than 'er now', Criseyde's words highlight the ambivalence of her consent. Louise Fradenburg and Christopher Cannon have pointed to the other elements of this scene that undermine Criseyde's apparent consent, observing that 'just previous to this moment, the narrator has posed the following rhetorical question: "What myghte or may the sely larke seye, / Whan that the sperhauk hath it in his foot?"', detracting from her claim that she has already yielded and is with Troilus willingly.[63] Criseyde's passive declaration that she has 'ben yolde' is also intriguing in this respect (as Somerset notes), as it could imply she has *been* yielded up,[64] perhaps subtly alluding to the way in which Pandarus has yielded her to Troilus.[65] Criseyde's words of apparent consent within this scene are complicated by Chaucer in a more subtle and pervasive way than Troilus's. Although Troilus and Criseyde are both initially reluctant to love, their resistance is explored in different ways and to different extents by Chaucer, positioning romantic a(nti)pathy as a more complex or problematic issue when expressed by women than by men. There may also be an additional factor at work here: Criseyde's status as a widow in Boccaccio's and Chaucer's narratives may have encouraged a

---

[62] For a recent subtle analysis of Criseyde's shifting thoughts, see Stephanie Trigg, 'Cloudy Thoughts: Cognition and Affect in *Troilus and Criseyde*', in *Gender, Poetry, and the Form of Thought in Later Medieval Literature: Essays in Honor of Elizabeth A. Robertson*, ed. by Jennifer Jahner and Ingrid Nelson (Bethlehem: Lehigh University Press, 2022), pp. 25–46.

[63] Fradenburg, 'Loss, Gender and Chivalry', pp. 99–100; Christopher Cannon, 'Chaucer and Rape: Uncertainty's Certainties', in *Representing Rape*, pp. 255–79 (pp. 268–9; first publ. in *Studies in the Age of Chaucer*, 22 (2000), 67–92). See also Rushton, 'The Awful Passion of Pandarus', p. 152; Perkins, *The gift of narrative*, pp. 141–2. For an alternative reading, see Jill Mann, 'Troilus's Swoon', in *Life in Words: Essays on Chaucer, the Gawain-Poet, and Malory*, ed. by Mark David Rasmussen (Toronto: University of Toronto Press, 2014), pp. 3–19 (pp. 16–17).

[64] Somerset, 'Consent/Assent', p. 38.

[65] On Pandarus's role, see Cathy Hume, *Chaucer and the Cultures of Love and Marriage* (Cambridge: D. S. Brewer, 2012), pp. 167–8; Rushton, 'The Awful Passion of Pandarus'; Gretchen Mieszkowski, *Medieval Go-Betweens and Chaucer's Pandarus* (New York: Palgrave Macmillan, 2006).

greater exploration of the ways in which she might be coerced into another relationship by a family member. In the later medieval period, 'kings and feudal superiors as well as heads of families continued to play a major role in the remarriage of widows of the elite – sometimes with the assent and even the encouragement of these widows, but often by exerting pressure in a number of ways', while widows were the most common victims of bride-theft, a problem Caroline Dunn notes was increasingly the subject of legislation in the fifteenth century.[66] *Troilus and Criseyde* does not directly confront the coercion of widows into remarriage, remaining focused upon love and sexuality in keeping with the classical setting of the romance, but the coercion Criseyde faces may comment on this contemporary social issue.

In addition to addressing the particular vulnerability of the widow, Chaucer's interest in the complexity and problematics of women's resistance and consent is notable in view of the broader preoccupations with *raptus* in *Troilus and Criseyde*. As Elizabeth Robertson notes,

> Various kinds of rape permeate *Troilus and Criseyde*. Helen's rape, or abduction, instigates the war against Troy. Throughout the work, Criseyde is threatened with rape as forced coitus, first from Troilus, and then from Diomedes. Before she is given over to the Greeks, Troilus considers the possibility of 'ravishing' Criseyde.[67]

Just as Chaucer uses the term 'consent' for Troilus's acceptance of love, so too does he use the term 'rape' later in the poem, 'for nearly the first time in English literature', as Robertson observes; Carolyn Dinshaw notes that this word occurs rarely in Chaucer's work, further heightening its significance.[68] When Troilus is reluctant to abduct Criseyde to prevent her being exchanged for Antenor, Pandarus declares

> It is no rape, in my dom, ne no vice,
> Hire to witholden that ye love moost. (IV. 596–7)

Troilus and Pandarus's explicit discussion of rape and *raptus* calls the problematic aspects of Criseyde's consent to the reader's attention perhaps more starkly than anywhere else in the poem, retrospectively adding to the uncertainty of Criseyde's consent compared to Troilus's. Pandarus's own perspective on what is or is not a rape is particularly provocative in view of

---

[66] Rhoda L. Friedrichs, 'The Remarriage of Elite Widows in the Later Middle Ages', *Florilegium*, 23.1 (2006), 69–83 (p. 71); Caroline Dunn, *Stolen Women in Medieval England: Rape, Abduction, and Adultery, 1100–1500* (Cambridge: Cambridge University Press, 2012), pp. 87–97.

[67] Robertson, 'Public Bodies and Psychic Domains', p. 298. See also the discussion in Cannon, 'Chaucer and Rape', pp. 263–5.

[68] Robertson, 'Public Bodies and Psychic Domains', p. 281; Dinshaw, *Chaucer's Sexual Poetics* (Madison: University of Wisconsin Press, 1989), p. 8.

his coercive influence on Criseyde throughout the poem. In addition, this conversation takes place between Troilus and Pandarus, when 'this discussion should not be taking place between two men, but rather between Troilus and Criseyde'.[69] It later does, with Criseyde herself rejecting the possibility of eloping (IV. 1528–1652), but the order of these conversations draws attention to the prioritisation of Troilus's and Pandarus's desires over Criseyde's. This exchange thus again draws out the differences between Troilus's and Criseyde's resistance and consent, highlighting that these issues were treated differently in accordance with gendered constructs.

Troilus and Criseyde raises important and often uncomfortable questions about the significance of consent, the power of coercion, and the gendered dynamics of the transition from resistance to participation in romantic and sexual relationships. But while it attends to differences in how gender might influence experiences of resistance and consent, on a narrative level the connections between Troilus's and Criseyde's resistance to love are also important. By prefiguring Criseyde's reluctance, Troilus places additional pressure upon her to accept love, as he has already modelled this narrative trajectory for her, indicating the normative function that could be served by pairing two reluctant lovers together. This expected trajectory is exploited by Pandarus in the poem, both to persuade Criseyde to love Troilus and to reassure Troilus of the likelihood that she will love him, telling him that there

> Was nevere man or womman yet bigete
> That was unapt to suffren loves hete,
> Celestial, or elles love of kynde. (I. 977–9)

Troilus himself aptly illustrates this point, supporting Pandarus's reasoning. Referring to Criseyde specifically, Pandarus then declares 'it sit hire naught to ben celestial' (I. 983);

> it sate hire wel right nowthe
> A worthi knyght to loven and cherice,
> And but she do, I holde it for a vice. (I. 985–7)

Commenting on Pandarus's conversations with Criseyde, Cathy Hume observes that

> if Pandarus plays on Criseyde's obedience and reliance on him as a familial protector, he also works on her as a courtly friend. These roles parallel two kinds of cultural pressure, which can be represented by the rival voices of moralising advice literature and love-glorifying romance, but surely reflect a more general tension in late medieval society. Pandarus combines these competing pressures in one person and makes them act together, to powerful

---

[69] Robertson, 'Public Bodies and Psychic Domains', p. 294.

effect [...] tr[ying] to invoke a sense of love as something she is obliged to do rather than something she is obliged to resist.[70]

Troilus and Criseyde provocatively explores the tension between contemplative life and erotic love, not only through Pandarus's comments but also in Criseyde's own sense that 'a widewes lif' (II. 114) should be to 'rede on holy seyntes lyves' (II. 118), and perhaps most extremely in the narrator's declaration after the consummation scene that

> Now is this bet than bothe two be lorn.
> For love of God, take every womman heede
> To werken thus, if it comth to the neede. (III. 1223–5)

By combining a plea 'for love of God' with advising women to be sexually active, Chaucer draws attention to *Troilus and Criseyde*'s dramatisation of a fundamental division within medieval culture, between the lay world of love, marriage, and procreation, and the rejection of sexuality and (to some extent) marriage in clerical and ascetic circles. Resistance to love is an apt motif through which to address this division, as reluctant lovers can be positioned between these two worlds. Criseyde is given religious associations from the start, as she is described as 'aungelik', 'an hevenyssh perfit creature', but she is ultimately led away from piety towards earthly love and consciously rejects a religious model of life in her monologue on her feelings for Troilus, declaring 'I am naught religious'.[71] *Troilus and Criseyde* depicts loving as the expected and accepted course of action, reflecting the generic priorities of romance, but the narrative trajectory also holds this up to question and critique. While Troilus's own modelling of the transition from reluctant to willing lover provides a powerful example that sets the reader's expectations for Criseyde, Chaucer is not straightforwardly extolling love and secular life above chastity and virginity.

Instead, Chaucer's dramatisation of the conflict between earthly and heavenly love is part of *Troilus and Criseyde*'s provocative and ambivalent approach to love.[72] The ending of the poem, with Troilus's ascent into the

---

[70] *Chaucer and the Cultures of Love and Marriage*, p. 169.

[71] 'Troilus and Criseyde', I. 102, I. 104, II. 759. Although Saunders observes that Criseyde's 'presence opens the way to the celestial' for Troilus, for Criseyde Troilus's love perhaps has the opposite effect, moving her from a life of chaste widowhood to her involvement in multiple love affairs: see 'Love and the Making of the Self', p. 142.

[72] For further discussions of love in *Troilus and Criseyde*, indicative of some of the different views of the poem, see Marcia Smith Marzec, 'What Makes a Man? Troilus, Hector, and the Masculinities of Courtly Love', in *Men and Masculinities in Chaucer's 'Troilus and Criseyde'*, ed. by Tison Pugh and Marcia Smith Marzec (Cambridge: D. S. Brewer, 2008), pp. 58–72; Saunders, 'Love and the Making of the Self'; Derek Brewer, 'Chivalry', in *A Companion to Chaucer*, ed. by Peter Brown (Oxford: Blackwell, 2000), pp. 58–74 (pp. 70–1).

heavens and his sense of the futility of love, has been particularly but perhaps misleadingly significant for interpreting its attitude towards love. Noting that 'modern criticism has interpreted the poem through a retrospect', while Chaucer's later retraction 'would have been scarcely necessary if he shared the religiose modern interpretation of the poem as a cumulative critique of earthly love', Barry Windeatt suggests

> It is not too soon to seek a reading of the poem's approach to love that attempts to match the openness and open-endedness of *Troilus* itself as inseparably both a humanist and experimental work. [...] It has been uncommon – yet logical and timely – for the poem's conclusion itself to be included as not more than one among that multiplicity.[73]

Rather than condemning love, Chaucer questions the performance of love – its rituals, tropes, and social mannerisms – throughout the poem.[74] Troilus's initial hostility to love is more important to this than has previously been acknowledged, as Chaucer adds to his questioning of the tropes of romance and courtly love by framing Troilus within the Ovidian and romance framework of resisting love as arrogance. Notably, Chaucer seems to express doubt about the trope of the reluctant lover's conversion when Criseyde starts to favour Troilus, as the narrator suggests that some might think

> This was a sodeyn love; how myght it be
> That she so lightly loved Troilus
> Right for the firste syghte. (ii. 667–9)

This doubting perspective is partly affirmed when the narrator clarifies,[75]

> I sey nought that she so sodeynly
> Yaf hym hire love, but that she gan enclyne
> To like hym first. (ii. 673–5)

No such question of the plausibility of love at first sight was raised in relation to Troilus falling in love, and yet the connections between Troilus's and Criseyde's transformation from reluctant to willing lover ensure that any question raised about Criseyde's love may also reflect back upon Troilus's.[76] This is not to say that Chaucer, or his narrator, is cynically disavowing Troilus's love: the implied contrast perhaps suggests that love at first sight does exist and may even happen to those who wished to avoid it.[77] Chaucer seems to find

---

[73] Windeatt, 'Love in a Manner of Speaking', pp. 82, 95.
[74] See further Windeatt, 'Love in a Manner of Speaking', p. 86.
[75] Although, for a contrary view, see Mann, 'Troilus's Swoon', p. 8.
[76] Fradenburg also notes that this passage 'pushes the point of the contrast upon us': 'Loss, Gender and Chivalry', p. 103.
[77] For a contrasting perspective, see Rushton, 'The Awful Passion of Pandarus', p. 160.

the romance trope of resistance to love good to think with, as it intersects with ideas about the will and its violation, consent and *raptus*, and the operations of human, divine, and supernatural agency. Crucially, Chaucer also seems to recognise resistance to love as a trope particularly associated with romance. It recurs elsewhere in his *Knight's Tale*, *Wife of Bath's Tale* (not in relation to the rape at the beginning but the knight's resistance to loving the loathly lady), *Man of Law's Tale*, *Franklin's Tale*, and *Merchant's Tale*, works that between them make up a significant proportion of Chaucer's romances.[78] In portraying both Troilus and Criseyde as reluctant to love in different ways, and for different reasons, and making their romantic a(nti)pathy part of his interrogation of romance tropes and the stylisation of love, Chaucer reveals the capacious functions to which resistance to love could be put and highlights the understanding of this *as* a generic trope.

Un/Willingness to Love: *Sir Degrevant's* Emotional Lacunae

The anonymous *Sir Degrevant*, roughly contemporary with Chaucer's *Troilus and Criseyde*, describes the eponymous hero's feud with the neighbouring Earl, his sudden love for the Earl's daughter Melidor, and the eventual resolution of both the feud and the love-plot in Degrevant and Melidor's marriage. *Sir Degrevant* follows the same pattern as *Amadas et Ydoine* and *Troilus and Criseyde* in doubling the portrayal of resistance to love and depicting romantic a(nti)pathy as gendered both in the attitudes it elicits and the ways it is resolved. Like Troilus and Amadas, Degrevant is primarily known as a lover, 'Sir Degriuaunt þat amerus'.[79] His resistance to love is even more briefly represented than Troilus's and Amadas's: after a description of his military might, his royal connections as Arthur's nephew, and his love of music and hunting, we are told

> Certus, wyff wold he non,
> Wench ne lemon,
> Bot as an anker in a ston
> He lyved ever trew. (61–4)

Degrevant is entirely uninterested in women, love, and marriage, but this is described almost as an afterthought, placed in the last four lines of a sixteen-line stanza that otherwise focuses on hunting (and, briefly, attending church). L. F.

---

[78] Resistance to love is also mentioned briefly in *The Book of the Duchess*, perhaps more in the form of *dangier* (lines 1242–3), and is a major thematic concern in *The Parliament of Fowls*.

[79] *The Romance of Sir Degrevant*, ed. by L. F. Casson, EETS, o. s., 221 (London: Oxford University Press, 1949; repr. 1970), Cambridge University Library, MS Ff.1.6 (the Findern manuscript), line 671. All quotations from *Sir Degrevant* are taken from the Findern manuscript version in this edition unless otherwise stated.

Casson is one of only a few scholars to note Degrevant's resistance, commenting that 'there are a number of detailed resemblances between *Sir Degrevant* and the *Lay of Guigemar* by Marie', including the protagonists being 'indifferent to the charms of women'.[80] However, the recognition of resistance to love as a widespread romance motif in this book calls into question Casson's suggestion that a version of *Guigemar* was known to the author of *Sir Degrevant*. This is far from the only place the *Degrevant*-poet could have found this motif and is not the work most closely resembling Degrevant's romantic a(nti)pathy, which seems more akin to Amadas's and Troilus's. It is possible that *Sir Degrevant* may be directly influenced by *Amadas et Ydoine*, which is alluded to in the description of Melidor's bed (1494). However, there is no evidence that *Amadas et Ydoine* was circulating in England at the time *Sir Degrevant* was written, and it is not possible to tell whether the author knew the romance well or was just familiar with the characters' names.[81] *Sir Degrevant* may be borrowing a motif from *Amadas et Ydoine*, but both the early description of Degrevant's resistance to love and the later use of it as a contrast to Melidor's resistance to love and marry Degrevant (she says she will not 'loue my lordys enemy' but also 'nel non housbond haue ʒyte', 998, 1002) suggest a deeper engagement with this motif than simply imitating an earlier work.

The curious reference to Degrevant living 'as an anker in a ston' particularly stands out, suggesting an unusual perspective on romantic a(nti)pathy rather than a straightforward borrowing. This could be an ironic comment: although anchoritic solitude 'rarely involved total isolation', with his love of music and hunting Degrevant very clearly does not live 'as an anker'.[82] This comparison may imply that anchorites were not living as solitary a life as they were supposed to, an anxiety evident in the early thirteenth-century *Ancrene Wisse*, which warns that the devil may bring an anchoress 'aleast makien feaste ant wurthen al worldlich, forschuppet of ancre to huse-wif of halle' [at last to make feasts and become entirely worldly, deformed from an anchoress into a housewife of a hall].[83] However, the comparison of Degrevant to an anchorite may also reflect ironically upon Degrevant and the romance tradition, suggesting the hyperbole of romance representations of resistance to love.

---

[80] L. F. Casson, 'Introduction', in *The Romance of Sir Degrevant*, ed. by Casson, pp. ix–lxxv (p. lxvi). Sylvester also notes Degrevant's initial resistance but reads this as typical for 'the perfect romance hero', which I do not. See *Medieval Romance and the Construction of Heterosexuality*, p. 18.

[81] See further Arthur, 'Introduction', in *Amadas and Ydoine*, ed. & trans. by Arthur, pp. 9–16 (p. 11).

[82] Cate Gunn and Liz Herbert McAvoy, 'Introduction: "No Such Thing as Society"? Solitude in Community', in *Medieval Anchorites in their Communities*, ed. by Cate Gunn and Liz Herbert McAvoy (Cambridge: D. S. Brewer, 2017), pp. 1–12 (p. 5).

[83] *Ancrene Wisse*, ed. by Robert Hasenfratz, TEAMS (Kalamazoo: Medieval Institute Publications, 2000), IV. 552–3. My translation.

Another possibility is that this could be a serious and unintentional instance of that very same hyperbole. Degrevant is a pious man, who 'lovede well almosdede, / Powr men to cloth and fede' (81–2): living 'as an anker' may simply be an exaggerated instantiation of his piety and virginity, or a uniting of religious and lay perspectives on virginity and masculinity. While we cannot know how medieval readers interpreted this reference, the differing content of the two manuscripts of *Sir Degrevant* may have fostered alternative interpretations. Cambridge University Library, MS Ff.1.6 (the Findern manuscript) is comprised mostly of 'lyrics and texts meditating on aristocratic conventions of love', within which Degrevant's anchoritic lifestyle might well seem an ironic or satirical feature.[84] Lincoln Cathedral Library, MS 91 (the Lincoln Thornton manuscript), on the other hand, includes works by Richard Rolle – a hermit and mystic – alongside which a comic reference to anchoritism seems more unlikely.[85] These broader contexts may have encouraged different interpretations of the striking comparison between Degrevant's romantic a(nti)pathy and anchoritic life.

While the reference to anchoritism is intriguing and unusual, the primary significance of Degrevant's resistance to love is, as for Amadas and Troilus, its interaction with and reflection upon the resistance of the romance heroine, Melidor. Although Degrevant is initially averse to love and marriage, when he sees Melidor, his enemy's daughter, the impact is instant:

> Wyth loue she wondus þe kny3t;
> In hert trewly he hyeght
> That he shall loue þat swet wy3t,
> Acheue how hit wold. (477–80)

While there is a brief, conventional reference to how Melidor 'wondus' Degrevant, Degrevant's conversion to love is accomplished briefly and unproblematically. There is little sense of Degrevant being subjected to love, or of any contradiction between his earlier reluctance to take a wife and his sudden passion for Melidor. Degrevant simply does not wish to love, then sees Melidor and changes his mind. There is some suggestion that this acceptance

---

[84] Michael Johnston, *Romance and the Gentry in Late Medieval England* (Oxford: Oxford University Press, 2014), p. 129.

[85] For a full list of the Lincoln Thornton manuscript's contents, see Susanna Fein, 'The Contents of Robert Thornton's Manuscripts', in *Robert Thornton and His Books: Essays on the Lincoln and London Thornton Manuscripts*, ed. by Susanna Fein and Michael Johnston (York: York Medieval Press, 2014), pp. 13–65 (pp. 21–48). Fein also discusses the religious focus of many of the texts Robert Thornton copied and the way 'he considered scribal work to be pious work', pp. 15, 19–20 (quotation at p. 19). In the Thornton manuscript, *Sir Degrevant* appears between the *Life of Saint Christopher* and *Sir Eglamour of Artois*.

of love is the correct course of action, as the Earl (Degrevant's enemy) later declares that

> Couþe he loue par amoure,
> I knew neuer hys mak. (1063–4)

This positions Degrevant's initial a(nti)pathy towards love as a flaw. The narrative trajectory also endorses Degrevant's acceptance of love, as this benefits him socially and financially, and eventually reconciles him with the Earl. Yet Degrevant is not criticised for his resistance to love when it is first introduced: although Casson's marginal summaries suggest that Degrevant 'was fond of music / and hunting, / *but* would have nothing to do with women', this adversative conjunction is not implied by the romance.[86] In some ways, *Sir Degrevant* offers the most idealistic conversion from resistance to acceptance of love, as it relies solely upon the beauty and attractions of one particular woman – in contrast to the more subversive portrayal in *Guigemar*.

However, Melidor's own conversion to loving Degrevant is not so clear-cut or idealised; as in *Amadas et Ydoine* and *Troilus and Criseyde*, women's resistance and consent seem to be perceived as more complex and problematic issues than men's attitudes towards love and marriage. Melidor's feelings for Degrevant are often described in ambiguous ways. When they first see each other,

> Þe Eorlus doughder be-held
> That borlich and bolde;
> For he was armed so clen
> [...]
> Was ioy to be-hold. (467–72)

The passive construction implies that Melidor enjoys looking at Degrevant but avoids stating this outright: as Louise Sylvester argues, 'the author of the romance is careful to reveal only Degrevant's feelings', as he instantly falls in love.[87] The protagonists' attitudes to love are thus contrasted through their initial reactions to each other. Similarly, when Degrevant breaks into the Earl's castle, fully armed but seeking to plight troth with Melidor, her response is ambiguous: she

> was gretely affraid,
> But naþeles hoo was wel paid,
> He was so ryally arayd. (701–3)

Melidor's fear and her complaint that Degrevant 'not dost ryȝth', because 'þou comyst armid on werre / To maydenus to afferre' (707–10) emphasise

[86] *Sir Degrevant*, p. 5 (my emphasis).
[87] Sylvester, *Medieval Romance and the Construction of Heterosexuality*, p. 18.

the coercive elements within this scene of two armed men surprising two women relaxing in their castle gardens.[88] As James Brundage notes, canon lawyers took a broad view of the kind of force necessary to constitute coercion: 'the sight of a group of armed men under the command of the attacker might be held to constitute violent force, even if no physical assault actually occurred'.[89] This may be reflected in Degrevant's 'martial approach to courtship' here, which is further echoed in his second attempt to win Melidor's love by interrupting a feast hosted by her father, where he 'chalangys þat fre' (1220), claiming Melidor as his tournament prize.[90] While these strategies do not succeed, Degrevant may be seen as first threatening Melidor and then making her consent irrelevant.

Their next encounter does focus on Melidor's will but only as mediated through her actions, as she leads a horse to Degrevant in the tournament and declares she will ride 'by my lemmanus syde' (1319). The Middle English text is a little unclear here, but Melidor seems to be supporting Degrevant and even going so far as to declare him her lover. By this point, then, her reluctance has apparently transformed into love, but the process by which this happens has been obscured from the reader, leaving an emotional lacuna in place of narrating her feelings and therefore offering no insights into how and why she decides to develop their relationship. The contrast between representing Melidor's transformation from unwilling to willing lover through actions only and Degrevant's own transformation, where his emotions are communicated to the reader, reveals the opacity with which romance sometimes treats women's emotional lives. The vital thing here is the outcome of Melidor's acceptance of Degrevant – their marriage, the end of Degrevant's feud with Melidor's father, and his social advancement as her husband – rather than the process through which she accepts him. The elision of how Melidor's feelings for Degrevant change is only compounded when she later tells him

> þe ferste tyme Y þe mette,
> Myn hert on þe was sette. (1538–9)

This erases her own resistance and offers a further comparison with Degrevant as she remodels her desire upon his. Degrevant's unwillingness may seem insignificant, barely commented upon and swiftly overcome, but it provides an important contrast to Melidor's resistance to love or marry Degrevant. Melidor's reluctance combines elements of anxiety about her familial

---

[88] For an analysis of Melidor's and Degrevant's agency in terms of speech acts during this encounter, see *Ibid.*, pp. 22–5.

[89] James A. Brundage, *Sex, Law and Marriage in the Middle Ages* (Aldershot: Variorum, 1993), p. 68.

[90] Arlyn Diamond, '*Sir Degrevant*: what lovers want', in *Pulp Fictions of Medieval England: Essays in Popular Romance*, ed. by Nicola McDonald (Manchester: Manchester University Press, 2004), pp. 82–101 (p. 86).

obligations, as she rejects Degrevant when she knows he is her father's enemy (733–60), a dual fear and fascination of Degrevant's intrusions into the castle, and potentially some concern with social status, as Melidor's maid comments that Degrevant's status is below that of Melidor's other suitors (857–60). While Degrevant's attitude to love changes according to his spontaneous desire, Melidor's reluctance is grounded in social concerns and is susceptible to both consensual and coercive persuasion, rather than solely responsive to her own feelings. Like *Amadas et Ydoine* and *Troilus and Criseyde*, *Sir Degrevant* demonstrates that both the means of overcoming resistance and the challenge it poses are differently inflected in relation to gender. These representations not only respond to, but actively construct, contemporary ideas of gender, suggesting that women *ought* to consider the social consequences of love.

Queer Alternatives: Thomas Malory's Dynadan

Sir Dynadan from Malory's late medieval Arthurian prose romance, *Le Morte Darthur*, contrasts with the other examples discussed in this chapter. Thus far, resistance to love was mentioned briefly (with the exception of *Guigemar*) at the start of each text and then swiftly overcome, turning reluctant lovers into exemplary ones. In contrast, Dynadan's resistance to love is introduced very late in Malory, after he has already played a significant role in the adventures of Tristram. This may seem to minimise the importance of Dynadan's romantic a(nti)pathy, making it merely a part of his widely recognised role as a comic questioner of chivalry.[91] However, this late introduction is appropriate to the different function of Dynadan's resistance. In contrast to the usual pattern of reluctance to love being overcome to facilitate narrative resolution, Malory's Dynadan never falls in love (as is the case in most – but not all – versions of Malory's source for this part of the *Morte*, the *Tristan en prose*).[92] His roman-

---

[91] See Carolyne Larrington, 'Gender/Queer Studies', in *Handbook of Arthurian Romance: King Arthur's Court in Medieval European Literature*, ed. by Leah Tether and Johnny McFadyen (Berlin: de Gruyter, 2017), pp. 259–72 (p. 269); Gergely Nagy, 'A Fool of a Knight, a Knight of a Fool: Malory's Comic Knights', *Arthuriana*, 14.4 (2004), 59–74; Dorsey Armstrong, *Gender and the Chivalric Community in Malory's 'Morte d'Arthur'* (Gainesville: University Press of Florida, 2003), p. 142; D. Thomas Hanks, Jr., 'Characterization or Jumble? Sir Dinadan in Malory', *Medieval Perspectives*, 2.1 (1987), 167–76 (p. 173); Donald L. Hoffman, 'Dinadan: The Excluded Middle', *Tristania*, 10.1–2 (1984–85), 3–16 (p. 14); Keith Busby, 'The Likes of Dinadan: The Rôle of the Misfit in Arthurian Literature', *Neophilologus*, 67.2 (1983), 161–74 (p. 166).

[92] Version I of the *Tristan* does include a brief episode where Dynadan falls in love: see *Le Roman de Tristan en prose: Version du manuscrit fr. 757 de la Bibliothèque nationale de Paris*, ed. by Joël Blanchard and Michel Quéreuil, Classiques français du moyen âge, 123, 5 vols (Paris: Champion, 1997), I, 113–4 (28). However, Malory used a version of the *Tristan* combining Versions II and IV, so was likely unaware of this episode.

tic a(nti)pathy persists and endures, marking him out as an alternative, queer figure who stands at odds with the normative patterns of romance.[93]

While Dynadan does not reinforce sexual and marital norms through his own narrative trajectory, there is a sense in which his character can be seen to reinforce romance norms through the contrast he offers to Tristram, the superior knight and lover. As D. Thomas Hanks comments,

> Dinadan as foil is perhaps an idea that explains itself as soon as voiced. Where Tristram is invariably brave, Dinadan is as likely as not to flee danger [...]. Where Tristram loves Isolde faithfully (excepting his inexplicable marriage to Isolde of the White Hands), Dinadan refuses to love at all. Tristram shines the brighter through his contrast with Dinadan.[94]

Dynadan as a foil to Tristram in some ways replicates the use of romantic a(nti)pathy as a contrast to subsequent passion in the romances discussed previously, albeit through two different figures rather than within one character (although Dynadan is sometimes thought of as a double for Tristram).[95] Their unequal martial prowess is evident from Dynadan's first major appearance in the *Morte*, when he rides to Cornwall to seek Tristram, jousts with him, is unhorsed by him, and joins him in fellowship.[96] The contrast between them is linked to love when Dynadan complains 'in all the worlde ar nat such too knyghtes that ar so wood as ys Sir Launcelot and ye Sir Trystram!' (p. 400), railing against the eagerness to fight of the two 'trewyst lovers' in the Arthurian court (p. 57). This anticipates the later and more extensive contrast drawn between Dynadan and Tristram, when Dynadan's disinterest in love is revealed in full for the first time. As Dynadan scorns lovers, declaring 'fye on that crauffte!', Tristram counters that 'a knyght may never be of proues but yf he be a lovear' (p. 544), voicing what 'is virtually an equation of chivalric

---

See Ralph Norris, *Malory's Library: The Sources of the 'Morte Darthur'* (Cambridge: D. S. Brewer, 2008), p. 96.

[93] My interpretation here departs from Johnson's suggestion that Dynadan's rejection of love is a rejection of a specific kind of love, *fin amor*. In comparison with other representations of men's romantic a(nti)pathy I think Dynadan's resistance appears much more thoroughly subversive and queer. See David F. Johnson, '"A grete bourder and a passynge good knyght": Sir Dinadan: "Gareth with a Twist"', *Arthurian Literature*, 37 (2022), pp. 49–65 (p. 64).

[94] D. Thomas Hanks, Jr., 'Foil and Forecast: Dinadan in *The Book of Sir Tristram*', *Arthurian Yearbook*, 1 (1991), 149–63 (p. 159).

[95] See Busby, 'The Likes of Dinadan', p. 165; Stefano Mula, 'Dinadan Abroad: Tradition and Innovation for a Counter-Hero', in *The European Dimensions of Arthurian Literature*, ed. by Bart Besamusca, Frank Brandsma, and Keith Busby (= *Arthurian Literature*, 24 (2007)), pp. 50–64 (pp. 54–5).

[96] Johnson has recently drawn attention to the potential significance of the earlier mentions of Dynadan, but I concentrate on the later, more substantial episodes in which he appears: 'Sir Dinadan: "Gareth with a Twist"'.

behavior'.[97] Yet although Władysław Witalisz misleadingly claims that 'in his reaction Dinadan questions this romance truth', in fact Dynadan tells Tristram 'ye say well'.[98] Dynadan does not challenge the romance equation of love with prowess through his response but accepts this paradigm and his own disconnection from it. This acceptance may seem to uphold the normative expectations of romance, but Dynadan may also be read as offering a kind of 'yes, and...' here. His acceptance of this equation *and* his own distance from it marks him out as an alternative to the norm, opening up different, more subversive and queer possibilities.

These queer potentialities may be read as celebrated or contained within dominant norms, depending on how we understand Dynadan's comic role to function. Dynadan's comic role is directly related to his resistance to love in his dialogue with Isode, when he arrives at Joyous Gard looking for Tristram in the second book of 'Sir Tristram de Lyones'. Isode and Dynadan discuss Dynadan's resistance to love and its merits or disadvantages, Isode ultimately asking Dynadan whether he would live up to the example set by Sir Bleoberys de Ganys by fighting three knights for her, going so far as to say 'insomuche as ye bene a knyght of Kynge Arthurs, I requyre you to do batayle for me' (p. 549). Dynadan responds,

> 'I shall sey you ye be as fayre a lady as evir I sawe ony, and much fayrer than is my lady Quene Gwenyvere, but wyte you well, at one worde, I woll nat fyght for you wyth thre knyghtes, Jesu me defende!'

> Than Isode lowghe, and had good game at hym. So he had all the chyre that she myght make hym, and there he lay all that nyght. (p. 549)

Isode responds to Dynadan with laughter, a response that Dorsey Armstrong reads as acceptance, aligning with recent work by Stephanie Trigg and Debra Best, who have argued that the ability to make someone laugh is a knightly or courtly accomplishment.[99] In this sense, Dynadan's comic role could indeed be seen as 'a positive alternative to the standard "knights who serve ladies"

---

[97] Dhira Mahoney, '"Ar ye a knyght and ar no lovear?": The Chivalry Topos in Malory's *Book of Sir Tristram*', in *Conjunctures: Medieval Studies in Honor of Douglas Kelly*, ed. by Keith Busby and Norris J. Lacy (Amsterdam: Rodopi, 1994), pp. 311–24 (p. 311).

[98] Władysław Witalisz, 'A (Crooked) Mirror for Knights – The Case of Dinadan', *Studia Anglica Posnaniensia*, 44 (2008), 457–62 (p. 460); Malory, *Le Morte Darthur*, p. 544.

[99] Armstrong, *Gender and the Chivalric Community*, p. 141; Stephanie Trigg, '"Laughe and pleye so womanly": Feeling Happy' (presented at the 22nd Biennial New Chaucer Society Congress, Durham, 2022); Debra E. Best, '"A lowed laghtur that lady logh": Laughter, Snark, and Sarcasm in Middle English Romance', in *Words that Tear the Flesh: Essays on Sarcasm in Medieval and Early Modern Literature and Cultures*, ed. by Stephen Alan Baragona and Elizabeth Louise Rambo (Berlin: de Gruyter, 2018), pp. 143–64.

paradigm'; Dynadan the famous japer may be celebrated not despite but in part because of his resistance to love, which he mobilises to comic effect.[100] The 'chyre' Dynadan receives from Isode certainly indicates a positive reaction to his answer. However, might we not stop and ask: is Dynadan actually joking here?

Dynadan's response to Isode is entirely characteristic: while he displays bravery at times in the *Morte*, he is no stranger to weighing up the odds and, if he decides they are not in his favour, doing everything in his power to avoid fighting. There are some notable exceptions, including his offer to fight Palomydes for Tristram when Tristram is wounded, even if this would result in his death. However, this seems to testify to his particular love for Tristram more than his innate bravery. While Dynadan's response may be intended to make Isode laugh, then, it also seems likely to be true. So where exactly does the humour come from here? Theories of camp, specifically camp conceived as queer discourse and as performative, may be a helpful way to understand the humour of Dynadan's response. Dynadan often deliberately performs and exaggerates his chosen roles of japer or coward, aligning with the queerness of camp as an exaggeration of a stereotype that functions as 'a survivalist strategy (working through a reinscription of stigma) for the subordinated, the excluded, the unnatural, the fake'.[101] That is, Dynadan recognises that a good knight is required to be brave and to be in love with a woman, and that he is neither, and he responds to this difference not by hiding it or denying it but by exaggerating it. This maps onto understandings of the humour of camp: Esther Newton has argued that 'camp humor is a system of laughing at one's incongruous position instead of crying', while Ann Pellegrini suggests with regard to Jewish camp that 'when the joke's on you, perhaps the best defence is getting there first'.[102] This seems to me an apt model for Dynadan's humorous role-playing, and particularly his exchange with Isode. Dynadan may recognise that refusing to fight three knights for Isode is shameful, but he also realises that her beauty and encouragement do not motivate him. He responds to the threat of shame not by shying away from it but by making this truth comic, sharing it as a joke with Isode rather than allowing her to mock him: getting to the joke first.

---

[100] Armstrong, *Gender and the Chivalric Community*, p. 141.

[101] Fabio Cleto, 'Introduction: Queering the Camp', in *Camp: Queer Aesthetics and the Performing Subject*, ed. by Fabio Cleto (Edinburgh: Edinburgh University Press, 1999), pp. 1–42 (p. 8).

[102] Esther Newton, *Mother Camp: Female Impersonators in America* (Chicago: University of Chicago Press, 1972), p. 109; Ann Pellegrini, 'After Sontag: Future Notes on Camp', in *A Companion to Lesbian, Gay, Bisexual, Transgender, and Queer Studies*, ed. by George E. Haggerty and Molly McGarry (Oxford: Blackwell, 2007), pp. 168–93 (p. 178).

This shared joke, however, acts as a survival strategy not only for Dynadan but also for Isode. When Armstrong considers the use of laughter elsewhere in the *Morte*, in the episode where Dynadan is forced to don women's clothing, she suggests that laughter is not only 'reflecting the dissipation of gender anxiety, but rather, functioning as a strategy to diffuse such anxiety'.[103] Dynadan and Isode's exchange may also operate in this dual direction, both marking and diffusing anxiety over Dynadan's response and its challenge to romance's chivalric and romantic priorities. Dynadan must present himself as camp, comic, playing a role in order not to be read as deviating threateningly from expected norms, while Isode must read Dynadan this way in order to overlook his challenge to these norms, both tacitly agreeing that it is 'only' a joke. However, this strategy of assimilation may not be entirely successful, because identifying Dynadan as only telling a joke draws attention to the performative nature of the opposite role against which Dynadan defines himself: the role of the brave lover–knight, which is no less performative than Dynadan's cowardly persona. The performativity of knighthood is indeed foregrounded in the comparison and contrast between Tristram and Dynadan because of the episode where Tristram pretends to be a coward and Dynadan berates him for this, performing a direct reversal of their roles (pp. 544–6, 549–52). Tristram, too, is revealed as a master role-player here, denaturalising not only Dynadan's posturing but the posturing of all knights, even – or perhaps especially – the 'good' ones.

To read Dynadan as camp, with a focus on camp as intertwined with queer gender or sexuality, both aligns with and opens up the wider queer resonances of his role in the *Morte Darthur*. That Dynadan has queer potential is suggested in gendered terms when he is forced to wear women's clothing at the tournament of Surluse, making Guenevere and the court laugh so hard they fall down.[104] Again, pausing to ask exactly what is funny here highlights Dynadan's camp role, as well as the way in which laughter might enable or contain subversive potential. Guenevere laughs at Dynadan 'ibrought in so amonge them all' (p. 530), but she does not seem to be laughing at the sight of a knight dressed in women's clothing, as Launcelot has just donned women's clothing with no humorous effects. Instead, it seems to be the sight of *Dynadan* dressed in women's clothing that is humorous. Why might this be? Is it a matter of intention – is it amusing that Dynadan has been forced to wear women's clothing as a token of humiliation before the court, where Launcelot

---

[103] Armstrong, *Gender and the Chivalric Community*, p. 140. See further Sandra M. Hordis, 'Gender Anxiety and Dialogic Laughter in Malory's *Morte Darthur*', in *Medieval English Comedy*, ed. by Sandra M. Hordis and Paul Hardwick (Turnhout: Brepols, 2007), pp. 145–70.

[104] On this episode, see Armstrong, *Gender and the Chivalric Community*, pp. 135–40; Molly Martin, *Vision and Gender in Malory's 'Morte Darthur'* (Cambridge: D. S. Brewer, 2010), pp. 91–3; Hoffman, 'Dinadan: The Excluded Middle', pp. 9–12.

wore such clothing as a deliberate disguise on the battlefield? Or is Dynadan the source of humour because of something about him? Newton writes that drag 'is a double inversion that says, "appearance is an illusion". Drag says "my 'outside' appearance is feminine, but my essence 'inside' [the body] is masculine". At the same time it symbolizes the opposite inversion; "my appearance 'outside' [my body, my gender] is masculine but my essence 'inside' [myself] is feminine"'.[105] Is Guenevere laughing because she recognises that Dynadan's enforced drag expresses his difference, a difference that he himself expresses comically and that others receive as comic – perhaps in part to assimilate it rather than be forced to recognise it?

Dynadan being forced to wear women's clothing imposes queerness upon him in relation to gender, but he could with more accuracy and more attention to his self-expression be seen as queer in terms of sexuality. Indeed, this may be what Guenevere and the court are picking up on in framing Dynadan as different through the enforced drag. Dynadan's love of Tristram is well known. It is perhaps most clearly illuminated during the tournament at the Castle of Maidens, when Dynadan uncharacteristically bravely volunteers to fight Palomydes for Tristram, who is wounded, telling him 'yf I be slayne ye may pray for my soule' (p. 419). In addition, Gareth remarks upon Dynadan's love for Tristram at Lonezep, telling Tristram 'ye ar the man in the worlde that he lovyth beste' (p. 589), while Dynadan himself tells Palomydes 'I love my lorde Sir Trystram abovyn all othir knyghtes, and hym woll I serve and do honoure' (p. 479). Although Corinne Saunders suggests that in Dynadan's declaration of love, 'the reader is drawn away from the individual erotics of love by Malory's inclusion of Lamorak's affirmation of this sentiment', Lamerok's response has a rather different emphasis to Dynadan's, as he declares 'so shall I […] in all that I may with my power'.[106] While Dynadan articulates his love for Tristram and his intention to serve him, Lamerok affirms his service without expressing his love. Of course, love for another knight is not necessarily erotic: references to knights' love of each other are fairly frequent and often platonic in the *Morte*. However, the eroticism of Dynadan's love for Tristram is suggested by his comment in the scene with Lamerok that 'I woll nat abyde, for I have suche a talente to se Sir Trystram that I may nat abyde longe from hym' (p. 479). P. J. C. Field glosses 'talente' as 'longing';[107] it can also mean 'desire', 'inclination', 'inherent physical urge or drive', or 'resolve'

[105] Newton, *Mother Camp*, p. 103.

[106] Corinne Saunders, '"Greater love hath no man": Friendship in Medieval English Romance', in *Traditions and Innovations in the Study of Medieval English Literature: The Influence of Derek Brewer*, ed. by Charlotte Brewer and Barry Windeatt (Cambridge: D. S. Brewer, 2013), pp. 128–43 (p. 138); Malory, *Le Morte Darthur*, p. 479.

[107] P. J. C. Field, 'Glossary', in *Le Morte Darthur: Apparatus, Commentary, Glossary, and Index of Names*, ed. by P. J. C. Field, 2 vols (Cambridge: D. S. Brewer, 2013), II, 893–988 (p. 974).

('talent' is also the Anglo-Norman word used to describe Guigemar's lack of desire to love).[108] 'Talente' is rare in Malory's *Morte*: Tomomi Kato's concordance records it only once, in this scene.[109] This unusual term marks out Dynadan's powerful attachment to Tristram as unusual and perhaps excessive, going beyond the normative boundaries of chivalric attachment to indicate a queer connection. Analogous figures to Dynadan provide further support for a queer reading: Keith Busby explores the parallels between Dynadan and Galehaut of the *Lancelot en prose* in the Vulgate *Lancelot-Grail* Cycle, commenting that 'the intensity of Galehaut's love for Lancelot can be illustrated from practically every page of the "Galehaut" section'.[110] Of course, the fact that Dynadan's love for Tristram is less intense and less frequently commented upon in Malory and the *Tristan en prose* is significant: Galehaut's love for Lancelot is of a different quality. But the influence of Galehaut upon both the *Tristan en prose* and directly on Malory suggests that Dynadan's love for Tristram carries a queer residue. This is not fully activated by Malory, but in combination with Dynadan's resistance to love (or, more accurately, his resistance to love *women*) and his camp and comic expressions of gender and alternative sexuality, it reveals the presence of queer identities in the *Morte*.[111] The humorous role attributed to Dynadan therefore also illustrates how queer identities can be subsumed into the dominant courtly culture. Yet such assimilation is not complete: Dynadan's performance of comedy and cowardice may foreground the ways in which more normative roles are themselves performed and constructed, inhabiting both the radical and conservative possibilities of camp and leaving them open for the reader to activate. Like *Guigemar*, then, the role of Dynadan in the *Morte* both reveals the strategies romance deploys to circumscribe queerness and indicates the queer potential of the motif of resistance to love.

Conclusion

While men's expressions of romantic a(nti)pathy form a sporadic and often briefly represented motif, this is nonetheless a significant one, situated at the nexus of romance's generic concerns with love, gender, and chivalric performance. Two of the romances discussed in this chapter reveal the queer potential of resistance to love, *Guigemar* resonating with modern understandings of asexuality and retaining elements of dissonance even in the normative

---

[108] 'Talent n.', *Middle English Dictionary* <https://quod.lib.umich.edu/m/middle-english-dictionary/dictionary/MED44433> [accessed 19 July 2023].

[109] Tomomi Kato, *A Concordance to the Works of Sir Thomas Malory* (Tokyo: University of Tokyo Press, 1974), p. 1192.

[110] Busby, 'The Likes of Dinadan', p. 164.

[111] The Vulgate *Lancelot-Grail* Cycle was one of Malory's main sources for the *Morte*: see Norris, *Malory's Library*, pp. 4, 11, 70–3.

ending and Malory's Dynadan offering a more permanent queer alternative both masked and preserved by his camp performance. Both narratives to some extent circumscribe their depictions of queerness, though they do not do so completely. They therefore indicate romances' investment in upholding sexual and gendered norms, but also their failure to maintain these norms entirely. Similarly, *Amadas et Ydoine, Troilus and Criseyde*, and *Sir Degrevant* both perpetuate and question gendered norms. They indicate that consent and coercion are gendered issues in romance, positioning women's romantic a(nti) pathy as both more problematic and more vulnerable to forms of coercion than men's resistance to love. But at times they also invite questions about why men's and women's romantic a(nti)pathy is treated and resolved so differently. Taken together, the five romances discussed in this chapter illustrate romance's self-conscious negotiation of gender, sexuality, and generic expectations, suggesting the generative potential medieval writers found in romantic a(nti)pathy as a motif that encourages exploration of contemporary expectations. Do romances primarily focused upon women's romantic a(nti) pathy, and particularly those portraying the figure of the proud lady in love, raise the same questions and uphold the same norms? Chapter 2 investigates the proud lady's role in exploring, questioning, and upholding cultural ideas of love, marriage, and gendered behaviour.

2

'But of love to lere': The Proud Lady in Love[1]

*B*lanchardyn and Eglantine, translated from the fifteenth-century French prose redaction of *Blancandin et l'Orgueilleuse d'amours* by William Caxton in 1489, tells of how Blanchardyn leaves his parents' home upon learning of chivalry and sets out to prove himself as a knight. Entering the neighbouring country of Darye, he hears of the queen of that land, Eglantine, who is known as 'the proude lady in loue' because she refuses all suitors.[2] The Knight of the Ferry, one of Eglantine's vassals, urges Blanchardyn to try and kiss Eglantine and then help defend her against the attacks of the Muslim King Alymodes, claiming that this will result in Blanchardyn and Eglantine falling in love. Events follow largely as he predicts: initially furious about the kiss, Eglantine's heart softens as she sees evidence of Blanchardyn's chivalric prowess and courtly behaviour. The fulfilment of their love in marriage, while apparently expected from the start, is delayed by various battles, maritime mishaps, and betrayals, but the end of this lengthy romance sees the couple married and ruling their joint realms together. Eglantine's transformation from a proud and scornful attitude to love towards acceptance of an exemplary knight is echoed in other Middle English romances. While Eglantine is the only romance heroine directly labelled 'the proud lady in love', I suggest that this offers an appropriate appellation for a wider group of heroines in Middle English romances of the fourteenth and fifteenth centuries.

---

[1] Quotation from *Ipomadon*, ed. by Rhiannon Purdie, EETS, o. s., 316 (Oxford: Oxford University Press, 2001), line 108.

[2] The land the proud lady rules is also known as Tormaday, after its main city. Eglantine's name is not used at all within the body of William Caxton's edition, so far as I can find. It is used in the dedication and the heading of Caxton's table of contents but does not seem to appear anywhere within the romance itself. Her name is used more in the 1595 adaptation by Thomas Pope Goodwine (printed by William Blackwall and available on EEBO), but in Caxton's she is usually referred to as 'the proude mayden in amours' or 'the proude pucelle in amours'. I refer to her as Eglantine to avoid any confusion with my use of 'the proud lady' as a broader label. All references are to William Caxton, *Blanchardyn and Eglantine, c. 1489*, ed. by Leon Kellner, EETS, e. s., 58 (Oxford: Oxford University Press, 1890). See p. 2 of the 'Dedication' and p. 3 for the table of contents.

This group encompasses Felice from *Guy of Warwick* (c. 1300), the Fere from *Ipomadon* (c. 1390–1400), Winglayne from *Eger and Grime* (c. 1450), Ettarde from Thomas Malory's *Morte Darthur* (1469–70), and of course Eglantine herself.[3] These women all resist love and/or marriage (with the exception of the *Morte*, love is usually aligned with marriage in these works),[4] rejecting suitors outright or issuing a difficult, if not impossible, condition for their hand to be won. They are usually referred to as proud or portrayed as proud in some way, they rule or are heiresses to significant lands and wealth, and they generally accept love and marriage by each romance's conclusion. While each of these works, with the exception of *Eger and Grime*, is a translation or adaptation of an earlier Anglo-Norman or French romance, the linguistic, geographic, and chronological range of their French sources means that they have not been considered together, despite their similarities.[5] Focusing on the adaptation of these works in Middle English romances of the fourteenth and fifteenth centuries illuminates the proud lady in love as a more cohesive and discrete motif, opening up new possibilities for interpretation, and bringing to light a group of romances that combines canonical texts (*Guy of Warwick* and Malory's *Morte*) with more understudied works that tend to be dismissed as straightforward translations of French romances (such as *Blanchardyn and Eglantine*). The proud lady clearly comes from the French tradition, but I argue that she is an important figure in Middle English romance who offers key insights into the functions of romantic a(nti)pathy expressed by women.

The proud ladies upon whom I focus in this chapter are not the only women in Middle English romance who are hostile or indifferent to love. In addition to those considered in the previous chapter, Emelye from Geoffrey Chaucer's *Knight's Tale* attempts to resist love but is married by the end of the narrative, while the group of haughty damsels who scorn unproven knights could also be thought of as resisting love (though they do not usually become the knights' wives). There is also a broader conceptual link between pride and

---

[3]   *Eger and Grime* is a Scottish text but circulates in an anglicised form and context in London, British Library, MS Additional 27879 (the Percy Folio).

[4]   In *Ipomadon* the Fere makes a vow refusing to be the 'wyffe' of an unworthy knight, but she is labelled 'provde of love' for this (lines 117, 104). In *Blanchardyn and Eglantine*, Eglantine is described as resisting love, but the concerns of her vassals clearly align this with the stakes of marriage. *Eger and Grime* depicts the opposite scenario: Winglayne's vow relates a condition for her marriage, but there is no suggestion that she could love Eger or any other knight in a context separate from her proposed marriage. *Guy of Warwick* provides a particularly interesting example because Felice and Guy seem to shift the negotiation from love to marriage, as I discuss briefly below.

[5]   *Guy of Warwick* and *Ipomadon* translate and adapt the Anglo-Norman *Gui de Warewic* and Hue de Rotelande's *Ipomedon*. Malory's Pelleas and Ettarde episode adapts a section of the Post-Vulgate *Suite du Merlin*, while *Blanchardyn and Eglantine* is a translation of the fifteenth-century French prose *Blancandin et l'Orgueilleuse d'amours*, itself an adaptation of the thirteenth-century verse *Blancandin et l'Orgueilleuse d'amour*.

women's rejections of love in the romance tradition. In addition to *Guigemar* and *Amadas et Ydoine*, discussed in Chapter 1, Chrétien de Troyes's works sometimes describe women as proud when they reject love, and occasionally the women themselves indicate that they know they may be thought of as proud if they refuse a knight's advances.[6] Early French *lais* also associate women's resistance to love with pride, in *Narcisus et Dané*, the *Lai du Trot*, *Graelent*, and *Doon*.[7] This association recurs in the later *Belle dame sans mercy* tradition, where the lady is sometimes referred to as proud, though she is primarily described as cruel.[8] These associations are often brief, sometimes having little to no narrative impact, but such cursory references suggest that presenting women's resistance to love as a form of pride would be widely understood. Although these references are particularly common in French texts, the appearance of the proud ladies I discuss in this chapter in the Middle English tradition, together with the circulation of several of the French texts mentioned above in medieval England, suggests that the conceptual link between women's romantic a(nti)pathy and pride would have been recognised by medieval English readers.[9] This preconditions interpretation of women's resistance to love by presenting it in a negative light: pride is, of course, one of the seven deadly sins, commonly represented in medieval literature and cultural artefacts, and thus a point of reference readily available to medieval

---

[6]   For example, Blancheflor tells the eponymous protagonist of *Perceval* 's'ele vos ert escondite, / Vos le tendriiez a orgueil' ['you'd think me proud if [my love] were denied you']: Chrétien de Troyes, *Le Roman de Perceval ou Le Conte du Graal*, ed. by Keith Busby (Tübingen: Niemeyer, 1993), lines 2110–11; Chrétien de Troyes, 'The Story of the Grail (Perceval)', in *Chrétien de Troyes: Arthurian Romances*, ed. & trans. by William W. Kibler (London: Penguin, 1991), pp. 381–494 (p. 407).

[7]   'Graelent', in *French Arthurian Literature IV: Eleven Old French Narrative Lays*, ed. & trans. by Glyn S. Burgess and Leslie C. Brook, Arthurian Archives, 14 (Cambridge: D. S. Brewer, 2007), pp. 375–412 (line 218); 'Doon', in *Eleven Old French Narrative Lays*, ed. & trans. by Burgess and Brook, pp. 259–73 (lines 18–36, 66).

[8]   References to pride include Alain Chartier, 'La belle dame sans mercy', trans. by Joan E. McRae et al., in *Alain Chartier, The Quarrel of the Belle dame sans mercy*, ed. by McRae (London: Routledge, 2014; first publ. Taylor & Francis, 2004), pp. 43–95 (lxxxv. 680); Baudet Herenc, 'Accusations against the Belle dame sans mercy', in *Alain Chartier, The Quarrel of the Belle dame sans mercy*, ed. & trans. by McRae, pp. 127–68 (xxv. 198, xxvi. 202, 204, 207); Achilles Caulier, 'The Cruel Woman in Love', in *Alain Chartier, The Quarrel of the Belle dame sans mercy*, ed. & trans. by McRae, pp. 229–93 (civ. 828).

[9]   For example, the Anglo-Norman works *Guigemar* and *Amadas et Ydoine*. Chrétien's works seem to have been known in England: *Perceval* and *Yvain* both influenced Middle English adaptations or retellings, and there are indications that his other works were known, too. See Michelle Szkilnik, 'Medieval Translations and Adaptations of Chrétien's Works', in *A Companion to Chrétien de Troyes*, ed. by Norris J. Lacy and Joan Tasker Grimbert (Cambridge: D. S. Brewer, 2005), pp. 202–13 (pp. 206–7); Keith Busby, 'The Manuscripts of Chrétien's Romances', in *A Companion to Chrétien de Troyes*, pp. 64–75 (pp. 67, 68, 70).

readers. Names or references that associate women's resistance to love with pride already indicate their ideological orientation, identifying these women as departing from a generic norm in a negative way. This goes against the attention to women's shamefastness Mary Flannery has observed in other literary genres, and indeed the wider cultural valuation of female chastity and virginity; in romances, women who guard themselves from love are usually viewed negatively.[10] The negative implications of pride and its specific connection with women's romantic a(nti)pathy suggest that this is seen as an especially problematic form of resistance to love, according with the gendered contrasts discussed in the previous chapter. As the motif of the proud lady in love makes the ideological stakes of women's romantic a(nti)pathy particularly clear, it is the focus of this chapter.

As in the previous chapter, I explore each work in turn to evaluate the nuanced functions of individual examples of romantic a(nti)pathy. I trace the proud ladies through Middle English romance in a broadly chronological trajectory, though I combine my discussion of *Ipomadon* and *Blanchardyn and Eglantine* because of their particularly close similarities. For each romance, I explore the extent to which the proud lady's resistance provokes anxieties about women's autonomy, the sometimes fragile construction of masculinity in romance, and the challenging of generic norms and expectations. I also evaluate to what degree these anxieties are resolved by the (usually) normative ending. The proud ladies can be seen as forming a kind of spectrum, with some functioning more conservatively and others raising more subversive questions and possibilities. While the proud lady is usually a figure of female autonomy, this is not necessarily threatening if she uses her power in ways that accord with dynastic priorities or the promotion of chivalric masculinity, as is the case with Felice in *Guy of Warwick*. But in the other works discussed in this chapter, the proud ladies can be seen as raising questions about the prerogative of male rule or the celebration of chivalric masculinity. The reliance upon forms of coercion to bring about the 'happy ending' in many of these narratives suggests the forceful containment of the proud lady and thereby indicates the potential for disruption she embodies. These romances exhibit a marked and sometimes forceful drive to reintegrate the proud lady into the normative expectations of romance and secular society, but in most cases their conventional endings do not entirely erase the questions posed by the proud lady's initial resistance to love.

---

[10] Mary C. Flannery, *Practising shame: Female honour in later medieval England* (Manchester: Manchester University Press, 2020).

Women's Pride and Men's Prowess:
Directing Chivalric Masculinity in *Guy of Warwick*

Felice, the heroine of the Middle English *Guy of Warwick* narratives, can be placed at one end of the spectrum of proud ladies in love, playing a relatively conventional and conservative role by facilitating Guy's chivalric achievements and marrying in accordance with dynastic interests.[11] After initially rejecting Guy, Felice sets him a series of increasingly difficult conditions he must meet in order to become her lover, and ultimately her husband – interestingly, Felice seems to shift from considering Guy as a lover to viewing him as a potential husband as he proves himself worthy of raising the stakes, perhaps indicating the factors that might have shaped medieval women's decisions to pursue particular relationships.[12] When he meets her final condition of proving himself the best knight in the world, the couple are married, concluding the first part of the romance. The subsequent sections detail Guy's religious penitence (though the extent to which this is really a shift in priorities, given that he continues to prove his prowess in battle, has been debated),[13] leaving Felice

---

[11]   *Guy of Warwick* survives in five independent redactions in Middle English, across three manuscripts and two sets of fragments. I focus here on the most extensive versions: Edinburgh, National Library of Scotland, Advocates' MS 19.2.1 (the Auchinleck manuscript); Cambridge, Gonville and Caius College, MS 107; Cambridge University Library, MS Ff.2.38 (henceforth CUL). I generally cite the Auchinleck version first and foremost, following most other commentators and the manuscript's earlier date. For a full discussion see Alison Wiggins, 'The Manuscripts and Texts of the Middle English *Guy of Warwick*', in *Guy of Warwick: Icon and Ancestor*, ed. by Alison Wiggins and Rosalind Field (Cambridge: D. S. Brewer, 2007), pp. 61–80. All citations of the Auchinleck and Caius manuscripts are from *The Romance of Guy of Warwick: The First or Fourteenth-Century Version*, ed. by Julius Zupitza, EETS, e. s., 42, 49, 59 (London: Paul, Trench, and Trübner, 1883), though the Caius manuscript has now been dated to the late fifteenth rather than the fourteenth century (see Wiggins, cited above). All citations of the CUL manuscript are from *The Romance of Guy of Warwick: The Second or Fifteenth-Century Version*, ed. by Julius Zupitza, EETS, e. s., 25–6 (London: Trübner, 1875).

[12]   In the early sections of *Guy of Warwick* their relationship is referred to primarily in terms of love and/or sex, and Felice seems to see Guy's initial advances as sexually motivated rather than as seeking marriage. In Auchinleck, Guy and Felice start to refer to their relationship in terms of marriage only in the stanzaic *Guy*. This begins after 7306 lines of the couplet *Guy*; the texts are probably by different authors, and were pieced together in the compilation of the manuscript: see Alison Wiggins, 'Imagining the Compiler: *Guy of Warwick* and the Compilation of the Auchinleck Manuscript', in *Imagining the Book*, ed. by Stephen Kelly and John J. Thompson (Turnhout: Brepols, 2005), pp. 61–73. In Caius the only references to marriage come after Felice's father enquires about her marital plans, lines 7339–44. In CUL, this shift occurs much earlier, as Felice announces her plan to become Guy's wife only if he proves himself the best knight in the world at lines 807–20.

[13]   See, for example, Robert Allen Rouse, 'An Exemplary Life: Guy of Warwick as Medieval Culture-Hero', in *Guy of Warwick: Icon and Ancestor*, pp. 94–109 (pp. 102–4);

behind with their son Reinbrun. Because Felice's role is concentrated in the first half of the romance, I focus primarily on these early sections.

The more conventional aspects of Felice's role come in part from the fact that she, unlike the other proud ladies discussed in this chapter, appears to have good reason to reject Guy's advances: his lower social status. This legitimises her romantic a(nti)pathy, as differing status was an accepted – and, indeed, expected – reason to reject a marriage.[14] Felice may therefore seem less clearly aligned with the motif of the proud lady in love. Indeed, she is not directly referred to as proud in the Middle English versions of *Guy*: while versions of the Anglo-Norman *Gui* refer to her 'fere de corage' ['proud heart'],[15] this is omitted in Cambridge University Library, MS Ff.2.38 (CUL), does not appear in the Auchinleck manuscript because the first leaf is missing, and is ambiguously translated as 'she was a woman of grete corage' (93) in the Caius manuscript (which may or may not indicate pride).[16] Yet Felice's rejection of

---

Paul Price, 'Confessions of a Godless Killer: Guy of Warwick and Comprehensive Entertainment', in *Medieval Insular Romance: Translation and Innovation*, ed. by Judith Weiss, Jennifer Fellows, and Morgan Dickson (Cambridge: D. S. Brewer, 2000), pp. 93–110.

[14] See Cathy Hume, *Chaucer and the Cultures of Love and Marriage* (Cambridge: D. S. Brewer, 2012), p. 16; Noël James Menuge, 'The Wardship Romance: A New Methodology', in *Tradition and Transformation in Medieval Romance*, ed. by Rosalind Field (Cambridge: D. S. Brewer, 1999), pp. 29–43 (p. 37). This concern is often discussed in relation to the Paston family's dissatisfaction with Margery Paston's clandestine marriage to Richard Calle, the family's bailiff: see *Paston Letters and Papers of the Fifteenth Century*, ed. by Norman Davis, EETS, s. s., 20, 3 vols (Oxford: Oxford University Press, 2004; first publ. Oxford: Clarendon Press, 1971), I, 341–3 (letter 203), 409 (letter 245), 541–2 (letter 332). See the further discussion of social status and resistance to love in Chapter 3.

[15] *Gui de Warewic: roman du XIIIe siècle*, ed. by Alfred Ewert, Classiques français du moyen âge, 74, 2 vols (Paris: Champion, 1933), I, line 69; trans. in 'Gui de Warewic', in *'Boeve de Haumtone' and 'Gui de Warewic': Two Anglo-Norman Romances*, ed. & trans. by Judith Weiss, FRETS, 3 (Tempe: Arizona Center for Medieval and Renaissance Studies, 2008), pp. 97–243 (p. 98). I generally refer to Ewert's edition and Weiss's translation of the Anglo-Norman *Gui*, both based on London, British Library, MS Additional 38662. Although Ivana Djordjević argues that it is reductive to focus only on the Anglo-Norman *Gui* in Ewert's edition, she acknowledges that the other versions are largely inaccessible: see Ivana Djordjević, '*Guy of Warwick* as a Translation', in *Guy of Warwick: Icon and Ancestor*, pp. 27–43 (pp. 29, 36). Parts of *Gui de Warewic* from Cambridge, Corpus Christi College, MS 50, however, are included in *The Fourteenth-Century Guy of Warwick*, where Zupitza supplies it in place of Auchinleck's missing leaf: line 93 includes the reference to Felice's 'fere de corage'.

[16] Neither the *Middle English Dictionary* or Peggy Knapp include 'pride' as a meaning of 'corage' (of the meanings they list, 'heart' seems the only one potentially appropriate to Felice), but the *OED* does: 'Corāge n.', *Middle English Dictionary*, ed. by Frances McSparran et al., Middle English Compendium (Ann Arbor: University of Michigan Library, 2000–18) <https://quod.lib.umich.edu/m/middle-english-dictionary/dictionary/MED9682> [accessed 19 July 2023]; Peggy Knapp, 'Corage/Courage',

'Erles, Dukes, fro the worldes ende' (Caius, 96), her scorn of Guy, and her insistence on all but impossible conditions before she will agree to marry him align her with the other proud ladies in love. While Felice represents a less extreme form of the proud lady, recognising her connections with this motif uncovers the more subversive aspects of her character, such as her striking autonomy, as well as indicating the central and affirmative role the proud lady could play in the construction of chivalric masculinity.

The conditions that Felice requires Guy to meet before she will agree to love him and be his wife directly motivate Guy's chivalric prowess, as she first asks him to become a knight, then to prove himself in battle, then to become the best knight in the world. Felice presents this final demand as representing Guy's own interests, saying that if she were to accept him without further trial, 'ich þi manschip schuld schone' (Auchinleck, 1145). While recalling romance perceptions of marriage as detrimental to chivalric reputation,[17] her words also focus specifically upon 'manschip', indicating this romance's particular interest in chivalric masculinity. Felice's final command might seem extreme, as Guy indicates when he initially despairs of ever achieving it, as well as when he blames her for the death of his knights while pursuing her condition.[18] However, the point seems to be that Guy *is* capable of achieving this condition, and this seems to justify Felice's demand. In *Guy of Warwick*, the proud lady and her resistance to love act as a catalyst for the creation of chivalric masculinity, illustrating the more conservative function this motif can serve.

The way that Felice's romantic a(nti)pathy motivates Guy's prowess is particularly important because this enables him to compensate for his lower status. His achievements prove him to be a worthy and valuable partner for Felice, and her subsequent acceptance of him thus indicates the value placed upon chivalric reputation in assessing romantic or marital offers. In this respect, Felice's resistance to love and deferral of marriage align with dynastic and masculine priorities and may function as a form of *dangier* by creating a space in which she can negotiate the terms of their partnership. This all contributes to the less subversive representation of romantic a(nti)pathy in this work. Indeed, Felice's role to some extent overlaps with the figure of the

---

in *Time-Bound Words: Semantic and Social Economies from Chaucer's England to Shakespeare's* (Basingstoke: Macmillan, 2000), pp. 13–27; 3. c., 'Courage, n.', *Oxford English Dictionary*, ed. by Michael Proffitt et al. (Oxford: Oxford University Press, 2020) <https://www.oed.com/view/Entry/43146> [accessed 27 May 2023].

[17] See Neil Cartlidge, *Medieval Marriage: Literary Approaches, 1100–1300* (Cambridge: D. S. Brewer, 1997), p. 102.

[18] See Auchinleck and Caius, lines 1555–66, and CUL, lines 1155–60. The British Library *Gui* does not blame Felice for the knights' deaths, but the Corpus Christi *Gui* does. Scenes like this may prime the reader for the reversal of priorities in the second half of the romance.

'actively desiring heiress' in that they both facilitate fantasies of social advancement, though their relationship to desire is different: Felice eventually responds to Guy's desire but does not initiate their romantic connection.[19] Felice's conditions also support her family's priorities: her father, Rohaud, belatedly concerns himself with his dynasty in the CUL manuscript, telling Felice

> Hyt were tyme, þou toke an husbonde
> Aftur my day to kepe my londe.[20]

The ability to 'kepe my londe', a quality the proud ladies are often urged to seek in their potential partners, is exactly what Guy's supreme prowess proves him capable of doing.[21] Dynastic concerns of this kind may have been particularly significant within some of the reading contexts for the *Guy of Warwick* narratives. Although the concept of 'ancestral romance' is questionable, particularly in relation to *Guy*, which circulated widely, Marianne Ailes notes that the Earls of Warwick 'did "adopt" Gui early on'.[22] The Beauchamps of Warwick and their circle have been tentatively associated with a number of Guy of Warwick texts, including the Caius and CUL versions of the Middle English *Guy*.[23] Alison Wiggins notes the dynastic concerns faced by the Beauchamps in the fifteenth century, suggesting that the Rous Rolls and *Beauchamp Pageants*

> should almost certainly be seen in the context of the struggles of Anne Beauchamp [...] to regain her rightful inheritances. From the death of her

---

[19] Helen Cooper, *The English Romance in Time: Transforming motifs from Geoffrey of Monmouth to the death of Shakespeare* (Oxford: Oxford University Press, 2004), p. 223; on these fantasies, see p. 225.

[20] CUL, lines 7015–16. Caius, but not Auchinleck, alludes to dynastic priorities, as Rohaud reminds Felice 'thou art heire to all my londe' (line 7340), but the CUL reference is the most explicit.

[21] This also offers the 'reassuring colouring' Cooper argues frequently accompanies social climbing in medieval romance: *The English Romance in Time*, p. 225.

[22] Marianne Ailes, '*Gui de Warewic* in its Manuscript Context', in *Guy of Warwick: Icon and Ancestor*, pp. 12–26 (p. 25; see pp. 23–4 for a discussion of the problems with 'ancestral romance').

[23] See Wiggins, 'Manuscripts and Texts', pp. 75–6, 64; Martha W. Driver, '"In her owne persone semly and bewteus": Representing Women in Stories of Guy of Warwick', in *Guy of Warwick: Icon and Ancestor*, pp. 133–53 (p. 139). On the Beauchamps' connections with other Guy of Warwick texts, see A. S. G. Edwards, 'The *Speculum Guy de Warwick* and Lydgate's *Guy of Warwick*: The Non-Romance Middle English Tradition', in *Guy of Warwick: Icon and Ancestor*, pp. 81–93 (pp. 87–8); John Frankis, 'Taste and Patronage in Late Medieval England as Reflected in Versions of *Guy of Warwick*', *Medium Ævum*, 66.1 (1997), 80–93 (pp. 84, 88–9); Driver, 'Representing Women in Stories of Guy of Warwick', pp. 136–9; Ailes, '*Gui de Warewic* in its Manuscript Context', p. 25.

husband at Barnet in 1471 almost up until the restoration of her estates in 1487, Anne was excluded from her possessions and 'kept' by her son-in-law, Richard, Duke of Gloucester. During this period she wrote numerous letters appealing for the restoration of her rightful inheritances.[24]

If CUL Ff.2.38 (dated to the late fifteenth or early sixteenth century) was produced within the Beauchamp circle, as Martha Driver suggests, its particular concern with marrying well 'to kepe my londe' (7016) may have been especially poignant, and seemed especially prudent, in this context.[25] Felice's initial resistance to loving Guy, and the way it motivates his prowess and social advancement, serves dynastic interests as well as the couple's own desires: romance unites individual fantasy with familial preoccupations here.

However, this alignment can also serve more subversive purposes, as adherence to convention at times seems to become merely a gesture of compliance that belies the real operations of agency and power. The arrangement of Felice's marriage in particular anticipates the more subversive manifestations of the proud lady in later Middle English romances, whose autonomy sometimes challenges male rule. It is Rohaud who eventually offers Guy Felice's hand and the Warwickshire lands, a conventional marriage agreement that seems to accord with Rachel Moss's description of elite marriage as negotiated 'not between a man and a woman, but between two men'.[26] However, Rohaud's apparent significance is undermined by the reader's knowledge of Guy and Felice's prior relationship. The CUL *Guy* reflects particularly ironically upon Rohaud's role, as he declares

> Now wote y [...] full well,
> That ye loue me, be seynt Mychell,
> That ye wyll my doghtur take.[27]

Rohaud's emphasis on Guy's love for him and his impression that he has arranged the marriage belies the fact that it is Felice, not Rohaud, who has

[24] Wiggins, 'Manuscripts and Texts', p. 76 n. 46.
[25] Wiggins suggests a late fifteenth- or early sixteenth-century date, while Johnston argues for the last quarter of the fifteenth century: see Wiggins, 'Manuscripts and Texts', p. 64; Michael Johnston, *Romance and the Gentry in Late Medieval England* (Oxford: Oxford University Press, 2014), p. 120. Johnston does not link this manuscript to the Beauchamp circle, however: he associates it with mercantile readers and suggests it may have been produced on a commercial basis for a patron in the Leicestershire area: 'Two Leicestershire Romance Codices: Cambridge, University Library MS Ff.2.38 and Oxford, Bodleian Library MS Ashmole 61', *Journal of the Early Book Society*, 15 (2012), 85–100 (pp. 88–9).
[26] Rachel E. Moss, *Fatherhood and its Representations in Middle English Texts* (Cambridge: D. S. Brewer, 2013), p. 124.
[27] CUL, lines 7073–5. The British Library *Gui* offers a similar emphasis to the CUL *Guy*: *Gui de Warewic*, ed. by Ewert, II, lines 7517–19; trans. by Weiss, p. 179.

negotiated with Guy. Felice's active negotiating role and the sidelining of this role in the formal marriage agreement thus align with Amy Vines's argument that in late medieval romance, 'despite the heroines' show of silence and submissiveness, the audience is always aware of the actual circumstances of their behavior'.[28] But *Guy of Warwick* takes the implications of this further, as the exposure of Rohaud's control as a façade raises questions about fathers' typical roles in arranging marriages. The subtle comedy of Rohaud assuming his own pre-eminence asks whether fathers ought to be so sure of their control over their daughters' relationships, and whether homosocial bonds are really more important than romantic love, hinting that women may be more actively involved in the marriage process than their fathers might realise. The romance treats this possibility as comic rather than threatening – all parties are, after all, satisfied with the arrangement. But the discrepancy between Rohaud's knowledge, Felice's, and the reader's highlights the subversive possibilities of her role, even as she appears to conform to tradition.

Felice asserts her power in her interactions with Guy, shaping his identity through her conditions: she tells him he will 'haue þe loue of me, / Ʒif þow be swiche *as y telle þe*' (Auchinleck, 673–4; my emphasis). Far from a 'courted nonentit[y]' who plays an 'essentially marginal role in the hero's life', Felice constructs Guy's chivalric reputation and actively negotiates her relationship with him.[29] As the second half of *Guy of Warwick* shifts into a penitential mode, the initial celebration of Guy's secular prowess and, correspondingly, Felice's role in motivating this is called into question, as Guy himself now rejects romantic love and marriage as part of a renunciation of worldliness. However, Felice still has a role in the latter half of the romance, not only providing Guy with a son and heir, but performing her own pious and moral acts. Felice serves the most socially conservative function of the proud ladies in Middle English romance, and is accordingly the most positively presented, but her agency also anticipates the more subversive functions of the proud lady in love in later narratives.

Enforcing Desire and Interrogating Masculinity:
Ipomadon and *Blanchardyn and Eglantine*

In the Middle English *Ipomadon*, the eponymous hero falls in love with the Fere when he hears of her noble reputation; he travels to her court, where he spends his time hunting. He is scorned by the other knights for this but

---

[28] Amy N. Vines, *Women's Power in Late Medieval Romance* (Cambridge: D. S. Brewer, 2011), p. 6.

[29] Judith Weiss, 'The wooing woman in Anglo-Norman romance', in *Romance in Medieval England*, ed. by Maldwyn Mills, Jennifer Fellows, and Carol M. Meale (Cambridge: D. S. Brewer, 1991), pp. 149–61 (p. 150); Geraldine Barnes, *Counsel and Strategy in Middle English Romance* (Cambridge: D. S. Brewer, 1993), p. 75.

becomes beloved of the Fere despite her vow to marry only the best knight in the world. Through a series of separations, misunderstandings, and incognito chivalric performances, Ipomadon and the Fere are estranged and brought together again, and the romance eventually concludes with their marriage – though the lengths to which the narrative and Ipomadon himself delay this are notable.[30] *Ipomadon*'s structure is broadly similar to *Blanchardyn and Eglantine*'s and both romances adopt a very similar attitude to the figure of the proud lady; I therefore consider these works together. I focus on one redaction of *Ipomadon*, the tail-rhyme *Ipomadon* or *Ipomadon A* contained in Manchester, Chetham's Library, MS Chetham 8009, which offers a complete version of the story similar to Hue de Rotelande's Anglo-Norman *Ipomedon* and the Middle English prose *Ipomedon*.[31]

Both romances overtly identify their heroines as proud ladies. While Eglantine's byname is 'the proude lady in loue', the Fere (La Fière in Anglo-Norman) means 'the Proud One'. Although 'fere' may also be glossed as 'companion' in Middle English, the redactor of *Ipomadon* puns on the meaning of pride, noting that 'she was namyd prowde / But of love to lere' (107–8), which suggests that the connotation of pride was still recognised.[32] As I have already mentioned, the focus on pride preconditions responses to these women through pride's negative cultural valences, which *Blanchardyn and Eglantine* augments by associating pride with military enemies (p. 104) and with the knight Subyon's attempt to force Eglantine to marry him and usurp her rule (p. 176). Both *Ipomadon* and *Blanchardyn and Eglantine* present the heroine's pride as transgressive and establish tension between her celebrated characteristics and her resistance to love. These romances use the motif of the proud lady to explore disruptions to normative desires and gender roles, ultimately reinforcing the importance of marriage. However, while desire

---

[30] On these deferrals, especially in the Anglo-Norman *Ipomedon*, see Rebecca Newby, 'The Three Barriers to Closure in Hue de Rotelande's *Ipomedon* and the Middle English Translations', in *Cultural Translations in Medieval Romance*, ed. by Victoria Flood and Megan G. Leitch (Cambridge: D. S. Brewer, 2022), pp. 135–52.

[31] Hue de Rotelande's twelfth-century Anglo-Norman *Ipomedon* was translated into three distinct Middle English versions: *Ipomadon A* (here referred to as *Ipomadon*), *Ipomydon B* (or the couplet *Lyfe of Ipomydon*), and *Ipomedon C* (the prose *Ipomedon*). Each version follows the same broad storyline but diverges in form, style, and detail. The *Lyfe of Ipomydon* survives in more manuscripts than the other two versions, but I use *Ipomadon* for its greater similarities with the prose and Anglo-Norman versions. For discussions of the relationships between these versions, see Purdie, 'General Introduction: *Ipomedon* in Middle English', in *Ipomadon*, ed. by Purdie, pp. xiii–xvi (p. xiv); Jordi Sánchez-Martí, 'Reading Romance in Late Medieval England: The Case of the Middle English *Ipomedon*', *Philological Quarterly*, 83.1 (2005), 13–39 (pp. 25–7).

[32] On the alternative meaning of 'fere' in Middle English, see Helen Cooper, 'Passionate, eloquent and determined: Heroines' tales and feminine poetics', *Journal of the British Academy*, 4 (2016), 221–44 (p. 232).

is reimposed upon the proud lady, these works also question romance constructions of masculinity, moving away from the affirmative role the proud lady plays in *Guy of Warwick*. *Ipomadon* and *Blanchardyn and Eglantine* thus exemplify romance's ability to both reinforce and question socio-cultural expectations, playing with some gendered expectations while at times punitively enforcing others. To this extent, their portrayal of resistance to love overlaps with Angela Chen's theorisation of asexuality as able to 'draw attention to sexual assumptions and sexual scripts […] and interrogate the ways that these norms make our lives smaller'.[33] Neither heroine entirely fits into modern thinking on asexuality or aromanticism, as they seem to voice resistance to love at least partly as a political strategy for autonomy, and both later desire the hero. However, their initial resistance does challenge normative sexual scripts and reveals the restrictive stakes of these scripts, though these subversive effects are disavowed by the negative perspective from which each work presents its heroine.

Blanchardyn and Eglantine expresses a negative attitude towards Eglantine's romantic a(nti)pathy early on – almost as soon as she is introduced. The Knight of the Ferry's early speech to Blanchardyn, wishing that Eglantine will fall in love 'som daye / yf god be plesed', aligns God's grace with the expectation of love in romance, while Eglantine's 'prowde corage' and 'obstynate wylle' are criticised (p. 37). As Rosalind Brown-Grant notes, these criticisms of l'Orgueilleuse d'amours are much more prominent in the fifteenth-century French prose *Blancandin et l'Orgueilleuse d'amours* than the thirteenth-century verse *Blancandin et l'Orgueilleuse d'amour*; this perhaps suggests the increasingly negative or threatening perception of the proud lady in love towards the later medieval period, a trajectory borne out in this chapter.[34] This shift in perception may have been influenced by increased anxieties about the efficacy of chivalric masculinity following crusading failures.[35] While key moments such as the loss of Acre occurred in the late thirteenth century, significantly predating the French prose *Blancandin* and Caxton's translation, Katherine Lewis suggests that anxieties about crusading and masculinity continued to affect writers in later medieval England and directly shaped Caxton's literary output.[36] *Blanchardyn and Eglantine* does seem to engage with crusading discourses: it depicts Alymodes's men as 'sarrasyns' (p. 87)

---

[33] Angela Chen, *Ace: What Asexuality Reveals About Desire, Society, and the Meaning of Sex* (Boston: Beacon, 2020), pp. 6–7.

[34] Rosalind Brown-Grant, *French Romance of the Later Middle Ages: Gender, Morality, and Desire* (Oxford: Oxford University Press, 2008), p. 42.

[35] See Katherine J. Lewis, '"…doo as this noble prynce Godeffroy of boloyne dyde": Chivalry, masculinity, and crusading in late medieval England', in *Crusading and Masculinities*, ed. by Natasha R. Hodgson, Katherine J. Lewis, and Matthew M. Mesley (Abingdon: Routledge, 2019), pp. 311–28.

[36] *Ibid.*, pp. 311–13, 317, 319.

but also indicates concern with distinguishing Christians and Muslims, in the episodes where Blanchardyn serves the Muslim King of Marienburg and Eglantine's provost fails to recognise him, perceiving him as a Muslim knight. Leon Kellner also speculates that the author of the prose *Blancandin* altered the location of these scenes from Athens to Marienburg because of an interest in the Teutonic orders' battles with their non-Christian neighbours in central Europe at this time.[37] For Caxton, a backdrop of concerns about masculinity and crusading failures may have influenced his interest in this romance, which he claims to have sold to Lady Margaret Beaufort in French and to translate at her request.[38] The French prose version already offered a means to consider the construction and disruption of chivalric masculinity, as well as a way of resolving these concerns by disavowing the problems posed by the proud lady in love through repeated criticisms of her.

These critiques of Eglantine often come from characters who owe loyalty to her, as the Knight of the Ferry does (he is her vassal), priming the reader to view Eglantine's pride as a negative characteristic because these opinions stem from within her realm rather than from enemies to her country. Her provost tells Blanchardyn 'we sholde wel desyre' Eglantine to fall in love (p. 75), while her foster-mother warns her 'youre pryde shalbe cause / but yf ye take hede, of the totall distruction of your royalme' (p. 65). The foster-mother projects larger socio-political concerns onto Eglantine's resistance to love, indicating the way that women's sexuality becomes a public issue when the woman in question holds political power. The foster-mother's fear of the realm's 'distruction' also points to a specific anxiety about female rulers' inability to defend their lands in military action, a particular concern in *Blanchardyn and Eglantine* in the context of Alymodes's attack.[39] Eglantine's pride is further criticised by the narrator, who disavows her 'haulte corage insaucyble' (p. 52) and 'dismesurable herte' (p. 68), lending narratorial authority to this condemnation. While Eglantine is initially praised for her beauty and virtue,

---

[37] Leon Kellner, 'Introduction', in *Blanchardyn and Eglantine*, ed. by Kellner, pp. v–cxxvi (p. cxxv).

[38] William Caxton, 'Dedication', in *Blanchardyn and Eglantine*, pp. 1–2. Yu-Chiao Wang has drawn attention to the fact that the relationships Caxton describes in his prologues may be part of an advertising technique rather than reflecting real transactions, noting that his works seem primarily to have been read by people who probably considered themselves to be gentry rather than aristocracy or royalty: Yu-Chiao Wang, 'Caxton's Romances and Their Early Tudor Readers', *Huntington Library Quarterly*, 67.2 (2004), 173–88.

[39] This fear was not necessarily well grounded: Margaret Paston's letter to her husband requesting arms with which to defend their manor at Gresham indicates that women could organise military action. See *Paston Letters and Papers*, ed. by Davis, I, 226–7 (letter 130). I am indebted to Diane Watt's work on this letter. For a broader investigation of women's roles in war, see Sophie Harwood, *Medieval Women and War: Female Roles in the Old French Tradition* (London: Bloomsbury Academic, 2020).

presenting her as a desirable partner for Blanchardyn, her positive features exist in tension with her proud repudiation of love. This perhaps develops a feature of troubadour and *trouvère* poetry, where, as Helen Dell writes,

> *la dame* must be constituted as of great worth in order for the lover and the desire itself to be accepted as correspondingly worthy [...]. She must be the best. And yet, [...] her necessary unattainability requires her to refuse the lover, so she *cannot* be the best. She must be split. The genre's contradictory requirements necessitate her having both a good and a bad aspect.[40]

The portrayal of Eglantine seems to reflect this split between the desirable object of love and the unattainable, recalcitrant, and thus flawed figure, but the narrative form of romance allows these two attributes to interweave in varied ways at different times, opening up different possibilities for resolving and reassuring the anxieties provoked by romantic a(nti)pathy.

The same tension is evident in *Ipomadon*, where the celebration of the Fere as 'the beste in all degre / That euer on erthe myghte trede' (92–3) is soon qualified, as

> Yf she were semelyeste vnder schrovde
> Of other poyntys, she was namyd prowde
> But of love to lere. (106–8)

Again, the Fere's proud rejection of love is what disrupts her status as a supremely desirable lady. However, views of the Fere's pride in *Ipomadon* are more varied than the criticisms of Eglantine, as the Fere's pride is perceived, at times, as a form of chastity:

> Nowghte she covthe of love amowre
> And held hur howse wyth so grette honoure
> [...]
> And dyd so worthely and so well,
> All prayd God gyffe her happe and sell. (127–31)

The references to 'honoure' and acting 'worthely' and the connection between her honour and her innocence about 'love amowre' present her resistance as chastity, which was usually a worthy reason to resist love. But as *Ipomadon* continues and she remains unmarried, more negative views of the Fere's pride surface, illuminating the valuation of love and virginity particular to Middle English romance. Her barons blame her for the discord in Calabria, insisting

> Oure lady dothe full ylle
> That she will not take a lord
> To mayneteyme vs in good acord.

---

[40] Helen Dell, *Desire by Gender and Genre in Trouvère Song* (Cambridge: D. S. Brewer, 2008), p. 80.

We will goo witte hure wille,

For folly makythe she wyth her pride. (1777–81)

They describe her behaviour as 'synne' (1783) that has created 'grett warre' (1772), emphasising its disruptive impact. As in *Blanchardyn and Eglantine*, this perspective comes from those who are supposed to be loyal to the Fere, although here this primarily highlights the political consequences of her romantic a(nti)pathy. These political consequences are again connected to military weakness, as the barons perceive a female ruler as incapable of resolving military strife, a repeated concern across several of these narratives. Yet moments of ambiguity about the Fere's pride do remain: at one point, Imayne asks the Fere 'whate pryde', claiming 'that hard I speke neuer or nowe' (1424–5). Onlookers admiring the Fere also think that it is 'no wondere yf she be daungerus / To take an onworthy spowsse' (2058–9), positioning her resistance as a form of *dangier*. This may not reflect the Fere's own understanding of her resistance to love, however, as even if her vow starts out as a deliberate strategy, it becomes an impediment to her own desires. Varied perspectives on the Fere's romantic a(nti)pathy exist, but her refusal to love remains the primary obstacle to her ability to fulfil the normal expectations of love and marriage in medieval romance, even once this becomes her own desire.

The specific focus of these criticisms in *Ipomadon* and *Blanchardyn and Eglantine* – the need for the women to take a lord – suggests that the Fere and Eglantine not only threaten normative expectations of desire but arguably inspire greater anxiety and critique by disrupting patriarchal rule. Eglantine and the Fere are both sole female rulers, having already come into their inheritance. This places them, together with Ettarde, the final proud lady I will discuss in this chapter, in an unusual position for women in late medieval literature and society. Corinne Saunders notes that 'the system of male primogeniture did not allow women to inherit land except in the absence of a male heir and then only with circumscribed rights; heiresses were therefore married at the earliest opportunity'.[41] While the 'actively desiring heiress' is a prominent romance motif, female rulers appear most often as fairies or enchantresses (in the *Lanval* narratives and *Partonope of Blois*, for example), or as women whose lands are under threat and who are happy to accept the love of a knight who rescues them, with no resistance (such as Blancheflor in Chrétien's *Perceval*, the Lady of Synadowne in *Lybeaus Desconus*, and the lady Degaré marries in *Sir Degaré*).[42] Eglantine, the Fere, and Ettarde are unusual as human women who are rulers with significant power, and the threat this unusual position poses is suggested by the focus upon the political need for

---

[41] Corinne Saunders, *Rape and Ravishment in the Literature of Medieval England* (Cambridge: D. S. Brewer, 2001), p. 51.
[42] Cooper, *The English Romance in Time*, p. 223.

them to marry.[43] In *Blanchardyn and Eglantine*, the provost argues Eglantine's vassals should hope she does love Blanchardyn, 'to thende she myght take a goode lord for to deffende vs and her lande' (p. 75), suggesting that Eglantine is inadequate as a military leader and requires a husband to fulfil this role for her. Similar concerns are voiced in *Ipomadon*, where a male ruler is perceived as so essential to 'maynteyme vs and hyr lond, / Our stryffe to stabull and stille' (2089–90) that the Fere's barons threaten 'but she a lord take', 'they shuld þer omage make / To kyngys of other kynne' (1787–9). This criticism of the Fere's rule conflicts with the earlier description of her as 'ware and wyce', a ruler who would 'abowtte hur suffyr no debatte', and whom 'her meyny lovyd […] euer ilke one' (348–52). This inconsistency may imply that even an initially effective female ruler eventually requires a husband to keep her followers in check, or it may indicate a growing dissatisfaction with the Fere as her resistance to love persists. These anxieties often focus on the perceived vulnerability of a country ruled by a woman, implying that she is incapable of directing military strength.[44] But they also seem to express discomfort with women's rule and the effects it may have on the prerogative of male rule.

In this respect, the proud lady in love shares some perhaps surprising similarities with a figure in Old Norse literature: the maiden-king. Francophone influence upon the literary culture of both Iceland and England offers an explanation for this connection, but the maiden-king is usually considered unique to Old Norse literature.[45] The Old Norse narratives *are* 'unique in the large international corpus of narratives devoted to the taming of a haughty princess in that their plot is dominated by a misogamous female ruler who insists on being called *kongr* ("king") rather than *dróttning* ("queen")'.[46] This title offers a decisive difference from the proud ladies, as it foregrounds the maiden-king's transgression of a powerful role usually associated with men. Yet Icelandic maiden-kings are still recognised as maiden-kings without this title,[47] and Jóhanna Katrín Friðriksdóttir suggests that 'the crucial element is

---

[43] Dido in the *Roman d'Enéas* and Caxton's *Eneydos* (as well as, in the context of epic, Virgil's *Aeneid*) is another human ruler with significant power, although she is disempowered and commits suicide because of her love for Eneas.

[44] On the similar way in which the Old Norse maiden-kings' realms are perceived as vulnerable, see Jóhanna Katrín Friðriksdóttir, *Women in Old Norse Literature: Bodies, Words, and Power* (New York: Palgrave Macmillan, 2013), pp. 112–13.

[45] See Jóhanna Katrín Friðriksdóttir, 'From Heroic Legend to "Medieval Screwball Comedy"? The Origins, Development and Interpretation of the Maiden-King Narrative', in *The Legendary Sagas: Origins and Development*, ed. by Annette Lassen, Agneta Ney, and Ármann Jakobsson (Reykjavík: University of Iceland Press, 2012), pp. 229–49; Sif Ríkharðsdóttir, *Medieval Translations and Cultural Discourse: The Movement of Texts in England, France and Scandinavia* (Cambridge: D. S. Brewer, 2012).

[46] Marianne E. Kalinke, *Bridal-Quest Romance in Medieval Iceland* (Ithaca: Cornell University Press, 1990), p. 66.

[47] For example, in *Clári saga* and *Dínus saga drambláta*.

that the maiden-king is empowered to achieve her own aims and rule in practice if not in name'.[48] Elaborating on the characteristics of the maiden-king,
Friðriksdóttir writes that she is

> a young, noble, unmarried woman, usually depicted as haughty, cruel, and,
> early in the tradition, armed. She rules her own kingdom, rejects all her suit-
> ors and mistreats them physically, verbally, or both. However, ultimately the
> male hero finds a way to outwit and conquer the maiden-king, sometimes
> subjecting her to equal violence, and the story concludes with a traditional
> ending in which the two protagonists [...] marry, though sometimes they do
> not live so happily-ever-after from the woman's point of view.[49]

This raises a number of similarities with and differences from the proud ladies,
who could be seen as a less extreme version of the maiden-king. They are
young, noble, unmarried, haughty; rule or are heiresses to significant lands;
reject all suitors; and eventually marry in a traditional ending. However, the
proud ladies are not usually described as cruel (Ettarde is an exception), they
are not armed, and they do not usually mistreat their suitors – though their
suitors could sometimes be said to mistreat them, as I shall argue. The proud
ladies of Middle English romance have more in common with the Old Norse
maiden-kings than has previously been recognised, particularly in terms of
the anxieties they raise about women's autonomy and the humiliations that
are at times used to disempower them. Although Marianne Kalinke claims
that 'only Icelandic romance focuses on the dilemma of the powerful female
heiress who is faced with a conscious choice between a career as an unmarried regent and marriage, with the consequent abdication of authority [...] to
her husband', the political focus of concerns about Eglantine's and the Fere's
resistance to love subtly draws attention to this issue, while not addressing
it so explicitly.[50] Indeed, the fact that the Fere makes her vow to marry only
the best knight in the world on the day that she inherits control over her lands
approaches a more direct framing of this issue: because a single heiress could
rule the land she inherits, with that right passing to her husband when she
marries, this makes the timing of the Fere's vow a pointed statement about her
power and her determination to maintain it. In this light, her romantic a(nti)
pathy appears to be a deliberate strategy but one with rather different intentions to that of *dangier*. The proud ladies function in a similar, if less extreme,
way to the Old Norse maiden-king, placing women's rule as a challenge to
patriarchal power structures.

Women's romantic a(nti)pathy therefore has significantly different implications from men's resistance to love. Although men's acceptance of love and

[48] Friðriksdóttir, *Women in Old Norse Literature*, p. 109.
[49] *Ibid.*, p. 107. Thanks to Rebecca Merkelbach for advice here.
[50] Kalinke, *Bridal-Quest Romance*, p. 83.

marriage allows them to fulfil generic expectations and continue their lineage, its resolution rarely has political or economic implications. In *Guigemar*, we do not know if Guigemar and the lady marry (indeed, it would seem they cannot as she is presumably still married to her first husband), have children, or if the lady brings Guigemar any wealth or property; the emphasis is upon Guigemar's acceptance of love – although this partly reflects the different literary and historical context of Marie's courtly twelfth-century *Lais*. *Troilus and Criseyde* likewise focuses upon the experience of love itself, not wealth, property, or even dynasty. In *Amadas et Ydoine* and *Sir Degrevant*, the female love-object possesses significant wealth and property, but no explicit concerns are expressed about the impact the men's initial resistance might have on their economic and familial responsibilities. And there appears to be no question of how Dynadan, who never marries or falls in love, may compromise his familial, political, or economic interests. In contrast, anxieties about women's power in *Blanchardyn and Eglantine* and *Ipomadon* reveal a concern with preserving men's access to political and economic power through heiresses who accept marriage, highlighting what is really at stake in these romances – and, indeed, what is at stake in romances that emphasise 'desirable desire'.[51] While Moss argues that an heiress's 'marriage making must be controlled' as it 'could potentially threaten patriarchal authority', this risk was even greater if an heiress threatened not to marry at all.[52] The concerns about resistance to love with which romances engage vary in accordance with gendered perceptions: while men's acceptance of love and marriage aligns them with dominant models of chivalric masculinity, women's acceptance of love is more specifically an issue of economic and political power.

The resolution of the proud lady's resistance also has a dynastic function, as in each of the romances discussed in this chapter (except for Malory's Pelleas and Ettarde episode), the proud lady's acceptance of love leads to the birth of at least one son, ensuring that the political and economic power she initially wields is handed down to a male successor rather than repeating the cycle of female inheritance. The proud lady's romantic a(nti)pathy is taken seriously, then, and her pride viewed negatively, because of her political and economic power, which requires her desire for autonomy to be disavowed. Brown-Grant similarly argues that the prose *Blancandin*,

> In stressing how the Orgueilleuse d'amour's affective autonomy equates to a dangerous political independence, [...] presents her as a threat to the correct social order whereby a male should rule, and hence emphasizes the need for Blancandin to assert mastery over her.[53]

---

[51] See further Cooper, *The English Romance in Time*, pp. 221–3.

[52] Moss, *Fatherhood and its Representations*, p. 137.

[53] Brown-Grant, *French Romance of the Later Middle Ages*, p. 42.

While Brown-Grant suggests that *Blancandin* is influenced by sceptical attitudes to love and women in late medieval French chivalric treatises, the similarities between the Anglo-Norman *Ipomedon*, the Middle English *Ipomadon*, the prose *Blancandin*, and *Blanchardyn and Eglantine* reveal that anxieties about women's rule and independence are also found in earlier romances and may be inherent within narratives of the proud lady (appearing in *Guy of Warwick* in Rohaut's late but evident concern with Felice's marriage). *Blanchardyn and Eglantine* and *Ipomadon*, like other romances of the proud lady in love, are deeply invested in restoring normative attitudes to love and marriage so that political and economic power can be upheld as the preserve of men.

To reimpose normative attitudes to love and marriage in these romances, *Blanchardyn and Eglantine* and *Ipomadon* use episodes of physical and psychological coercion. These coercive actions fall outside of the medieval legal concept of *raptus* but seem to be recognised as coercive within each romance, suggesting an acknowledgement of extra-legal forms of coercion in the literary sphere. In *Blanchardyn and Eglantine*, a forced kiss marks Eglantine's first encounter with Blanchardyn, as he rides up behind her and seizes the opportunity to kiss her when she turns to see who approaches (an illustration of this episode from the French prose *Blancandin* is included on the cover of this book).[54] Blanchardyn does this at the Knight of the Ferry's suggestion, associating the kiss with collusion between men in a manner reminiscent of Carissa Harris's concept of 'felawe masculinity' as teaching men to perpetuate rape culture (though, again, the class context is rather different here).[55] The knight explicitly frames this kiss as the beginning of Blanchardyn and Eglantine's love, telling him 'yf ye may haue that onely cusse [...] hit shal be occasyon of a loue inseparable betwyx her and you' (p. 39). But the kiss is entirely undesired and non-consensual on Eglantine's part: she describes it at first as 'this Iniurye' (p. 43) and 'this vyolence' (p. 45), and desires restitution for Blanchardyn's behaviour, threatening to have him killed. Unwanted kissing was not a crime in medieval English law – and indeed attempts to prosecute it as sexual assault in modern legal cases have had mixed results – so there would have been no legal recompense available to Eglantine. However, other literary works do depict kissing as comparable to sexual violation. For example, Chrétien's Perceval forcibly kissing the maiden in the pavilion is described in terms akin to rape, as he 'mist le soz lui tote estendue [...] desfense mestier n'i ot' ['stretched her out beneath himself [...] her resistance was in vain'], while the lady's abusive partner later claims

---

[54] The image is taken, with kind permission from the ÖNB, from *Blancandin ou l'Orgueilleuse d'Amour*, 1450–74, Wien, Österreichische Nationalbibliothek, Cod. 3438, fol. 16v.

[55] Carissa M. Harris, *Obscene Pedagogies: Transgressive Talk and Sexual Education in Late Medieval Britain* (Ithaca: Cornell University Press, 2018), pp. 29–30.

> ce ne querroit ja nus
> Qu'il le baisast sanz faire plus,
> Que l'une chose l'autre atrait.[56]

Kissing and sexual assault are also conflated in Malory's *Morte Darthur*, when Hallewes the enchantress elides propositioning Launcelot for a kiss with her necrophilic desire for his dead body.[57] The kissing scene in *Blanchardyn and Eglantine* is less extreme, as for it to lead to a relatively idealised relationship, the use of force cannot be too openly acknowledged.[58] That this scene occurs shortly after Blanchardyn rescues another lady from rape may be intended to differentiate Blanchardyn's actions from those of the rapist knight he kills (pp. 25–9), and indeed any parallels between the distress of the lady Blanchardyn rescues and Eglantine may be supposed to position Eglantine's reaction as hyperbolic and inappropriate. This is how her foster-mother responds to her tears, telling her 'I haue right grete merueylle, how a prynces of so grete renounne as ye be of, may make so grete a sorowe of a thynge of nought'.[59] However, it also seems possible to read the relation between these scenes in the opposite direction, positioning the forced kiss as a less extreme violation.

The kissing scene 'resonates with sexual violence', as Jennifer Summit argues.[60] When Blanchardyn approaches Eglantine, he 'gaf the spore to þe hors & forced hym as moche as he coude', until 'bothe theyre mouthes recountred' (p. 41). Not only is the spectre of force raised in the description of Blanchardyn forcing his horse onwards, but 'recountred' identifies the kiss as a form of violence. This term is unique to Caxton's translation: the prose *Blancandin* says that their mouths 's'entrebaisierent' [kissed each other], and the verse *Blancandin* that Blancandin 'baisie' [kissed] her.[61] To 'recountre' usually refers to 'encounter[ing] (an enemy or his force) in battle', meeting

[56] *Le Roman de Perceval*, lines 703, 706, 3857–9. 'No one will ever believe he kissed her without doing more, for one thing leads to another': trans. by Kibler, pp. 389, 428.
[57] On Hallewes, see the discussion pp. 216–19 of this book.
[58] See Corinne Saunders, 'A Matter of Consent: Middle English Romance and the Law of *Raptus*', in *Medieval Women and the Law*, ed. by Noël James Menuge (Woodbridge: Boydell Press, 2000), pp. 105–24 (p. 116).
[59] *Blanchardyn and Eglantine*, p. 43. For more on the foster-mother's role in downplaying Blanchardyn's actions, see Jennifer Alberghini, '"A kysse onely": The Problem of Female Socialization in William Caxton's *Blanchardyn and Eglantine*', *Studies in the Age of Chaucer*, 44 (2022), 'Colloquium: Historicizing Consent: Bodies, Wills, Desires', ed. by Carissa M. Harris and Fiona Somerset, 347–57.
[60] Jennifer Summit, 'William Caxton, Margaret Beaufort and the Romance of Female Patronage', in *Women, the Book, and the Worldly*, ed. by Lesley Smith and Jane H. M. Taylor (Cambridge: D. S. Brewer, 1995), pp. 151–65 (p. 162).
[61] *Blancandin et l'Orgueilleuse d'amours: Versioni in prosa del XV secolo*, ed. by Rosa Anna Greco, Bibliotheca Romanica: Studi e Testi, 3 (Alessandria: Edizioni dell'Orso, 2002), p. 95 (10. 8); *Blancandin et l'Orgueilleuse d'amour: Roman d'aventures*, ed. by H. Michelant (Paris: Librairie Tross, 1867), line 702.

'in a hostile encounter, fight'.[62] This casts the kiss as a military encounter or, more specifically, a joust.[63] The scene shares several parallels with jousting, as Blanchardyn charges his horse towards Eglantine to 'recountre' with her, with the result that she 'fell doune from her amblere' in shock (p. 43), while he rides on. These parallels are latent in the French *Blancandin*, but Caxton's use of 'recountre' augments them, emphasising the violence of the forced kiss.[64]

Yet the military language describing the kiss also opens up possibilities for questioning this violence and its place in chivalric practices, as at times it seems humorously incongruous. The high register in which Blanchardyn considers his task, being 'affrayed and replenysshed wyth grete fere lest he shold faylle of his entrepryse' (p. 40), the description of it as a 'fayre aduenture' (p. 42), as well as the framing of the kiss as a joust, have an absurd, self-aggrandising quality. This is coupled with the comically fortuitous meeting of the couple's lips (with no injury to either party, despite Blanchardyn apparently riding at full speed) and the performance of Blanchardyn's subsequent ride through Eglantine's company 'gyuyng a gracyouse and honourable salutacion to them all' (p. 42). The exaggerated, comic, and performed qualities of these moments become more prominent in the later texts: in the verse *Blancandin*, the hero does think that he 'vivrai petit' [will live but a short time] after kissing l'Orgueilleuse, and 'fu angoissous' [was anxious] to kiss her, but the later texts inflate this sense of fear and corresponding gravitas more, perhaps responding to increased anxieties about chivalric masculinity in the later medieval period.[65] While the forced kiss is certainly a coercive attempt to enforce the role of beloved upon Eglantine, there may also be scope to read it in a more critical and questioning light.

While *Blanchardyn and Eglantine* uses physical force to initiate Eglantine's acceptance of love, *Ipomadon* turns to psychological coercion to reinforce the importance of normative desires. Ipomadon is both a master manipulator and a master of disguise: the two go together in his performance at the three-day tournament held to determine whom the Fere ought to marry, as well as in his concluding battle with Lyolyne. At the tournament, Ipomadon appears in a different guise each day, apparently to ensure he can earn his reputation anew each time. However, his disguises also make the Fere despair as she thinks that a new knight has won the field each day. Similarly, when Ipomadon defeats the Fere's enemy Lyolyne in a concluding battle, he then takes up Lyolyne's standard to pretend that it was he who won; once again, Ipomadon's

---

[62] 'Recŏuntren v.', *Middle English Dictionary* <https://quod.lib.umich.edu/m/middle-english-dictionary/dictionary/MED36231> [accessed 27 May 2023].

[63] Summit notes that the scene uses the 'language of masculine enterprise' but does not draw a specific parallel with a joust: 'The Romance of Female Patronage', p. 161.

[64] The imagery of jousting offers an unusual variation on the metaphor of love as warfare or as a siege, found in the works of Ovid as well as *Le Roman de la Rose*.

[65] *Blancandin et l'Orgueilleuse d'amour*, ed. by Michelant, lines 607, 690.

overt motive is to earn more prowess before he can ask the Fere to be his bride, but this causes the Fere to further despair and attempt to leave Calabria. While Ipomadon is not on either occasion trying to manipulate the Fere's emotional responses, the narrative nonetheless makes the emotional impact of his actions clear. This is not what inspires the Fere's love for Ipomadon as she began to desire him long before this point, but her increasing dependence and desperation do suggest that these episodes partly rebuke her initial transgression of normative gender and sexual roles. In this respect, they operate in a similar though much less extreme way to the humiliations inflicted upon the maiden-kings in Old Norse literature, which encompass loss of status, physical abuse, and rape.[66]

The three-day tournament and Ipomadon's fight with Lyolyne follow the same narrative trajectory as in Hue's *Ipomedon*, which, as Roberta Krueger argues, thwarts romance expectations and deprives La Fière of her agency.[67] However, the Middle English *Ipomadon* offers potentially differing views of these episodes because of this redaction's reduced misogyny.[68] *Ipomadon* portrays the Fere more positively during the three-day tournament, removing the Anglo-Norman *Ipomedon*'s description of her desire for the hero in each of his disguises (which, because she does not realise it is Ipomedon, is used to suggest indiscriminate lust) to instead emphasise her fidelity.[69] Given the significance of fidelity for female virtue in the Middle Ages, this may have encouraged greater sympathy with the Fere's distress. *Ipomadon* does not disguise but rather emphasises this distress: on the first day, the Fere 'þought for pur tene / Her hert wold breke in thre' (3406–7) when she hears Ipomadon has left, cursing her pride and proclaiming 'dothe he þus, he dothe grette synne!' (3417). In Hue's *Ipomedon*, this line is given to Jason rather than the Fere, ensuring that the heroine herself does not question Ipomedon's behaviour.[70]

---

[66] See Friðriksdóttir, *Women in Old Norse Literature*, pp. 120–5; Kalinke, *Bridal-Quest Romance*, pp. 66–8, 78–9, 101–2; Erik Wahlgren, 'The Maiden King in Iceland' (unpublished PhD thesis, University of Chicago, 1938), pp. 36–8.

[67] Roberta Krueger, 'Misogyny, Manipulation, and the Female Reader in Hue de Rotelande's *Ipomedon*', in *Courtly Literature: Culture and Context*, ed. by Keith Busby and Erik Kooper (Amsterdam: Benjamins, 1990), pp. 395–409 (p. 400).

[68] See Cooper, *The English Romance in Time*, pp. 235–7; Brenda Hosington, 'The Englishing of the Comic Technique in Hue de Rotelande's *Ipomedon*', in *Medieval Translators and Their Craft*, ed. by Jeanette Beer (Kalamazoo: Medieval Institute Publications, 1989), pp. 247–63.

[69] See further Susan Crane, *Insular Romance: Politics, Faith, and Culture in Anglo-Norman and Middle English Literature* (Berkeley: University of California Press, 1986), p. 205.

[70] See Hue de Rotelande, *Ipomedon: poème de Hue de Rotelande (fin du XIIe siècle)*, ed. by A. J. Holden, Bibliothèque française et romane, série B, éditions critiques de textes, 17 (Paris: Éditions Klincksieck, 1979), lines 5192, 6316.

Jason continues to warn Ipomadon against leaving the Fere in both versions,[71] even issuing the stark caution that

> Trewly, goo ye this fro her,
> My lady herselff shal shend. (4659–60)

But this warning has no effect, heightening the tension between Ipomadon's behaviour and the chivalric ideal of saving a lady from a desperate situation. Ipomadon acts conventionally by attempting to win the Fere's hand through prowess, but he simultaneously places her in a position of despair. In other lines again introduced by the Middle English writer, Ipomadon himself briefly acknowledges that he may be acting wrongly, declaring

> Hereafter I shall amendys make
> To that myld off chere. (5006–7)

These moments voice discomfort with Ipomadon's behaviour, problematising Hue's celebration of Ipomedon's triumph in humbling La Fière to reflect more soberingly on the negative impact of Ipomadon's behaviour.

The distress Ipomadon causes the Fere becomes even more evident in the Lyolyne episodes, where the Fere's behaviour suggestively indicates the traumatic effects Ipomadon's abandonment has on her sense of autonomy.[72] When she sees her cousin Cabanus approach after Lyolyne's apparent victory, she introduces herself as

> a sympull woman, syr,
> That yesterday owght Calaber:
> Today I am in drede. (8295–7)

This emphatically reveals her transformation from the proud lady who 'thought no prynce her pere' (105) into this humble woman, indicating how Ipomadon's manipulation of her feelings changes her sense of autonomy. These lines thus reveal the interest narratives of the proud lady have in subduing women's autonomy, aligning them again with the Icelandic maiden-king romances. The Fere's perception of external events also indicates the impact of Ipomadon's machinations. She assumes Cabanus's men are Lyolyne's forces coming to abduct her, and Cabanus has to reassure her:

---

[71] *Ibid.*, lines 6313–18.
[72] While trauma is culturally specific and symptoms and understandings shift over time, I perceive it to be a useful term for the Fere's experiences of 'shock or stress beyond the limits of [her] psychic ability to cope'. See Wendy J. Turner and Christina Lee, 'Conceptualizing Trauma for the Middle Ages', in *Trauma in Medieval Society*, ed. by Turner and Lee (Leiden: Brill, 2018), pp. 3–12 (p. 8).

> Drede you for no gile!
> I am your cosyne Cabanus. (8306–7)

The reference to 'gile' is introduced by the Middle English redactor, perhaps as a more pointed reflection on Ipomadon's conduct.[73] Similarly, when one of Cabanus's men returns from the fight with 'Lyolyne' (Ipomadon in disguise), the Fere assumes 'slayne is my cosyne Cabanus!' (8626). The effects of Ipomadon's repeated manipulation and abandonment are illustrated through the Fere's constant assumption of the worst-case scenario. While Ipomadon's treatment of the Fere is explicitly motivated by his determination to prove himself, the romance recognises the impact this might have upon the Fere and takes this seriously. Today we could read Ipomadon's behaviour as a form of psychological coercion because it humiliates the Fere, makes her dependent on him, and causes her significant distress (attributes used to define coercive control in modern UK law).[74] While modern law may not be an appropriate framework through which to read medieval literature, the similarities between Ipomadon's behaviour and modern definitions, and the recognition of the impact his actions have upon the Fere within the romance, are suggestive, again indicating how literature is able to acknowledge the existence of a wider range of coercive behaviours outside of contemporaneous legal structures.

The reduction of the Fere's pride also takes on didactic meaning, however. She repeatedly blames herself for her misfortune, saying 'aftur pryde comythe grette reprove' (942), and declaring

> Prowde in hertte ay haue I been,
> Therefore I haue a falle, I wene. (944–5)

This proverbial wisdom, stemming ultimately from the Bible, may lend additional authority to her self-castigation.[75] She also extends this moral lesson to others:

> Cursyd pryde, woo worthe þe aye!
> Off all women so may I say. (3414–15)

This opens up her experience for the reader to learn from. While these reflective speeches may invite further sympathy, this sympathy functions in line with the didactic message to restore normative desires and gender roles. It therefore illuminates the role of readers' emotional responses in maintaining dominant emotional regimes, as sympathising with the Fere influences the

---

[73] Compare *Ipomedon*, lines 10036–8.

[74] See 'Controlling or Coercive Behaviour in an Intimate or Family Relationship', The Crown Prosecution Service (2017) <https://www.cps.gov.uk/legal-guidance/controlling-or-coercive-behaviour-intimate-or-family-relationship> [accessed 27 July 2022].

[75] Proverbs 16. 18.

extent to which the message that pride can lead to a painful fall is absorbed by the reader.[76]

Like the forced kiss in *Blanchardyn and Eglantine*, these episodes of psychological coercion in *Ipomadon* are portrayed ambivalently: while they impose a normative role upon the Fere, they also highlight the coercive effects of Ipomadon's behaviour and raise questions about the performative nature of masculinity in *Ipomadon* and romance more widely. As with the kiss in *Blanchardyn and Eglantine*, but this time on a broader basis across the narrative, masculinity is repeatedly highlighted as something that is constructed in *Ipomadon* because of Ipomadon's propensity for disguise. His disguises are particularly subversive because they often take the form of figures antithetical to the role of the chivalric Christian knight: the fool, the coward, and finally the threatening knight who besieges the Fere, Lyolyne. This final disguise is the most disruptive, not only because it ruptures the Fere's and the reader's expectations of a climactic (re)union but also because this disguise is both closer to the Christian chivalric knight than the fool or the coward and furthest from this identity. While Lyolyne is a knight, he is also a black man from 'Ynde Mayore' (6138) who embodies the trope of the 'hostile pagan outsider's desire to possess the woman'.[77] Somewhat surprisingly, Lyolyne is not explicitly described as pagan or Muslim, unlike Alymodes in *Blanchardyn and Eglantine*, whom Eglantine refuses to marry because 'neuer the dayes of her lyff she sholde wedde paynem nor noo man infydele'.[78] However, Lyolyne's association with 'Ynde Mayore' may link him to the trope of what Geraldine Heng refers to as 'black Saracens', who 'abound from the twelfth century on – in the shape of [...] enemies whose bodies may also bear nonhuman characteristics', recalling the description of Lyolyne.[79] Ipomadon's disguise as Lyolyne could be seen as a kind of blackface here: while he masquerades as a black person successfully,

---

[76] On emotional regimes as 'the normative order for emotions' within a particular political structure, see William M. Reddy, *The Navigation of Feeling: A Framework for the History of Emotions* (Cambridge: Cambridge University Press, 2001), pp. 124–5.

[77] Saunders, 'A Matter of Consent', p. 115. I follow Jonathan Hsy's distinction between Black as 'signal[ling] contemporary sociopolitical identities shaped by African diaspora experiences', while black 'is not always capitalized in earlier historical instances': Hsy, *Antiracist Medievalisms: From 'Yellow Peril' to Black Lives Matter* (Leeds: Arc Humanities Press, 2021), p. 16 n. 98.

[78] *Blanchardyn and Eglantine*, p. 65. On the importance of using the term 'Muslim' instead of 'Saracen' to call attention to Islamophobia in medieval literature, see Shokoofeh Rajabzadeh, 'The depoliticized Saracen and Muslim erasure', *Literature Compass*, 16.9–10 (2019) <https://doi.org/10.1111/lic3.12548>.

[79] Geraldine Heng, *The Invention of Race in the European Middle Ages* (Cambridge: Cambridge University Press, 2018), pp. 187–8. Heng notes that people from India are imagined as black in *Parzival*, p. 209. See *Ipomadon*, lines 6145–64.

Lyolyne cannot cross racial borders so easily.[80] Ipomadon's masquerade as a black, presumably non-Christian character, against whom Christian knights are often purposefully contrasted in medieval romance, may raise questions about constructions of race alongside the broader exploration of chivalric masculinity in these episodes of disguise.[81] The centrality of disguise and deception in *Ipomadon* may even suggest that masculinity itself is a form of disguise or deception, aligning with modern views of gender as performative.[82] Several scholars have commented on the way other romances, particularly Malory's *Morte*, align with this model, but *Ipomadon* perhaps takes this further to suggest that masculinity is also a perpetual work of deception, of pretending to be (or performing as) something you are not.[83] This may stem from Hue de Rotelande's ironic and satirical approach to romance and gender, but the Middle English text opens up other possibilities for exploring and questioning chivalric masculinity through its subtle critiques of Ipomadon.

Blanchardyn and Eglantine and *Ipomadon* both reassert normative models of desire and gender, at times forcefully emphasising the necessity of marriage to maintain male rule. These romances expose the political significance of the proud lady's marriage, which ensures that her lands return to patriarchal control. However, both narratives also explore possibilities outside the norm by interrogating romance constructions of masculinity, moving beyond the affirmative role of the proud lady in the first half of *Guy of Warwick* and starting to denaturalise gendered roles and sexual scripts, opening up possibilities for comparing women's romantic a(nti)pathy with Chen's sense of how asexuality can help us to interrogate sexual norms. This interrogation of masculinity is developed further in *Eger and Grime* and Malory's episode of Pelleas and Ettarde.

---

[80] For scholarship on blackface and medieval performance, see Erik Wade, '*Ower Felaws Blake*: Blackface, Race, and Muslim Conversion in the Digby *Mary Magdalene*', *Exemplaria*, 31.1 (2019), 22–45; Wade's insights into the way blackface is used as a contrast to a sense of white Christian identity as stable and God-given align with my reading of *Ipomadon* here. I am indebted to Dorothy Kim for suggesting the focus on blackface to me at the 2018 Gender and Medieval Studies Conference.

[81] I elaborate on race and medieval race-making in Chapter 4.

[82] See Judith Butler, *Gender Trouble: Feminism and the Subversion of Identity* (New York: Routledge, 2002; first publ. 1990).

[83] See, for example, Molly Martin, *Vision and Gender in Malory's 'Morte Darthur'* (Cambridge: D. S. Brewer, 2010), pp. 12–13; Dorsey Armstrong, *Gender and the Chivalric Community in Malory's 'Morte d'Arthur'* (Gainesville: University Press of Florida, 2003), pp. 38, 68–9, 129. Armstrong discusses Malorian masculinity as masquerade, pp. 86–9, but this is not quite the same as masculinity as disguise or even pretence in *Ipomadon*.

Chivalric Failures and the Censoring of the Proud Lady in *Eger and Grime*

The late medieval Scottish romance of *Eger and Grime* follows a model of the proud lady similar to the Fere in *Ipomadon*, but Winglayne, heiress to Earl Bragas/Diges (depending on the redaction), makes a vow that holds more subversive implications for the construction of chivalric masculinity. At the beginning of *Eger and Grime*, we are told that she has pledged to marry only a knight who is undefeated in battle. While this seems to accord with chivalric priorities, the repercussions of sticking to this vow push chivalric masculinity to its limits. When Eger attracts Winglayne's attention, they are apparently engaged to be married, until Eger returns home from fighting the mysterious knight Gray-steele, sorely wounded, his little finger and his weapons missing. Winglayne repudiates him and Eger's companion Grime takes up the challenge of fighting Gray-steele while pretending to be Eger, in an attempt to restore his friend's lost reputation and regain his bride. Grime is successful, Eger and Winglayne are married, and Grime marries Loosepaine, the heiress of lands that border on Gray-steele's. Yet this is not the ending – or at least not the only one. *Eger and Grime* survives in two different versions: an anglicised version in the Percy Folio (London, British Library, MS Additional 27879) and a Scottish version represented by three prints from 1669, 1687, and 1711, known as the Huntington-Laing redaction (HL). While the Percy Folio text concludes with the conventional ending described above, Huntington-Laing has a further twist: Grahame (Grime) dies, Eger confesses that it was Grahame who defeated Gray-steele, Winliane (Winglayne) repudiates Eger, enters a nunnery, and dies, and Eger eventually remarries Lilias (Loosepaine). The differences of these two redactions hold important implications for considering the representation of the proud lady and the extent to which each questions or upholds chivalric masculinity as a source of celebration. The two versions also offer different reading contexts, a snapshot of the wide range of audiences amongst which this story apparently circulated. While the early audience for the Percy Folio is uncertain, Aisling Byrne and Victoria Flood's work on its 'Stanleyite' connections aligns with Michael Johnston's assessment of *Eger and Grime* as a gentry romance; the printed texts point to wider circulation, while the earliest recorded reference to the story is a performance of 'Graysteil' before King James IV of Scotland in 1497.[84] This varied readership is another factor that needs to be taken into account when

---

[84] Aisling Byrne and Victoria Flood, 'The Romance of the Stanleys: Regional and National Imaginings in the Percy Folio', *Viator*, 46.1 (2015), 327–51; Johnston, *Romance and the Gentry*, pp. 82, 84; James Ralston Caldwell, 'Introduction', in *Eger and Grime: A parallel-text edition of the Percy and the Huntington-Laing Versions of the Romance*, ed. by Caldwell (Cambridge, MA: Harvard University Press, 1933), pp. 3–176 (pp. 6, 10–12).

considering the particular portrayal of the proud lady and the implications she holds for chivalric masculinity in this romance.

Winglayne is characterised more negatively than any of the women discussed so far. She is shown to be fickle and scornful, speaking 'words [...] both strange & drye' to Eger when she eventually visits him on his sickbed.[85] Her scorn is contrasted with Loosepine's care for Eger's injured body and 'Loosepine serves as Winglaine's foil' more generally in the romance, as Tison Pugh notes.[86] Intradiegetic responses, similarly to those in *Ipomadon* and *Blanchardyn and Eglantine*, encourage the reader to share this critical view of Winglayne: 'all that euer stoode her by, / did Marueill her answer was soe dry' (Percy, 639–40), while Grime, arguably the romance's real hero, laments that

> thy great pride of thy daughter free
> made him in this great perill to bee;
> alas that euer shee was borne! (Percy, 1319–21)

Winglayne does have some redeeming features: we are granted a rare insight into her feelings for Eger when we are told that she only overhears the conversation about Eger's defeat because

> of Sir Egar shee soe sore thought
> that shee lay wakened, & sleeped nought.
> (Percy, 367–8, phrased similarly in HL, 457–8)

However, this more neutral or positive description is extremely rare. We are repeatedly confronted with a negative view of Winglayne, which ensures that the demands she makes are positioned as unreasonable. Whereas military strength is desirable and necessary for ruling women's husbands in *Guy of Warwick*, *Ipomadon*, and *Blanchardyn and Eglantine*, Winglayne is perceived as taking this condition too far, demanding too much for any knight to fulfil. This is made to reflect upon her character rather than upon the failure of chivalric masculinity.

This negative view of Winglayne is also built into the plot of *Eger and Grime*, as the marriage between Eger and Winglayne is brought about through deception – the pretence that it was Eger, and not Grime, who finally defeated Gray-steele.[87] This is the foundation upon which their marriage rests, and the romance does not hide this but openly accepts and indeed celebrates it at the end of the Percy text, applauding Grime for having 'proued soe weele' that 'he

---

[85] *Eger and Grime*, ed. by Caldwell, Percy, line 672; HL, lines 715–16; Percy, line 450.
[86] Tison Pugh, *Sexuality and its Queer Discontents in Middle English Literature* (New York: Palgrave Macmillan, 2008), p. 136.
[87] See the discussion in Antony J. Hasler, 'Romance and Its Discontents in *Eger and Grime*', in *The Spirit of Medieval English Popular Romance*, ed. by Ad Putter and Jane Gilbert (London: Routledge, 2013; first publ. 2000), pp. 200–18 (pp. 210–13).

gate to his brother Sir Egar / an Erles Land & a ladye faire' (1445–8). Praising Grime's actions implies that there is nothing wrong with deceiving Winglayne into marriage and by extension suggests that she was wrong to make such an extreme condition for her marriage in the first place, and wrong to hold to this when Eger failed to meet it. Grime's intervention does not only serve the romance's primary focus on the love between him and Eger,[88] then, in keeping with the pattern of works like *Ywain and Gawain* or *Amis and Amiloun*, but also reaffirms the negative portrayal of Winglayne by suggesting that she deserves to be tricked into marriage.[89]

Indeed, Winglayne apparently merits not only deception but also a taste of her own medicine through Eger's scorn, as Grime instructs Eger to

> looke thou as strange to her bee
> as shee in times past hath beene to thee;
> for & thou doe not as shee hath done before,
> thou shalst loose my loue for euermore. (Percy, 1305–8)

Because this instruction comes from Grime and threatens a loss of the male protagonists' all-important love, the reader is encouraged to agree that Winglayne deserves Eger's scorn. The idea that this is a taste of her own medicine is explicit in Huntington-Laing, where Eger exclaims 'as ye have brewd, so shal ye drink' (2384), this proverbial statement, as Michael Cichon argues, 'us[ing] aspects of traditional wisdom to endorse the action of the narrative

[88] Their love has often been discussed in terms of the romance prioritising friendship: see Mabel Van Duzee, *A Medieval Romance of Friendship: Eger and Grime* (New York: Franklin, 1963), pp. 33–4, 38–9; Deanna Delmar Evans, 'Scott's *Redgauntlet* and the Late Medieval Romance of Friendship, *Eger and Grime*', *Studies in Scottish Literature*, 31.1 (1999), 31–45; Michael Cichon, '"As ye have brewd, so shal ye drink": The Proverbial Context of *Eger and Grime*', in *Medieval Romance, Medieval Contexts*, ed. by Rhiannon Purdie and Michael Cichon (Cambridge: D. S. Brewer, 2011), pp. 35–46 (p. 42); Hasler, 'Romance and Its Discontents', p. 212; and, for a queer interpretation, Pugh, *Sexuality and its Queer Discontents*, pp. 123–44. I refer to their relationship as one of love rather than friendship to leave open the queer resonances of this romance.

[89] *Ywain* or *Ywain and Gawain* have sometimes been proposed as sources for *Eger and Grime*: see James Wade, *Fairies in Medieval Romance* (Basingstoke: Palgrave Macmillan, 2011), p. 87; Laura A. Hibbard, *Mediæval Romance in England: A Study of the Sources and Analogues of the Non-Cyclic Metrical Romances* (New York: Franklin, 1924; repr. 1969), pp. 314–15; David E. Faris, 'The Art of Adventure in the Middle English Romance: *Ywain and Gawain, Eger and Grime*', *Studia Neophilologica*, 53.1 (1981), 91–100. For comparisons with *Amis and Amiloun* see William Calin, *The Lily and the Thistle: The French Tradition and the Older Literature of Scotland – Essays in Criticism* (Toronto: University of Toronto Press, 2014), p. 213; Sergi Mainer, '*Eger and Grime* and the Boundaries of Courtly Romance', in *Joyous Sweit Imaginatioun: Essays on Scottish Literature in Honour of R. D. S. Jack*, ed. by Sarah Carpenter and Sarah M. Dunnigan (Amsterdam: Rodopi, 2007), pp. 77–95 (pp. 84–6); Hasler, 'Romance and Its Discontents', pp. 211, 212–13; Pugh, *Sexuality and its Queer Discontents*, pp. 123–5; Van Duzee, *A Medieval Romance of Friendship*, pp. 33–4, 38–9.

and the so-called wisdom that informs it'.[90] The Percy Folio text may indicate more discomfort with Eger's feigned scorn, as here the Earl offers Grime '40ˡⁱ of Land, / of florences that were fayre & round' (1349–50) to reconcile Eger with Winglayne, the narrator commenting 'I hope that was ethe to doe' (1352). That Grime profits from a problem that he has created may question the motivation for Eger's scorn, but given the acquisitive focus of this romance overall (the ending of the Percy Folio text openly celebrates the protagonists' material acquisitions, 1445–52), it is possible that Grime's easily won reward is supposed to be applauded and Eger's scorn viewed as a just rebuke for Winglayne's earlier pride. The romance drive towards a happy ending is able to silence any reservations about deception or monetary motives. Indeed, *Eger and Grime* suggests that these are part of romance fulfilment: acquisitive and economic fantasies are included within the desires that 'are, or rather *can be*, satisfied' within this genre.[91]

The only person to question the means by which Eger and Winglayne's marriage is brought about is Winliane herself, at the end of Huntington-Laing, where she considers it a serious enough issue to merit their separation:

> Now may I live in lasting pain:
> I should never have made you band,
> Ye should never have had mine hand,
> And ye should never have been mine,
> Had I kend it had been sir Grahame. (HL, 2822–6)

Although the condition Winliane argues was invalid (Eger's false claim to have defeated every knight he has fought) is a hyperbolic demand typical of romance literature, her reasoning seems to draw on medieval legal precedents for divorce. Her complaint recalls the law of divorce *a vinculo*, which constituted 'a release from the bond of marriage, granted on the grounds that the marriage had never been valid': 'ye should never have been mine', she states.[92] However, while this may endow Winliane's complaint with a quasi-legal status, the romance is quick to refute her claim of injustice, asserting

> Thus she was so set all to ill,
> As wanton women that gets their will:
> Amongst thousands there is not one
> Can govern them but wit of none. (HL, 2827–30)

---

[90] Cichon, 'The Proverbial Context of *Eger and Grime*', pp. 43–4.

[91] Nicola McDonald, 'Desire Out of Order and *Undo Your Door*', *Studies in the Age of Chaucer*, 34 (2012), 247–75 (p. 255). Emphasis in original.

[92] Conor McCarthy, *Marriage in Medieval England: Law, Literature and Practice* (Woodbridge: Boydell Press, 2004), p. 140. Although McCarthy focuses upon an English context, Karras notes that 'the canon law rules about the formation and dissolution of marriage were well established and uniform across Europe': Ruth Mazo Karras, *Sexuality in Medieval Europe: Doing Unto Others*, 2nd edn (London: Routledge, 2012), p. 79.

Rather than the wrong Eger has done to Winliane, this passage focuses on the wrong Winliane does to Eger by separating from him, discrediting her complaint of deception. This drive to demerit Winliane suggestively aligns with Huntington-Laing's concluding marriage between Eger and Lilias, a marriage that implies that Winliane does not deserve a happy ending because of her proud adherence to her vow at all costs, while Eger does. Winliane's exclusion provides a definitive final condemnation, which positions her as the problem rather than as a figure who reveals the problems inherent within chivalric masculinity.

Unlike the Fere and Eglantine, Winglayne is not the sole ruler of her lands, as her father is still alive, suggesting that her negative depiction is not prompted by her threatening autonomy. Instead, Winglayne's negative portrayal seems to be motivated by the difficult questions the condition she sets for her marriage poses, questions that reflect upon the failure of chivalric masculinity. The Fere's conditions are primarily aspirational, seeking to marry

> the best knyghte
> Of all this world in armus bryghte
> Assayde vnder his shelde. (118–20)

In contrast, Winglayne issues a prohibition: she will not take a husband

> without he would with swords dent
> win euery battell where he went. (Percy, 13–14)

She adheres strictly to this prohibition by rejecting Eger after his defeat and, in the Huntington-Laing version, separating from him on discovering his deception. While romance often focuses on exceptional knights capable of the most demanding deeds, *Eger and Grime* raises a question the genre rarely addresses: what happens when a romance hero is defeated?[93] The difficulties posed by this question seem to be what motivates the negative representation of Winglayne, ensuring that masculinity can be questioned but that challenges to it are refracted through Winglayne and thus dissociated from the author and reader.

Eger and Grime, as many critics have suggested, is preoccupied with masculinity above all else, with frequent references to 'manhood' (Percy, 68, 81, 84, 90, 668), a prioritisation of love between men, and the unsubtle symbolic castration figured by Gray-steele cutting off defeated knights' little fingers.[94] Yet the romance provides no convincing answers to the questions

---

[93] There is some acknowledgement of this possibility elsewhere, including in Malory's *Morte Darthur*, when Palomydes unhorses Tristram and Lamerok: see *Le Morte Darthur*, ed. by P. J. C. Field, 2 vols (Cambridge: D. S. Brewer, 2013), I, 379.

[94] On this symbolic castration, see Wade, *Fairies in Medieval Romance*, p. 88; Pugh, *Sexuality and its Queer Discontents*, pp. 123–44; Cooper, *The English Romance in*

that Winglayne's vow raises about defeat and knightly identity.[95] Eger's defeat is resolved only through deception and his masculinity is reinforced only by association with Grime. This diverges from the analogous tale of Sadius and Galo in Walter Map's *De Nugis Curialium*, where Galo turns down Sadius's offer to fight the giant in his place.[96] In contrast, the focus of chivalric exceptionality in *Eger and Grime* passes from Eger to Grime. While this may seem to reassert masculinity, replacing Eger with Grime as the triumphant hero of the romance whose prowess is infallible, this transference draws attention to the provisional nature of masculine prowess. If Eger had formerly 'euermore [...] wan the honour' (Percy, 31), only to be defeated in battle, might not the same thing happen to Grime? Huntington-Laing partly explores this possibility, as Eger is apparently restored as the hero of the romance after Grahame's death. He goes crusading, where

> A better man then sir Eger,
> Was not counted that day to live.[97]

This secondary transferral of exceptional chivalric masculinity from Grahame back to Eger again underscores the fragility of masculine identities that are dependent on the outcome of each battle, an iterative and always incomplete performance. As Pugh suggests,

> Under cultural conditions in which manhood always needs to be proved, it faces the likelihood of eventually being disproved. Masculinity must be repeatedly performed, but the performance is so complex and demanding that even the most masculine of men will eventually trip up in its enactment.[98]

Eger and Grime acknowledges the possibility that chivalric masculinity may fail, but if Grime appears happy to accept the possibility of failure (Percy,

---

Time, p. 82; Calin, *The Lily and the Thistle*, p. 218; Mainer, 'The Boundaries of Courtly Romance', p. 82.

[95] Mainer makes a similar argument, although he sees the romance as 'a consciously self-parodic meta-romance' because of this, which I do not: see 'The Boundaries of Courtly Romance', p. 94. Likewise, Hasler questions 'how far [...] Grime's extemporized romance make[s] good Eger's loss', although he proposes a different reason for this, approaching the romance through psychoanalytic theories: 'Romance and Its Discontents', p. 216.

[96] For discussions of this story and its relation to *Eger and Grime*, see Neil Cartlidge, '"Vinegar upon Nitre"? Walter Map's Romance of "Sadius and Galo"', in *Cultural Translations in Medieval Romance*, pp. 117–33; Wade, *Fairies in Medieval Romance*, pp. 91–3.

[97] HL, lines 2846–7. Mainer does not view this as an uncritical idealisation of Eger, however, as he argues that 'by the end of the fifteenth century, crusades had partly or completely lost their originally idealised significance': 'The Boundaries of Courtly Romance', p. 93.

[98] *Sexuality and its Queer Discontents*, p. 127.

87–9), the romance itself does not seem comfortable with the idea that knights are 'as like to loose as win' (Percy, 354). Instead, it attempts to reassert masculine prowess first through Grime's defeat of Gray-steele and then, in Huntington-Laing, through the attempt to rehabilitate Eger with his victories at Rhodes and his marriage to Lilias. Yet this does not seem to be successful because it draws attention to the provisional nature of chivalric masculinity.

Eger and Grime arguably occupies a place in literary history where concerns about masculinity and sexual dissidence were particularly likely to be taken seriously by readers. This romance was read (and listened to) by people from a wide range of social classes, in the context of changes in the class system such as the emergence of the gentry as a distinct and significant class, a cultural development that Johnston has argued profoundly impacted the romance genre, including works like *Eger and Grime*.[99] These societal changes must also have affected contemporary understandings of and performances of gender roles.[100] This is not to posit a 'crisis of masculinity' in late medieval Scotland and England: as Derek Neal has argued, 'these crises have happened rather too often [...] for the concept to have much use'.[101] But as a later medieval romance read by different social classes, which consciously reflects on the problematic results of class systems like primogeniture and invokes a crusading context associated with the promotion of particular kinds of masculinity, *Eger and Grime* is well-placed to testify to, comment on, and either exacerbate or reassure concerns about changes in the performance and celebration of particular kinds of masculinity.[102] Yet its response to Eger's failure relies upon deception (as does *Ipomadon*'s approach to chivalric masculinity): because no better resolution can be offered to the questions it raises, these questions must be contained within a character who is represented negatively, distancing these problems from the romance's writer, though leaving them open for the reader to pursue. *Eger and Grime* illustrates a shift in views and uses of the proud lady in romance literature, perhaps in response to changing understandings of chivalric masculinity. This process undertakes a further step in Malory's portrayal of Pelleas and Ettarde.

---

99 See *Romance and the Gentry*.
100 See Pugh, *Sexuality and its Queer Discontents*, p. 52.
101 Derek G. Neal, *The Masculine Self in Late Medieval England* (Chicago: University of Chicago Press, 2008), p. 6.
102 See Lewis, 'Chivalry, masculinity, and crusading', pp. 311–13.

The Proud Lady beyond Redemption
in Malory's Tale of Pelleas and Ettarde

Pelleas's unrequited love for the proud lady Ettarde appears early in the *Morte*, as part of the adventures of Gawain in 'King Uther and King Arthur'.[103] This episode is drawn from the anonymous thirteenth-century *Suite du Merlin*'s story of Pellias and Arcade, but Malory 'radically alter[s]' this source, which he 'follows quite closely until this point'.[104] In the *Suite*, Pellias cannot approach Arcade 'pour ce qu'il est de bas lignage et elle est extraicte de haulte gent' ['because he's of low descent and she is of the nobility']; 'il n'estoit pas de tel lignage que elle le deust amer' ['he was not of such birth that she should love him'].[105] Arcade is still criticised for rejecting Pellias – she is 'orgueilleuse [...] encor plus que nulle autre' (p. 403, 25. 452) ['arrogant [...] more than any other', p. 227] – but she has a reason for rejecting Pellias, and a reason medieval readers may have considered compelling. While Eugène Vinaver suggests that Malory alters Pelleas's status because he was 'reluctant [...] to have a protagonist of low birth', the motivations for and consequences of this change are more significant than Vinaver acknowledges.[106] Removing social status as a factor, Malory highlights Ettarde's transgressive refusal to accept a suitable, well-tested knight as her lover, exploring the disruptions proud women can cause to the construction of chivalric masculinity, while also disavowing this disruption as the result of female pride rather than masculine failure.

The proud lady more directly disrupts chivalric masculinity in this tale than any other discussed so far, as Ettarde rejects any involvement in recognising Pelleas's virtue as a knight and lover. As Carolyne Larrington argues, Ettarde 'refuses to follow the courtly script': within the romance economy of love and prowess, she 'has no right *not* to grant her love to Pelleas, since he is brave and loves her faithfully, especially once Malory has removed the *Suite*'s mitigating circumstance: that Pelleas is of low birth'.[107] Ettarde's disruption of

---

[103] This section draws on material from my article on 'Desire, Consent and Misogyny in Post-medieval Adaptations of the Pelleas and Ettarde Story', in *Arthurian Medievalism*, ed. by Andrew B. R. Elliott and Renée Ward (= *JIAS*, 10.1 (2022)), pp. 5–28. I follow the same broad argument set out in the first two paragraphs of that article, providing more detail and a new focus on Ettarde as a proud lady in love here. The article goes on to discuss rewritings of this story in nineteenth- and twentieth-century literature.

[104] Carolyne Larrington, *King Arthur's Enchantresses: Morgan and Her Sisters in Arthurian Tradition* (London: Tauris, 2006), p. 115.

[105] *La Suite du Roman de Merlin*, ed. by Gilles Roussineau, Textes littéraires français, 472, 2 vols (Geneva: Droz, 1996), II, 402–3 (23. 450, 452); *The Post-Vulgate Cycle: The Merlin Continuation*, trans. by Martha Asher, Lancelot-Grail: The Old French Arthurian Vulgate and Post-Vulgate in Translation, 10 vols (Cambridge: D. S. Brewer, 2010), VIII, 227.

[106] Eugène Vinaver, 'Commentary', in *The Works of Sir Thomas Malory*, ed. by Eugène Vinaver, 2nd edn, 3 vols (Oxford: Clarendon, 1967), III, 1261–1663 (p. 1358).

[107] Larrington, *King Arthur's Enchantresses*, p. 115.

chivalric and romantic scripts partly aligns her with Chen's work on asexuality as highlighting restrictive norms, as her (deliberate) refusal to conform draws attention to normative patterns through its difference. Situating Ettarde within the romance tradition of the proud lady in love can further our understanding of the specific nature of her transgression in the *Morte*, Malory's punitive response to it, and the wider challenges and opportunities the proud lady in love offers to chivalric masculinity. Ettarde is the most negatively represented, punitively treated, and in some ways most subversive incarnation of a proud lady in love; as such, she reveals the functions this motif can serve at its furthest extreme.

The rupture of expectations Ettarde's refusal to love Pelleas creates is repeatedly emphasised in this episode. When Gawain first encounters Pelleas, Pelleas tells him that 'sorow and shame commyth unto me after worshyppe' (p. 128), emphasising Ettarde's fracturing of the chivalric economy, where 'worshyp' should result in reward rather than 'sorow and shame'. Malory also asserts that while Ettarde is 'so prowde that she had scorne of [Pelleas], and seyde she wolde never love hym thoughe he wolde dye for hir',

> all ladyes and jantyllwomen had scorne of hir that she was so prowde; for there were fayrer than she, and there was none that was there but and Sir Pelleas wolde have profyrde hem love they wolde have shewed hym the same for his noble prouesse. (p. 131)

These other 'ladyes and jantyllwomen' model the normative behaviour expected of Ettarde, behaviour she herself later rehearses when she tells Gawain his lady (an invention of Gawain as part of his seduction of Ettarde) 'is to blame [...] and she woll nat love you, for ye that be so well-borne a man and suche a man of prouesse, there is no lady in this worlde to good for you' (p. 133). Although Ettarde does agree to a sexual relationship with Gawain, marking a difference from the other proud ladies, this may not so much mitigate as further condemn her refusal to love Pelleas, given Malory's negative representation of Gawain in this episode.[108] Her acceptance of Gawain pinpoints the issue Malory is targeting through Ettarde: the failure to reward a deserving knight with love. This indicates the preoccupation with the will – or wilfulness – of women characteristic of the motif of the proud lady. It is not so much women's right to consent to love or retain their virginity that is at issue in this motif (though these may seem the most pressing issues to modern readers) as it is concerns about women's ability to dictate the terms of bestowing (and withdrawing) their love however they desire, and the impact this may have on constructions of masculinity. In this way, the motif of the proud lady in love

---

[108] Ettarde's feelings also remain less clear than in the *Suite*: see Siobhán M. Wyatt, *Women of Words in 'Le Morte Darthur': The Autonomy of Speech in Malory's Female Characters* (New York: Palgrave Macmillan, 2016), p. 46.

to some extent rewrites the motif of 'desirable desire', revealing some of the anxiety the focus on women's desires may have provoked.[109] In opposition to modern conceptions of asexuality and aromanticism, the proud ladies' unwillingness to love is seen as wilful, and this wilfulness is 'judged as a problem by others' because it threatens to become 'nonproductive and nonreproductive', both by resisting marriage and procreation and by attempting to opt out of the construction of chivalric masculinity.[110] As Megan Arkenberg comments, 'one of the romance genre's most powerful strategies for normalizing sexual desire lies in its linking of desire to productivity, specifically the production of future knightly deeds': the proud ladies in love temporarily resist this model of sexual desire, and their wilfulness in doing so requires condemnation to close off the questions they pose about the dependency of chivalric masculinity upon women's ratification.[111]

Malory's precise condemnation of Ettarde's wilful refusal to reward a deserving knight with her love is supported by his entirely altered resolution of the episode. In the *Suite*, Gauvain repents his betrayal and convinces Arcade to love Pellias instead. While Gauvain argues Pellias's case, Arcade's priorities are taken into account: she asks Gauvain 'le dictes vous sur vostre loyauté que vous cuidés que ce soit mon preu?' (p. 421, 24. 465) ['do you tell me on your faith that you believe this is to my benefit?', p. 237] and tells her knights 'ja n'en dirés […] chose que je n'en face, pourquoy je y voie mon preu et mon honnor' (p. 425, 24. 468) ['I'll do everything you say […] provided I see my welfare and honor in it', p. 239]. Arcade thus abides by courtly and chivalric priorities in reflecting on whether Pellias's noble character surpasses his lower birth, and in attending to these concerns the *Suite* considers her will and consent. In Malory, however, Ettarde's will is disavowed and indeed violated. Here, Gawain does not repent and a very different kind of resolution is provided by Nyneve, Malory's Lady of the Lake, who enchants Ettarde to love Pelleas.[112] However, Pelleas now scorns Ettarde, for reasons that are not entirely clear: Nyneve has enchanted Pelleas so that he 'fell on slepe' (p. 135) and when Pelleas praises God for his sudden hatred of Ettarde, Nyneve tells him to 'thanke me therefore' (p. 136), so it may be implied though not clearly stated that Nyneve has also enchanted Pelleas. Nyneve then becomes his lover and wife herself, leaving Ettarde to die of sorrow. While other uses of magic

---

[109] See Cooper, 'Desirable desire: "I am wholly given over unto thee"', in *The English Romance in Time*, pp. 218–68.

[110] Sara Ahmed, *Willful Subjects* (Durham, NC: Duke University Press, 2014), pp. 19, 20.

[111] Megan Arkenberg, '"A Mayde, and Last of Youre Blood": Galahad's Asexuality and its Significance in *Le Morte Darthur*', *Arthuriana*, 24.3 (2014), 3–22 (p. 7).

[112] Malory's altered ending may partly reflect a desire to portray Gawain more negatively, as Ralph Norris suggests: *Malory's Library: The Sources of the 'Morte Darthur'* (Cambridge: D. S. Brewer, 2008), p. 45. However, this does not seem to sufficiently account for the inclusion of Nyneve.

for coercive purposes are portrayed negatively in the *Morte*, Nyneve's enchantment is framed as an appropriate punishment for Ettarde's refusal to love Pelleas. Inna Matyushina's claim that 'in the realm of *amour courtois*, any hint of punishing a lady would have struck a discordant note' does not, it seems, apply to women who disobey the rules of *amour courtois*.[113] Nyneve tells Ettarde 'ye oughte to be ashamed for to murther suche a knyght', insisting that Ettarde's sudden love for Pelleas is 'the ryghteuouse jugemente of God' (pp. 135–6). Positioning her enchantment as divine justice, Nyneve's words and actions imply that Ettarde merits death for her refusal to love Pelleas. There is some ambiguity as to the appropriateness of this judgement: Siobhán Wyatt argues that her proclamation 'comes close to being associated with blasphemous words', opening up a space in which readers may question it.[114] However, the episode as a whole appears to support Nyneve's perspective. Pugh has argued (in relation to *Amis and Amiloun*) that 'normative sexuality kills in medieval romance [...]. Death [...] serves a regulatory function in narrative. It frequently codes characters as heroes and as villains'.[115] Ettarde's death defines her (and not just Gawain) as the villain of this episode, condemning her wilful rejection of Pelleas, and not just reducing the focus upon Arcade's will in the *Suite* but actually violating Ettarde's will through Nyneve's enchantment. The role-reversal occasioned by this enchantment (turning Pelleas's sorrow and wish for death into Ettarde's) positions Nyneve as giving Ettarde a taste of her own medicine in a manner similar to, but more extreme than, Eger's scorn of Winglayne. Winliane, too, of course, ultimately dies in the Huntington-Laing *Eger and Grime*, perhaps similarly indicating the regulatory function of death in that narrative. The ending of Malory's Pelleas and Ettarde episode precisely and deliberately identifies Ettarde's wilful rejection of Pelleas as transgressive, superseding any focus on representing Gawain negatively to establish Ettarde as a villain within this episode. The *Morte* offers the most punitive and condemnatory representation of a proud lady in love, which both reveals the subversive potential of this figure and violently eliminates it.

Malory's more extreme punitive approach to the motif of the proud lady in love perpetuates and promotes what we would now think of as rape culture. In this light, the accusations against Malory of two counts of the *raptus* of Joan Smith may offer a sobering reminder of the potential connections between literary and real-life violence. We do not and may never know what actually happened between Malory and Joan Smith, and focusing restrictively upon the binaries of guilty and innocent seems misdirected, particularly if we allow

---

[113] Inna Matyushina, 'Treacherous Women at King Arthur's Court: Punishment and Shame', in *Treason: Medieval and Early Modern Adultery, Betrayal, and Shame*, ed. by Larissa Tracy (Leiden: Brill, 2019), pp. 288–319 (p. 312).

[114] Wyatt, *Women of Words*, p. 47.

[115] Pugh, *Sexuality and its Queer Discontents*, pp. 118–19.

these binaries to govern our interpretations of *Le Morte Darthur*. As we have already seen in Chapter 1, and as we will return to in Chapter 5, the *Morte* is a work of huge variety, including in its approach to issues of coercion and gender. At times it seems highly nuanced and sensitive in its account of the pressures of love or the shock of violation. But recalling potential echoes of the Pelleas and Ettarde episode in Malory's biography may fruitfully remind us that literature forms part of the means by which real-life misogyny and violence are normalised and perpetuated, urging us to recognise how the *Morte* is imbricated in and actively upholds the values of late medieval rape culture.

The misogynistic implications of the Pelleas and Ettarde episode are perhaps particularly long-lasting, as later rewritings of and references to this story continue to blame Ettarde for her refusal to love Pelleas, upholding misogynistic ideas about women and consent.[116] In doing so, they reveal the wider cultural impact of the motif of the proud lady in love and of the ideas and ideologies upheld by the romance genre. Malory's *Morte Darthur*, of course, has become a particularly canonical romance (albeit, within academia, relatively recently) and so holds greater cultural reach.[117] But despite its unusual influence on later literature, the *Morte* indicates (if more prominently and extremely) the impact of romance's engagement with resistance to love. The works discussed in this chapter often incorporate powerful condemnations of resistance to love and forceful reassertions of normative desires and conventional gendered roles. However, they also raise some questions about these gender roles, particularly chivalric masculinity and the extent to which it depends upon women for its successful construction. There are, then, suggestions of gender roles and sexual practices that sit outside of medieval norms encoded within these narratives, and the proud ladies' resistance at times functions as a means of queering normative behaviour and assumptions. Even in the *Morte*, where we are presented with a narrative that overtly condemns Ettarde, from a perspective focused on consent it is not Ettarde's but Pelleas's behaviour that is unreasonable. By the time Malory was writing, consent was well established as (at least in theory) paramount to medieval marriages and, as Elisabeth van Houts has argued, consent had also been adopted as 'a tool that could be used [by

---

[116] See my discussion of post-medieval adaptations of this story in 'Desire, Consent and Misogyny'.

[117] Leitch and Rushton's *New Companion to Malory* observes that 'Malory is now canonical and widely taught', positioning this as a change that has occurred between the publication of *A Companion to Malory* in 1996 and the *New Companion* in 2019: Megan G. Leitch and Cory James Rushton, 'Introduction', in *A New Companion to Malory*, ed. by Leitch and Rushton (Cambridge: D. S. Brewer, 2019), pp. 1–10 (p. 1). On the afterlives of Malory's *Morte* more generally, see A. S. G. Edwards, 'The Reception of Malory's *Morte Darthur*', in *A Companion to Malory*, ed. by Elizabeth Archibald and A. S. G. Edwards (Cambridge: D. S. Brewer, 1996), pp. 241–52.

laypeople] to push their own demands for self-determination'.[118] Understandings of consent were thus not entirely limited to marital contexts, suggesting
that this was an available framework of reference for the Pelleas and Ettarde
episode. From this perspective, Ettarde simply wants to be rid of Pelleas: we
are told that 'all she doth hit is for to cawse hym to leve this contrey and to
leve his lovynge' (p. 131), while she later tells Gawain that 'I hated hym
moste, for I coude never be quytte of hym' (p. 133). Ettarde's desire to be rid
of Pelleas is one reason I do not find convincing Amy Kaufman's suggestion
that 'the female characters against which Nynyve pits herself are arguably the
constructions of patriarchal fantasy more than they can be said to represent
"real" women': Ettarde too seems to be resisting the constructions of patriarchal fantasy.[119] However, the rarity of these insights into Ettarde's desires
corresponds with Kaufman's suggestion that 'a female character's struggle
within Malory's text is, quite frequently, a struggle of competing narratives':
'a woman's pleas for her own sovereignty and safety must struggle against
a privileged male narrative just to be heard'.[120] Ettarde's pleas for her right
to choose – or refuse – a romantic partner are almost entirely erased by the
narrative's overt sympathy with Pelleas, deploying Nyneve to further encourage readers (perhaps particularly female readers) to accept the condemnation
of Ettarde as appropriate.[121] But while later narratives and the *Morte* itself
overtly condemn Ettarde, this cannot entirely confine readers' responses. As
Jeff Rider argues,

> Narrative literature educates rather than indoctrinating since […] it often
> both offers examples of 'resistance' to the standards it purveys and inevi-
> tably encourages, or at least inevitably leaves open, the possibility of such
> resistance in its audience. […] Readers, in other words, always retain some
> degree of agency.[122]

Ettarde's subversive potential to reveal the weaknesses and dependencies of
chivalric masculinity is contained by Malory's punitive depiction, but this
confinement is not complete: the proud lady's transgressive potential remains
latent, waiting to be activated by medieval and modern readers.

---

[118] Elisabeth van Houts, *Married Life in the Middle Ages, 900–1300* (Oxford: Oxford University Press, 2019), p. 4.
[119] Amy S. Kaufman, 'The Law of the Lake: Malory's Sovereign Lady', *Arthuriana*, 17.3
(2007), 56–73 (p. 63).
[120] Amy S. Kaufman, 'Malory and Gender', in *A New Companion to Malory*, pp. 164–76
(pp. 172, 174).
[121] Roberta Davidson argues that Malory uses Nyneve 'to voice his own interpretations,
guiding us to read the episodes "correctly"': 'Reading Like a Woman in Malory's
"Morte Darthur"', *Arthuriana*, 16.1 (2006), 21–33 (p. 27).
[122] Jeff Rider, 'The Inner Life of Women in Medieval Romance Literature', in *The Inner
Life of Women in Medieval Romance Literature: Grief, Guilt, and Hypocrisy*, ed. by Jeff
Rider and Jamie Friedman (New York: Palgrave Macmillan, 2011), pp. 1–25 (p. 6).

Conclusion

The motif of the proud lady in love can be socially subversive as well as conservative, raising questions about the performance of gender (especially masculinity) in medieval romance, even while reimposing normative desires. These romances' ultimate adherence to norms reveals the political investment they have in female (heterosexual) desire: while Felicity Riddy argues that in romance, 'the woman [...] simply moves, plotlessly, from daughterhood to wifehood', the romances discussed in this chapter reveal the plot within this pattern and the politics within that plot.[123] Romantic a(nti)pathy is a gendered motif, as I have argued, which differentiates between men's and women's expressions of romantic a(nti)pathy, resolves them to different extents and for different purposes. Women's desires emerge as not solely about love but as holding important implications for the transfer of political and economic power and the continuance of patriarchal structures, revealing the ideological functions of romance literature and exposing the ways in which its approach to love is at times more pragmatic than idealistic. However, at the same time as these romances' conclusions adhere to sociocultural expectations and set a pattern for women's behaviour in secular society, they also raise questions about normative assumptions, particularly with regard to chivalric masculinity. The fact that they seem to problematise gender roles even while trying to reassert the importance of love and marriage may suggest the difficulty of imposing binaries that do not account for the complexity and variety of human expressions of gender and sexuality. Even in a genre – and with a motif – that seems particularly concerned to uphold marriage, love, and procreation (with, that is, what have become the 'cultural appurtenances' of heterosexuality), formulations of gender and sexuality are not absolute, and attempts to impose norms are undermined by the questions that remain unanswered, the suggestions of alternative and queer practices, and the necessity of coercion.[124] The next chapter continues to explore the coercive strategies at work in medieval romance, uncovering the ways in which resistance to *mésalliance* opens up coercive situations that reveal men's sexual vulnerability as a concern of this genre.

---

[123] Felicity Riddy, 'Middle English romance: family, marriage, intimacy', in *The Cambridge Companion to Medieval Romance*, ed. by Roberta L. Krueger (Cambridge: Cambridge University Press, 2000), pp. 235–52 (p. 240). McDonald also argues that in romance, 'women's lives [...] are conventionally plotless': 'Desire Out of Order', p. 271.

[124] Karma Lochrie, *Heterosyncrasies: Female Sexuality When Normal Wasn't* (Minneapolis: University of Minnesota Press, 2005), p. xiii.

3

'Ne feolle hit þe of cunde / To spuse beo me bunde': Resisting *Mésalliance*

When Horn, a foundling and the orphaned son of the King and Queen of Suddenne, is propositioned by Rymenhild, daughter and heir to the King of Westernesse, he responds carefully, having first thought 'what he speke miȝte'.[1] Horn's hesitancy suggests he considers the position in which Rymenhild has placed him to be a difficult one: as a foundling who has been taken in by her father, he cannot accept her offer without fear of the consequences if the King were to discover their relationship, but nor can he afford to offend Rymenhild. The offer of a relationship with a woman of such importance may seem like a typical romance fantasy, but Horn responds with an awareness of the problematic status such relationships would have in real life: as Elisabeth van Houts notes, '*mésalliance*, or disparagement (marrying below one's social standing), was seen as deeply dishonourable, a shame that not only affected the parents of the couple but also their wider kin'.[2] Yet what constituted *mésalliance* was highly ambiguous:

> Within the elite (earls, barons, and knights) there was sufficient flexibility for parties to agree on marriages if the circumstances called for them. In other words, what in one case might be deemed an unsuitable marriage, in another might be acceptable. [...] It was a surmountable problem but only if all parties were happy with the arrangement. If not, the social issue was made into a stumbling block.[3]

The relationships discussed in this chapter span the range from those van Houts describes as more socially acceptable (a knight being matched with a duke's daughter) to more extreme cases, including the deliberate disparagement of royalty and a marriage between a knight and a woman of unknown status.

---

[1] *King Horn: A Middle-English Romance*, ed. by Joseph Hall (Oxford: Clarendon Press, 1901), lines 421–2, 412. All quotations are taken from the text of Cambridge University Library, MS Gg.4.27.2 unless otherwise stated.

[2] Elisabeth van Houts, *Married Life in the Middle Ages, 900–1300* (Oxford: Oxford University Press, 2019), p. 30.

[3] *Ibid.*, p. 31.

Romances often create additional layers of complexity through generic tropes such as disguise and secret identities: Horn claims he is 'icome of þralle' (419) as he rejects Rymenhild's advances, but he is actually the rightful heir of Suddenne. The complexities of these relationships and the ways in which they are initiated, resisted, and negotiated offer fruitful material for rethinking the importance of status and its relationship to fantasy and morality, consent and coercion in medieval romance.

Four romances in particular stand out as offering especially significant portrayals of attempts to resist *mésalliance*: the early Middle English romances of *King Horn, Amis and Amiloun,* and *Havelok,* and the later *Wife of Bath's Tale* by Geoffrey Chaucer.[4] These works all devote significant attention to how and why relationships between partners of (apparently) differing status might be rejected or negotiated. In doing so, they go against the grain of the more common romance trope of social status as an external barrier to a relationship, where it may be mutually desired by the people involved but face opposition from parents or other figures. This motif occurs in works like *Le Fresne* and *Lay le Freine, Amadas et Ydoine, Sir Eglamour of Artois, William of Palerne, The Franklin's Tale, Sir Torrent of Portingale, The Squire of Low Degree* (*Undo Your Door*), and William Caxton's *Paris and Vienne.* This pattern is often thought to 'serve the wishful thinking of male readers' for whom 'marriage provided the best way to rise in life', as social disparity usually, although not always, takes the form of a higher-status woman being paired with a lower-status man.[5] This gender imbalance is also a feature of the romances discussed in this chapter, as all but *The Wife of Bath's Tale* focus on relationships between higher-status women and (apparently) lower-status men. The frequency of this form of status imbalance suggests that there are gendered differences in who is able to 'marry up' in romance. But while the works explored here depict men's status as open to improvement through marriage, they also offer a caution to any such aspiration, exposing the anxieties and coercive dynamics that might characterise such relationships. These works therefore reflect on, question, and even challenge the priorities of other romances, where the offer of improved status through marriage is more readily accepted as an emphatic good.

---

4   *King Horn* is usually thought to date from c. 1225–75; Rosamund Allen argues for the 1270s: 'The Date and Provenance of *King Horn*: Some Interim Reassessments', in *Medieval English Studies Presented to George Kane*, ed. by Edward Donald Kennedy, Ronald Waldron, and Joseph S. Wittig (Cambridge: D. S. Brewer, 1988), pp. 99–125 (pp. 102–3, 122, 125). *Amis and Amiloun* dates from either the late thirteenth or early fourteenth century, *Havelok* from the late thirteenth century, and *The Wife of Bath's Tale* from the late fourteenth century.

5   Helen Cooper, *The English Romance in Time: Transforming motifs from Geoffrey of Monmouth to the death of Shakespeare* (Oxford: Oxford University Press, 2004), p. 225.

King Horn, Amis and Amiloun, Havelok, and Chaucer's *Wife of Bath's Tale*
are not the only romances that portray social status as a reason to resist a
romantic or marital relationship. Several other works discussed in this book,
including *Sir Degrevant, Guy of Warwick, Ipomadon, Eger and Grime*, and
Sir Bevis of Hampton also engage with this theme, but subordinate it to another kind of resistance to love, such as romantic a(nti)pathy or resistance
on the basis of race or faith. They offer, however, a useful background and
complement to the romances explored in this chapter, where status emerges as
a primary issue. As status was a key concern in real-life marital arrangements,
it is perhaps unsurprising that the works discussed here often focus on the
context of marriage, although they also frequently emphasise love within such
relationships. Rymenhild tells Horn 'þu schalt haue me to þi wif' (408), but
she also says she has 'þe luued stronge' (304). In *Havelok*, Goldeborw emphatically refuses to 'wedde', 'but he were king or kinges eyr', while Havelok
asks 'hwat sholde Ich with wif do?'; love and marriage are eventually aligned,
however, as 'so mikel loue was hem bitwene'.[6] The loathly lady of *The Wife of
Bath's Tale* demands that the knight 'me take unto thy wyf', but their relationship eventually brings them 'parfit joye'.[7] Belisaunt and Amis's relationship
in *Amis and Amiloun* is more ambiguous, as Belisaunt forces Amis into a
sexual relationship with her, perhaps partly as a marital strategy. The marital
qualities of their relationship are emphasised in the language of Belisaunt's
demand that Amis

> Pliȝt me þi trewþe þou schalt be trewe
> & chaunge me for no newe
> Þat in þis world is born,
> & y pliȝt þe mi treuþe al-so,
> Til god & deþ dele ous ato,
> Y schal neuer be forsworn.[8]

Coupled with their subsequent sexual relationship, Belisaunt's demands seem
to reflect contemporary ideas of what made a valid marriage and indeed effect
such a marriage between herself and Amis. Following the ruling of Pope Alexander III, it was believed that 'future consent freely given between a man and
a woman of marriageable age makes an indissoluble union from the moment
intercourse takes place', while 'present consent freely given, even in the most

[6] *Havelok*, ed. by G. V. Smithers (Oxford: Clarendon Press, 1987), lines 1114, 1116, 1138, 2968.
[7] Geoffrey Chaucer, 'The Wife of Bath's Tale', in *The Riverside Chaucer*, ed. by Larry D. Benson, 3rd edn (Oxford: Oxford University Press, 2008), pp. 116–22 (lines 1055, 1258).
[8] *Amis and Amiloun*, ed. by MacEdward Leach, EETS, o. s., 203 (London: Oxford University Press, 1937), lines 583–8. This edition is based upon the text in the Auchinleck manuscript.

informal of circumstances, between a man and a woman of marriageable age constitutes an indissoluble marriage'.[9] The gap between Amis and Belisaunt's first and second meeting suggests they have exchanged words of future consent, possibly followed by words of present consent (that 'þai plaid in word & dede' may imply this, 766). However, their sexual relationship also ensures that they have created a valid marriage with or without words of present consent. *Amis and Amiloun* thus seems to engage closely with the legal realities of marriage, revealing how a *mésalliance* desirable to the higher-status partner might be upheld in the face of parental opposition. In this light, Belisaunt appears a crafty and unethical strategist with detailed knowledge of how to achieve her desires. *Amis and Amiloun* thus demonstrates the complex and at times provocative reflections the works discussed in this chapter offer on how social status might impact power dynamics in romance and real life.

The relationship between romance and real-life perspectives on social status is a complex one: while depicting an heiress desiring a subordinate man goes against the priorities of real upper-class marriages, the common desire for social advancement through the medieval marriage market also suggests that social mobility is not always transgressive. Cathy Hume notes that although 'parity of social class was thought crucial for the maintenance of the individual's and family's social position', 'marriages between adjacent classes of society were commonplace: Rosenthal shows that only two-thirds of his sample of English peers, for example, married nobility, and similarly merchant daughters frequently married the gentry and the gentry the nobility'.[10] She also suggests that 'an oldest son would probably marry a bride of equal status or financial prospects, whereas daughters and younger sons would marry into families of lower status or with less money – but ideally still make some kind of useful local alliance'.[11] The focus on increasing wealth and status; making socially advantageous alliances; the intermarriage between the nobility, gentry, and merchant classes; and the likelihood of younger sons and daughters marrying slightly lower-status partners point to the presence of social mobility within the medieval marriage market. While families sought to increase their wealth and status through marriage, logically the people who provided this increase in wealth and status were themselves marrying people of a lower status or of less wealth (while not necessarily reducing their own social standing). Of course, I am not suggesting that interclass marriages were not controversial and transgressive: that they were is clearly evidenced by the much-discussed case of Margery Paston's clandestine marriage to her

---

[9]   van Houts, *Married Life*, p. 1.
[10] Cathy Hume, *Chaucer and the Cultures of Love and Marriage* (Cambridge: D. S. Brewer, 2012), pp. 16–17. See also Barbara J. Harris, *English Aristocratic Women, 1450–1550: Marriage and Family, Property and Careers* (Oxford: Oxford University Press, 2002), pp. 43–4.
[11] Hume, *Chaucer and the Cultures of Love and Marriage*, p. 15.

family's bailiff, Richard Calle, which met with hostility and threats from her family.[12] But attitudes to social status are more complex than one example conveys: representations of relationships between people of different status need not always be socially subversive. They replicate an important part of the medieval marriage market, albeit often in a more extreme way; similarly, the balance between resistance and negotiation in the examples I discuss may also reflect real-life behavioural expectations. The romances discussed in this chapter both shape and echo understandings of appropriate conduct, and their focus on conduct intertwines with their use of consensual and coercive forms of negotiation.

Modelling Consent and Coercion in *King Horn* and *Amis and Amiloun*

King Horn, *Amis and Amiloun*, and *Havelok* (discussed in the next section) are all translated from earlier Anglo-Norman or continental French works, but the changes they make to their sources and antecedents indicate a particular interest in social status upon the part of the Middle English redactors. The precise connections between the Middle English and Anglo-Norman versions of the Horn and Amis stories are uncertain: Judith Weiss suggests that both *King Horn* and *Horn Childe and Maiden Rimnild* 'appear ultimately to depend on the *Romance of Horn*, though in ways impossible to unravel totally',[13] while Susan Dannenbaum argues that despite the similarities between the Anglo-Norman and Middle English *Amis* narratives, they 'cannot be considered strictly as source and descendant'.[14] John Ford has subsequently suggested that the redactor of the Middle English *Amis* may have used an Anglo-Norman manuscript similar to Karlsruhe and connected to the other Anglo-Norman manuscripts, as well as drawing upon remembered knowledge of the Old French *Ami et Amile* in a version close to that of Paris, Bibliothèque

---

[12] See *Paston Letters and Papers of the Fifteenth Century*, ed. by Norman Davis, EETS, s. s., 20, 3 vols (Oxford: Oxford University Press, 2004; first publ. Oxford: Clarendon Press, 1971), I, 541 (letter 332), 342–3 (letter 203).

[13] Judith Weiss, 'Introduction', in *The Birth of Romance in England: The 'Romance of Horn', The 'Folie Tristan', The 'Lai of Havelok', and 'Amis and Amilun'*, ed. & trans. by Weiss, FRETS, 4 (Tempe: Arizona Center for Medieval and Renaissance Studies, 2009), pp. 1–43 (p. 5). Joseph Hall's approach to the relationships between these texts is now outdated: 'The Story', in *King Horn*, ed. by Hall, pp. li–lvi.

[14] Susan Dannenbaum [Crane], 'Insular Tradition in the Story of Amis and Amiloun', *Neophilologus*, 67.4 (1983), 611–22 (p. 621). See further Françoise Le Saux, 'From *Ami* to *Amys*: Translation and Adaptation in the Middle English *Amys and Amylion*', in *The Formation of Culture in Medieval Britain: Celtic, Latin, and Norman Influences on English Music, Literature, History, and Art*, ed. by Françoise Le Saux (Lewiston: Mellen, 1995), pp. 111–27 (p. 111).

nationale de France, français 860 (MS Colbert 658).[15] The textual relationships between the Anglo-Norman (and Old French) and Middle English versions are complex, but the Middle English works typically emphasise issues of status more than their antecedents.

In Thomas's *Roman de Horn*, Rigmel's father, King Hunlaf, is well aware that Horn is of royal blood: when Horn washes ashore in Brittany, he tells the King and Herland the steward that he is 'fiz Aälof, al bon rei coruné, / Ki out a justisier Suddene, le regné' ['Aalof's son, the good crowned king, ruler of the realm of Suddene'].[16] Hunlaf then agrees to protect Horn and 'vus aïderai purchacer voz regnez' (336) ['help you acquire your kingdom', p. 51]. Thomas thus indicates that Hunlaf knows Horn's status throughout his wardship and intends Horn to regain his kingdom when he is of age. In contrast, Horn's identity is much vaguer in the Middle English versions. In Cambridge University Library, MS Gg.4.27.2, an early manuscript of *King Horn*,[17] Horn tells King Aylmar

> We beoþ of Suddenne,
> Icome of gode kenne,
> Of Cristene blode
> & kynges suþe gode. (175–8)

Horn alludes to his status, being of 'kynges suþe gode', but provides no further information, and Aylmar does not offer to help restore Horn's kingdom as Hunlaf did. More significantly, in the other manuscripts of *King Horn* (London, British Library, MS Harley 2253 and Oxford, Bodleian Library, MS Laud Misc. 108), Horn does not allude to his royal lineage. Instead, the line referring to kingly descent is replaced with the more general 'of cunne swyþe gode' (Harley, 186) and 'of swiþe gode' (Laud, 188), suggesting that Aylmar remains unaware of Horn's royal lineage in these versions. This opens up greater possibilities for exploring the challenges and opportunities differing status can pose to love.

---

[15] John Ford, 'From *Poésie* to Poetry: *Remaniement* and Mediaeval Techniques of French-to-English Translation of Verse Romance' (unpublished PhD thesis, University of Glasgow, 2000), pp. 57, 286–7 <http://theses.gla.ac.uk/2690/> [accessed 20 January 2021]. The manuscript has been given a new call number since Ford's thesis was written, which I use here.

[16] Thomas, *The Romance of Horn*, ed. by Mildred K. Pope, Anglo-Norman Texts, 9–10, 2 vols (Oxford: Blackwell, 1955), I, lines 169–70; Thomas, 'The Romance of Horn', in *The Birth of Romance in England*, trans. by Judith Weiss, pp. 45–137 (p. 48).

[17] MS Gg.4.27.2 was previously thought to be the oldest manuscript, dated to c. 1250–60, but Allen notes that the more recent estimate of c. 1300 for the Cambridge manuscript would postdate Oxford, Bodleian Library, MS Laud Misc. 108 (dated to c. 1290). Nonetheless, she describes the Cambridge manuscript as 'the most accurate MS of *KH* (though neither the earliest nor the most complete)': Allen, 'The Date and Provenance of *King Horn*', pp. 103, 116.

In both the Anglo-Norman and Middle English versions, Horn tries to reject Rigmel/Rymenhild's affection because he deems himself unworthy. In the
Anglo-Norman *Roman*, he declares

> ne sui si vaillant
> Ke me devez offrir de vus chose taunt grant.
> Povre sui orphanin, n'ai de terre plein gant.[18]

In the Middle English, he insists 'ihc am ibore to lowe', 'ihc am icome of
þralle' (417, 419). Even these claims indicate a slightly different approach
to Horn's status, as in the *Roman* Horn correctly says that he is a 'povre [...]
orphanin', implying that his lack of land results from his orphaned status,
while in *King Horn* he falsely declares he is 'ibore to lowe', 'icome of þralle'
– which, as the rightful ruler of Suddenne, he is not. More significantly, in the
Roman Rigmel refutes Horn's claim, saying

> Ke me voillez amer dreiz est que vus requere:
> Del parage estes bien, kar reis fu vostre pere
> E de real lignage fud née vostre mere,
> E vostre aol si fud d'Alemagne enperere.[19]

In contrast, in *King Horn* Rymenhild 'gan [...] mis lyke / & sore gan to sike'
(425–6), indicating the Middle English author's differing approach to Horn's
status: here, Rymenhild cannot refute Horn's claim because in this version
Horn's true status is unknown in her father's court, meaning he may indeed
be 'ibore to lowe'. The 'essentially hypothetical' obstacle of different status in
the *Roman* becomes more significant in the Middle English redaction, offering
opportunities to reflect on how status might impact resistance to love.[20] That
this is an innovation of the Middle English redactor is further supported by
the absence of this focus on status in the later Middle English *Horn Childe
and Maiden Rimnild*, which is thought to be an independent adaptation from
the *Roman*; their differing representations of status in turn support this.[21] *Horn
Childe* makes social status even less of an issue than the *Roman*, as Horn is
not only presented to King Houlac as Haþeolf's son, but he makes no attempt

---

[18] *The Romance of Horn*, I, lines 1110–12. 'I am not worthy of so great an offer. I am a
poor orphan, I haven't a scrap of land': trans. by Weiss, p. 65.

[19] *The Romance of Horn*, I, lines 1122–5. 'It is only right that I should ask you to love me:
you are of noble birth, for a king was your father, your mother was of royal stock and
your grandfather the emperor of Germany': trans. by Weiss, p. 65.

[20] John H. Perry, 'Opening the Secret: Marriage, Narration, and Nascent Subjectivity in
Middle English Romance', *Philological Quarterly*, 76.2 (1997), 133–57 (p. 146).

[21] Judith Weiss, 'Introduction', in *The Birth of Romance in England*, p. 5. Matthew Holford provides a good overview of and argument for the significantly different emphases
of *Horn Childe and Maiden Rimnild*: 'History and Politics in *Horn Child and Maiden
Rimnild*', *Review of English Studies*, 57.229 (2006), 149–68.

to reject a relationship with Rimnild on the basis of differing status, accepting her love as soon as she offers it.[22] The differing representation of Horn and Rymenhild's relationship in terms of social status can be attributed to the redactor of *King Horn*, then, and can perhaps be related to the different audience and social context of this redaction, as I will explore later.

The Middle English *Amis and Amiloun*, written within a century of *King Horn*, focuses on the relationship between the eponymous heroes. The pursuit of Amis by the Duke's daughter, Belisaunt, is important to the plot because when Amis is challenged by the jealous steward to accept a fight in which he is guilty rather than innocent of engaging in a sexual relationship with Belisaunt, Amiloun is required to take up the trial by combat for his sake. This romance survives in four different manuscripts: Edinburgh, National Library of Scotland, Advocates' MS 19.2.1 (the Auchinleck manuscript); London, British Library, MS Egerton 2862; Oxford, Bodleian Library, MS Douce 326 (Bodleian 21900); London, British Library, MS Harley 2386. The Auchinleck manuscript is closest to the original redaction, which (like *King Horn*) differs from its Anglo-Norman antecedent in its representation of resistance to *mésalliance*.[23]

In *Amys e Amillyoun*, Amys does not reject Florie (as Belisaunt is known here) outright. Instead, we are told

> Quideit que ele fuit devee
> Qe ele pout pur hounte descoverir
> Sa volunté e son desir.[24]

Amys seems shocked because Florie is so open about her desires – not, in this version, because of their differing status (although other versions of *Amys e Amillyoun* are less clear about this: neither Cambridge, Corpus Christi College, MS 50 nor Karlsruhe, Badische Landesbibliothek, MS 345 include the line about Florie's desire, meaning that in these texts Amys's shock perhaps could be interpreted as relating to social status).[25] Florie does not wait for Amys to respond before she upbraids him, and the most we hear of Amys's

---

[22]   'Horn Childe and Maiden Rimnild', in *King Horn*, ed. by Hall, pp. 179–92 (lines 253–71, 409–14).

[23]   See the discussion in Ford, 'From *Poésie* to Poetry', pp. 56–8.

[24]   *Amys e Amillyoun*, ed. by Hideka Fukui, Plain Texts Series, 7 (London: Anglo-Norman Text Society, 1990), lines 266–8. 'He thought she was out of her mind', 'that she could shamefully reveal her will and her desire': 'Amis and Amilun', in *The Birth of Romance in England*, trans. by Judith Weiss, pp. 171–88 (p. 175 and 175 n. 23).

[25]   See Weiss, 'Amis and Amilun', p. 175; *Anglo-Norman 'Amys e Amilioun': The Text of Karlsruhe, Badische Landesbibliothek, MS 345 (olim Codex Durlac 38) in parallel with London, British Library, MS Royal 12 C. XII*, ed. by John Ford, Medium Ævum Monographs, 27 (Oxford: Society for the Study of Medieval Languages and Literature, 2011), Karlsruhe MS, lines 446–9.

reluctance is that he 'talent ne aveit / Q'il mesprist vers son seignur' (270–1) ['did not want to harm his lord', p. 175] and refuses to

> Vers vous ne mesprendroie mye
> Par quei vous en averez vilenye
> Ne de vostre corps hontage.[26]

Although a concern with status is indicated by Florie's outrage that Amys will not 'me dedeignez avere amye! / Tant gentils hommes m'ount prié' (280–1) ['deign to have me as your mistress: so many noble men have begged me', p. 175], this is not developed. Likewise, after they marry it is clear Florie was of higher status, since

> est mout en astage,
> Car cru li est par mariage
> Grant seignurie e grant honur.[27]

But while Amys ascends socially by marrying Florie, the exact disparity between them is unclear. Amys and Amillyoun are identified as 'fiz […] de barons' (11) [barons' sons]; when Amillyoun marries 'une gentile femme […] / Qe fille d'un counte' (172–3) ['a high-born lady, a count's daughter', p. 174], we are told that

> Bien furent entre eux couplés
> De parage e de beautez.[28]

As Florie's father is also a count, this suggests a similarity in rank between Florie and Amys. Florie's father, after his initial anger, does not seem reluctant to allow Florie to marry Amys because of Amys's social status, as when he sees Amillyoun (pretending to be Amys) arrive to fight the steward,

> li dist suef en son oraille
> Qe, s'il pout deffendre la bataille,
> Sa fille a femme ly dorreyt
> E de tote sa terre heir li freit.[29]

---

[26] *Amys e Amillyoun*, lines 297–9. 'Do you wrong, to bring you discourtesy or bodily shame': trans. by Weiss, p. 176.

[27] *Amys e Amillyoun*, lines 771–3. 'He had risen to a high rank, for through marriage he accrued great power and great estates': trans. by Weiss, p. 182.

[28] *Amys e Amillyoun*, lines 179–80. 'They were well matched in beauty and rank': trans. by Weiss, p. 174.

[29] *Amys e Amillyoun*, lines 581–4. 'He whispered in his ear that if he could win the fight, he would give him his daughter to wife and make him heir to all his land': trans. by Weiss, p. 179.

In *Amys e Amillyoun*, then, there is some disparity between Amys and Florie, but its extent is unclear and it is not highlighted in Amys's attempt to reject Florie, which focuses instead on his position as her father's retainer and his fear of slander.

In contrast, the Middle English *Amis and Amiloun* makes social status central to Amis's resistance. Although Amis and Amiloun remain barons' sons in this version, the romance reduces the suggestions of equality between Amis and Belisaunt, for example by telling us only that Amiloun marries 'a leuedy briȝt in bour' (334), not that he marries a count's daughter with whom he is well matched. Moreover, here Amis explicitly rejects Belisaunt because of their social inequality, saying

> Kinges sones & emperour
> Nar non to gode to þe;
> Certes, þan were it michel vnriȝt,
> Þi loue to lain opon a kniȝt
> Þat naþ noiþer lond no fe. (596–600)

Amis does also protest against doing 'mi lord þis deshonour' (607), but the disparity between his status and Belisaunt's is more central to his rejection of her. In this focus upon social class, the Middle English *Amis* seems to develop an emphasis of the Old French *Ami et Amile* that is not carried over into the Anglo-Norman *Amys*. As Ford notes, Amis's focus on class recalls the Old French Amile's rejection of Belissant (the roles of Ami and Amile are swapped between the Old French and Anglo-Norman redactions, with the Middle English adhering to the Anglo-Norman pattern), which also focuses on their differing status.[30] In addition, the Old French *Ami* also focuses on class in the episode where Belissant overcomes Amile's resistance by climbing into his bed and allowing him to think that she is a servant (with whom he is willing to have sex). This episode is not recounted in the Middle English *Amis*, whether because the author did not know of it, did not remember it, or did not approve of it. However, the Middle English *Amis* and the Old French *Ami* both explore issues of status, albeit in rather different ways: the Old French poet's inclusion of Amile's willingness to have sex with a lower-class girl seems to go against the Middle English poet's focus on conveying morally and socially appropriate behaviour through Amis's initial rejection of Belisaunt.

The Middle English *King Horn* and *Amis and Amiloun* both invite reflection upon appropriate conduct, but they draw upon different frameworks of

---

[30] Ford, 'From *Poésie* to Poetry', p. 118; *Ami et Amile: Chanson de Geste*, ed. by Peter F. Dembowski, Classiques français du moyen âge, 97 (Paris: Champion, 1969), lines 631–42; trans. in *Ami and Amile: A Medieval Tale of Friendship*, trans. by Samuel N. Rosenberg and Samuel Danon (Ann Arbor: University of Michigan Press, 1996; first publ. York, SC: French Literature Publications Company, 1981), p. 50.

consent or coercion in doing so. While discussions of coercion in romance have often focused on more extreme cases, mostly in relation to men's sexual coercion of women,[31] the works discussed here highlight the extent to which 'consent has to be read through power dynamics' – and not exclusively gendered power.[32] Horn and Amis are both wooed by the high-status daughter of their lord, a lord who has fostered them and to whom they therefore owe loyalty and gratitude. While this might seem to be a fantasy scenario, given the power and wealth the women possess, Horn's and Amis's resistance to this apparent fantasy brings the coercive dynamics of relationships between people of unequal status to the fore. Status disparity does seem to have been a risk factor for the rape and assault of women in the Middle Ages, according to the evidence of court cases; it also features in the literary genre of the *pastourelle*, where such inequalities are more pronounced than in the romances discussed here.[33] Horn's and Amis's situations may reflect other, more specific, preoccupations with status, however: although Horn's situation is extreme, given his dependence on Aylmar because of his exile, Noël James Menuge notes that it 'touch[es] briefly upon wardship issues', providing some

---

[31] See, for example, Amy N. Vines, 'Invisible Woman: Rape as a Chivalric Necessity in Medieval Romance', in *Sexual Culture in the Literature of Medieval Britain*, ed. by Amanda Hopkins, Robert Allen Rouse, and Cory James Rushton (Cambridge: D. S. Brewer, 2014), pp. 161–80; Corinne Saunders, *Rape and Ravishment in the Literature of Medieval England* (Cambridge: D. S. Brewer, 2001); Kathryn Gravdal, 'The Poetics of Rape Law: Chrétien de Troyes's Arthurian Romance', in *Ravishing Maidens: Writing Rape in Medieval French Literature and Law* (Philadelphia: University of Pennsylvania Press, 1991), pp. 42–71. Some critics have focused on the sexual violence experienced by men in romance, but have concentrated on the more extreme examples: Elizabeth Harper, 'Teaching the Potiphar's Wife Motif in Marie de France's *Lanval*', in *Teaching Rape in the Medieval Literature Classroom: Approaches to Difficult Texts*, ed. by Alison Gulley (Leeds: Arc Humanities Press, 2018), pp. 128–37; David Grubbs, 'The Knight Coerced: Two Cases of Raped Men in Chivalric Romance', in *Teaching Rape in the Medieval Literature Classroom*, pp. 164–82; Catherine Batt, 'Malory and Rape', *Arthuriana*, 7.3 (1997), 78–99.

[32] Lucia Akard and Alice Raw, 'Global Response: Futures of Medieval Consent', *Studies in the Age of Chaucer*, 44 (2022), 'Colloquium: Historicizing Consent: Bodies, Wills, Desires', ed. by Carissa M. Harris and Fiona Somerset, 363–7 (p. 363).

[33] See Katherine Harvey, *The Fires of Lust: Sex in the Middle Ages* (London: Reakton, 2021), pp. 188, 192–3; Lucia Akard, 'Unequal Power and Sexual Consent: The Case of Cassotte la Joye', *Studies in the Age of Chaucer*, 44 (2022), 'Colloquium: Historicizing Consent', ed. by Harris and Somerset, 285–92; Sarah Baechle, Carissa M. Harris, and Elizaveta Strakhov, 'Introduction: Recovering the Pastourelle', in *Rape Culture and Female Resistance in Late Medieval Literature*, ed. by Baechle, Harris, and Strakhov (University Park: Penn State University Press, 2022), pp. 1–14; Baechle, Harris, and Strakhov, 'Reassessing the Pastourelle: Rape Culture, #MeToo, and the Literature of Survival', in *Rape Culture and Female Resistance*, pp. 17–28; Carissa M. Harris, 'Pastourelle Encounters: Rape, Consent, and Sexual Negotiation', in *Obscene Pedagogies: Transgressive Talk and Sexual Education in Late Medieval Britain* (Ithaca: Cornell University Press, 2018), pp. 103–49.

engagement with the relatively common practice of wardship in the case of an orphaned (or fatherless) child.[34] Amis's situation is perhaps more akin to the wider experiences of the medieval nobility and gentry, as within these social classes many 'children were sent to other households for their education', as Amis and Amiloun are after the Duke volunteers to foster them in his service from the age of twelve.[35] Horn's and Amis's situations therefore share some similarities with the potential experiences of the audiences for these romances (discussed later in this chapter), illuminating some of the possible difficulties and vulnerabilities associated with such experiences.[36]

As young men raised by another family, Horn and Amis occupy a somewhat precarious position. Being pursued by their lord's daughter puts them at the mercy of this high-status woman, who holds a more established position in court than they do. The men are also placed at the mercy of their lord, should he discover this relationship. Parents are often concerned about children forming attachments to foster-children or wards in other romances, such as *William of Palerne* and *Sir Torrent of Portingale*. *King Horn* and *Amis and Amiloun* pick up on this anxiety and to some extent invert it, presenting it from the protagonist's perspective: while Amis is concerned about doing 'mi lord [...] deshonour' (607), Horn alludes to his relationship with Rymenhild's father by reminding her that he is 'fundling bifalle' (420). In both cases, the vulnerability of Horn and Amis to their lord's revenge is later made clear by Aylmar exiling Horn and the Duke attacking Amis and wishing to have him executed. These episodes thus highlight the potentially serious consequences of relationships considered disparaging. However, it is also clear that, despite the men's attempts to resist their lord's daughter, she wields significant enough influence that to refuse her carries its own risk, as Amis in particular discovers. That the women hold greater social and political power in their fathers' courts, while

---

[34] Noël James Menuge, *Medieval English Wardship in Romance and Law* (Cambridge: D. S. Brewer, 2001), p. 6.

[35] *Women of the English Nobility and Gentry, 1066–1500*, ed. & trans. by Jennifer Ward (Manchester: Manchester University Press, 1995), p. 48. See also Ruth Mazo Karras, *From Boys to Men: Formations of Masculinity in Late Medieval Europe* (Philadelphia: University of Pennsylvania Press, 2003), pp. 29–30; Nicholas Orme, *From Childhood to Chivalry: The Education of the English Kings and Aristocracy 1066–1530* (London: Methuen, 1984), p. 45.

[36] While each may have reached varied social audiences, some of the manuscript versions of these romances have been associated with a middle- to upper-class readership: see Derek Pearsall, 'The Auchinleck Manuscript Forty Years On', in *The Auchinleck Manuscript: New Perspectives*, ed. by Susanna Fein (York: York Medieval Press, 2016), pp. 11–25 (p. 13); Susanna Greer Fein, 'The Complete Harley 2253 Manuscript, Volume 2: Introduction', in *The Complete Harley 2253 Manuscript*, ed. by Fein, trans. by Susanna Greer Fein, David Raybin, and Jan Ziolkowski, TEAMS, 3 vols (Kalamazoo: Medieval Institute Publications, 2014), II, 1–13 (pp. 10–11); see also Susan Crane, *Insular Romance: Politics, Faith, and Culture in Anglo-Norman and Middle English Literature* (Berkeley: University of California Press, 1986), pp. 13–14, 32.

the young men occupy a more precarious position, separated from their family, suggests that coercive power dynamics were recognised as operating along the vector of status as well as gender.[37] *King Horn* and *Amis and Amiloun* take different approaches to resolving these coercive dynamics, Horn negotiating with Rymenhild to retain control over the situation, while *Amis and Amiloun* directly confronts the issue of coercion and demonstrates the potential vulnerability of men in situations akin to Horn and Amis.

In *King Horn*, Rymenhild is established as a powerful figure who initiates a relationship with Horn on her terms. He is brought to her bower, ensuring their encounter takes place at a time and in a location of Rymenhild's choosing. The bower carries specific implications for understanding the power dynamics between this couple: Hollie Morgan has argued that 'there was a cultural understanding that women had a degree of power in the chamber, which they did not have elsewhere', suggesting that 'male anxieties surrounding the powers allowed to women [...] manifest themselves in stories in which women become powerful when they are in the chamber', a situation that seems to be reflected in *King Horn*.[38] Rymenhild is clearly marked as the active partner determining their actions: she 'tok him bi þe honde', 'sette him on pelle', gives him wine, 'makede him faire chere / & tok him abute þe swere', 'him custe' often, and instructs Horn 'þu schalt haue me to þi wif' (400–8). Although Megan Leitch argues that Rimnild in *Horn Childe and Maiden Rimnild* exhibits more 'strategic awareness' of how to 'manipulat[e] her space both to declare erotic intent and to seek to elicit a similar response', as she 'strategize[s] inwardly about what she will do', Rymenhild's actions perform a similar kind of spatial manipulation and erotic control, the lack of a thoughtful strategy perhaps indicating the reduced focus upon internal subjectivity in earlier Middle English romances rather than the absence of such a strategy altogether.[39] Indeed, Rymenhild's agency has been developed from the *Roman*, where it is not so pronounced, in part because Herland's intermediary comments dilute the focus on Rigmel.[40] While the Middle English Rymenhild starts to shift the balance of power by asking Horn to 'haue of me rewþe' (409), aligning more with the *Roman*, where Rigmel says 'joe vus otrei m'amur, si l'estes otreiant' (1104) ['I offer you my love, if you consent', p. 65], Rymenhild's control over the situation at this point in *King Horn*

37 For a contrasting view of this dynamic in the Anglo-Norman *Roman de Horn*, see Nicholas Perkins, *The gift of narrative in medieval England* (Manchester: Manchester University Press, 2021), p. 35.
38 Hollie L. S. Morgan, *Beds and Chambers in Late Medieval England: Readings, Representations and Realities* (York: York Medieval Press, 2017), pp. 188, 213.
39 Megan G. Leitch, 'Enter the Bedroom: Managing Space for the Erotic in Middle English Romance', in *Sexual Culture in the Literature of Medieval Britain*, pp. 39–53 (p. 44).
40 See *The Romance of Horn*, I, lines 1075–88; trans. by Weiss, p. 65.

remains evident, hinting at the potentially coercive dynamics of seduction by a higher-status woman.

However, *King Horn* ultimately diverts the potential for coercion, as Horn manoeuvres the relationship from one controlled by Rymenhild to one that benefits him. He initially rejects Rymenhild in terms that clearly indicate the problems with an apparent *mésalliance*, telling her

> Ne feolle hit þe of cunde
> To spuse beo me bunde. (421–2)

But this attempted rejection is short-lived, as he begins to change his mind barely ten lines later. Addressing Rymenhild as 'lemman [...] dere' (433), Horn requests that she

> Help me to kniȝte
> Bi al þine miȝte,
> To my lord þe king,
> Þat he me ȝiue dubbing.
> Þanne is mi þralhod
> Iwent in to kniȝthod,
> & ischal wexe more
> & do, lemman, þi lore. (435–42)

While Horn is initially reluctant to accept Rymenhild's love because of their (apparently) different social status, he swiftly agrees to fulfil her wishes if she persuades her father to knight him. This instant reversal may imply that Horn's resistance ought not to be taken too seriously, but concerns about status continue to shape the relationship between Horn and Rymenhild and thus suggest that we should attend to his initial hesitancy. Horn's counter-request to Rymenhild's proposition exemplifies this focus. Not only does it bring his social status closer to hers (recalling the function of Felice's conditions in *Guy of Warwick*), but it provides Horn with a means of social advancement through Rymenhild's influence over her father. According with Rosalind Field's conception of 'the somewhat calculating affections of the standard exile-and-return hero', this pattern of conditions that benefit Horn continues.[41] When Horn is knighted, Rymenhild demands he 'do nu þat þu er of spake', 'to þi wif þume take', 'nu þu hast wille þine' (535–9), but Horn again refuses, saying that first he will 'mi kniȝthod proue, / Ar ihc þe ginne to woȝe' (545–6). Rymenhild agrees again, this time giving him a ring that has such power that he need not be afraid of any blows in battle – or, in the *Roman* and the Harley 2253 *King Horn*, protects him from death. After Horn has proven himself in

---

[41] Rosalind Field, 'The King Over the Water: Exile-and-Return Revisited', in *Cultural Encounters in the Romance of Medieval England*, ed. by Corinne Saunders (Cambridge: D. S. Brewer, 2005), pp. 41–53 (p. 46).

battle, he at last consents to love Rymenhild. The Middle English versions seem to disagree as to whether the couple remain chaste or embark on a sexual relationship at this point: in both the Laud and Harley manuscripts, Fikenhild's accusation that Horn is sleeping with Rymenhild causes Horn to be 'modi for þat fable' (Harley, 716; see also Laud, 737), suggesting that the couple remain chaste. In the Cambridge manuscript, however, this line is absent, and the reference to Rymenhild as 'his wyue' (722) may suggest that they do not lie innocently in each other's arms in this version. Either way, their love (and possibly their sexual relationship) is almost immediately disrupted when Fikenhild betrays Horn and Horn is exiled by Rymenhild's father. Horn later insists on one more delay after he eventually returns to Westernesse, declining to wed Rymenhild until he has regained his rightful lands. Horn's initial refusal of Rymenhild is thus overcome by a series of conditions he outlines for Rymenhild and himself – conditions it is often up to Horn to meet but with which Rymenhild frequently assists him, enabling him to be knighted and offering him the magical protection of the ring.

These conditions effectively rewrite the relationship between Horn and Rymenhild, from one in which Rymenhild propositions and commands Horn to love her to one where Horn must accomplish a series of feats before the couple can be united. This re-establishes Horn as the active partner, the one who will 'woʒe' (546) rather than being wooed, in accordance with the contemporary expectation that during courtship, 'the man should take the lead while the woman followed'.[42] Horn's conditions thus reassert normative gender roles, overturning the potentially coercive situation of Rymenhild wooing him to instead ensure that the relationship is based upon male chivalric achievement rather than female desire. More specifically, the conditions Horn sets out demonstrate his need to perform his gender and status, as he insists on proving himself as a knight despite his true identity as the rightful King of Suddenne. This accords with romance's characteristic representation of masculinity as reliant on display, constituted by 'highly ritualized performances' that 'define knights' masculinity and espouse a specific model of maleness' premised on action.[43] The emphasis on Horn's abilities also serves a dynastic function, as Horn prioritises reclaiming his own family heritage rather than what he can gain through marriage to Rymenhild, suggesting 'the hero's unease at losing the quest to regain his own lands amid the easier acquisition of lands through marriage'.[44] While advancement and property acquired through marriage are usually celebrated in romance, as well as in real-life arrangements, *King Horn*

[42] Shannon McSheffrey, *Marriage, Sex, and Civic Culture in Late Medieval London* (Philadelphia: University of Pennsylvania Press, 2006), p. 48.
[43] Molly Martin, *Vision and Gender in Malory's 'Morte Darthur'* (Cambridge: D. S. Brewer, 2010), p. 13.
[44] Rosalind Field, 'Children of Anarchy: Anglo-Norman Romance in the Twelfth Century', in *Writers of the Reign of Henry II: Twelve Essays*, ed. by Ruth Kennedy and Simon

prioritises making Horn a ruler in his own right.[45] Dynastic preoccupations, particularly in relation to political power, are thus shown to be a concern for men when considering relationships that are socially mismatched, even though this seems surprisingly absent from the representations of men's romantic a(nti)pathy discussed in Chapter 1.

The conditions Horn sets also reinforce traditional boundaries of status, conveying with them a critique of Rymenhild's desires. She is criticised fairly directly in the romance for offering her love to Horn, as her father's steward, Aþelbrus, is concerned that Rymenhild summoning Horn 'nas for none gode' (282):

> Sore ihc me ofdrede
> He wolde horn misrede. (291–2)

We might expect Aþelbrus's concern to be with Rymenhild lowering herself to love Horn – as indeed it is in the *Roman de Horn*, where the equivalent character Herland is reluctant to bring Horn to Rigmel because she is the 'fille le rei', 'si çoe ne fust par lui, mut sereit avilé' (666–7) ['daughter to the king', 'if this is not done through him, she will be greatly dishonoured', pp. 57–8]. But in the Middle English redaction Aþelbrus instead suggests that Rymenhild poses a danger to Horn. Although this diverges from the issue of disparagement, it may indicate an awareness of coercive status dynamics, as Aþelbrus fears for Horn's safety. Aþelbrus's anxiety also censures Rymenhild's desires, saying they are 'for none gode' (282) even while abstracting them from the issue of social status. However, it is Horn himself who provides the strongest disavowal of Rymenhild's desires, telling her

> Ne feolle hit þe of cunde
> To spuse beo me bunde. (421–2)

This emphasis on disparaging marriages being against 'cunde' is repeated in *Havelok*, where Goldeborw is said to be sorrowful 'þat she were yeuen unkyndelike' (1251), while Amis insists it is

> michel vnriȝt
> Þi loue to lain opon a kniȝt
> Þat naþ noiþer lond no fe. (598–600)

This may have carried strong moral implications, given the association between the unnatural and the immoral in medieval thinking.[46] These brief suggestions

---

Meecham-Jones (New York: Palgrave Macmillan, 2006), pp. 249–62 (p. 252); Field makes this point in relation to the *Roman de Horn*.

[45] See van Houts, *Married Life*, p. 249, on real-life contexts.
[46] See Victoria Blud, 'What Comes Unnaturally: Unspeakable Acts', in *The Unspeakable, Gender and Sexuality in Medieval Literature 1000–1400* (Cambridge: D. S. Brewer,

130

that *mésalliance* is unnatural combine with Aþelbrus's and Horn's criticisms of Rymenhild to convey a moral and socially conservative warning against (the desire for) disparaging relationships, drawing upon misogynistic ideas about female desire as a disruptive force.

As Horn renegotiates his relationship with Rymenhild, however, the romance also seems to consider the circumstances in which relationships between two partners of (apparently) differing status may be acceptable and the appropriate way in which such relationships might be formed. The conditions Horn sets before he will love (and marry) Rymenhild help overcome their apparent difference in status, while also adhering to 'the romance model of the strenuous processes involved in winning the lady' in order to give 'a reassuring colouring' to the ability of socially mobile young men 'to manage well the power they acquired through their wives'.[47] While Horn's conditions ensure that he benefits from their relationship, in a way that perhaps mitigates its inherent risks – a strategy that might not have seemed ignoble to participants in a real-life marriage market shaped by desire for social advancement – his conditions also seem to orient Rymenhild towards a different kind of desire. He effectively suggests the things she ought to seek in a partner: as Nicholas Perkins argues of the *Roman de Horn*, Horn 'ticks [Rigmel] off for apparently pricing herself too low', modelling what she should request before granting her love.[48] This reassertion of appropriate desires is particularly evident in comparison with *Guy of Warwick*. Although the Anglo-Norman *Gui de Warewic* may have been influenced by the *Roman de Horn*, the *Roman* differs from the later works by having Horn set all three conditions at once, while *Gui de Warewic*, *King Horn*, and *Guy of Warwick* include three separate episodes in which one partner sets a different and increasingly demanding condition.[49] In the Guy of Warwick story, the tasks Felice sets compensate for Guy's lower status by elevating his chivalric renown to prove him a worthy partner. The conditions Horn sets arguably serve the same function, but the imposition of these conditions by Horn and not Rymenhild reconfigures the gendered dynamics here, not positing these things as what women want but what they

---

2017), pp. 61–106; Ruth Mazo Karras, *Sexuality in Medieval Europe: Doing Unto Others*, 2nd edn (London: Routledge, 2012), p. 20; Karma Lochrie, *Heterosyncrasies: Female Sexuality When Normal Wasn't* (Minneapolis: University of Minnesota Press, 2005), p. xxii.

47 Cooper, *The English Romance in Time*, p. 225.

48 Perkins, *The gift of narrative*, p. 34.

49 Weiss suggests '*Gui* is indebted to its insular romance predecessors, *Horn*, *Boeve de Haumtone*, the Havelok story' and others: Judith Weiss, 'Introduction', in *'Boeve de Haumtone' and 'Gui de Warewic': Two Anglo-Norman Romances*, ed. & trans. by Weiss, FRETS, 3 (Tempe: Arizona Center for Medieval and Renaissance Studies, 2008), pp. 1–24 (p. 14). Any potential relationship between *Gui*, *King Horn*, and *Guy* is unclear. The texts do not appear in any of the same manuscripts, although they are relatively close chronologically.

should want. *King Horn* thus explores how differences in status may be appropriately overcome through romance models of chivalric prowess and inner worth, while at the same time avoiding any socially subversive representation of social mobility because the reader knows throughout that Horn *is* of an eminently suitable status for Rymenhild. The romance can therefore explore the possibilities for negotiating social mobility through romantic relationships while also retaining a conservative sense of social boundaries.

King Horn's exploration of social mores, both in terms of whether class boundaries ought to be overcome and how this might be appropriately negotiated, seems particularly suitable for some of the probable reading contexts of this romance. The moral or didactic focus fits in a general sense with the contents of MS Laud Misc. 108 (late thirteenth century): as well as *King Horn* and *Havelok*, this codex includes one of the earliest versions of the *South English Legendary* alongside other religious and didactic works, such as the *Sayings of St Bernard*, the *Vision of St Paul*, and the *Dispute Between the Body and the Soul* (which are placed between the *South English Legendary* and the romances in the manuscript).[50] Cambridge University Library, MS Gg.4.27.2 (c. 1300) contains a fragment of *Floris and Blauncheflour*, along with the *Assumpcion de nostre Dame*, but its fragmentary nature makes it difficult to advance any conclusions about reading contexts and interpretative possibilities here.[51] However, MS Harley 2253 (late thirteenth to early fourteenth century) offers a more fruitful context for *King Horn*'s exemplary potential. Susanna Fein argues that

> If an externally directed pattern is perceptible here, it runs toward edification and instruction. It would seem likely that the Ludlow scribe had some responsibility in the inculcation of manners and learning for a male heir or heirs in a well-bred, perhaps aristocratic setting.[52]

---

[50] See further 'MS. Laud Misc. 108', Medieval Manuscripts in Oxford Libraries (Bodleian Library, University of Oxford, 2017) <https://medieval.bodleian.ox.ac.uk/catalog/manuscript_6917> [accessed 22 January 2021]; Kimberly K. Bell and Julie Nelson Couch, 'Introduction: Reading Oxford, Bodleian Library, MS Laud Misc. 108 as a "Whole Book"', in *The Texts and Contexts of Oxford, Bodleian Library, MS Laud Misc. 108: The Shaping of English Vernacular Narrative*, ed. by Bell and Nelson Couch (Leiden: Brill, 2011), pp. 1–18.

[51] See *A Catalogue of the Manuscripts Preserved in the Library of the University of Cambridge*, ed. by C. Hardwick et al., 5 vols (Cambridge: Cambridge University Press, 1858), III, 174; Joseph Hall, 'Introduction', in *King Horn*, ed. by Hall, pp. vii–xv (p. x).

[52] Fein, 'Introduction', II, 10. See further Daniel Birkholz, *Harley manuscript geographies: Literary history and the medieval miscellany* (Manchester: Manchester University Press, 2020), p. 3.

As Fein suggests, 'the inclusion of the adventure stor[y] of *King Horn* [...] seems well explained as directed toward an audience of boys whose morals were to be shaped by a clerical tutor or schoolmaster',[53] while

> The Harley lyrics' recurrent interest in exploring male/female love relationships is realized narratively in the romance. One can readily imagine how *Horn* would have appealed viscerally to adolescent boys in a well-to-do household, where such entertainment would have helped to inculcate social skills and good morals in prospective heirs.[54]

However, Carter Revard also points out that the manuscript seems to include women in its imagined audience, while Daniel Birkholz suggests it may have had 'a strong female patron', making *King Horn*'s redirection of Rymenhild's desires perhaps of more direct relevance to its audience.[55] *King Horn* carefully depicts a relationship between two people of (apparently) different status, exploring how this social difference might be overcome and the kinds of negotiations and conditions that might make this permissible. This offers suitable material for an audience of young upper-class readers developing a sense of social mores, correct conduct, and courtship patterns. Moreover, the way Horn and Rymenhild negotiate their changing relationship indicates the capacity of romance to 'conceive of good conduct as a shifting idea whose correct manifestation might change from one situation to the next'.[56] The reading contexts offered by the Harley and Laud manuscripts suggest that *King Horn* may have been read in environments where its exploration of nuanced models of behaviour for negotiating social status and romantic relationships, and its reinforcement of gender (and, to some extent, class) boundaries, would have found a receptive audience.

Amis and Amiloun goes further than *King Horn* in exploring how status could enable coercion but does so primarily to emphasise Amis's chastity – uncomfortably for the modern reader. Belisaunt's agency is more extreme

---

[53] Fein, 'Introduction', II, 10.
[54] Fein, 'Explanatory Notes', in *The Complete Harley 2253 Manuscript*, II, 371–454 (p. 449). See further Susanna Fein, 'Compilation and Purpose in MS Harley 2253', in *Essays in Manuscript Geography: Vernacular Manuscripts of the English West Midlands from the Conquest to the Sixteenth Century*, ed. by Wendy Scase (Turnhout: Brepols, 2007), pp. 67–94 (p. 73).
[55] Revard, 'Oppositional Thematics and Metanarrative in MS Harley 2253, Quires 1–6', in *Essays in Manuscript Geography*, pp. 95–112 (p. 104); Birkholz, *Harley manuscript geographies*, p. 9.
[56] Rory G. Critten, 'Bourgeois Ethics Again: The Conduct Texts and the Romances in Oxford, Bodleian Library MS Ashmole 61', *Chaucer Review*, 50.1–2 (2015), 108–33 (p. 124).

than Rymenhild's, as she effectively blackmails Amis into a relationship with her.[57] She declares:

> Mi loue schal be ful dere abouȝt
> Wiþ pines hard & strong;
> Mi kerchef & mi cloþes anon
> Y schal torende doun ichon
> & say wiþ michel wrong,
> Wiþ strengþe þou hast me todrawe;
> Ytake þou schalt be þurch londes lawe
> & dempt heiȝe to hong! (629–36)

Belisaunt's proposition turns into a 'Potiphar's wife' motif as she threatens to falsely accuse Amis of rape.[58] The *Middle English Dictionary* includes Belisaunt's use of 'todrawe' under the meaning 'to cause affliction […] injure (sb.), harm; […] oppress',[59] apparently a euphemism for sexual violation, which is supported by Belisaunt's mention of the 'londes lawe' and its 'legal emphasis [that] […] is unusual in its historical accuracy'.[60] The Middle English *Amis* is more explicit than the Anglo-Norman, where Florie more ambiguously says she will

> A mon pere le conteray
> Qe vers li estes e moy forfet,
> E serrés des chivals destret.[61]

Other considerations of this scene and the Potiphar's wife motif more broadly have focused on how it presents a 'mirror image' of rape, obscuring the greater prevalence of violence against women.[62] While this is a vital line of inquiry, I want to take seriously the threat of women's violence against men and draw attention to this less common but even less frequently acknowledged possibility. Amis tries to resist Belisaunt's advances, but her threatening behaviour

---

[57] See also Le Saux, 'From *Ami* to *Amys*', p. 119. Pugh sees this as a 'coercive seduction': Tison Pugh, *Sexuality and its Queer Discontents in Middle English Literature* (New York: Palgrave Macmillan, 2008), p. 110.

[58] See the discussion of this motif in Amy N. Vines, 'The Many Wives of Potiphar: Rape Culture in Medieval Romance', in *Rape Culture and Female Resistance*, pp. 97–113; Harper, 'Teaching the Potiphar's Wife Motif'.

[59] d)., 'tọ̄drauen v.', *Middle English Dictionary*, ed. by Frances McSparran et al., Middle English Compendium (Ann Arbor: University of Michigan Library, 2000–18) <https://quod.lib.umich.edu/m/middle-english-dictionary/dictionary/MED46122> [accessed 11 February 2021].

[60] Saunders, *Rape and Ravishment*, p. 197.

[61] *Amys e Amillyoun*, lines 286–8. 'Tell my father you have wronged both me and him, and you will be torn to pieces by horses': trans. by Weiss, p. 175.

[62] Harper, 'Teaching the Potiphar's Wife Motif', p. 132; Vines, 'The Many Wives of Potiphar'.

overcomes his resistance, clearly indicating the coercive force that could characterise relationships with a status imbalance between people of any gender.
In contrast to perspectives that emphasise men's sexual aggression, here male
vulnerability is clearly and sympathetically portrayed.

Indeed, there seems to be some moral condemnation of Belisaunt's behaviour at the start of their relationship, even if the later happy nature of
their marriage (in contrast to Amiloun's) suggests that 'the end justifies the
means'.[63] Not only do Belisaunt's own words, declaring she will 'say wiþ
michel wrong' (633), hover ambiguously between a reference to her false
accusation being itself 'michel wrong' and her accusing Amis of behaving
with 'michel wrong', but the Potiphar's wife motif would have had strong
negative connotations for medieval – and, indeed, modern – readers. It would
have readily recalled its namesake in the Bible, but it is also associated with
negative characters who are usually unsuccessful in their sexual pursuit elsewhere in romance literature, in *Lanval*, *Protheselaus*, and *Generydes*, for
example. Readers of *Amis and Amiloun* in the Auchinleck manuscript had an
even more immediate point of comparison: *The Seven Sages of Rome*, which
Nicole Clifton argues occupies a midpoint in Auchinleck that 'may encourage
readers to reflect on both earlier and later items in the book', also includes a
Potiphar's wife motif.[64] This highlights the negative impression a reader of
Auchinleck may gain of Belisaunt, as the Empress in this version of the *Seven
Sages* is presented as a thoroughly negative character who falsely accuses
her stepson of rape as part of a plot to have him killed and thereby secure her
own dynastic interests. *Amis and Amiloun* seems to raise more challenging
questions than the *Seven Sages* in its use of the Potiphar's wife motif, in that
Belisaunt's threat to falsely accuse Amis of raping her may draw attention to
her successful sexual coercion of him. Amis's experience probably would not
have been directly considered as rape by medieval readers, because *raptus*
was a gendered crime, as discussed in the Introduction. However, the mirroring between the Potiphar's wife motif and Belisaunt's coercion of Amis
suggests an awareness of sexual violence as an issue that could affect men as
well as women, regardless of whether this could be punished in law. This adds
to the implicit condemnation of Belisaunt's behaviour.

This condemnation, and Belisaunt's coercion of Amis, serves an important moral and social function in the romance: carefully monitoring and to
some extent warning against pursuing a relationship with a partner of different
status. While Weiss notes that Amis is a rare 'sexually unchaste' hero, it is

[63] Judith Weiss, 'The wooing woman in Anglo-Norman romance', in *Romance in Medie-
val England*, ed. by Maldwyn Mills, Jennifer Fellows, and Carol M. Meale (Cambridge:
D. S. Brewer, 1991), pp. 149–61 (p. 159).
[64] Nicole Clifton, 'The Seven Sages of Rome, Children's Literature, and the Auchinleck
Manuscript', in *Childhood in the Middle Ages and the Renaissance*, ed. by Albrecht
Classen (Berlin: de Gruyter, 2005), pp. 185–201 (p. 187).

because Belisaunt coerces him into a relationship with her that he is allowed to be sexually unchaste and socially mobile without condemnation.[65] This use of sexual coercion as a mitigating moral factor is deeply uncomfortable for the modern reader but appears to align with contemporary moral perspectives. In the Old French *Ami*, Amile's complicity is also effectively mitigated by Bellisant's deception of him, but there Amile is acknowledged to have sexual desires, although he considers it acceptable to act on them only with a lower-class woman. In contrast, the Middle English Amis remains apparently undesiring because he is coerced into a sexual relationship: Amis's chastity, not his sexual agency or (lack of) consent, is the concern here. While this is unusual amongst romance representations of resistance, it accords with the hagiographical interests of this particular work, discussed further below.

While *King Horn* mitigates the potentially subversive nature of an apparent *mésalliance* by aligning it with the romance focus on chivalric prowess, and above all by ensuring that Horn is actually of an appropriate status to marry Rymenhild, the Potiphar's wife motif ensures that Amis is not implicated in a desire for social mobility, and that Belisaunt is to some extent portrayed negatively for her desires. However, here *Amis and Amiloun* very much has it both ways: while Belisaunt is implicitly compared to the negative characters associated with the Potiphar's wife motif, the poet simultaneously praises her, introducing her as 'fair & bold' (422), 'gentil & auenaunt' (427), and characterising her as a 'bird briȝt' (661) even during her coercion of Amis. Belisaunt is also portrayed positively in the remainder of the narrative, in contrast to Amiloun's wife. Rather than the 'ironic sarcasm' that Jean Jost perceives in such descriptions, the two approaches – criticising Belisaunt by associating her with negative narrative patterns, while also overtly praising her – seem to accord with the ways in which *Amis and Amiloun* uses resistance to *mésalliance*.[66] Belisaunt is both praised and criticised; the romance both permits social mobility for a deserving protagonist and simultaneously warns against pursuing this by focusing on the potential for coercion and danger. To this extent, *Amis and Amiloun* does seem to offer the 'educational material relating to spiritual, family or political matters, or [...] social order' that Raluca Radulescu suggests it eschews.[67]

Like *King Horn*, the socially moralising aspects of *Amis and Amiloun* resonate with and may have been amplified by the manuscript contexts in which it survives, while the differing genre of *Amis*, with its hybrid interests in romance and hagiography, may also have influenced its didactic aspects

[65] Weiss, 'The wooing woman', p. 158.

[66] Jean E. Jost, 'Hearing the Female Voice: Transgression in *Amis and Amiloun*', *Medieval Perspectives*, 10 (1995), 116–32 (p. 119).

[67] Raluca L. Radulescu, 'Genre and Classification', in *A Companion to Medieval Popular Romance*, ed. by Raluca L. Radulescu and Cory James Rushton (Cambridge: D. S. Brewer, 2009), pp. 31–48 (p. 43).

and presentation of sexual coercion.[68] Versions of this story survive in hagiographical form, such as the Latin *Vita Amici et Amelii*, where elements such as the Lombard campaign in which Amici and Amelii die a martyred death, or the miracle of their tombs appearing together when they had previously been buried in separate churches, are added to (or exaggerated from) the romance versions.[69] The Middle English *Amis and Amiloun* is not a hagiographical version: it emphasises the traditional romance aspects such as the fight with the steward and the companions' loyalty above the miracle of the children's resurrection and the voice that speaks to Amiloun before the trial by combat.[70] While mentioned, their theological import is not elaborated and their role does not surmount what we would expect in a pious romance. However, given the emphasis on virginity and threats to virginity in hagiography, *Amis and Amiloun*'s more direct confrontation of sexual coercion is perhaps facilitated or encouraged by its hagiographical affinities.[71] Indeed, hagiographical romances such as *The Man of Law's Tale* may offer a helpful parallel: while fulfilling romance expectations of marriage and the continuation of the family line, neither Custance nor Amis seems to enjoy sexual encounters or romantic attention.[72] Ambivalence about sexuality seeps into romances that are aligned with or influenced by hagiography, demonstrating the fundamental impact genre has upon the valuation of love, sexuality, and desire.

The manuscript contexts of *Amis and Amiloun* both support and refine this view of hagiographical connections, indicating a more general focus upon education and conduct. The four surviving manuscripts of *Amis and Amiloun*,

---

[68] For further discussion of *Amis and Amiloun*'s relationship to hagiography, see Sheila Delany, 'A, A and B: Coding same-sex union in *Amis and Amiloun*', in *Pulp Fictions of Medieval England: Essays in Popular Romance*, ed. by Nicola McDonald (Manchester: Manchester University Press, 2004), pp. 63–81 (pp. 65–7); Crane, *Insular Romance*, pp. 117–18, 122–5, 127–8; Diana T. Childress, 'Between Romance and Legend: "Secular Hagiography" in Middle English Literature', *Philological Quarterly*, 57.3 (1978), 311–22 (pp. 318–19); Ojars Kratins, 'The Middle English *Amis and Amiloun*: Chivalric Romance or Secular Hagiography?', *PMLA*, 81.5 (1966), 347–54.

[69] See Kathryn Hume, 'Structure and Perspective: Romance and Hagiographic Features in the Amicus and Amelius Story', *Journal of English and Germanic Philology*, 69.1 (1970), 89–107.

[70] *Ibid.*

[71] On the threat of sexual violence in hagiography, see Suzanne M. Edwards, 'Medieval Saints and Misogynist Times: Transhistorical Perspectives on Sexual Violence in the Undergraduate Classroom', in *Teaching Rape in the Medieval Literature Classroom*, pp. 12–28; Saunders, 'The Threat of Rape: Saintly Women', in *Rape and Ravishment*, pp. 120–51; Simon Gaunt, *Gender and Genre in Medieval French Literature* (Cambridge: Cambridge University Press, 1995), pp. 197–8; Gravdal, 'Plotting Rape in the Female Saints' Lives', in *Ravishing Maidens*, pp. 21–41. See also Pugh's discussion of how the affinities with hagiography at the end of *Amis and Amiloun* erase the protagonists' potential queerness: *Sexuality and its Queer Discontents*, pp. 116–21.

[72] See further Chapter 4.

as mentioned above, are the Auchinleck manuscript, MS Egerton 2862, MS Douce 326, and MS Harley 2386. Although Auchinleck's focus on romance has often been emphasised, A. S. G. Edwards observes that 'the early sections of the Auchinleck manuscript [...] differ markedly in content from the later, predominantly romance sections [...] compris[ing] poems on religious subjects'.[73] *Amis and Amiloun* (as well as *The King of Tars*) is included in this early, religious section, between the *Speculum Gy de Warewyke* and the *Life of St Mary Magdalene*. Edwards suggests that *Amis and Amiloun* may have been regarded as a religious narrative here.[74] However, *Amis and Amiloun*'s focus on social mores also accords with arguments that this narrative and other Auchinleck texts (as well as other Middle English romances) may have been aimed partly at an audience inclusive of children.[75] Phillipa Hardman suggests that popular romances 'were seen as particularly suitable texts for transmitting core parental cultural values to young readers', noting that 'six of Reiss's pre-1300 child-centred romances are found in the Auchinleck MS' (Edmund Reiss's list includes *Amis and Amiloun*), which has been identified as 'a household, family book'.[76] Clifton also observes that the long list of names of the Browne family written in the Auchinleck manuscript in the late Middle Ages 'suggests that during the 15th century, the manuscript belonged to a family – a large family, with children of varying ages to be educated and entertained'.[77] The Auchinleck romances engage with 'lessons on chivalric or courtly accomplishments', while Amis's encounter with Belisaunt highlights correct and subversive forms of desire. The preoccupation with status may have been thrown into sharp relief in a household reading context such as that proposed by Nicholas Orme, where 'reading aloud was a means of social entertainment', which took place in 'households [that] often included children: sons and daughters of the family, pages and wards being brought up and educated, and young servants'.[78] The wards and pages fostered away from their nuclear family offer a particularly immediate connection with *Amis and Amiloun*'s cautious depiction of a relationship between a duke's daughter and a young man being fostered by that duke.

---

[73] A. S. G. Edwards, 'Codicology and Translation in the Early Sections of the Auchinleck Manuscript', in *The Auchinleck Manuscript: New Perspectives*, pp. 26–35 (p. 26).

[74] *Ibid.*, p. 30 n. 14.

[75] See Cathy Hume, 'The Auchinleck *Adam and Eve*: An Exemplary Family Story', in *The Auchinleck Manuscript: New Perspectives*, pp. 36–51; Clifton, 'The Seven Sages of Rome'; Nicholas Orme, 'Children and Literature in Medieval England', *Medium Ævum*, 68.2 (1999), 218–46.

[76] Phillipa Hardman, 'Popular Romances and Young Readers', in *A Companion to Medieval Popular Romance*, pp. 150–64 (p. 154).

[77] Clifton, 'The Seven Sages of Rome', p. 189.

[78] Orme, 'Children and Literature', p. 229.

MS Egerton 2862 and MS Douce 326 provide less contextual scaffolding for *Amis and Amiloun*'s insights into appropriate conduct. Egerton 2862 is comprised entirely of romances: while romances can and do contain didactic material, the content of Egerton 2862 does not suggest a particularly didactic intent.[79] Douce 326 contains only *Amis and Amiloun* and a Marian lyric, limiting its reading contexts.[80] Harley 2386, however, offers a particularly intriguing context for *Amis and Amiloun*'s focus on social status: this manuscript was owned by William Cresset, 'a household servant residing in Herefordshire' around 1510–30.[81] Cresset's name appears four times in the manuscript, including once after its fragmentary copy of *Amis and Amiloun*, where Cresset wrote what Michael Johnston describes as 'the whimsical phrase "wyllyaum cresett was a lorde a lorde"'.[82] Of course, we cannot know why Cresset wrote this phrase or what he meant by it, but it is tempting to connect its appearance after *Amis and Amiloun* to the theme of social status in this romance.[83] While only the first part of *Amis and Amiloun*, lines 1–890 and 1013–58, is included in the manuscript, this encompasses the section with Amis and Belisaunt (but not the more religiously oriented sections).[84] Even without this phrase, Cresset's status as a household servant, whose annotations indicate that he 'served in the kitchen and pantry of some institution, be it a gentry household or a religious house', seems to indicate his particular potential to be aware of and interested in the treatment of social class.[85] However, 'wyllyaum cresett was a lorde a lorde' does not seem to accord with an exemplary or cautious reading of *Amis and Amiloun*, which I posited may have been invited by its place in the Auchinleck manuscript. Instead, it suggests a more subversive attitude to class, perhaps a reader viewing *Amis and Amiloun*'s advancement of social status through marriage as a vehicle for their own fantasies. We can see here again the agency afforded to readers of romance, the extent to which

[79] For discussion of this manuscript, see Michael Johnston, *Romance and the Gentry in Late Medieval England* (Oxford: Oxford University Press, 2014), pp. 92, 94, 103–4, 110–12.
[80] Ford, 'From *Poésie* to Poetry', pp. 48, 49.
[81] Michael Johnston, 'New Evidence for the Social Reach of "Popular Romance": The Books of Household Servants', *Viator*, 43.2 (2012), 303–31 (p. 306). Johnston establishes that Cresset was not the original owner of the manuscript, pp. 311–13.
[82] *Ibid.*, p. 306.
[83] Wiggins comments that the 'annotations at the end of *Amis and Amiloun* express his active interest in the story', although Wiggins's understanding of Cresset as a 'young learner [...] undergoing elementary education with other boys' is cast in a different light by Johnston's work: Alison Wiggins, 'Middle English Romance and the West Midlands', in *Essays in Manuscript Geography*, pp. 239–55 (p. 251).
[84] Ford gives the line numbers at which *Amis and Amiloun* breaks off: 'From *Poésie* to Poetry', p. 49.
[85] Johnston, 'New Evidence for the Social Reach of "Popular Romance"', p. 306.

the genre 'educates rather than indoctrinating'.[86] The education romance offers may be ignored; careful constructions of relationships between partners of differing status may instead be interpreted more freely as the material of wish-fulfilment and fantasy.

King Horn and *Amis and Amiloun* use the motif of resistance to love to probe the repercussions of socially mismatched relationships, deploying strategies to mitigate their potentially subversive representation of social advancement. The two romances diverge in their approaches to the consensual or coercive possibilities of such relationships: while Rymenhild initially controls her wooing of Horn, Horn negotiates their relationship to his own benefit and satisfaction, moving from the potential for coercion to consent. In contrast, *Amis and Amiloun* openly depicts Belisaunt's sexual aggression but uses this to indicate disapproval of socially imbalanced relationships and to mitigate Amis's involvement. While social advancement through marriage can be an acceptable and celebrated romance motif, these romances use resistance to love to set out a cautious and conservative approach to such relationships while not entirely prohibiting them. In doing so, they not only complicate ideas about consent and coercion, social fantasy and social conservatism, but also draw attention to the nuanced moral functions romance literature could serve – even if these functions were not always effective.

The Politics of Coercion and Exemplarity in *Havelok*

The late thirteenth-century romance of *Havelok* differs from *King Horn* and *Amis and Amiloun* because it depicts a couple who are both unwilling to marry. Abuses of power are the subject of this romance from the start, with its parallel storylines of how Godrich and Godard, close friends of the dying Kings of England and Denmark, are made regents and use this opportunity to disinherit the rightful heirs (Goldeborw and Havelok) and seize power for themselves. Part of Godrich's strategy to disinherit Goldeborw is to marry her to Havelok, who appears to be a poor young man working as a kitchen servant. Coercion is not a strategy levelled by a desiring partner upon an undesiring one here: it is a political tactic, exerted by someone in a position of power over two subordinates. *Havelok* therefore situates the relationship between desire, resistance, and social status differently to *King Horn* and *Amis and Amiloun*, amplifying the undesirability of interclass relationships. *Havelok* uses resistance to marriage to highlight the importance of maintaining class boundaries, perhaps challenging the interest in social mobility through marriage elsewhere in romance. Havelok and Goldeborw do come to love one another, but they do

---

[86] Jeff Rider, 'The Inner Life of Women in Medieval Romance Literature', in *The Inner Life of Women in Medieval Romance Literature: Grief, Guilt, and Hypocrisy*, ed. by Jeff Rider and Jamie Friedman (New York: Palgrave Macmillan, 2011), pp. 1–25 (p. 6).

so (or at least Goldeborw, the apparently higher-status partner, does so) only after their status parity is revealed. Havelok's and Goldeborw's resistance and its development into love offer exemplary and socially conservative models for their medieval readers, functioning in ways that align with and elaborate on the identification of *Havelok* as a *vita* in the incipit added to it in MS Laud Misc. 108 (the only complete surviving manuscript, in which it appears with *King Horn*).[87] My reading of *Havelok*'s exemplarity draws on Kimberly Bell and Julie Nelson Couch's work situating *Havelok* within its manuscript context but explores how *Havelok*'s portrayal of resistance to marriage brings secular forms of exemplarity into dialogue with spiritual concerns, not simply echoing the focus of the more religious texts in the manuscript but inviting readers to draw connections between hagiographical material, secular love, and their own conduct.[88]

Goldeborw's resistance to marrying Havelok offers a more worldly and potentially quite immediate set of concerns for the romance's audience, concentrating specifically on the issue of social class.[89] Goldeborw tells Godrich that 'hire sholde noman wedde' 'but he were king or kinges eyr' (1114–16), emphasising her fear of *mésalliance* while also anticipating the providential outcome of her marriage to Havelok, who is actually the 'kinges eyr' of Denmark. Like *King Horn* and *Amis and Amiloun*, the focus on status is more emphatic in the Middle English romance, adapting the more courtly narratives of Geffrei Gaimar's *Estoire des Engleis* (written for Constance Fitz Gilbert,

---

[87] See further Kimberly K. Bell, 'Resituating Romance: The Dialectics of Sanctity in MS Laud Misc. 108's *Havelok the Dane* and Royal *Vitae*', *Parergon*, 25.1 (2008), 27–51 (pp. 32, 41–2, 51). *Havelok* is also referred to as a 'gest' within the text itself. For a full discussion of *Havelok*'s genre, see K. S. Whetter, '*Gest* and *Vita*, Folktale and Romance in *Havelok*', *Parergon*, 20.2 (2003), 21–46. As well as MS Laud Misc. 108, fragments of *Havelok* survive in Cambridge University Library, MS Add. 4407 (19), along with fragments of the *Elegy on the Death of Edward I*, *The Proverbs of Hendyng*, and a poem based on the first elegy of Maximianus. See further Smithers, 'Introduction', in *Havelok*, pp. xi–xciii (pp. xiv–xvi).

[88] See Bell, 'Resituating Romance'; Julie Nelson Couch, 'Defiant Devotion in MS Laud Misc. 108: The Narrator of *Havelok the Dane* and Affective Piety', *Parergon*, 25.1 (2008), 53–79; and their edited volume, *The Texts and Contexts of MS Laud Misc. 108*.

[89] Little is known about the initial audience of *Havelok*. For a discussion of the audience for MS Laud Misc. 108, see Bell and Nelson Couch, 'Introduction', pp. 14–16. For the *South English Legendary*, of which the Laud manuscript offers an early witness, O. S. Pickering has suggested an initial audience of 'enclosed religious', quickly broadening to encompass devout lay readers. Annie Samson suggests 'regional gentry and perhaps secular clergy' for the early *South English Legendary* readers, while Crane proposes a baronial readership for *Havelok* and *King Horn*. While a wider audience may have heard these narratives read aloud, a gentry or noble audience does not seem unlikely for *Havelok*. See Pickering, 'The *South English Legendary*: Teaching or Preaching?', *Poetica*, 45 (1996), 1–14 (pp. 6, 10, 12–13); Samson, 'The South English Legendary: Constructing a Context', *Thirteenth Century England*, 1 (1986), 185–95 (p. 194); Crane, *Insular Romance*, pp. 43–52.

1135–37) and the *Lai d'Haveloc* (late twelfth to early thirteenth century) to a socially conservative focus on status.[90] In Gaimar's *Estoire*, Argentille (as Goldeborw is named in the Anglo-Norman works) starts to love Havelok before she knows his true status, as when 'il firent primes lur deduit: / mult s'entreamerent e joïrent' ['they made love for the first time. They showed great affection to each other and found great pleasure'].[91] Likewise, in the *Lai d'Haveloc*, while Argentille is initially ashamed of Haveloc,

> puis s'asseürerent tant,
> Et par parole et par semblant,
> Qu'il l'ama et od lui geut
> Come od s'espouse fere deut.
> [...]
> Et la meschine s'endormi;
> Son braz getta sus son ami.[92]

These lines establish a loving relationship between Haveloc and Argentille after their marriage but before the revelation of Haveloc's true status in the *Lai d'Haveloc*, as well as in Gaimar's *Estoire*: in both cases this reflects a courtly focus upon sexuality, which the Middle English romance eschews.

In doing so, *Havelok* makes social class a more significant preoccupation, expanding the focus from the couple's initial resistance to consider how the development of love is influenced by social status. When Goldeborw travels to Grimsby with Havelok, 'sory and sorwful was she ay', 'þat she were yeuen unkyndelike' (1249, 1251), 'unkyndelike' potentially conveying the moral implications indicated above in relation to *King Horn*'s portrayal of *mésalliance* as against 'cunde'. Whereas love develops between Haveloc and Argentille in the *Estoire* and the *Lai* before Haveloc's status is revealed, in the Middle English romance it is only when Goldeborw sees the light coming from Havelok's mouth and the cross on his shoulder and thinks 'he beth heyman yet' (1261) that her attitude towards him starts to change. This episode yokes together immediate, practical, and worldly concerns about social class

[90] On FitzGilbert as Gaimar's patron, see Emily Dolmans, 'The View from Lincolnshire: Gaimar's *Estoire des Engleis* as Regional History', in *Writing Regional Identities in Medieval England: From the 'Gesta Herwardi' to 'Richard Coer de Lyon'* (Cambridge: D. S. Brewer, 2020), pp. 64–96 (pp. 65–6, 68, 70–2); Ian Short, 'Introduction', in *Estoire des Engleis | History of the English*, ed. & trans. by Ian Short (Oxford: Oxford University Press, 2009), pp. ix–liii (pp. ix–xii). On the relationships between the *Havelok* stories, see Crane, *Insular Romance*, p. 40; Smithers, 'Introduction', p. liv.
[91] Geffrei Gaimar, *Estoire des Engleis*, ed. & trans. by Short, lines 192–3, trans. p. 13.
[92] 'Later they became so trusting of each other, / In both their words and their expressions, / That he loved her and lay with her / As it was his duty to do with his wife. / [...] / And the maiden slept, / Throwing her arm over her lover': *The Anglo-Norman Lay of 'Haveloc': Text and Translation*, ed. & trans. by Glyn S. Burgess and Leslie C. Brook (Cambridge: D. S. Brewer, 2015), lines 387–96.

with religious symbolism: Bell notes the holy and specifically Christological connotations of the light and king-mark as symbols of Havelok's status, and this combination of religious and secular concerns is developed as Goldeborw is told by an angel to 'lat þi sorwe be! / For Hauelok [...] is kinges sone and kinges eyr'.[93] Only after the angel's message, which echoes the terms in which Goldeborw earlier attempted to set a condition for her marriage, does she become 'so fele siþes bliþe' (1278) that she kisses Havelok and calls him 'lemman' (1323). The time frame here is unclear: it is possible that the angel appears to Goldeborw 'on their wedding night', as Emma O'Loughlin Bérat suggests, but this is not clearly stated.[94] Goldeborw may actually fall in love with Havelok more quickly than Argentille in Gaimar or the *Lai*, but the time frame is perhaps less important than whether Argentille/Goldeborw knows her husband's true status before loving him. The way in which Goldeborw's developing love for Havelok is impacted by her understanding of his class status positions her desire firmly within a conservative framework, where she may function as an exemplary model of how a middle- to upper-class family might wish their daughters to consider their romantic attachments.

Such a focus may have suited the audience of *Havelok* aptly: although earlier scholarship argued that it may have appealed to a lower-class audience,[95] this view has been refuted by scholars who have revealed that the aspects presumed to appeal to lower-class audiences also appear in the earlier Haveloc narratives (associated with the upper classes), emphasising the romance's primarily baronial and bourgeois sympathies.[96] Scholarship has also focused on the textual evidence for readership provided by the only complete manuscript, MS Laud Misc. 108.[97] Although little is known about the readership of the Laud manuscript, Andrew Taylor suggests that it may have been 'a purposeful commission from a prosperous, sophisticated, and highly literate patron'.[98] Amongst middle- to upper-class readers, social class and *mésalliance* appear

[93] Bell, 'Resituating Romance', pp. 44–50; *Havelok*, lines 1266–8.
[94] Emma O'Loughlin Bérat, 'Constructions of Queenship: Envisioning Women's Sovereignty in *Havelok*', *Journal of English and Germanic Philology*, 118.2 (2019), 234–51 (p. 248).
[95] Henk Aertsen, '*Havelok the Dane*: A Non-Courtly Romance', in *Companion to Early Middle English Literature*, ed. by N. H. G. E. Veldhoen and Henk Aertsen, 2nd edn (Amsterdam: VU University Press, 1995), pp. 29–50; Roy Michael Liuzza, 'Representation and Readership in the Middle English *Havelok*', *Journal of English and Germanic Philology*, 93.4 (1994), 504–19.
[96] Crane, *Insular Romance*, p. 43; Sheila Delany and Vahan Ishkanian, 'Theocratic and Contractual Kingship in *Havelok the Dane*', *Zeitschrift für Anglistik und Amerikanistik*, 22 (1974), 290–302.
[97] Nelson Couch, 'Defiant Devotion', pp. 56–7, 63–4; see also the broader discussion in Bell and Nelson Couch, *The Texts and Contexts of MS Laud Misc. 108*.
[98] Andrew Taylor, '"Her Y Spelle": The Evocation of Minstrel Performance in a Hagiographical Context', in *The Texts and Contexts of MS Laud Misc. 108*, pp. 71–86 (p. 85).

to have been matters of considerable concern. Menuge notes that five out of six of the works she defines as wardship romances 'share the connected themes of wardship marriage, marriage abuse and disparagement', indicating the relatively popular nature of this subject; Menuge also interprets the presence of legislation against disparaging marriages in medieval law as indicating that such marriages were occurring, revealing the real-life problems wardship romances confront.[99] *Mésalliance* may have been a real concern for the early readers of *Havelok*, opening up connections between the romance's possible audience and Goldeborw, which may have enhanced her exemplary potential by prompting empathy for her.

Goldeborw's experience of marital disparagement and coercion is extreme, but, as Menuge argues, it closely engages with legal and social realities, as the 'marriage [is] thrust upon [Goldeborw] with the threat of "force and fear"', following the legal identification of forced marriages, while the constraints upon Goldeborw to accept Godrich's command 'must be representative of the legal difficulties female wards faced'.[100] These emphases are particularly characteristic of the Middle English *Havelok*, which is more preoccupied with consent and the law throughout (for example, in the praise of Aþelwold's laws, the description of Godrich establishing his reign, and the judgement and punishment scenes at the end), as well as specifically in Goldeborw and Havelok's marriage.[101] In Gaimar, Argentille's non-consent is evident only after the marriage has taken place, when she

> sovent son uncle maldisseit
> ki si l'aveit desheritee
> e a un tel home donee.[102]

---

[99] Noël James Menuge, 'The Wardship Romance: A New Methodology', in *Tradition and Transformation in Medieval Romance*, ed. by Rosalind Field (Cambridge: D. S. Brewer, 1999), pp. 29–43 (pp. 33, 37). See also the discussion of disparaging marriages and the interest in prospective husbands' rank in Harris, *English Aristocratic Women*, pp. 54, 56.

[100] Menuge, 'The Wardship Romance', p. 31; Noël James Menuge, 'Female Wards and Marriage in Romance and Law: A Question of Consent', in *Young Medieval Women*, ed. by Katherine J. Lewis, Noël James Menuge, and Kim M. Phillips (Stroud: Sutton, 1999), pp. 153–71 (p. 159).

[101] For further discussion, see Corinne Saunders, 'A Matter of Consent: Middle English Romance and the Law of *Raptus*', in *Medieval Women and the Law*, ed. by Noël James Menuge (Woodbridge: Boydell Press, 2000), pp. 105–24 (p. 113); Crane, *Insular Romance*, p. 48; Robert Rouse, 'English Identity and the Law in *Havelok the Dane, Horn Childe and Maiden Rimnild* and *Beues of Hamtoun*', in *Cultural Encounters in the Romance of Medieval England*, pp. 69–83 (pp. 75–7).

[102] 'Kept cursing her uncle for having disinherited her and for having given her to a man like this': *Estoire des Engleis*, lines 188–90, trans. p. 13.

The *Lai*, meanwhile, gives more prominence to the barons' dissent than to Argentille's:

> Entre eus dient en apert
> Que ceo n'ert ja par eus suffert.[103]

Their resistance is overcome when Alsi summons his soldiers to force their acceptance. The emphasis on the barons may relate to contemporary aristocratic concerns, as Susan Crane notes that the Angevin kings (who ruled during the period in which the *Estoire* and *Lai* were written) extended their powers over the barony 'to include forced marriages of the king's choice'.[104] While the *Lai* makes the barons' opposition clear, all we hear of Argentille herself is that Alsi

> Sa niece lur fet amener
> Et a Cuaran esposer.
> Pur lui aviler et honir
> La fist la nuit lez lui gisir.[105]

While this highlights Argentille's lack of agency, her consent is not expressly declined; instead, it is absent. This contrasts with the Middle English narrative, which makes consent an individual issue and gives significant prominence to Goldeborw's experiences of coercion.

Havelok adds the scene in which Goldeborw and Godrich discuss her marriage before it occurs and focuses significantly on her emotional response to coercion during the wedding itself:

> Sho was adrad for he so þrette,
> And durste nouth þe spusing lette,
> But þey hire likede swiþe ille,
> Þouthe it was Godes wille. (1164–7)

These details are very different to the omission of Argentille's feelings in the *Lai* and the mention of her non-consent only after marriage in Gaimar. The Middle English writer establishes Goldeborw's anger and fear, focusing on her emotions both as they are externally manifested and internally experienced by Goldeborw. She is said to have 'gret and yaf hire ille' when she is first told she will marry Havelok (1130), but she also 'was adrad' and 'durste nouth' protest,

---

[103] 'They said openly among themselves / That they would never tolerate this': *The Anglo-Norman Lay of 'Haveloc'*, lines 373–4. For further discussion of this baronial emphasis, see my article, 'The Ethics of Community in the *Lai d'Haveloc*', *Le Cygne: Journal of the International Marie de France Society*, 3rd ser., 8 (2022), 53–71.

[104] *Insular Romance*, p. 19.

[105] 'Had his niece brought forward / And married her to Cuaran. / To disgrace and dishonour her / He made her lie next to him that night': *The Anglo-Norman Lay of 'Haveloc'*, lines 377–80.

privileging the reader with knowledge of Goldeborw's fear and dissatisfaction to elicit sympathy for this coerced bride. This offers a striking contrast to the lack of detailed interest in women's emotional experiences characteristic of several of the romances discussed in Chapter 1. As Nelson Couch notes, the narrator of *Havelok* repeatedly 'shape[s] an audience response of sympathy for the victimized heroine', 'mapping out expected actions for the external audience' and 'priming us to suffer with her'.[106] While Nelson Couch connects this to *Havelok*'s emphasis upon affective, meditative reading, the sympathy evoked for Goldeborw may also reflect an implicit connection between Goldeborw's experiences and the more moderate experiences of or fears about marital coercion relevant to middle- and upper-class readers. Goldeborw's experiences emphasise the violating nature of disparaging marriages and suggest the importance of status parity for a successful partnership.

However, while Goldeborw protests her forced marriage, she also accepts the need to abide by God's will: 'þey hire likede swiþe ille, / [she] þouthe it was Godes wille' (1166–7). The ensuing comment that 'God […] / Formede hire wimman to be born' (1168–9) resonates with Custance's famous reflection that 'wommen are born to thraldom and penance' in Chaucer's *Man of Law's Tale*, an echo that highlights that Goldeborw is not accepting the marriage as a positive outcome but is rather criticising gendered constructions and the coercion of female wards.[107] However, her acceptance of God's will even while she opposes the marriage further develops her exemplary function, indicating the importance of faith in God even at an apparently disastrous moment. This reference to accepting God's will in the face of crisis is particular to the Middle English romance, as Gaimar and the *Lai* only refer to God's will in positive contexts. Crane notes that 'a sense of providential favor suffuses the story's developments' in the *Lai*, while Gaimar affirms at the comparable point that 'ore est mesters de Deus aït' (170) '['what is needed at this stage is God's help', p. 11], appealing for God's assistance with restoring good fortune rather than acknowledging his providence at work even in an apparently negative outcome.[108] The different emphasis of the Middle English romance again heightens its engagement with exemplary behaviour, aligning *Havelok* with other pious romances that emphasise accepting God's will, such as *Sir Isumbras* and *Sir Amadace*. Goldeborw's focus on God's providence offers a model of pious behaviour, which may explain her particular prominence in *Havelok*, as in this light she shares similarities with hagiographical-romance

---

[106] Nelson Couch, 'Defiant Devotion', p. 70.

[107] Geoffrey Chaucer, 'The Man of Law's Tale', in *The Riverside Chaucer*, pp. 87–104 (line 286).

[108] *Insular Romance*, p. 41. There is no exact counterpart in the *Lai*, but it emphasises the positive nature of God's providence: 'mult fut einçois desesperee, / Mes ore l'ad Dieus reconfortee' ['earlier she had been in great despair, / But now God had comforted her'], lines 977–8.

heroines like Custance or Emaré, whose heroism focuses on enduring and accepting suffering while upholding faith.[109] Although her acceptance of God's will is mentioned only briefly, it is supported by the greater prominence of religious concerns in the Middle English work compared to its Anglo-Norman antecedents, such as the emphasis on confession and prayer in Aþelwold's and Birkabeyn's deaths, the focus on religious objects in the oaths Godrich and Godard swear, the references to Godard and Godrich as Judas, and the appearance of the angel to Goldeborw.[110] The brief indication of Goldeborw's acceptance of God's will broadens our sense of *Havelok*'s appeal and didacticism, indicating some of the more immediately imitable models *Havelok* may have offered its audience.

While Bell suggests that *Havelok* 'exerts its own influence on the *vitae* [in the Laud manuscript] by offering a more complete picture of royal sanctity', the romance also presents models of exemplary behaviour more immediately relevant to its readers through the dual focus on Goldeborw and Havelok.[111] I am suggesting, then, that the Laud romances add to the hagiographical narratives' focus, providing models of behaviour that readers might more readily be called upon to imitate. The presence of these intermediary models of behaviour may encourage readers to broaden their emulation of exemplary actions from the more easily imitated romance models to encompass religious models, too. While Goldeborw's resistance to marrying Havelok reinforces class boundaries and opposes coercive practices associated with wards' marriages, she also offers an exemplary model of worldly piety through the brief but significant focus on God's providence.

Havelok's unwillingness to marry further extends the moral remit of this motif by using it to elicit consideration of and sympathy with experiences of poverty. His situation reflects a(n apparently) much more extreme situation of class difference than that in *King Horn* and *Amis and Amiloun*, as Havelok lacks basic necessities. When Godrich asks if Havelok wants to marry, Havelok responds,

> Hwat sholde Ich with wif do?
> J ne may hire fede ne cloþe ne sho.
> Wider sholde Ich wimman bringe?
> J ne haue none kines þinge –
> J ne haue hws, Y ne haue cote,
> Ne I ne haue stikke, Y ne haue sprote,

---

[109] On Goldeborw's prominence, see Bérat, 'Constructions of Queenship', p. 236; Whetter, '*Gest* and *Vita*', pp. 43–6. On Custance and similar heroines as models of female endurance, see Holly A. Crocker, 'Virtue's Grace: Custance and Other Daughters', in *The Matter of Virtue: Women's Ethical Action from Chaucer to Shakespeare* (Philadelphia: University of Pennsylvania Press, 2019), pp. 111–53.

[110] Bell discusses these aspects: 'Resituating Romance', pp. 38–9, 44.

[111] *Ibid.*, p. 28.

J ne haue neyþer bred ne sowel,
Ne cloth but of an hold with couel. (1138–45)

Havelok's reservations about marriage are not concerns about the boundaries between degrees of rank but reflect his urgent material need. The extent to which Havelok considers his situation unsuitable to allow him to marry anyone, let alone the heir to the throne, is emphasised by the vagueness of Godrich's offer. Asking 'mayster, wilte wif?' (1136), it is unclear whether Godrich has specifically mentioned Goldeborw at this point or whether Havelok is rejecting marriage in general because of his poverty. Havelok does not imagine marriage as enabling upward social mobility – again subtly conveying caution about this – but considers poverty a debilitating state that prevents him from marrying. *Havelok*, then, takes the didactic and moral potential of resistance to *mésalliance* further than the other romances discussed so far, broadening its audience's moral and social framework to elicit sympathetic consideration of social issues like poverty, which were probably outside of their lived knowledge. Sympathy with Havelok, however, does not inspire an interest in social mobility: while Goldeborw and Havelok's marriage is unambiguously forced, social mobility is also depicted negatively elsewhere in the romance. Grim almost murders the child Havelok 'for monetary gain and upward social mobility', while Godrich's treachery seems to be motivated by a desire for social advancement, as he demands of Goldeborw, 'hwor þou wilt be / Quen and leuedi ouer me?'.[112] The moral focus of this romance, its socially conservative and cautious representation of relationships between people of differing status, and its exploration of coercion, then, serve complementary functions, all of which can fruitfully be read within the Laud manuscript's exemplary framework. The portrayals of Goldeborw and Havelok develop these interests in new ways by emphasising the qualities middle- to upper-class readers ought to consider when determining whom to marry.

Interrogating Social Class in Chaucer's *Wife of Bath's Tale*

The Wife of Bath's contribution to *The Canterbury Tales* is Chaucer's only Arthurian romance, which describes how a rapist knight is set the challenge of finding out what women truly want in order for his death sentence to be commuted. He discovers the answer only with the help of a loathly lady, who demands an unspecified promise from him in return. When she announces her intention to marry him, he is reluctant, though he recognises that he must keep his word. Written in the late fourteenth century, this tale considerably postdates the romances discussed so far in this chapter, and I offer a briefer

---

[112] Bell, 'Resituating Romance', p. 48; *Havelok*, lines 1120–1.

reading of this work as a point of comparison to and development of earlier romances.[113]

The Wife of Bath's Tale both shares and develops some of the earlier uses of resistance to *mésalliance*, continuing the emphasis upon social morality that is often a focus of this motif but working against the conservative pattern established so far to turn moral consideration upon the class system itself. This emphasis seems to be a deliberate focus of Chaucer's, as once again this tale augments the focus on social status from its sources and analogues. Status is not the only reason why the knight in *The Wife of Bath's Tale* attempts to reject the loathly lady, as he also complains 'thou art so loothly, and so oold also' (1100). However, that she is 'comen of so lough a kynde' (1101), and the extent to which he will be 'disparaged' (1069) through this marriage, are significant factors in his reluctance. These reasons are specific to Chaucer's version of the narrative rather than being shared by the tale's sources and analogues, John Gower's 'Tale of Florent', *The Wedding of Sir Gawain and Dame Ragnelle*, and *The Marriage of Sir Gawain*. The precise textual relationships between these works are uncertain, though it is likely that Chaucer knew and drew upon Gower's version.[114] In Gower, the lady is twice described as wearing 'ragges', but this is all the attention that is given to her poverty, and Florent's main preoccupation is that

> His youthe schal be cast aweie
> Upon such on which as the weie
> Is old and lothly overal.[115]

Similarly, *The Wedding* does not seem to indicate that Ragnelle is poor, as when she initially appears to Arthur, she is riding 'a palfray was gay begon, / With gold besett and many a precious stone'.[116] Not only the decorative equipment but the term 'palfray' itself indicates a level of status, as palfreys 'would be destined for a wealthy person: a noble lady, a prelate, or as a knight's

---

[113] Larry D. Benson, 'Explanatory Notes', in *The Riverside Chaucer*, pp. 795–1116 (p. 872).

[114] See Marc Glasser, '"He nedes moste hire wedde": The Forced Marriage in the "Wife of Bath's Tale" and Its Middle English Analogues', *Neuphilologische Mitteilungen*, 85.2 (1984), 239–41 (p. 240 n. 2); *Sources and Analogues of The Canterbury Tales*, ed. by Robert M. Correale with Mary Hamel, 2 vols (Cambridge: D. S. Brewer, 2005), II, 407–9. *The Wedding of Sir Gawain and Dame Ragnelle* and *The Marriage of Sir Gawain* both post-date *The Wife of Bath's Tale*; while they may build on earlier sources, this is not certain, nor is it known if they use Chaucer's tale as their source.

[115] John Gower, 'Tale of Florent', in *Confessio Amantis*, ed. by Russell A. Peck, TEAMS, 2nd edn, 3 vols (Kalamazoo: Medieval Institute Publications, 2006), I, I. 1407–1882 (lines 1723, 1745, 1711–13).

[116] 'The Wedding of Sir Gawain and Dame Ragnelle', in *Sir Gawain: Eleven Romances and Tales*, ed. by Thomas Hahn, TEAMS (Kalamazoo: Medieval Institute Publications, 1995), pp. 47–70 (lines 246–7).

traveling horse'.[117] Likewise, in *The Marriage* the lady is wearing 'red scar-lett' when she first meets Arthur, a 'very costly product' and thus associated with the upper classes.[118] More significantly, *The Wife of Bath's Tale* is unique in not revealing the lady to be of high status. In the 'Tale of Florent', the lady turns out to be 'the kinges dowhter of Cizile', who had been enchanted by her wicked stepmother.[119] In *The Wedding* and *The Marriage*, the loathly lady is implicitly of an appropriate status, since she is the sister of Arthur's antagonist, referred to as Sir Gromer Somer Joure, 'a knyght fulle strong and of greatt myghte', in *The Wedding*, and as 'the Baron' in *The Marriage*.[120] She is thus established as one of the knightly class. In contrast, Chaucer occludes the lady's social status in the tale's ending, focusing instead on her restored beauty and youth. While the initial description of her appearance after twen-ty-four ladies dance and disappear hints that she may be a fairy, associated with wealth and power in medieval romance, this is not explicitly resolved. The lack of overt resolution means the relationship may be allowed to stand as at least potentially interclass, unusually for the works discussed in this chapter. This omission also supports the moral interrogation of social class in the tale, since, as Alastair Minnis notes, 'a woman who turned out to be ostentatiously aristocratic, rich, young, and beautiful would make a highly unconvincing advocate for virtuous poverty, the advantages of ugliness, and *gentilesse* by merit alone'.[121] Leaving the lady's social status unspecified while transforming her physical appearance may attest to the particular interest in social status and what it does and does not signify that is characteristic of *The Wife of Bath's Tale* above its sources and analogues.

The loathly lady's climactic discussion with the knight confronts his resist-ance to love someone of a lower status as a moral and ethical issue, an angle none of the other works discussed in this chapter explore. While *Havelok* invites sympathy with poverty and exposes abuses of power, Chaucer raises questions about the class system itself, as the lady openly queries whether 'gentillesse / [...] descended out of old richesse' (1109–10) equates to being 'the grettest gentil man' (1116). She defends her lower birth using the 'nobilitas virtus, non sanguis' trope and argues that poverty can be a virtuous state, again

---

[117] Jürg Gassman, 'Mounted Combat in Transition: The Transformation of the Eleventh Century: Early Medieval Cavalry Battlefield Tactics', in *The Horse in Premodern Euro-pean Culture*, ed. by Anastasija Ropa and Timothy Dawson (Berlin: de Gruyter, 2019), pp. 71–86 (p. 74).

[118] 'The Marriage of Sir Gawain', in *Sir Gawain: Eleven Romances and Tales*, ed. by Hahn, pp. 362–9 (line 56); Michel Pastoureau, *Red: The History of a Color*, trans. by Jody Gladding (Princeton: Princeton University Press, 2017), p. 90.

[119] Gower, 'Tale of Florent', i. 1841.

[120] 'Wedding', line 52; 'The Marriage of Sir Gawain', line 18.

[121] Alastair Minnis, 'The Wisdom of Old Women: Alisoun of Bath as *Auctrice*', in *Writings on Love in the English Middle Ages*, ed. by Helen Cooney (New York: Palgrave Mac-millan, 2006), pp. 99–114 (p. 111).

features that are unparalleled in other versions of this story. Her questioning of the upper classes' right to claim moral authority and respect is particularly provocative in view of the rape that opens the tale, which exposes the lack of *gentillesse* with which a knight can act. The Queen and her ladies' intercession on behalf of the knight may further develop this querying of *gentillesse*, as it perhaps implies an element of class solidarity, courtly figures intervening to defend their own rather than watch justice be done (an implication that seems regrettably topical even today).[122] This effect would be exacerbated if, as Bernard Huppé suggests, the survivor of the rape is a lower-class, perhaps peasant, woman.[123] However, as Corinne Saunders notes, we are 'told nothing of the victim except that she is a "mayde"', meaning that far from an attempt to excuse the crime on the basis of social class (as Huppé posits), it 'falls into the gravest category of theft of virginity'.[124] While the lady's status may affect our understanding of the axes of oppression that make possible the knight's rape of her and the court's forgiving attitude to this rape, her status does not change the fact that the rape exposes the knight, and the court that defends him, as far from inevitably *gentil*.

This questioning of *gentillesse* in part accords with the characterisation of the Wife as the tale's teller: the moral issue of 'nobilitas virtus, non sanguis' may reflect her interest in social status, evidenced in the *General Prologue*'s focus on her rich clothing and her need to be first to go to the offering in church. However, the specifically moral focus upon class seems to suit the Wife's character less well, and may reflect Chaucer's own interests and preoccupations.[125] Chaucer's interrogation of *gentillesse* does come from prior literary sources: the loathly lady's speech draws on Dante, and Chaucer's short poem 'Gentilesse', which echoes the perspective of the loathly lady, is a paraphrase of Boethius.[126] But Chaucer's decision to bring these sources to bear

---

[122] See the discussions in Alison Gulley, '"How do we know he really raped her?": Using the BBC *Canterbury Tales* to Confront Student Skepticism towards the Wife of Bath', in *Teaching Rape in the Medieval Literature Classroom*, pp. 113–27 (p. 114); Carissa M. Harris, 'Rape and Justice in the *Wife of Bath's Tale*', in *The Open Access Companion to the Canterbury Tales*, ed. by Candace Barrington et al. (2015–17) <https://open-canterburytales.dsl.lsu.edu/wobt1/> [accessed 1 February 2021]; Bernard F. Huppé, 'Rape and Woman's Sovereignty in the *Wife of Bath's Tale*', *Modern Language Notes*, 63.6 (1948), 378–81 (p. 379). The notion of class solidarity is developed in Dryden's rewriting of the *Wife of Bath's Tale*, as Christine M. Rose notes: 'Reading Chaucer Reading Rape', in *Representing Rape in Medieval and Early Modern Literature*, ed. by Elizabeth Robertson and Christine M. Rose (New York: Palgrave, 2001), pp. 21–60 (p. 38).

[123] Huppé, 'Rape and Woman's Sovereignty', pp. 379–80.

[124] Saunders, *Rape and Ravishment*, p. 302.

[125] Alistair Minnis offers a helpful perspective on this: 'Alisoun of Bath as *Auctrice*', pp. 109–10. See also Kathryn L. McKinley, 'The Silenced Knight: Questions of Power and Reciprocity in the *Wife of Bath's Tale*', *Chaucer Review*, 30.4 (1996), 359–78 (p. 361).

[126] Benson, 'Explanatory Notes', pp. 847, 1085.

on this tale suggests his personal interest in the topic, and this is borne out by his engagement with the *gentillesse* of deeds rather than birth elsewhere in *The Canterbury Tales*, such as in *The Franklin's Tale*.[127] As the son of a (wealthy) wine merchant who married a noblewoman, the daughter of a knight, Chaucer may have been keenly aware of what social class does and does not govern.[128]

Attending to resistance to *mésalliance* in Chaucer's tale reveals how it differs from its analogues to bring out an ethical theme, while comparison with earlier romances uncovers some of the ways in which Chaucer was building on established traditions in romance writing, even while pushing at their boundaries. Some of the preoccupations Chaucer – and/or the Wife – explores through the motif of resistance to love find comparable emphases in earlier romances. The shifting experiences of consent and coercion evident in the knight being required to keep his promise of marriage to the loathly lady, for example, recall some of the coercive practices in earlier texts.[129] While Chaucer takes the moral function of the motif beyond the earlier works' more socially conservative perspectives, the seeds of this use of resistance to love to explore the privileges of the gentry and nobility were perhaps evident in *Havelok*'s sympathy for the poor, as well as in the more conventional social morality of *King Horn* and *Amis and Amiloun*. Reading resistance to love because of social status from *King Horn* to *The Wife of Bath's Tale* can thus reveal traces of earlier romances influencing Chaucer, despite his apparent ambivalence towards the genre.[130]

Conclusion

From *King Horn* through to *The Wife of Bath's Tale*, resisting *mésalliance* is consistently used for moral and didactic purposes, often warning against socially mismatched relationships even while permitting them in exceptional cases. Other forms of resistance to love also engage with appropriate models of behaviour, but resistance to *mésalliance* repeatedly evokes a more pointed didactic message, perhaps suggesting the immediacy of concerns about social status for the middle- and upper-class readers of romances. These romances'

[127] Geoffrey Chaucer, 'The Franklin's Tale', in *The Riverside Chaucer*, pp. 178–89 (lines 1611–12).
[128] See Marion Turner, *Chaucer: A European Life* (Princeton: Princeton University Press, 2019), pp. 64–5; Paul Strohm, *Social Chaucer* (Cambridge, MA: Harvard University Press, 1989), pp. 10–13.
[129] On the loathly lady's coercion of the knight, see Carissa Harris, 'Rape and Justice'; McKinley, 'The Silenced Knight'; Gerald Richman, 'Rape and Desire in *The Wife of Bath's Tale*', *Studia Neophilologica*, 61.2 (1989), 161–5.
[130] See Corinne Saunders, 'Chaucer's Romances', in *A Companion to Romance from Classical to Contemporary*, ed. by Corinne Saunders (Malden, MA: Blackwell, 2004), pp. 85–103.

cautious approach to relationships between partners of differing status can also be seen as a response to the relatively common representation of such relationships as desirable elsewhere in romance literature, taking seriously a problem that other works gloss over. They thus reveal the complexity of the genre's engagement with social advancement, and the ways in which it might reflect on the real-life medieval marriage market and its opportunities for social mobility. Presenting relationships between people of a different class as undesirable and dangerous, these romances indicate the ways in which resistance to love in medieval romance does not just mandate desire but mandates particular kinds of desire, shaping its readers' sense of what they ought to look for in romantic and marital relationships. The next chapter turns to racially motivated resistance to love to further consider the active construction of who is and is not considered desirable in medieval romance, revealing race as another vector along which coercion and desire are shown to operate, and demonstrating romance's political shaping of desire in the service of upholding contemporary social boundaries and structures of power.

4

'What wonder is it thogh she wepte'?
Hierarchies of Desire, Race, and Empathy[1]

In her field-changing book *The Invention of Race in the European Middle Ages*, Geraldine Heng sets out her 'working minimum hypothesis of race':

> 'Race' is one of the primary names we have – a name we retain for the strategic, epistemological, and political commitments it recognizes – that is attached to a repeating tendency, of the gravest import, to demarcate human beings through differences among humans that are selectively essentialized as absolute and fundamental, in order to distribute positions and powers differentially to human groups. […] Race is a structural relationship for the articulation and management of human differences, rather than a substantive content.[2]

While this is a broad definition,[3] Heng elaborates on it by detailing more specific kinds of race-making (or racialisation), focusing on 'religious race, colonial race, cartographic race, and epidermal race'.[4] I use Heng's widely accepted and influential definition of race in this chapter to reflect the way in which race is not a fixed category but a flexible construct that, as Michael Hames-García writes, 'emerges from the intra-action of history, culture, economics, and material human bodies' in configurations that 'var[y] across time and space'.[5]

---

[1] Quotation from Geoffrey Chaucer, 'The Man of Law's Tale', in *The Riverside Chaucer*, ed. by Larry D. Benson, 3rd edn (Oxford: Oxford University Press, 2008), pp. 87–104 (line 267).

[2] Geraldine Heng, *The Invention of Race in the European Middle Ages* (Cambridge: Cambridge University Press, 2018), p. 3.

[3] See further Adam Hochman, 'Is "Race" Modern? Disambiguating the Question', *Du Bois Review*, 16.2 (2020), 647–65 (p. 655).

[4] Heng, *The Invention of Race*, p. 6. Hochman prefers the term 'racialisation' to race, but most medievalists now agree that 'race' is a helpful term for premodern constructions. For Hochman's argument, see 'Is "Race" Modern?', pp. 656–61.

[5] Michael Hames-García, 'How Real Is Race?', in *Material Feminisms*, ed. by Stacy Alaimo and Susan Hekman (Bloomington: Indiana University Press, 2008), pp. 308–39 (pp. 331, 326). I am indebted to Dorothy Kim's use of Hames-García's work in her 'Introduction to Literature Compass Special Cluster: Critical Race and the Middle Ages', *Literature Compass*, 16.9–10 (2019) <https://doi.org/10.1111/lic3.12549>.

Specific forms of premodern race-making have been explored by scholars working in premodern critical race studies. This field began with the work of Black feminist early modernists Margo Hendricks and Kim F. Hall, and continues today in scholarship by medievalists like Geraldine Heng, Dorothy Kim, Mary Rambaran-Olm, Jeffrey Jerome Cohen, Jonathan Hsy, and Cord J. Whitaker.[6] Drawing upon their work and seeking to foreground the voices of Black and Indigenous scholars and people of colour who have shaped this field, this chapter explores how resistance to love demarcates who is and is not desirable along racialised lines.[7]

I draw particularly upon Kim F. Hall's work on 'the ideology of white beauty [as] a "racial formation"'.[8] Hall's foundational studies of the representation of black people in early modern literature and the construction of whiteness as beauty resonate with the one-sided portrayal of interracial desire in the romances discussed in this chapter: white people can be desirable to people of colour in English romances, but while there was a counter-discourse that described black women as desirable, it does not seem to have influenced Middle English romance.[9] Like Hall, I attend to the intersections between the personal and the political when desire is imbricated in racialisation. Hall argues powerfully that 'the desirability and over-valuation of a seemingly abstract whiteness [...] has material effects', tracing the relation between the whiteness of beauty in Renaissance lyrics and the violence of the slave trade and colonialism but also attending to how 'the opposition of dark and light

---

[6] For further examples and full citations, see the excellent bibliographies: Mary Rambaran-Olm and Erik Wade, 'Race 101 for Early Medieval Studies (Selected Readings)', Medium (2020) <https://mrambaranolm.medium.com/race-101-for-early-medieval-studies-selected-readings-77be815f8d0f> [accessed 26 August 2022]; Jonathan Hsy and Julie Orlemanski, 'Race and Medieval Studies: A Partial Bibliography', *postmedieval*, 8 (2017), 500–31. See also Kim's discussion of the genealogies of premodern critical race studies and premodern race studies: Kim, 'Introduction: Critical Race and the Middle Ages', pp. 4–7.

[7] I use 'Black, Indigenous, and people of colour' in accordance with the RaceB4Race community, which is producing some of the most exciting and important work on premodern critical race theory: 'RaceB4Race', Arizona Center for Medieval and Renaissance Studies <https://acmrs.asu.edu/RaceB4Race> [accessed 20 September 2022]. I acknowledge, however, that this terminology is imperfect and can be reductive. When referring to medieval representations, I generally use the term 'people of colour'. I capitalise Black when 'signal[ling] contemporary sociopolitical identities shaped by African diaspora experiences' but not in relation to medieval people, following the distinction made by Jonathan Hsy: *Antiracist Medievalisms: From 'Yellow Peril' to Black Lives Matter* (Leeds: Arc Humanities Press, 2021), p. 16 n. 98.

[8] Kim F. Hall, *Things of Darkness: Economies of Race and Gender in Early Modern England* (Ithaca: Cornell University Press, 1995); Hall, '"These bastard signs of fair": Literary whiteness in Shakespeare's sonnets', in *Post-Colonial Shakespeares*, ed. by Ania Loomba and Martin Orkin (London: Routledge, 1998), pp. 64–83 (quotation at p. 80).

[9] See Heng, *The Invention of Race*, pp. 211–12.

has materially affected black women's lives, destroying our self-image and disfiguring our bodies', including through 'a Eurocentric beauty culture that privileges one skin color over another'.[10] The consequences of what Hall calls 'the ideology of fairness' vary according to their historical contexts, but these consequences remain real, political, and material; as Dorothy Kim argues, 'race is not an intellectual debate. Race has a body count. Race is political' – and it still is when considered in relation to desire.[11] In tracing the 'ideology of fairness' through a series of crusading romances written in the fourteenth and fifteenth centuries, I attend to the real and harmful consequences of this ideology in that historical moment and indicate how this is reflected in modern white supremacist violence.

Hall's work on the ideology of white beauty situates race primarily (though not exclusively) in relation to the body, indicating the importance of embodied race. As Dorothy Kim and Jeffrey Jerome Cohen argue, 'we cannot discuss race without discussing it as embodied' – although race is socially constructed, 'the body is the battleground where identities are perpetually sought, forced, expressed'.[12] The embodied performance of race, however, is not reducible to an 'ocularcentric fixation' on the epidermal and 'visual': as Cord Whitaker observes, 'color lacks the overwhelming primacy in medieval race that it lays claim to in modern racial ideology', enabling medieval race to be 'characterized by religious and political differences in addition to and often instead of phenotypic differences'.[13] Heng has explored 'how religion, the state, economic interests, colonization, war, and international contests for hegemony, among other determinants, have materialized race', while Cohen lists 'religion, descent, custom, law, language, monstrosity, geographical origin, and species' as 'essential to the construction of medieval race' and its embodied performance.[14] This chapter focuses particularly on the construction of religious race, which functions 'both socioculturally and biopolitically', and its imbrication with 'epidermal race', cultural customs, and geographical provenance.[15] All of the relationships I discuss involve a white Christian and a Muslim, religious categories of identity that were racialised in the Middle Ages (as they sometimes are today): Heng notes that 'the streaming of diverse

[10] Hall, 'Literary whiteness', p. 66; Hall, *Things of Darkness*, p. 264.
[11] Hall, *Things of Darkness*, pp. 86, 264; Kim, 'Introduction: Critical race and the Middle Ages', p. 13.
[12] Kim, 'Introduction: Critical race and the Middle Ages', p. 7; Jeffrey Jerome Cohen, 'Race', in *A Handbook of Middle English Studies*, ed. by Marion Turner (Chichester: Wiley-Blackwell, 2013), pp. 109–22 (p. 115).
[13] Kim, 'Introduction: Critical race and the Middle Ages', p. 4; Cord J. Whitaker, 'Race and Racism in the *Man of Law's Tale*', in *The Open Access Companion to the Canterbury Tales*, ed. by Candace Barrington et al. (2017) <https://opencanterburytales.dsl.lsu.edu/mlt1/> [accessed 26 August 2022], n.p.
[14] Heng, *The Invention of Race*, pp. 181–2; Cohen, 'Race', p. 111.
[15] Heng, *The Invention of Race*, pp. 3, 6.

Muslims […] into a corporate entity by virtue of religion alone suggests an extraordinary ability on the part of the Latin West to grant an essence-imparting power to Islam'.[16] Because different kinds of race-making intersect, I refer to both interracial and interfaith relationships in this chapter, using these terms flexibly to reflect how religion can be racialised or religious conversion can occur while other forms of difference maintain a particular racialised identity.

The romances discussed in this chapter – *The King of Tars*, Geoffrey Chaucer's *Man of Law's Tale*, *Sir Bevis of Hampton*, *Sir Ferumbras*, and *The Sowdone of Babylone* – present relationships between a Christian and Muslim as undesirable. In some cases, these relationships are portrayed as undesirable even after the non-Christian partner has offered to convert or actually has converted, implying that even a relationship with a convert is viewed negatively – either because of their status as a convert or because conversion does not surmount other racialised differences. This positions white Christians at the top of their own constructed hierarchy of desire and relegates people identified as of a different race and/or faith to the bottom of that hierarchy; that many of the Muslim characters who do form relationships with Christians in these works are described as white or white-passing supports this by permitting them, but not other Muslim figures, to be desirable. There are also gendered differences in these portrayals: Christian men marrying Muslim women seems to provoke less anxiety than Christian women marrying Muslim men, which I argue reflects long-embedded patterns of weaponised white female vulnerability and racist stereotypes of 'the encroachments of foreign others'.[17] These romances therefore offer insights into the intersections of gender and race as well as the political construction of desire – the latter a subject to which contemporary feminist thought has only recently returned. As Amia Srinivasan writes, the dominance of sex-positive feminism over the past few decades threatens to treat sexual preferences and prejudices as pre-political, which 'risks covering not only for misogyny, but for racism, ableism, transphobia and every other oppressive system that makes its way into the bedroom through the seemingly innocuous mechanism of "personal preference"'.[18] The use of un/desirability to effect race-making offers a clear example of how 'who is desired and who isn't is a political question, a question often answered by more general patterns of domination and exclusion'.[19] In drawing attention to this dynamic, this chapter seeks also to prompt consideration of less obvious sexual prejudices today.

These patterns of domination and exclusion within romance reflect historical practices of division along the lines of religious race. Most significantly,

---

[16]   *Ibid.*, p. 111. See Heng's discussion of the racialisation of Muslim identity today, p. 20.
[17]   Hall, *Things of Darkness*, p. 52.
[18]   Amia Srinivasan, *The Right to Sex* (London: Bloomsbury, 2021), p. 84.
[19]   *Ibid.*, p. 90.

Canon 68 of the Fourth Lateran Council in 1215 required Jews and Muslims in Christian lands to dress differently from Christians so that they 'shall be marked off in the eyes of the public from other peoples', avoiding the possibility 'that through error Christians have relations with the women of Jews or Saracens, and Jews and Saracens with Christian women'.[20] This decree aimed to prevent sexual contact between Christians and Muslims or Jews but betrays anxiety about the recognisability of these racial-religious categories, suggesting that they *required* enforcing because they were not self-evident. Attempts to enforce racial-religious difference by legislating against interfaith marriages and sexual encounters recur: James Brundage records that Gratian prohibited marriages between Christians and non-Christians; the Council of Nablus in 1120 forbade sex and marriage between Muslims and Christians; and the thirteenth-century Italian lawyer Benencasa of Arezzo warned Christians against marrying non-Christians even when conversion to Christianity had been agreed.[21] Benencasa was not alone in advocating the avoidance of intermarriage even after conversion: 'Pope Clement IV in 1268 rebuked Alfonso III of Portugal for allowing marriages of Christian men to women of Saracen and Jewish *origin*', while in late fourteenth-century Aragon (a context associated with particularly extreme persecution), King John I 'restated in 1393 the death penalty for all sex relations between Jews and Christians, including new converts'.[22] Romance sometimes treats conversion as an absolute and immediate phenomenon, but the works I discuss are more cautious, expressing concern about the desirability of marriage between a Christian and a (former) Muslim even after conversion. This reflects contemporary anxieties about how and to what extent converts should be assimilated into the Christian church. Converts from Judaism to Christianity were often treated as a separate

---

[20] 'Medieval Sourcebook: Twelfth Ecumenical Council: Lateran IV 1215', *Medieval Sourcebook*, ed. by Paul Halsall (1996) <https://sourcebooks.fordham.edu/basis/lateran4.asp> [accessed 28 September 2022].

[21] James A. Brundage, *Law, Sex, and Christian Society in Medieval Europe* (Chicago: University of Chicago Press, 1987), pp. 238, 207, 361. For further discussion of these and similar prohibitions, see David M. Freidenreich, 'Muslims in Eastern canon law, 1000–1500', in *Christian-Muslim Relations: A Bibliographical History, Volume 4 (1200–1350)*, ed. by David Thomas et al., 7 vols (Leiden: Brill, 2012), IV, 45–57; Freidenreich, 'Muslims in Western canon law, 1000–1500', in *Christian-Muslim Relations: A Bibliographical History, Volume 3 (1050–1200)*, ed. by David Thomas and Alexander Mallett, 7 vols (Leiden: Brill, 2009), III, 41–68; Siobhain Bly Calkin, *Saracens and the Making of English Identity: The Auchinleck Manuscript* (London: Routledge, 2005), pp. 80–2; Steven F. Kruger, 'Conversion and Medieval Sexual, Religious, and Racial Categories', in *Constructing Medieval Sexuality*, ed. by Karma Lochrie, Peggy McCracken, and James A. Schultz (Minneapolis: University of Minnesota Press, 1997), pp. 158–79 (pp. 167–9, 178 n. 32).

[22] Kruger, 'Conversion and Medieval Sexual, Religious, and Racial Categories', p. 169; Salo Wittmayer Baron, *A Social and Religious History of the Jews*, 20 vols (New York: Columbia University Press, 1952), XI, 79.

group, *conversos* or New Christians, not fully assimilated into Christian society but not considered Jewish either.[23] As Steven Kruger notes, 'converts clearly occupied an uncomfortable position in relation to both their old and their new religions', and 'what remains unassimilated or unassimilable to the dominant is often involved in the sexual realm'.[24] This is borne out in some of the romances discussed in this chapter, where a gendered pattern emerges, in which Muslim men are less easily assimilated than Muslim women.

This gendered pattern is also reflected in historical perspectives on inter-faith marriage, where

> the gender of the people involved was key. Christian men who had relations with minority women could, in some sense, be seen to reinforce hierarchies, by subjugating them to their will. Relationships between Christian women and non-Christian men, on the other hand, dishonoured families, and threatened patriarchal authority and Christian rule. Indeed, medieval men of all religions argued that their women should not have sex with men of other faiths, because this led to apostasy and was a form of submission.[25]

Women's sexual relations with people of another religion were also the primary concern for Muslim and Jewish writers,[26] which was probably influenced by 'the assumption that the husband, as head of the family, would be likely to convert his wife, whereas the wife, as the subordinate partner, would be unable to convert her husband to her religion'.[27] This shaped Christian attitudes, too, combining with politicised perceptions of white women as vulnerable victims and Muslim men as sexual aggressors to present relationships between Christian women and Muslim men as particularly fraught.

While all of the romances I discuss considerably postdate most of these historical examples, historical resonances remind us that romances draw upon and perpetuate real-life racism and violence rather than existing in a neatly sealed-off fictional space. It is in part for this reason that I refer to characters of Islamic faith as Muslim rather than 'Saracen',[28] following Shokoofeh Rajabzadeh's argument that

---

[23] Kruger, 'Conversion and Medieval Sexual, Religious, and Racial Categories', pp. 173, 172; see further the discussion of conversion anxieties in Daisy Black, *Play time: Gender, anti-Semitism and temporality in medieval biblical drama* (Manchester: Manchester University Press, 2020), pp. 59–64; Heng, *The Invention of Race*, pp. 75–80.

[24] Kruger, 'Conversion and Medieval Sexual, Religious, and Racial Categories', p. 171.

[25] Katherine Harvey, *The Fires of Lust: Sex in the Middle Ages* (London: Reaktion, 2021), p. 150.

[26] *Ibid.*, pp. 153–5.

[27] Jessica Coope, *The Martyrs of Córdoba: Community and Family Conflict in an Age of Mass Conversion* (Lincoln: University of Nebraska Press, 1995), p. 12.

[28] There are some cases in which 'Saracen' is used to mean 'pagan' more generally, or where the term is more ambiguous, but all of the cases I explore involve characters who are clearly supposed to be Muslim. For discussion, see Kathy Cawsey, 'Disorienting

with few exceptions and unless it is a direct quotation, all qualified and unqualified uses of Saracen should be replaced with the word Muslim [...]. It may seem as though using Muslim erases the recognition that the people in these stories are *misrepresented* Muslims. We may fear that, if we do not capture this misrepresentation by using Saracen we are softening the harsh racism of the primary material in our scholarship. [...] But [...] it is by using Muslim that we acknowledge that a misrepresentation exists and legitimize the violence of that misrepresentation. [...] The most simple and powerful way [...] to produce racially conscious scholarship [is to call] these primary texts what they are: racist, Islamophobic, and hateful.[29]

Heng has also detailed the racist lie upon which the term 'Saracen' relies.[30] Referring to the figures discussed in this chapter as Muslim highlights the real stakes of Islamophobic prejudice and violence expressed in crusading romances. These stakes continued to be relevant throughout the period in which these romances were written: Marianne Ailes and Phillipa Hardman have drawn attention to the topical interest in reconquering Spain in the later Middle Ages, the personal commitments made to crusading enterprises throughout the period, and the progress of Ottoman Turkish forces in Europe (including the fall of Constantinople in 1453) in the fifteenth century, to high-light the ongoing relevance of crusading romances in the later Middle Ages.[31]

The romances discussed in this chapter occupy a distinct space between historical violence and the Christian fantasies of other romances. The trope of the Christian man marrying a beautiful Muslim woman is reasonably common in romance and *chansons de geste*: in addition to the works discussed in this chapter, Muslim princesses who convert to Christianity for love appear in *La Chanson de Roland*, *Fierabras* (the source for several of the works discussed here), the *Guillaume d'Orange* cycle, *Aiol*, *Anseis de Cartage*, *Elie de Saint Gille*, *Floovant*, and *Gaufrey*.[32] In a romance context, interfaith or interracial

Orientalism: Finding Saracens in Strange Places in Late Medieval English Manu-scripts', *Exemplaria*, 21.4 (2009), 380–97.

29 Shokoofeh Rajabzadeh, 'The depoliticized Saracen and Muslim erasure', *Literature Compass*, 16.9–10 (2019) <https://doi.org/10.1111/lic3.12548>. Rajabzadeh diverges from previous academic practice, which used 'Saracen' to indicate this misrepresenta-tion: see Jeffrey Jerome Cohen, 'On Saracen Enjoyment', in *Medieval Identity Ma-chines* (Minneapolis: University of Minnesota Press, 2003), pp. 188–221 (p. 136 n. 3; first publ. in *Journal of Medieval and Early Modern Studies*, 31.1 (2001), 113–46); Bly Calkin, *Saracens and the Making of English Identity*, pp. 2, 213 n. 3; Norman Daniel, *Heroes and Saracens: An Interpretation of the 'Chansons de Geste'* (Edinburgh: Edin-burgh University Press, 1984), pp. 9–10.

30 Heng, *The Invention of Race*, pp. 110–12.

31 Marianne Ailes and Phillipa Hardman, *The Legend of Charlemagne in Medieval Eng-land: The Matter of France in Middle English and Anglo-Norman Literature* (Cam-bridge: D. S. Brewer, 2017), pp. 172, 279–80, 195, 220, 277.

32 See Suzanne Conklin Akbari, *Idols in the East: European Representations of Islam and the Orient, 1100–1450* (Ithaca: Cornell University Press, 2009), pp. 173–89; Sharon

relationships occur in *Parzival* and *Octavian*, while religious conversion is a widespread theme from the Otuel narratives to Henry Lovelich's *History of the Holy Grail*, *Sir Isumbras* to *Amoryus and Cleopes*.[33] In these works, conversion is the assumed goal and is generally endorsed even when motivated by love. However, these are recognisably fantastic tropes: the idea of crusaders converting Muslim women 'ha[s] little historical basis' and can be seen as a compensatory fantasy for the failures of the crusading era.[34] In the works discussed in this chapter, these fantasy tropes are avoided, subverted, or become the subject of doubt, as resistance to loving a convert disrupts the easy fantasies of other romances, problematising straightforward acceptance of conversion in a manner perhaps similar to the trope of unsuccessful conversion.[35] While most of these romances ultimately reimpose essentialised racial differences, including in and through hierarchies of desire, they can also open up a space in which to question these ideological formations through their divergence from the patterns set by other romances.

'Y nold hir ȝiue a Sarazin': Desire, History, and Fantasy in *The King of Tars*

In *The King of Tars*, an anonymous early fourteenth-century romance that has attracted a significant amount of scholarship focusing on race, the Sultan of Damascus besieges the titular Christian King to force a marriage between himself and the King's daughter.[36] The Princess is clearly unwilling to marry the Sultan, declaring, when her father asks whether she would 'for tresour, / Forsake Ihesus our saueour' (55–6),

> Nay lord, so mot y þriue!
>
> Ihesu, mi Lord in trinite,
> Lat me neuer þat day yse
> A tirant forto take. (60–3)

Kinoshita, *Medieval Boundaries: Rethinking Difference in Old French Literature* (Philadelphia: University of Pennsylvania Press, 2006), pp. 35–73; Geraldine Heng, *Empire of Magic: Medieval Romance and the Politics of Cultural Fantasy* (New York: Columbia University Press, 2003), p. 186; Mohja Kahf, *Western Representations of the Muslim Woman: From Termagant to Odalisque* (Austin: University of Texas Press, 1999), pp. 21–33; Jacqueline de Weever, *Sheba's Daughters: Whitening and Demonizing the Saracen Woman in Medieval French Epic* (New York: Garland, 1998); Dorothee Metlitzki, *The Matter of Araby in Medieval England* (New Haven: Yale University Press, 1977), pp. 160–77.

[33] On *Parzival*, see Heng, *The Invention of Race*, p. 196; Kahf, *Western Representations of the Muslim Woman*, pp. 40–3.

[34] Heng, *The Invention of Race*, p. 141.

[35] See Ailes and Hardman, *The Legend of Charlemagne in Medieval England*, p. 162.

[36] *The King of Tars, ed. from the Auchinleck MS, Advocates 19.2.1*, ed. by Judith Perryman, Middle English Texts, 12 (Heidelberg: Winter, 1980), line 43.

The Princess does not focus upon the Sultan's identity as Muslim in her rejection of his proposal, referring to him only as 'a tirant' (which presents him negatively, but not in terms particularly associated with Muslim figures). However, she does clearly reject the proposed marriage in a way that highlights her Christian identity as paramount to her resistance. Her focus upon religion may reflect the 'strategic essentialisms' that link the Princess of Tars to her medieval English readers.[37] While Sierra Lomuto has argued that 'many scholars erase her Mongol identity', this seems to me to reflect not so much scholarly as textual erasure – what the narrative itself is trying to achieve.[38] Lomuto's reconstitution of the Princess as an 'exotic ally' and Mongol figure is a helpful critical approach, but the relegation of these aspects within *The King of Tars* is also significant for understanding its construction of race.[39] The focus on her Christianity may reflect a tendency among Christian crusaders at the time, who 'reached across lines of country, region, ethnicity, tribe, and caste to constitute themselves as a people defined by their religion alone'.[40] Such race-making 'is contingent and functional', as Heng notes, and as Jamie Friedman has drawn attention to in discussing *The King of Tars*'s insistent and provisional construction of whiteness.[41] This contingency leaves open alternative possibilities such as reading the Princess's race on the basis of her geographic provenance, but the portrayal of her Christianity and white skin identifies her as similar to the white Christian readers of this romance, enabling her to act as a model for whom they ought and ought not to desire.

The normative hierarchy of desire constructed by the Princess's rejection of the Sultan is supported by its converse: her desirability *to* the Sultan, which specifically presents whiteness as desirability, as Cohen and Heng also note.[42] References to colour saturate the description of the Princess's beauty in the first two stanzas of the poem: 'non *feirer* woman miȝt ben', she is '*white* as feþer of swan', 'wiþ rode *red*', 'eyȝen stepe & *gray*', and a '*white* swere', making the Sultan desire to 'haue hir to wiue / Þat was so *feir* a may' (11–12, 14–16, 23–4; all emphases mine). The Princess is the image of 'normative female beauty in medieval European literature', as Heng argues, and this normative beauty is defined by colour: it is her white skin, red lips, and grey eyes that are said to be attractive to the Sultan.[43] The emphasis on the corporeal

---

[37] Heng, *The Invention of Race*, p. 27.
[38] Sierra Lomuto, 'The Mongol Princess of Tars: Global Relations and Racial Formation in *The King of Tars* (c. 1330)', *Exemplaria*, 31.3 (2019), 171–92 (p. 183).
[39] *Ibid.*, p. 174.
[40] Heng, *The Invention of Race*, p. 124.
[41] *Ibid.*; Jamie Friedman, 'Making whiteness matter: *The King of Tars*', in *Making Race Matter in the Middle Ages*, ed. by Cord J. Whitaker (= *postmedieval*, 6.1 (2015)), pp. 52–63.
[42] Cohen, 'Race', p. 119; Heng, *Empire of Magic*, p. 231.
[43] Heng, *Empire of Magic*, p. 231.

features associated with whiteness here align with Friedman's argument that 'the white racial body is precisely what is being constructed and continually held together across the narrative's trajectory', assembling white racial identity from the sum of the Princess's body parts.[44] While the Sultan's race is barely remarked in the opening of the poem – as Siobhain Bly Calkin notes, 'we don't know until line 799 that the sultan is black' – the Princess's repeatedly is.[45] But the detailed description of the Princess's features does not just construct whiteness but constructs whiteness *as* desirability, endorsing the 'ideology of white beauty' that Hall exposes as a 'racial formation'.[46]

Desire functions on a political level to essentialise selective differences as race, and this is further developed by the King's response to the Sultan's proposal. The King condemns this more stridently than the Princess did, focusing directly upon the Sultan's Muslim identity. He tells the Sultan's messengers 'Y nold hir ȝiue a Sarazin' (43) and, according to their report, calls him a 'heþen hounde' (93). The King mobilises these racist stereotypes to a greater extent than the Princess and unites them with a focus on patriarchal ownership. 'Y nold hir ȝiue a Sarazin' potently yokes together racism and misogynistic anxieties about transferring patriarchal ownership of (white) women to people of colour, an anxiety Hall identifies in William Shakespeare's *The Tempest*, where she argues it 'strikes at the heart of European fears of the putative desire of the native other for European women'.[47] The King of Tars, like Prospero, is positioned as the rightful owner of (white) women and as protecting them from the sexual threat of racialised others, purportedly justifying patriarchal control. As Hall writes, 'female bodies serve as the testing ground for the symbolic boundaries of culture and race', but white women do so specifically through what Ruby Hamad categorises as their (or our) 'sanctioned victim' status.[48] Positioned as desirable to racialised others (therefore maintaining the 'ideology of white beauty'), white women's supposed vulnerability justifies white patriarchal authority and characterises people of colour as sexually threatening – as abductors, proponents of forced marriage, or even as rapists. This racialised pattern also deflects attention away from the sexual abuse of women of colour. This dual operation of racism and patriarchal justification

---

[44] Friedman, 'Making whiteness matter', p. 53.

[45] Siobhain Bly Calkin, 'Marking Religion on the Body: Saracens, Categorization, and *The King of Tars*', *Journal of English and Germanic Philology*, 104.2 (2005), 219–38 (p. 224 n. 19).

[46] Hall, 'Literary whiteness', p. 80.

[47] Hall, *Things of Darkness*, p. 143.

[48] Hall, *Things of Darkness*, p. 101; Ruby Hamad, *White Tears/Brown Scars: How White Feminism Betrays Women of Color* (New York: Catapult, 2020), p. 14.

through the motif of the vulnerable white woman is still being echoed in white supremacist violence and far-right conspiracy theories today.[49]

I am not trying to posit a direct link between *The King of Tars* and modern far-right violence but to point out that the correlation of racism and patriarchal anxiety about white female vulnerability is deeply embedded in European literature, culture, and politics, in the hope of disrupting this association. As a white woman working in medieval studies, I feel it is particularly vital to draw attention to how problematic the leveraging of white female vulnerability is.[50] Medieval studies has been characterised by Kim as an unbearably white field, in which people of colour have, as Whitaker has described, at times been made to feel 'out of place' – even as it is people of colour who have been doing the vital work of tackling racism in our discipline.[51] Challenging the weaponisation of whiteness may be an area in which white people can help-fully contribute to critical race theory: as Heather Blatt notes, 'white people need to take on more responsibility for speaking and educating about race', but we must also acknowledge that our privileged perspectives may lead us to miss important nuances.[52]

The link between racism and perceptions of white female vulnerability is evident not only in *The King of Tars* but across the works discussed in this chapter, which considered collectively show much greater concern about the marriage of a Christian woman to a Muslim or formerly Muslim man than they do for marriages between Christian men and (formerly) Muslim women. This may be influenced by the portrayal of epidermal race in narratives where Muslim women are described as white or white-passing, but it also seems to reflect anxieties about white female vulnerability. Within *The King of Tars*, the level of concern about a white Christian woman marrying a Muslim man is evident in the continued focus upon the Princess's unwillingness to love the

---

[49] See Laura Bates, *Men Who Hate Women* (London: Simon & Schuster, 2020), p. 176; Steve Rose, 'A deadly ideology: how the "great replacement theory" went mainstream', *The Guardian* (8 June 2022) <https://www.theguardian.com/world/2022/jun/08/a-deadly-ideology-how-the-great-replacement-theory-went-mainstream> [accessed 18 August 2022]. See also Sanyal's discussion of the Cologne attacks: Mithu Sanyal, *Rape: From Lucretia to #MeToo* (London: Verso, 2019), p. 91.

[50] This leveraging of white female vulnerability also characterises trans-exclusionary feminism: see the discussion in Alison Phipps, 'White Tears, White Rage: Victimhood and (as) Violence in Mainstream Feminism', in *The Politics of Victimhood*, ed. by Sarah Banet-Weiser and Lilie Chouliaraki (= *European Journal of Cultural Studies*, 24.1 (2021)), pp. 1–13 (pp. 8–9).

[51] Dorothy Kim, 'The Unbearable Whiteness of Medieval Studies', *In the Middle* (10 November 2016) <https://www.inthemedievalmiddle.com/2016/11/the-unbearable-white-ness-of-medieval.html> [accessed 22 April 2023]; Cord J. Whitaker, 'Race-ing the dragon: the Middle Ages, race and trippin' into the future', in *Making Race Matter in the Middle Ages*, ed. by Whitaker (= *postmedieval*, 6.1 (2015)), pp. 3–11 (p. 3).

[52] Heather Blatt, '"Whiteness seeps through": Resisting colorblind racism in Mandeville's *Travels*', *postmedieval*, 11.4 (2020), 484–92 (p. 486).

Sultan even after she marries him. She agrees to become his wife, but only when she sees there is no alternative after he defeats her father's forces. The Princess's words upon the healing of their child, born as a lump of flesh and miraculously restored through baptism,[53] reveal that she still does not love him, even if she has been forced to marry him:

> ʒif þe haluendel wer þin
> Wel glad miʒt þou be
> [...]
> Bot þou were cristned so it is
> þou no hast no part þeron, ywis,
> Noiþer of þe child ne of me. (809–16)

She effectively denies their marriage, as Lynn T. Ramey also notes, suggesting that neither she nor the child are connected with the Sultan unless he converts to Christianity.[54] While the Sultan forced her to marry him, he still cannot command her love and desire. This maintains Christian perspectives on desirability and perpetuates the stereotype of black men as perpetrators of force, ensuring that Christian superiority is upheld on the personal, if not the military, level throughout the romance.

In the field of national politics as opposed to the politics of desire, *The King of Tars* allows more doubt about racial-religious hierarchies, through the Sultan's military victory over the Christian forces. That the Sultan determines to win the Princess 'in batayl' (32) aligns with stereotypical romance depictions of Muslim–Christian relationships, particularly the trope of the Muslim knight besieging a Christian woman, which occurs in works like *Blanchardyn and Eglantine*, *Sir Gowther*, *Sir Percyvell of Gales*, and perhaps *Ipomadon*.[55]

---

[53] For discussions of the child, see Natalie Goodison, Deborah J. G. Mackay, and Karen Temple, 'Genetics, Molar Pregnancies and Medieval Ideas of Monstrous Births: The Lump of Flesh in *The King of Tars*', *Medical Humanities*, 45.1 (2019), 2–9; Molly Lewis, '"Blob Child" Revisited: Conflations of Monstrosity, Disability, and Race in *King of Tars*', in *Monstrosity, Disability, and the Posthuman in the Medieval and Early Modern World*, ed. by Richard H. Godden and Asa Simon Mittman (Cham: Palgrave Macmillan, 2019), pp. 147–62; Sarah Star, '*Anima Carnis in Sanguine Est*: Blood, Life, and *The King of Tars*', *Journal of English and Germanic Philology*, 115.4 (2016), 442–62; Jane Gilbert, 'Putting the pulp into fiction: the lump-child and its parents in *The King of Tars*', in *Pulp Fictions of Medieval England: Essays in Popular Romance*, ed. by Nicola McDonald (Manchester: Manchester University Press, 2004), pp. 102–23; Heng, *Empire of Magic*, pp. 227–30. I follow Lewis's example in referring to the baby simply as 'the child', avoiding more reductive terminology.

[54] Lynn T. Ramey, *Black Legacies: Race and the European Middle Ages* (Gainesville: University Press of Florida, 2014), p. 69; see also Gilbert, 'Putting the pulp into fiction', p. 108.

[55] On this trope, see Corinne Saunders, 'A Matter of Consent: Middle English Romance and the Law of *Raptus*', in *Medieval Women and the Law*, ed. by Noël James Menuge (Woodbridge: Boydell Press, 2000), pp. 105–24 (pp. 114–16).

In these romances, it usually upholds the perceived or desired moral, chivalric, and romantic supremacy of Christians: a Christian knight who arrives to defend the besieged lady reinforces the idea that marital consent is prioritised by Christians where Muslims seek to force marriage upon unwilling women; the Christian knight's military triumph ensures that Christian chivalry is upheld as the greater military force; the lady's usual offer of love to her Christian champion suggests the desirability of Christians compared to Muslim knights, while also continuing to contrast the coercive force of the Muslim suitor with the apparently free offer of love to the Christian defender. However, while clearly invoking this trope, *The King of Tars* decisively veers away from it, as no Christian hero arrives to defend the Princess and her father's forces suffer severe defeat, losing 'þritti þousend [...] / kniʒtes of Cristen lawe' (211–12). The effects of the Princess's resistance are not just to outline and impose a racial-religious hierarchy of desire, then, as they also function in the opposite direction. They expose romance fantasies *as* fantasies, as the Christian hero never materialises, leaving the Princess to surrender to the Sultan on his terms and casting doubt upon the racist hierarchy constructed by the operations of desire.

Instead of the fantasies of romance with which it begins, *The King of Tars* can be seen as turning to history to grapple with Christian defeat and loss. *The King of Tars* invites comparison with contemporary events: as Judith Perryman notes, 'the basis of the romance is a historical incident from the late thirteenth-century crusades', which 'appeared in a number of chronicles'.[56] The historical record concerns Ghazan, Khan of the Persians, who defeated the Sultans of Damascus and Babylon in 1299 and formed alliances with the Christian Kings of Armenia and Georgia.[57] Ghazan himself ultimately converted to Islam, but a number of chronicles record tales of a Mongol leader converting to Christianity. These layers of history and chronicle seem to have formed the basis for *The King of Tars* and may have influenced both the portrayal of the Christian King of Tars, a figure associated with the Tartars (as even if Tars refers to the Armenian city of Tarsus, this city was under Mongol rule), and the later conversion of the Sultan.[58] The King's defeat by the Sultan seems a provocative intrusion of the underlying history into its more common representation in narrative. As Bly Calkin notes, 'the late thirteenth century', shortly before *The King of Tars* was composed, was 'the period during which the Crusader kingdoms definitively fell to Muslim powers after a series of Christian military defeats and failures culminating in the Fall of Acre in

---

[56] Judith Perryman, 'Introduction', in *The King of Tars*, ed. by Perryman, pp. 7–72 (p. 42).
[57] See Friedman, 'Making whiteness matter', pp. 54–5.
[58] See Perryman, 'Introduction', pp. 47–8; Friedman, 'Making whiteness matter', p. 55.

1291'.[59] The loss of Acre in particular, Robert Rouse argues, 'had a profound impact on the culture and literature of Western Europe', as 'Christendom was left to face the undeniable fact that the Islamic foe had triumphed'.[60] *The King of Tars*'s stark depiction of Christian military defeat in its opening sequence challenges and disrupts contemporary fantasies of military supremacy, interpolating real-life losses into the fantasy context of romance.

However, this is not the full story. While the opening sequence reveals the lie of romance and its illusions of Christian supremacy, the end turns away from both romance and history to reaffirm Christian power through divine miracle. When the child is restored from a 'rond of flesche' (580) to a healthy baby upon being baptised, the Sultan agrees to accept Christianity, and his skin colour changes from black to white as he is given a Christian name, offering a double corporeal miracle that asserts the power of the Christian God to act in the world.[61] The Sultan's persecution of his own people who refuse to convert may have troubled medieval Christian readers insofar as it suggests continuity between his actions at the start and end of the romance, as Whitaker has argued, but it also effectively reverses the Christian forces' initial losses.[62] This return to and reversal of the opening may itself be unsettling, however, because if the opening exposed the motif of the Christian knight saving a woman besieged by a Muslim man as improbable, its refraction in the ending may question whether this is also an unlikely fantasy. However, the difference between these two types of fantasy is the centrality of Christianity. *The King of Tars* turns away from the illusions of romance, through and past historic losses, to assert the greater power of Christian miracle to achieve a desirable ending. That medieval readers may have perceived the narrative in this way is suggested by its manuscript contexts: the related manuscripts of Oxford, Bodleian Library, MS Eng. poet. a. 1 (the Vernon manuscript) and London, British Library, MS Additional 22283 (the Simeon manuscript) are codices focused on 'items of a moral or religious nature', which contain only two other romance-affiliated works, the pious works *Robert of Cisyle* (in both manuscripts) and *Joseph of Arimathia* (in the Vernon manuscript).[63] Commenting on *Robert of Cisyle* and *The King of Tars*, N. F. Blake suggests that

---

[59] Siobhain Bly Calkin, 'Saracens', in *Heroes and Anti-Heroes in Medieval Romance*, ed. by Neil Cartlidge (Cambridge: D. S. Brewer, 2012), pp. 185–200 (p. 191).

[60] Robert Allen Rouse, 'Crusaders', in *Heroes and Anti-Heroes in Medieval Romance*, pp. 173–83 (p. 182).

[61] As Whitaker notes, it is actually this transformation that precipitates the Sultan's true belief: Cord J. Whitaker, *Black Metaphors: How Modern Racism Emerged from Medieval Race-Thinking* (Philadelphia: University of Pennsylvania Press, 2019), pp. 26–7.

[62] *Ibid.*, p. 43.

[63] Perryman, 'Introduction', p. 9. For example, the Vernon manuscript includes the *South English Legendary*, the *Northern Homily Cycle*, the *Miracles of the Virgin*, *La Estorie del Evangelie*, *Piers Plowman*, works by medieval mystics like Richard Rolle, and a version of the *Ancrene Riwle*. See 'MS. Eng. poet. a. 1', Medieval Manuscripts in

'they are more in the nature of exempla exhibiting moral and religious truths, and as such they fit well into this section of the [Vernon] manuscript', while A. S. G. Edwards argues that *The King of Tars* pairs well with *The Pistel of Susan*, which it follows in the Simeon manuscript and precedes, a few texts apart, in the Vernon manuscript, as both emphasise 'female devotional figures who provide models of Christian conduct, and who, by their submission to Divine Will, enable the triumph of that Will'.[64] The other surviving manuscript of *The King of Tars*, the Auchinleck manuscript, supports these connections, as *The King of Tars* is grouped with religious narratives rather than romances there.[65] The manuscript contexts of *The King of Tars* therefore support a reading of it as turning away from the fantasies of romance to the promise of divine intervention.

The focus upon divine miracle may have appealed to Christian readers in the long aftermath of crusading defeats, which made an immediate military victory seem an unlikely fantasy indeed. Although Heng suggests that narratives like *The King of Tars* offer 'an elegant solution to holy war: The simple agency of a Christian princess, acting as a missionary for her faith and her people, obviates the need for large armies, territorial invasion, and bloody combat', *The King of Tars* also acknowledges the reality of brutal warfare.[66] It reassures anxieties about real crusading defeats not by sublimating those losses but by incorporating them into a story where accepting defeat results in ultimate victory. Although the Simeon and Vernon manuscripts postdate the loss of Acre by a hundred years, Rouse argues that the fall of Acre 'precipitated a collective trauma that would haunt the Christian peoples of western Europe for centuries to follow'.[67] In the late fourteenth century and into the fifteenth, divine miracle and Christian endurance might still have been seen to offer an important message, even as large-scale crusading movements faded into the past. While the connections between the opening and the ending of the romance may open up questions about its fantasy of Christian supremacy, *The King of Tars* ultimately permits both readings, offering its Christian readers a recuperation of loss through miracle and conversion, while also enabling some questioning of the ending. Desire is central to race-making in *The King*

Oxford Libraries (Bodleian Library, University of Oxford, 2018) <https://medieval. bodleian.ox.ac.uk/catalog/manuscript_4817> [accessed 12 February 2021].

[64] N. F. Blake, 'Vernon Manuscript: Contents and Organisation', in *Studies in the Vernon Manuscript*, ed. by Derek Pearsall (Cambridge: D. S. Brewer, 1990), pp. 45–59 (p. 54); A. S. G. Edwards, 'The Contexts of the Vernon Romances', in *Studies in the Vernon Manuscript*, pp. 159–70 (p. 167).

[65] See Edwards, 'Codicology and Translation', pp. 27, 30 n. 14.

[66] Heng, *The Invention of Race*, p. 139.

[67] Robert Rouse, 'Romance and Crusade in Late Medieval England', in *The Cambridge Companion to the Literature of the Crusades*, ed. by Anthony Bale (Cambridge: Cambridge University Press, 2019), pp. 217–31 (p. 217).

of Tars, offering an arena in which differentiation can be imposed even as Christian military supremacy is challenged. In this way, desire operates as another means by which, 'when the replication of colonial dominance in territorial and military terms falters, the preferred momentum of empire becomes cultural'.[68] Desire thus functions in accordance with the focus upon Christian miracle, as both assert Christian supremacy in contexts where this is called into doubt by military defeat.

'She knoweth nat his condicioun': Geography, Culture, and Prejudice in Chaucer's *Man of Law's Tale*

The late fourteenth-century *Man of Law's Tale* is 'Chaucer's sole textual confrontation with medieval Christianity's strongest religious rival, Islam'.[69] This tale is slightly at odds with the other works discussed in this chapter, for although it is sometimes thought of as a crusading romance,[70] it can also be considered a hagiographical romance, and it lacks the overt military violence directed at a Muslim population *because* they are Muslim characteristic of crusading works (military violence still exists but is motivated by the Sultana's attack on the Christians).[71] The approach to race is, accordingly, somewhat different, as the Sultan of Syria is here no fearful military leader threatening a Christian population but rather a courteous man who rules in a parliamentary style and converts to Christianity for Custance.[72] While *The Man of Law's Tale* maintains the perception of white Christians as desirable to Muslims, its attention to religious race differs. The Sultan's conversion prompts questions about 'the success or failure of religious conversion as a *techne* to effect racial transformation', leading to consideration of other ways in which a convert might be racialised as different to a white Christian.[73]

The Man of Law's Tale once again constructs 'an ideology of white beauty', as the Sultan falls in love with 'faire Custance' (245), while she is reluctant to marry him even though he has agreed to convert for her. His offer acknowledges the centrality of shared faith in contemporary requirements for marriage

---

[68] Heng, *Empire of Magic*, p. 190.

[69] 'The Man of Law's Tale', line 271; Susan Schibanoff, 'Worlds Apart: Orientalism, Antifeminism, and Heresy in Chaucer's Man of Law's Tale', in *Chaucer's Cultural Geography*, ed. by Kathryn L. Lynch (New York: Routledge, 2002), pp. 248–80 (pp. 248–9; first publ. in *Exemplaria*, 8 (1996), 59–96).

[70] For example, in Whitaker, 'Race and Racism'.

[71] See Manion's definitions of crusading romances: Lee Manion, *Narrating the Crusades: Loss and Recovery in Medieval and Early Modern English Literature* (Cambridge: Cambridge University Press, 2014), pp. 7–8.

[72] For discussion of how the political styles of different rulers in *The Man of Law's Tale* contribute to race-making, see Whitaker, 'Race and Racism'.

[73] Heng, *The Invention of Race*, p. 7.

as, in an episode unique to Chaucer's version of the tale,[74] the Sultan's council foresee 'swich difficultee',

> By cause that ther was swich diversitee
> Bitwene hir bothe lawes [...]
> They trowe that no 'Cristen prince wolde fayn
> Wedden his child under oure lawe sweete'. (218–23)

Interfaith relationships are acknowledged to be problematic in Islamic as well as Christian law (as is also the case in *The King of Tars*, lines 404–14), but the Sultan's solution is to give up his own faith and volunteer to convert his people. This evokes the kind of Christian fantasy that might well conclude a romance, but Custance's resistance to marrying the Sultan challenges this conversion fantasy, identifying him as undesirable despite his changed faith.[75] Custance's doubts do not revolve explicitly around the efficacy of conversion, as apart from a general reference to 'the Barbre nacioun' (281) she does not mention the Sultan's religious beliefs as a reason to be anxious about marrying him. Instead, she is reluctant to leave her home and family, lamenting to her parents 'ne shal I nevere seen yow moore with ye' (280). But her distress does juxtapose her familiar context with the unknown and foreign nature of the Sultan and the lands he inhabits, illuminating alternative forms of race-making beyond the emphasis on religion in *The King of Tars*.

Chaucer and his main source for *The Man of Law's Tale*, Nicholas Trevet's *Cronicles*, emphasise the differences of custom and geographical origin between Custance and the Sultan. In Trevet, Constance is sent 'hors de sa conoissaunce entre estranges barbaryns a grant deol et lermes et crie et noyse et plente de tote la cité de Rome' [from 'her acquaintances among foreign barbarians with great grief, tears, outcry, noise and lament from the whole city of Rome'].[76] This presents the Sultan as different from the citizens of Rome despite his conversion but conveys this in general terms rather than reflecting Constance's point of view. In *The Man of Law's Tale*, on the other hand, it is 'Custance, that was with sorwe al overcome' (264) on the day of her departure, and Chaucer describes her emotions with sympathy and pathos, asking

---

[74] In Trevet and Gower, the Sultan declares he will convert without consulting his council or giving them the opportunity to express reservations.

[75] See, for example, *The King of Tars, Sir Isumbras*, and *Amoryus and Cleopes*.

[76] Nicholas Trevet, 'De la noble femme Constance', ed. & trans. by Robert M. Correale, in *Sources and Analogues of the Canterbury Tales*, ed. by Robert M. Correale with Mary Hamel, 2 vols (Cambridge: D. S. Brewer, 2005), II, 297–329 (lines 67–8, trans. p. 300). Gower's 'Tale of Constance', another of Chaucer's sources, does not describe any sadness upon Constance's departure. See John Gower, 'Tale of Constance', in *Confessio Amantis*, ed. by Russell A. Peck, TEAMS, 2nd edn, 3 vols (Kalamazoo: Medieval Institute Publications, 2003), II, ll. 587–1612. It is now largely agreed that Gower's version pre-dates Chaucer's: see Peter Nicholson, 'The *Man of Law's Tale*: What Chaucer Really Owed to Gower', *Chaucer Review*, 26.2 (1991), 153–74.

Allas, what wonder is it thogh she wepte,
That shal be sent to strange nacioun,
Fro freendes that so tendrely hire kepte,
And to be bounden under subjeccioun
Of oon, she knoweth nat his condicioun? (267–71)

The 'strange nacioun' and unknown nature of the Sultan, in addition to her separation from friends and family, cause Custance's distress. Geographical origin played a constitutive role in medieval race-making, as writers like Isidore of Seville and Bartholomeus Anglicus argued that aspects of human difference such as skin colour, behaviour, and the humours were influenced by the varied climates of different geographies.[77] Custance's doubts about the Sultan's 'condicioun' are not borne out within the tale, as the rare phrases that characterise the Sultan describe his 'benigne curteisye' and 'good chiere' (179–80). These descriptions could equally apply to Christian knights, suggesting the Sultan may indeed share the '*sine qua non* of Christianity and chivalry' across which race can 'be bridged'.[78] However, more time is dedicated to conveying Custance's fear about what the Sultan may be like than to narrating what he actually *is* like: the tale effectively endorses prejudice on the basis of geographical origins through its sympathy with Custance. Such sympathy may also operate in accordance with epidermal race, as the description of Custance as 'ful pale' (265) perhaps pinpoints her white skin as an implicit contrast to her future husband's. Whitaker notes that the tale 'does not proclaim its sultan's blackness, but it does not disavow it either', suggesting that the delayed indication of the Sultan's blackness in *The King of Tars* may imply that 'medieval readers might very well have assumed the Muslim sultan's blackness – whether it is stated or not'.[79] Whether or not Custance's paleness evokes the Sultan's own skin colour as an implied contrast, the intersection of 'affect, religion, race, and sex' in paleness seems to invite the (pale) audience of *The Man of Law's Tale* to sympathise not only with Custance's plight but with her suspicion of a 'strange nacioun' and its unknown people.[80]

That Custance remains reluctant to marry the Sultan despite his conversion suggests that anxiety about Christian women marrying Muslim men persists even in instances where the men have converted. While this may reflect conversion anxieties, it may also indicate the separation of religion from race, if we see the anxieties that remain as motivated by a form of racial difference that is no longer tied to the Sultan's religious identity. Heng explores this possibility, concluding that it is epidermal race that establishes the Sultan as

---

[77] See Akbari, *Idols in the East*, pp. 41–50.

[78] Heng, *The Invention of Race*, p. 207.

[79] Whitaker, 'Race and Racism'.

[80] Carolyn Dinshaw, 'Pale Faces: Race, Religion, and Affect in Chaucer's Texts and Their Readers', *Studies in the Age of Chaucer*, 23 (2001), 19–41 (p. 27).

different here.[81] Drawing upon the contrast between Custance's relationship with the Sultan and with Alla (a pagan convert to Christianity), Heng argues that 'conversion to Christianity is insufficient *in and of itself* to cancel out differences of race and color'.[82] The insights Heng traces through the doubled role of the husband in this narrative share some similarities with Hall's discussion of the workings of desire, marriage, and racism in Lady Mary Wroth's manuscript continuation of *The Countess of Montgomerie's Urania* (c. 1620–30). Although reflecting a different context, where Rodomandro is much more explicitly racialised, there are some parallels between these works. In *Urania*, Rodomandro marries Pamphilia but then dies, leaving her to marry her true love. Hall argues that Rodomandro's 'blackness thereby marks that secondary status as if to assure the reader that the marriage is only temporary', offering 'a visual cue that he will never win Pamphilia's love or desire as it is valued in the romance'.[83] While the Sultan is not described as black, if medieval English readers perceived him as racialised – whether through his skin colour, his former religion, or his geographical and cultural differences from Custance and the Roman Christians – in a way that Alla is not, this may also have positioned him as only a temporary husband for Custance.

Rodomandro also offers a further parallel to Custance and the Sultan, as his son with Pamphilia 'dies shortly after Rodomandro [...] leaving no material trace of the marriage'.[84] This again resonates with Heng's discussion of the contrast between Custance's relationship with the Sultan and with Alla, the first abruptly ended before it can be consummated and the second consummated and resulting in a son.[85] The consummation of Custance's marriage to Alla is narrated oddly by the Man of Law, as he attempts to balance Custance's 'hoolynesse' (713) with the need to 'take in pacience at nyght / Swiche manere necessaries' as her husband deems fit (710–11). This reflects the generic hybridity of the tale itself, its hagiographical content steering it towards this genre's emphasis on chastity and virginity, while the romance framework calls for Custance and Alla's love and dynasty to be continued through the birth of an heir. The hagiographical resonances perhaps underlie an apparent aversion to sex both from the Man of Law and on the part of Custance: both figures could be read as asexual, though Custance could alternatively be seen as queer or lesbian, given her intense love for Hermengyld.[86] But while the

---

[81] Heng, *Empire of Magic*, pp. 226–37.

[82] *Ibid.*, p. 232. See also Ramey, *Black Legacies*, p. 83.

[83] Hall, *Things of Darkness*, pp. 206, 207.

[84] *Ibid.*, p. 208.

[85] Heng, *Empire of Magic*, pp. 227, 223.

[86] Karma Lochrie has commented on this as an intense friendship, while Daisy Black's critical and creative work has explored the queer or lesbian potential of their connection: Lochrie, 'Between women', in *The Cambridge Companion to Medieval Women's Writing*, ed. by Carolyn Dinshaw and David Wallace (Cambridge: Cambridge University

Man of Law negotiates the consummation scene awkwardly, he nonetheless *does* narrate it, again contrasting with the situation of Custance and the Sultan. Although there is no direct relationship between *The Man of Law's Tale* and the *Urania*, reading the resonances between these two narratives reveals the persistent forms of racism and erasure that affect interracial relationships.

The portrayal of the Sultana, whose violence prevents the consummation of Custance and the Sultan's marriage, is also revealing for the process of race-making and its entanglement with perceptions of gender. The Man of Law castigates the Sultana right from her first appearance, rebuking her as the

> roote of iniquitee!
> Virago, thou Semyrame the secounde!
> O serpent under femynynytee,
> Lik to the serpent depe in helle ybounde!
> O feyned womman, al that may confounde
> Vertu and innocence, thurgh thy malice,
> Is bred in thee, as nest of every vice!
>
> O Sathan, envious syn thilke day
> That thou were chaced from oure heritage,
> Wel knowestow to wommen the olde way!
> [...]
> Thou wolt fordoon this Cristen mariage.
> Thyn instrument so – weylawey the while! –
> Makestow of wommen, whan thou wolt bigile. (358–71)

This condemnation repeatedly focuses on the Sultana's gender, deploying misogynistic ideas about the associations between Satan and women, women and sin. This is also true of the later condemnation of Donegild, the second 'evil mother-in-law' figure in *The Man of Law's Tale*. She is identified as 'ful of tirannye' (696) from her first appearance, and some of the language used to describe her also seems gendered, such as the 'venym' (891) of her deed, perhaps recalling the serpent metaphor used for the Sultana. However, while both mothers-in-law are portrayed negatively, indicating anxieties about the figure of the mother-in-law such as feature in other accused queen narratives rather than specifically racialised portrayals, condemnations of the Sultana also subtly differ from those of Donegild.[87] Comparisons between the Sultana and the devil may draw upon prejudices about race and religion, as in *The*

Press, 2003), pp. 70–88 (pp. 74–5); Black, '"Diverse women said diverse things…": Storytelling, Research, and Shipping Custance and Hermengyld' (presented at Leeds International Medieval Congress, Leeds, 2021); Black, 'Broken Shells' (performed at 'Gender and Aliens', the annual Gender and Medieval Studies Conference, Durham University, 2019) <https://daisyblack.uk/storytelling/> [accessed 30 September 2022].

[87] *Cheuelere Assigne* and *Octavian*, for example, depict the mother-in-law as the false accuser.

Prioress's Tale Chaucer similarly invokes the devil as the motivator for the Jews' murder of the young boy.[88] The reference to Semiramis – an Assyrian queen who was sometimes said to have seized power from her husband (or to have done so after his death) – could also be motivated by race as well as gender. The Sultana thus seems to receive additional, racially motivated condemnation compared with Donegild. However, the portrayal of both mothers-in-law is united in the way the Man of Law simultaneously presents them negatively through gendered stereotypes and questions their femininity. The Sultana is called a 'Virago' (a standard antifeminist term, as Susan Schibanoff notes) and 'feyned womman', while Donegild is 'mannysh'.[89] These terms may open up the question of what a woman is or should be, in contrast to her feigned or 'mannysh' counterpart, contrasting the mothers-in-law to Custance. The misogynistic association between women and sin has its opposite and counterpart in the perception that women should be characterised by 'vertu and innocence', like Custance. While this contrast applies to both mothers-in-law, it may have specifically racist associations insofar as it draws upon the long-standing Western perception of white women's 'sanctioned victim status', in contrast to the construction of women of colour as illegible victims, even (here) as themselves agents of violence.[90] Both in itself and in the contrast with Custance, the portrayal of the Sultana combines misogyny and racism, as becomes evident in comparison with Donegild. This dual focus may recall and shed light upon Custance's resistance to loving the Sultan as a reflection of racist and misogynistic anxieties about white women marrying into Muslim society.

Custance's initial reluctance, the emphasis on foreign customs and distant geographical origins, the avoidance of consummation, and the portrayal of the Sultana indicate the imbrication of (un)desirability with race and racism in *The Man of Law's Tale*. There is explicit and repeated anxiety about Custance's marriage to the Sultan despite his conversion, suggesting that relationships between Christian women and (formerly) Muslim men are a significant concern for medieval Christian writers. In the works that deal with Christian men's relationships with Muslim (or formerly Muslim) women – *Sir Bevis of Hampton*, *Sir Ferumbras*, and *The Sowdone of Babylone* – there is much less explicit concern about race, and any anxieties associated with such partners tend to coalesce around different issues, reducing the importance of race (religious or otherwise) in hierarchies of desire.

---

[88] Geoffrey Chaucer, 'The Prioress's Tale', in *The Riverside Chaucer*, pp. 209–12 (lines 558–66).

[89] 'The Man of Law's Tale', lines 359, 362, 782; Schibanoff, 'Worlds Apart', p. 253.

[90] Hamad, *White Tears/Brown Scars*, p. 14.

'Y haue leuyd on false lore – / For þy loue y wyll no more': Faith, Status, and Isolation in *Sir Bevis of Hampton*

The fourteenth-century romance *Sir Bevis of Hampton* describes how the hero, Bevis,[91] is cast out by his mother and step-father as a child and grows up in the Muslim court of King Ermyne of Armenia (originally an Egyptian court in the Anglo-Norman *Boeve de Haumtone*).[92] The King's daughter, Josian, falls in love with Bevis and he eventually returns her love, while grappling (at times violently) with the difficulties of life in a court of another faith. Like many of the examples discussed in this book, resistance to love forms a small part of the narrative in *Bevis*, and indeed a small part of the structural delays to Bevis and Josian's marriage, which is more considerably held up by Josian being forced to marry two other men (through which she retains her virginity), and by Bevis's seven-year imprisonment by King Bradmond. However, despite its relatively minor role in the larger plot scheme, Bevis's initial resistance to loving and marrying Josian, and the negotiations through which this is resolved, reveal the processes and limits of race-making in and through constructions of desire in this work. *Bevis* does identify religious race as a key factor in resistance to love, according with the works discussed so far in this chapter, but this romance also foregrounds other potential issues in Bevis and Josian's relationship, reducing the primacy of the focus on race compared to *The King of Tars* and *The Man of Law's Tale*.

We are told immediately that Josian is 'whyte and swete' (581), according with the romance and *chanson de geste* image of the white Muslim princess that erases any presumed difference of epidermal race by imposing white European perceptions of beauty.[93] This 'strategic bleaching', as Heng notes, 'conduces, also, to the women's eventual baptism and assimilation into Christian European polities', but in *Bevis* Josian's religion is initially foregrounded as an issue.[94] When she is introduced, we are told

> Men knewe noon so feyre on lyue,
> So hende nor so wele ytaght,
> But of Crystes lawe cowde sche noght. (587–9)

Her positive qualities are listed first, with her lack of Christian faith positioned as a negative contrast to her beauty and nobility, once again placing non-Christians at the bottom of Christian hierarchies of desire. Similar to

---

[91] *Sir Bevis of Hampton*, ed. by Jennifer Fellows, EETS, o. s., 349, 2 vols (Oxford: Oxford University Press, 2017), I, lines 1328–9. All quotations are taken from this volume, specifically from the text of Cambridge University Library, MS Ff.2.38 unless otherwise stated.

[92] See the discussion in Amy Burge, *Representing Difference in the Medieval and Modern Orientalist Romance* (New York: Palgrave Macmillan, 2016), pp. 50–3.

[93] See further de Weever, 'Whitening the Saracen: The Erasure of Alterity', in *Sheba's Daughters*, pp. 3–52.

[94] Heng, *The Invention of Race*, p. 189.

the pattern in *The King of Tars*, Bevis as a white Christian is established as desirable, in contrast to the limiting effect Josian's Muslim faith has on her desirability. Josian's father admires Bevis, thinking that Muhammad would be pleased if he were to worship him; it is specifically Bevis's whiteness that the King praises, declaring 'a feyrer chylde neuyr y sye', 'nor fayrer colour had!' (599–601). Although the King does not desire Bevis for himself here, this arguably enhances the text's portrayal of whiteness as desirability, since the King recognises Bevis's beauty in a more impersonal, purportedly universal way. The King's concern for Bevis's situation, to the extent that he offers to make Bevis his heir if he converts, opens up a moment of interfaith empathy like those described by Marcel Elias.[95] However, the early scenes of encounter between Josian and Bevis establish Bevis as more desirable than Josian, aided by Josian's active pursuit of Bevis later in the narrative (for example, lines 786–91, 820–3, 854–63), again constructing a hierarchy of desire that reflects differences of religious race.

Race, religion, and desirability remain in correlation as the theme of religious conversion is swiftly introduced. Josian's father suggests to Bevis

> And þou wolde þy lorde forsake
> And Apolyn to þy lorde take,
> Hur wyll y geue þe to wyfe,
> And all my londe aftur my lyfe. (622–5)

While this may appear a tempting offer of land, riches, and a wife, especially to a young boy who has been disinherited, the King's proposition is quickly rejected by Bevis:

> That y nolde
> For all thy syluyr and þy golde;
> Ne for all þe gode vndur Heuyn lyght,
> Nodur for þy doghtur, þat ys so bryght.
> I wolde not forsake, on no manere,
> God þat boght me so dere.
> All be they brente to dethe
> That on odur false goddys beleuyth! (626–33)

His unwillingness to convert is explicitly the reason Bevis rejects the King's offer, violently refuting non-Christian beliefs. He acknowledges the appeal of the King's wealth and the beauty of Josian, ensuring that she, unlike the two sultans discussed above, is not described as undesirable (though she is perhaps less desirable than Bevis). However, he affirms his commitment to his faith above all, making it clear that he will not convert for Josian. The focus on religion is further emphasised in the scenes where Josian starts to offer Bevis

---

[95] Marcel Elias, 'Interfaith Empathy and the Formation of Romance', in *Emotion and Medieval Textual Media*, ed. by Mary C. Flannery (Turnhout: Brepols, 2018), pp. 99–124.

her love. She declares 'y haue leuyd on false lore – / For þy loue y wyll no more' (1328–9) and insists

> y schall, as y am mayde –
> My false goddys all forsake
> And Crystendome for þy loue take. (1335–7)

It is only after she has made these promises that Bevis agrees to love her, specifically saying 'on that maner [...] / I the graunt, my swete wyght!' (1338–9). *Bevis* engages clearly and directly with religious race as an issue in Christian men's relationships, as Bevis refuses to love Josian until she agrees to convert.

However, *Bevis* also complicates the fantasy trope of the converted Muslim princess through the context of Bevis and Josian's relationship. Compared to other similar romances, Bevis is in a particularly vulnerable position as he is the only Christian in Josian's father's court. While crusading romances, including the *Ferumbras* narratives discussed in the final section of this chapter, depict isolation in terms of war and imprisonment, *Bevis* is unusual in portraying the hero as the only Christian in a Muslim court. In some ways, Bevis's vulnerability and isolation position him similarly to Horn and Amis, according with the *Roman de Horn*'s influence on the Anglo-Norman *Boeve*.[96] Like *King Horn* and *Amis and Amiloun*, *Bevis* suggests that a young man living at another king's court was in a precarious position, depicting Bevis's vulnerability to accusations made by members of this court (lines 1347–79) and making Josian the active partner who pursues Bevis, although she does not coerce him into a relationship with her. However, the added issue of being a Christian in a Muslim court extends the isolation Bevis experiences, perhaps opening up anxiety about the potential for Bevis to be persuaded or coerced into converting to Islam himself – as the King initially suggests. As Bly Calkin notes, the romance 'conveys a fear of Christian assimilation into a non-Christian world', dramatising 'one of the historical anxieties prompted by crusade and settlement in the East [...] the fear that western Christians involved in these activities might lose their sense of proper mores and become too similar to their Muslim opponents'.[97] While *Bevis* does suggest that there were concerns about Christian men marrying Muslim women (even those who offer to convert), this may reflect the unusual situation within this narrative rather than a broader concern with Christian men marrying converts from Islam.

Indeed, while religion is a prominent concern in the conversation between Bevis and the King and when Bevis subsequently accepts Josian's love, the

---

[96] On *Boeve* and the *Roman de Horn*, see Judith Weiss, 'Introduction', in *'Boeve de Haumtone' and 'Gui de Warewic': Two Anglo-Norman Romances*, ed. & trans. by Weiss, FRETS, 3 (Tempe: Arizona Center for Medieval and Renaissance Studies, 2008), pp. 1–24 (p. 5).
[97] Siobhain Bly Calkin, 'The Anxieties of Encounter and Exchange: Saracens and Christian Heroism in *Sir Beves of Hamtoun*', *Florilegium*, 21 (2004), 135–58 (pp. 136–7).

romance overall reduces the importance of religious race in comparison with *The King of Tars* and *The Man of Law's Tale* by adding a secondary issue to Bevis and Josian's negotiation of their relationship: that of social status. This appears most prominently in an intermediary episode between the conversation with Josian's father and the couple's agreement to love each other, and it is emphasised more strongly in the Naples manuscript (Naples, Biblioteca Nazionale, MS XIII.B.29), which is closer to the Anglo-Norman *Boeve* at this point.[98] When Josian reveals her love to Bevis, Bevis replies

> For God [...] þat do I nelle!
> In alle this worlde is no suche man –
> King, prince ne soudan –
> That [t]he to wife hab nolde
> And he the onys had biholde.
> And I am a knyȝt of vnkouth lond
> And haue no more good þan I in stond. (Naples, 1231–7)

Rather than their differing faiths, Bevis here pinpoints the disparity in their social status – Josian a princess desired by many royal suitors and Bevis a disinherited knight being fostered by the foreign king whose daughter now woos him – as the reason for his resistance to Josian's advances, again recalling the scenario in *King Horn* and *Amis and Amiloun*. The focus upon social status is retained throughout this scene: after Bevis's rebuff, Josian insists that

> I haue the leuer to my leman,
> Al on thi shirt nakid,
> Than al the good that euer was makid. (Naples, 1241–3)

When Bevis still refuses her, she weeps and calls him a 'chorle' (1252), an insult predicated upon social status.[99] Josian then agrees with Bevis's argument that no king or knight would refuse her, and Bevis himself undergoes a similarly humorous reversal as he grows angry at her description of him as a churl, saying 'my fadir was bothe erle and knyȝt' (Naples, 1261). The sudden shifts in the protagonists' claims about social status in this scene may provide humour, indicating their quick tempers, but they also foreground the issue of

---

98 For the text of *Boeve*, see *Der Anglonormannische Boeve de Haumtone*, ed. by Albert Stimming, Bibliotheca Normannica, 7 (Halle: Niemeyer, 1899), lines 670–708; trans. in 'Boeve de Haumtone', in *'Boeve de Haumtone' and 'Gui de Warewic'*, ed. & trans. by Weiss, pp. 25–95 (p. 37). The relationships between the Middle English texts, and theirs to the Anglo-Norman version, are complicated, but Fellows describes the Naples manuscript as 'perhaps the most conservative version': Jennifer Fellows, 'Introduction', in *Sir Bevis of Hampton*, I, pp. xv–lxxviii (pp. lxi–lxii, lxix).

99 See 'Chĕrl n.', *Middle English Dictionary*, ed. by Frances McSparran et al., Middle English Compendium (Ann Arbor: University of Michigan Library, 2000–18) <https://quod.lib.umich.edu/m/middle-english-dictionary/dictionary/MED7461> [accessed 22 June 2023].

social status.[100] While Cambridge University Library, MS Ff.2.38 does not include Bevis's first speech insisting that he is too low-status to accept Josian's love, social status is still the primary focus of the scene in this manuscript, as Josian upbraids Bevis for rejecting her when kings and princes desire her and Bevis similarly takes offence at her description of him as a churl. In contrast, Josian's religion is not explicitly mentioned by Bevis in either version of this scene, even though she angrily curses 'Mahound yeue the tene and wrake!' (Naples, 1253; the line is almost identical in CUL Ff.2.38). This intermediary scene focuses consistently on social status, highlighting an issue that was not addressed in the works focused upon a woman involved in an interracial relationship but which potentially held much greater relevance for *Bevis*'s medieval readers. This dilution of the focus upon religious race suggests that there may be less concern about relationships involving Christian men and Muslim women than relationships involving Muslim men and Christian women, despite the focus on religion elsewhere in *Bevis*.

Bevis's initial resistance creates a space in which religious difference can be outlined and its undesirability conveyed, but also a space in which negotiation of religious and status difference can occur, as Bevis and Josian ultimately agree to a relationship on condition of Josian's conversion. This leaves intact the hierarchy of desire that privileges white Christians, as Josian is first described as white or white-passing, and then (perhaps with that causal implication) converts to Christianity, which enables Bevis to accept her offer of love. *Bevis* aligns with the use of resistance to love as a means of race-making in the other romances discussed so far, but also breaks with them by introducing the secondary issue of social status and thus making religious race of less central importance. The final two narratives discussed in this chapter, involving Christian men's relationships with (formerly) Muslim women, deprioritise religious race even further.

'Wyle I neuer take hire ner no woman': Homosociality and Social Pressure in *Sir Ferumbras* and *The Sowdone of Babylone*

The late fourteenth-century *Sir Ferumbras*, preserved in Oxford, Bodleian Library, MS Ashmole 33, and the early fifteenth-century *Sowdone of Babylone*, surviving in Princeton University Library, MS Garrett 140,[101] are derived ultimately and independently from the French *Fierabras* tradition.[102]

---

[100] On this humour, see Corinne Saunders, 'Gender, Virtue and Wisdom in *Sir Bevis of Hampton*', in *'Sir Bevis of Hampton' in Literary Tradition*, ed. by Jennifer Fellows and Ivana Djordjević (Cambridge: D. S. Brewer, 2008), pp. 161–75 (p. 169).

[101] *The Sowdone of Babylone*, ed. by Emil Hausknecht, EETS, e. s., 38 (London: Paul, Trench, and Trübner, 1881), line 1911.

[102] *Sir Ferumbras* derives ultimately from the Vulgate *Fierabras* tradition represented by the continental *chanson de geste* and the Anglo-Norman *Fierabras* in Hanover,

These works narrate the conflict between Charlemagne's forces and those of the Muslim Sultan Balan/Laban during or in the aftermath of the Sultan's sacking of Rome. When Charlemagne's peers are taken prisoner, the Sultan's daughter, Floripas, takes charge of them and seizes the opportunity to declare her love for Guy of Burgundy.[103] These romances demonstrate even less preoccupation with religious race than *Bevis*, though they still contribute to creating and maintaining a normative hierarchy of desire. This section focuses on Guy's attempt to reject Floripas in *Sir Ferumbras* and the *Sowdone*, drawing on some of their French sources – primarily the *chanson de geste*, Jean Bagnyon's prose *Fierabras*, and the anonymous prose version – as comparative material.[104]

When Floripas, who is 'fair & swet', asks for Guy of Burgundy's love in return for helping the imprisoned Christians, saying she will convert to Christianity for him, Guy's response does not focus on Floripas's race or faith at all.[105] Instead, Guy declares, 'wyuy nolde he noʒt, / With-oute assent of kyng Charloun ; þat had him vp i-broʒt' (2096–7). He elaborates on this further in *The Sowdone of Babylone*, where he swears

> By God [...] þat gafe me life,
> Hire wole I never haue,
> Wyle I neuer take hire ner no woman,
> But Charles the kinge hir me gife.

Niedersächsische Landesbibliothek, MS IV 578. *The Sowdone of Babylone* derives from the non-Vulgate or abbreviating tradition and probably shares a common source with the Anglo-Norman *Fierenbras* preserved in London, British Library, MS Egerton 3028. *Fierenbras* and the *Sowdone* combine the *Fierabras* story with that of the *Destruction de Rome*. See further Ailes and Hardman, *The Legend of Charlemagne in Medieval England*, pp. 266, 272–3, 316, 330; Marianne Ailes, 'A Comparative Study of the Medieval French and Middle English Verse Texts of the Fierabras Legend' (unpublished PhD thesis, University of Reading, 1989), pp. 270–7, 353–7, 420–6, 430–4, 443–4; Janet M. Cowen, 'The English Charlemagne Romances', in *Roland and Charlemagne in Europe: Essays on the Reception and Transformation of a Legend*, ed. by Karen Pratt (London: King's College London, Centre for Late Antique and Medieval Studies, 1996), pp. 149–68 (especially pp. 150–1, 159, 161–2).

[103] For a different interpretation of Floripas as herself undesiring, see Lucy M. Allen-Goss, 'Stony Femininity and the Limits of Desire in *The Sowdone of Babylon*', in *Female Desire in Chaucer's 'Legend of Good Women' and Middle English Romance* (Cambridge: D. S. Brewer, 2020), pp. 111–39.

[104] The Fillingham *Firumbras*, surviving in London, British Library, MS Add. 37492 (the Fillingham manuscript), is missing the early sections in which Guy and Floripas negotiate their relationship, so I do not consider it here. William Caxton's translation of the Bagnyon prose *Fierabras*, the *Lyf of the Noble and Crysten Prynce Charles the Grete* (1485), follows his source regarding Guy and Floripas's relationship.

[105] *Sir Ferumbras*, ed. by Sidney J. Herrtage, EETS, e. s., 34 (London: Paul, Trench, and Trübner, 1879), line 1201.

I hight him, as I was trewe man,
To holden it, while I lyve. (*SoB*, 1909–14)

Guy's resistance to marrying Floripas is not based upon racialisation or concerns about conversion; instead, he focuses upon the issue of homosocial loyalty through his reluctance to love any woman not given to him by Charlemagne. This reflects the value placed upon the social practice of kings rewarding their vassals through advantageous marriages rather than a concern with Floripas's own identity. *The Sowdone of Babylone* and *Sir Ferumbras* therefore significantly move away from the anxiety about racial-religious difference in *The King of Tars* and *The Man of Law's Tale*, suggestively indicating the extent to which marrying a Muslim (convert) was considered less of a fraught issue for Christian men compared to Christian women. This lack of concern about Floripas's faith is particularly striking in the Ashmole *Sir Ferumbras*, as the author of this version (which survives only in two draft, autograph copies preserved in the Ashmole manuscript) was apparently a cleric, though he may simply have been following his source material in this portrayal.[106]

Both Ferumbras romances use strategies to minimise, but not entirely erase, Floripas's racial-religious difference from Guy. Like Josian, Floripas is described as white. This is especially emphasised in the scene of her baptism at the end of *Sir Ferumbras*, in which 'hyr skyn' is said to be 'as whyt so þe melkis fom', her 'eʒene graye', and her hair 'of gold' (5879–82), but she is described as 'faire' in both works (for example, *SoB*, 124) and as 'whit as wales bon' in *Sir Ferumbras* (2429), suggesting that she is seen as white throughout both romances.[107] She also offers to convert for Guy's love. However, her proposed conversion does not seem to clearly resolve all possible concerns about her faith, as both the *Sowdone* and *Sir Ferumbras* include moments that characterise her religious beliefs as problematic. In *Sir Ferumbras*, after she has offered to convert, Floripas suggests the knights should pray to her idols, since 'ful litel ys ʒour god of myʒt ; þat vytailes ne sent ʒov none' (*SF*, 2526). Her commitment to conversion is reaffirmed after this, when the peers break her idols and she sees that they had no power to protect themselves, but her reversion to idolatry, falsely represented as a part of Islam, still expresses doubt about her commitment to Christianity. The *Sowdone* does not include the same reversion, in keeping with other texts

---

[106] See Ailes and Hardman, *The Legend of Charlemagne in Medieval England*, pp. 183–5.

[107] The *Sowdone* reduces the description of Floripas's beauty and whiteness greatly from *La Destruction de Rome*, one of the ultimate sources that lies behind it, but Floripas's later reference to Roland choosing one of her maidens who are 'white as swan' (2749) does seem to suggest that Floripas and her maidens are perceived as white here. See Emil Hausknecht, 'Notes', in *The Sowdone of Babylone*, ed. by Hausknecht, pp. 95–132 (pp. 100–1).

from the abbreviating tradition of *Fierabras*,[108] but it exhibits anxiety about religious difference when Roland refuses Floripas's offer for him to choose one of her maidens to love, saying

> þat were myscheve;
> Oure lay wole not, þat we with youe dele,
> Tille that ye Cristyn be made;
> Ner of your play we wole not fele,
> For than were we cursed in dede. (*SoB*, 2750–4)

Roland's refusal of Floripas's maidens sits uncomfortably alongside her relationship with Guy, as Roland apparently extends this concern to Floripas herself, saying Christians may not 'with *youe* dele, / Tille that *ye* Cristyn be made' (my emphasis). While Guy and Floripas's relationship is not depicted in detail, they do kiss as soon as they are betrothed, marking a departure from most of the French texts, where the sense of religious divides is stricter and they do not kiss initially 'por chen qu'ele iert paienne et il crestïennez' [because she was pagan and he Christian].[109] Roland's negative reaction to Floripas's offer contrasts with his positive response in *Sir Ferumbras* (3441–2) and the Fillingham *Firumbras*,[110] indicating some concern with interfaith relationships in the *Sowdone* and suggesting that despite Guy's lack of anxiety about Floripas's faith, some doubts about her conversion remain.

The oscillation between doubt and acceptance of Floripas in the Middle English texts is illuminated by comparing them with the anonymous French prose *Fierabras*. Unusually, this does not include Guy's resistance, as he accepts Floripas immediately.[111] The differing situation in the prose *Fierabras* can probably be attributed to the anonymous author or their immediate source, as this text is not a different recension of the narrative as a whole: Ailes situates it on the same side of the stemma as the Egerton manuscript of the Anglo-Norman *Fierabras* (London, British Library, MS Egerton 3028), the Middle English texts, and the Bagnyon prose version.[112] Nor does it seem to focus more emphatically on Floripas's willingness to convert: while she does say that in kissing her, 'ja vous n'y aurez pechié' [you will never have

---

[108] See Ailes and Hardman, *The Legend of Charlemagne in Medieval England*, p. 319.

[109] *Fierabras: Chanson de geste du XIIe siècle*, ed. by Marc Le Person, Classiques français du moyen âge, 142 (Paris: Champion, 2003), line 2930. My translation. The anonymous French prose *Fierabras* is an exception to the absence of the kiss, as I discuss below. See further Akbari, *Idols in the East*, pp. 183–4.

[110] *Firumbras and Otuel and Roland*, ed. by Mary Isabelle O'Sullivan, EETS, o. s., 198 (London: Oxford University Press, 1935), lines 860–2.

[111] *Fierabras: roman en prose de la fin du XIVe siècle*, ed. by Jean Miquet, Publications médiévales de l'Université d'Ottawa, 9 (Ottawa: Éditions de l'Université d'Ottawa, 1983), p. 92 (91. 1013–27).

[112] Ailes, 'The Fierabras Legend', pp. 291–320, 421, 444.

sinned] (a direct contrast to the Bagnyon prose version), her offer to convert is presented quite similarly to *Sir Ferumbras* and the *Sowdone*.[113] The omission of Guy's resistance does not seem to relate to a change in Floripas's conversion, then, but it does seem to correlate with a different approach to Floripas overall in this narrative, Suzanne Conklin Akbari suggesting that it 'presents a neutralized Floripas' as 'a model of feminine deportment'.[114] The omission of the rejection episode may contribute to or result from this change: the author of the anonymous prose version may have omitted Guy's initial rejection of Floripas to ensure she is presented as more conventionally desirable and thus does not need to resort to threats or violence to obtain her desired husband, or, in rendering Floripas a more neutral/positive figure, they may have seen no reason for Guy to reject her. These alterations can offer insights into the functions of the rejection episode in the other texts: if the rejection episode is omitted in accordance with changes to Floripas's character, then its inclusion may support a particular interpretation of Floripas. Despite his apparent absence of concern about her faith, and despite the courtlier and more romantic portrayal of Guy and Floripas in the Middle English texts more widely,[115] Guy's resistance to loving Floripas may work with the other moments that suggest anxiety about her beliefs to demarcate racial-religious difference by suggesting that she is an improper object of desire, even momentarily and without explicitly relating this to her faith. As I suggested in the introduction to this chapter, resistance to loving a convert can express concerns about the efficacy of conversion or can reveal the persistence of other forms of racialised difference, contrasting with the easy acceptance of conversion in other narratives of Muslim–Christian relations. Guy's resistance certainly seems to humiliate Floripas and, in *Sir Ferumbras*, to characterise her negatively through her angry and anti-Christian response to Guy's rejection (like Josian, Floripas curses 'by Mahoun', *SF*, 2099). While it seems odd that Guy's rejection of Floripas does not explicitly comment on her character or religion, his initial resistance may still implicitly serve the dual ideological function of race-making and demarcating normative desires along the lines of perceived racial-religious difference.

However, the focus on homosocial loyalty opens up different functions for Guy's resistance to love, diminishing the concern with racial-religious difference and instead turning to issues perhaps more rooted in medieval readers' realities. Kings influenced the marriages of their highest nobility in both literature and life, and Guy is noted to be Charlemagne's nephew in the *Sowdone* (1888) and to have been 'vp i-broȝt' by him in *Sir Ferumbras* (2097; and in

---

[113] *Fierabras: roman en prose*, p. 92 (91. 1014). My translation.

[114] Akbari, *Idols in the East*, pp. 179–80.

[115] See Ailes and Hardman, *The Legend of Charlemagne in Medieval England*, pp. 266, 284–6.

Charlemagne's description of Guy as 'of my blod', 1488), adding a familial or even paternal dimension to this relationship, where an even greater influence over marital choice would be expected.[116] Rachel Moss, writing about English gentry families, argues that

> Fathers played an important role in running negotiations. From the evidence of marriage contracts, it would seem that fathers were often responsible for having the contracts drawn up. [...] The case of William Stonor and Margery Blount demonstrates that whilst sons may have wooed women, they relied on their fathers for advice and permission – and that a father had the ability to stop negotiations.[117]

Shannon McSheffrey similarly observes that while 'there is little evidence to support the old chestnut that all medieval marriages were arranged by fathers or lords', 'a decision as important as the choice of spouse was not made without recourse to the advice, help, and sometimes the consent or even the coercion of the important people in a young man's or young woman's life'.[118] Guy's commitment to marry only a woman approved by Charlemagne therefore seems to reflect the real-life importance of fathers and guardians in marital arrangements, as well as the significance accorded to kings rewarding their followers with advantageous marriages. This focus on familial concern may have been apposite to the early readers of these romances: while the intended recipient of the fair copy that is presumed to have been planned (or actually produced) from the Ashmole *Sir Ferumbras* is unknown, Ailes and Hardman speculate on the basis of adaptations from its French source and the apparent care taken with work on the draft copies that the end product might have been intended for 'the noble or gentry families of the South-West', while the parchment manuscript of the *Sowdone* is of 'modest prestige' and makes 'no great effort [...] to economise on the use of this more expensive material', suggesting it may have been associated with readers of some wealth and status.[119] The probable social environments of these romances' readers are thus precisely those in which marriages are likely to have been negotiated through broader networks of agency.

---

[116] See *Women of the English Nobility and Gentry, 1066–1500*, ed. & trans. by Jennifer Ward (Manchester: Manchester University Press, 1995), pp. 15–16.

[117] Rachel E. Moss, *Fatherhood and its Representations in Middle English Texts* (Cambridge: D. S. Brewer, 2013), p. 94.

[118] Shannon McSheffrey, *Marriage, Sex, and Civic Culture in Late Medieval London* (Philadelphia: University of Pennsylvania Press, 2006), pp. 77–8.

[119] Ailes and Hardman, *The Legend of Charlemagne in Medieval England*, pp. 184–7 (quotation at p. 186); Carol M. Meale, 'Patrons, Buyers and Owners: Book Production and Social Status', in *Book Production and Publishing in Britain, 1375–1475*, ed. by Jeremy Griffiths and Derek Pearsall (Cambridge: Cambridge University Press, 1989), pp. 201–38 (p. 217).

While Guy's promise to Charlemagne is broken when he accepts Floripas's offer, this acceptance continues to highlight the range of people who might play a part in the making of a marriage. In *Sir Ferumbras*, Guy changes his mind when Roland appeals again to 'ys cosyn free', saying 'tak thys damesele by þe hand ; as þow louest me'. This time, Guy replies 'as þow wolt y wol done' (*SF*, 2102–4). While Guy partly reneges on his commitment to Charlemagne (although at the end of *Sir Ferumbras*, he says he will 'gladlych' marry Floripas 'so þat myn vncle assenty to', 5875), homosociality is still highlighted in his acceptance of her love. Likewise, in the *Sowdone*, Roland and Oliver both beseech Guy,

> Certyfyinge him of her myschefe,
> Tellinge him of the parelles, þat þay in wer,
> For to take this lady to his wedded wife.
> 'But thou helpe in this nede,
> We be here in grete doute.
> Almyghty god shalle quyte thy mede,
> Elles come we nevere hennys oute.'
> Thus thay treted him to and fro;
> At the laste he sayde, he wolde. (*SoB*, 1916–24)

Roland and Oliver make this decision about 'her myschefe' and 'parelles' rather than Floripas's qualities, appealing to Guy to help them and the other peers. They do tell Guy that 'almyghty god shalle quyte thy mede', perhaps implying reassurance about Floripas's faith and/or suggesting that Guy will be forgiven for breaking his promise to Charlemagne. But overall, the focus here seems to be on homosocial bonds and pressures, with Roland and Oliver's influence replacing Charlemagne's. While Guy's acceptance of Floripas diminishes his commitment to Charlemagne, it still prioritises homosocial influence.

Roland and Oliver's appeals reflect the manner in which Floripas has couched her proposal, combining her offer to convert with leveraging her power over the imprisoned Christian forces. Dorothee Metlitzki labels this 'blackmail', while Mohja Kahf suggests Floripas 'forces a proposal of marriage [...] on Sir Guy, whose options are understandably limited'.[120] Floripas tells Duke Neymes

> but he wole graunte me his loue,
> Of you askape shalle none here.
> By him, þat is almyghty aboue,
> Ye shalle abye it ellis ful dere. (*SoB*, 1899–1902)

---

[120] Metlitzki, *The Matter of Araby*, p. 174; Kahf, *Western Representations of the Muslim Woman*, p. 35.

In *Sir Ferumbras*, Floripas is not initially so explicit about threatening the peers, but she does instruct them, 'performyeþ ȝe my wille. / ȝif ȝe þynkeþ to askape away', 'do me haue a þyng ; þat al myn herte ys on' (*SF*, 2039–42). Floripas's assistance is dependent upon Guy accepting her offer, and this is augmented by an explicit threat when he initially rejects her, warning 'bote if Gy to wyue hure take [...] / Ecchone þay scholde for is sake ; or euene beo an-honge'.[121] As we have seen, concern for their own safety motivates Roland and Oliver to persuade Guy in the *Sowdone*, while this threat also prompts Roland's intervention in *Sir Ferumbras*. While Guy ultimately agrees to marry Floripas, and later seems to love her, the Middle English texts adding to their source material the language of precisely the kind of 'reciprocal married love' likely to be valued by romance and its readers,[122] the situation in which he accepts her love is marked by coercion and threats. Although Guy himself seems unconcerned about Floripas's Islamic heritage, her need to invoke threats and bribery and recruit the peers to make him accept her love suggests that she is not straightforwardly desirable, despite the descriptive emphasis on her fairness throughout. The *Sowdone* and *Sir Ferumbras* turn away from concerns with religious race, using Floripas's proposition to consider homosocial commitment instead. However, the presence of Guy's resistance in itself effects the political demarcation of who is and is not desirable, contributing to the creation of a hierarchy of desire.

Conclusion

Resistance to love because of racial-religious difference functions politically, drawing and at times redrawing dividing lines of desirability and racialisation. It purports to operate across pre-existing forms of difference but actually creates those differences, as is suggested by the variety of focal points resistance to love essentialises across the works discussed. These encompass religion, skin colour and physical features, and cultural differences, which are selectively overcome. The examples of resistance to love in this chapter operate as a form of race-making, focused primarily upon religious race. They create a hierarchy of desire that identifies white Christians as the most desirable figures and people of colour and/or of a different religion at the bottom of that hierarchy, with white converts as a middling group. They therefore not only highlight how fundamental a common faith was deemed to be for a successful partnership but construct and conform to the 'ideology of white beauty' Hall identifies in early modern literature, which functions as 'a "racial

---

[121] *Sir Ferumbras*, lines 2100–1. Floripas also issues this threat in the *chanson de geste*, lines 2918–19, and in *Charles the Grete*.
[122] See the discussion in Ailes and Hardman, *The Legend of Charlemagne in Medieval England*, pp. 185, 285–6 (quotation at p. 285).

formation" in that it helps construct a visual regime that uses human bodies and their signification to determine access to political, social and economic power'.[123] These romances largely uphold conventional ideas of whom white Christians should consider attractive – namely, each other and not anyone who is demarcated as different – marking out who ought to be granted access to the political, social, and economic power mediated through marriage. Hierarchies of desire thus have real political effect in the world. This is true of both the fictional world within which they are constructed and the real world outside of the text, as these works shape their readers' understanding of (un)desirability, preserving white Christian power structures. These hierarchies are intersectional, as gender is imbricated with race in portrayals of white female victimhood, and Christian women marrying Muslim men is a subject of much greater anxiety than Christian men marrying Muslim women. Racist stereotypes are thus entangled with misogynistic and patriarchal perspectives on the control of women. Hierarchies of desire also have an affective function, endorsing empathy with white female victims while positioning black and brown men as sexual aggressors and minimising any engagement with white men's victimisation of black and brown women. Race and national identity, as Heng notes, are constructed and sustained by 'affective communities mobilized by telling and retelling key stories of cultural power'.[124] The next chapter turns to resistance to adultery to further explore the interlinking of exemplarity and affective power.

---

[123] Hall, 'Literary whiteness', p. 80.
[124] Heng, *The Invention of Race*, p. 32.

5

'What deyntee sholde a man han in his lyf / For to go love another mannes wyf'? Resisting Adultery, Resisting Rape Culture[1]

Resisting adultery or infidelity appears to be the least transgressive form of resistance to love – or, more specifically, resistance to sex – discussed in this book.[2] Romances in which adultery is rejected conform to the priorities of monogamous Christian society, upholding the importance of fidelity within marriage and working in opposition to romances where adultery is endorsed. They therefore function as exemplary narratives, offering models of behaviour that sometimes display subtle nuances of appropriate conduct. Whether an example of perfect fidelity or acknowledging the difficulty of resisting adulterous temptations, exemplary figures invite empathy when viewed through the eyes of the dominant culture whose values they embody. This empathy is further elicited when such figures are subjected to coercion, violence, or revenge – as they are in each example discussed here. In the context of adultery, coercion and vengeance are associated with negative characters who are condemned both for their attempted violence and for its threat to marital fidelity. These portrayals operate in tension with the use of coercive practices to enforce normative desires, discussed in the earlier chapters of this book. At times this tension invites or permits the dominance of medieval rape culture and assumptions of the obligation of love to be questioned, although the focus on empathy for exemplary characters also upholds the idea of the perfect victim, itself a tenet of medieval and modern rape culture.[3] This chap-

---

[1] Quotation from Geoffrey Chaucer, 'The Franklin's Tale', in *The Riverside Chaucer*, ed. by Larry D. Benson, 3rd edn (Oxford: Oxford University Press, 2008), pp. 178–89 (lines 1003–4).

[2] I generally use the term 'adultery' in this chapter, except for when discussing Launcelot's relationships with women other than Guenevere, where I use 'infidelity' to indicate the distinction between extra-marital affairs and being unfaithful to a non-marital relationship.

[3] On the harm caused by the idea of the perfect victim and a singular narrative of what rape is, see Sarah Baechle, Carissa M. Harris, and Elizaveta Strakhov, 'Introduction: Recovering the Pastourelle', in *Rape Culture and Female Resistance in Late Medieval*

ter therefore uses portrayals of rejecting adultery to trace their potential to enable resistance to, as well as partial alignment with, medieval rape culture, illuminating the more subversive possibilities of this motif.

In its discussion of medieval rape culture, this chapter joins and builds upon the work of Carissa Harris in *Obscene Pedagogies* and Harris, Sarah Baechle, and Elizaveta Strakhov's recent volume *Rape Culture and Female Resistance in Late Medieval Literature*. As discussed in the introduction, rape culture can be defined as 'a complex of beliefs that encourages male sexual aggression and supports violence against women'.[4] As Harris outlines, these beliefs 'allow sexual violence to continue by blaming victims and failing to hold perpetrators accountable'; involve the 'erasure of cisgender male and transgender victim-survivors'; and include rape myths like 'she asked for it', 'he didn't mean to', and 'she wanted it'.[5] While such beliefs are evident throughout medieval literature and culture, including in romance writing, the works discussed in this chapter offer a different perspective. They do not tend to blame their victims, they often do hold perpetrators accountable, they expose rape myths as myths, and they depict cisgender men's experiences of sexual violation and victimisation. They do all of this within the framework of resisting adulterous sex, which reduces its radical implications by casting each victim as a model victim. In this respect, my chapter departs from the work of Harris, Baechle, and Strakhov, as while their focus on the *pastourelle* allows them to 'center marginalized women's voices and illuminate the intersecting inequalities that enable sexual violation', the romances I discuss portray the most privileged victim-survivors: high-status, often royal or at least noble, women and men.[6] Yet the alignments between their experiences and those of other victim-survivors of coercion and violence in romance acknowledge the harmful effects of medieval rape culture and challenge some of the ideas upon which it depends.

Rejections of adultery are a particularly common form of resistance to love in medieval romance, perhaps because of their exemplary potential. Resistance to adultery frequently occurs in the accused queen romances, such as *Syr Tryamowre*, *The Erle of Tolous*, *Le Bone Florence of Rome*, and *Valentine and Orson*; in the *Lanval* stories; in Geoffrey Chaucer's *Franklin's Tale*; in *Sir*

Literature, ed. by Baechle, Harris, and Strakhov (University Park: Pennsylvania State University Press, 2022), pp. 1–14 (p. 3); Baechle, Harris, and Strakhov, 'Reassessing the Pastourelle: Rape Culture, #MeToo, and the Literature of Survival', in *Rape Culture and Female Resistance*, pp. 17–28 (p. 26).

[4] Emilie Buchwald, Pamela R. Fletcher, and Martha Roth, 'Preamble', in *Transforming a Rape Culture*, ed. by Buchwald, Fletcher, and Roth, rev. edn (Minneapolis: Milkweed Editions, 2005), pp. i–xii (p. xi).

[5] Carissa M. Harris, *Obscene Pedagogies: Transgressive Talk and Sexual Education in Late Medieval Britain* (Ithaca: Cornell University Press, 2018), p. 10.

[6] Baechle, Harris, and Strakhov, 'Introduction: Recovering the Pastourelle', p. 3.

Gawain and the Green Knight and *The Greene Knight*; and several times in Thomas Malory's *Morte Darthur* (and its sources), although here the motif sometimes takes the form of trying to preserve fidelity to a relationship that is itself adulterous (as with the love of Launcelot and Guenevere or Tristram and Isode).[7] The examples discussed in this chapter are drawn from different kinds of romances and reflect the varied forms that rejecting adultery can take. From the accused queen group, I focus on *Syr Tryamowre* and *The Erle of Tolous*. These romances appear together in Cambridge University Library, MS Ff.2.38, facilitating direct comparisons that may have shaped medieval readers' experiences of these works. While *Le Bone Florence* and the Northern *Octavian* also appear in this manuscript, *Syr Tryamowre* and *The Erle of Tolous* offer a closer point of comparison and raise more searching questions about medieval rape culture through their deployment of narratives akin to the Biblical story of 'Susanna and the Elders' (Chapter 13 of the Vulgate Book of Daniel).[8] As in the story of Susanna, they include accusations of adultery that are made by characters the women rejected and that are initially accepted as true, positioning these accusations as a form of punishment or revenge for sexual rejection. They therefore offer greater potential for exploring how such accusations align with but also expose the operations of medieval rape culture, as they depict men responding violently to rejection and mobilising misogynistic stereotypes in order to present their point of view as the truth. The accusers are always eventually revealed to be lying, however, and this trajectory, as Alcuin Blamires and Helen Cooper have pointed out, positions these romances as challenging antifeminist stereotypes.[9] The first section of this chapter builds on their arguments, focusing on the exemplary and empathetic role of the heroines in *Syr Tryamowre* and *The Erle of Tolous*, and placing the coercion they experience in dialogue with other romance representations of resistance to love.

---

[7]   In addition to resisting infidelity, Isode's rejection of Palomydes could also have been discussed in Chapter 4, as another example of how religious race can impact constructions of desirability. Palomydes is an accomplished knight, but has no romantic success with Isode, largely because of her commitment to Tristram but potentially also because of Palomydes's racialised identity.

[8]   This is associated with the 'accused queen' motif surprisingly rarely, even though Jonathan Stavsky notes that the story of Susanna circulated widely in the Middle Ages, including in sources like prayers, suggesting illiterate people would also have known it: Jonathan Stavsky, '"Gode in all thynge": *The Erle of Tolous*, Susanna and the Elders, and Other Narratives of Righteous Women on Trial', *Anglia*, 131.4 (2013), 538–61 (p. 542 n. 18).

[9]   Alcuin Blamires, *The Case for Women in Medieval Culture* (Oxford: Clarendon Press, 1997), pp. 162–4; Helen Cooper, 'Women on trial', in *The English Romance in Time: Transforming motifs from Geoffrey of Monmouth to the death of Shakespeare* (Oxford: Oxford University Press, 2004), pp. 269–323.

The Erle of Tolous stands out within the accused queen tradition because it includes a secondary element to the story, the Empress Beulybon's relationship with the titular Earl. But the Empress's ambiguous relationship with a man who is not her husband finds a parallel in Chaucer's *Franklin's Tale*. These two works are not often compared but have many similarities.[10] Both identify themselves as Breton lays;[11] both were probably written in the later fourteenth century; both (arguably) take as their theme 'the sanctity of the marriage bond', as Carol Meale notes of *The Erle of Tolous*;[12] they are alone amongst the Middle English lays in 'focus[ing] alternatively and equally on two central characters'; in both cases the lady's (mis)adventures occur in the absence of her husband.[13] They also share in common the isolation of their female protagonist, who is the sole woman upon whom each work focuses: in *The Erle of Tolous*, no female friends of the Empress are mentioned, while *The Franklin's Tale* leaves Dorigen's 'freendes' (822) curiously and perhaps deliberately ungendered. Finally, both narratives offer more ambiguous portrayals of desire and morality than works like *Syr Tryamowre*. Given these similarities, I discuss *The Franklin's Tale* alongside *The Erle of Tolous* and *Syr Tryamowre*, exploring how all three works interrogate cultural formations of exemplarity, fantasy, and blame.

The other two romances discussed in this chapter involve men who resist infidelity. In *Sir Gawain and the Green Knight*, Gawain resists the lady's adulterous seduction; in Malory's *Morte Darthur*, Launcelot rejects or tries to reject many different women in order to remain faithful to his love for Guenevere – a love that is itself adulterous.[14] These two examples reflect different concerns to the other works discussed not only because they involve men rejecting adultery but because they configure infidelity differently. Gawain's rejection of the lady does not ensure his own fidelity but the lady's commitment to her husband, Bertilak. Launcelot is already committing adultery with Guenevere, and so Malory's *Morte* itself is not a rejection of infidelity to marriage. However, within the bounds of this adulterous relationship, Launcelot

---

[10] Some isolated similarities between the two tales, but no sustained attempts to compare them, are included in Shearle Furnish, 'The Modernity of *The Erle of Tolous* and the Decay of the Breton Lai', *Medieval Perspectives*, 8 (1993), 69–77.

[11] See 'The Erle of Tolous', in *Of Love and Chivalry: An Anthology of Middle English Romance*, ed. by Jennifer Fellows (London: Dent, 1993), pp. 231–65 (line 1214); Chaucer, 'The Franklin's Prologue', in *The Riverside Chaucer*, p. 178 (lines 709–15).

[12] Carol M. Meale, '"Prenes: engre": an early sixteenth-century presentation copy of *The Erle of Tolous*', in *Romance reading on the book: Essays on Medieval Narrative presented to Maldwyn Mills*, ed. by Jennifer Fellows et al. (Cardiff: University of Wales Press, 1996), pp. 221–36 (p. 231).

[13] Shearle Furnish identifies the last two commonalities listed: 'The Modernity of *The Erle of Tolous*', p. 71.

[14] The lady is not named in *Sir Gawain and the Green Knight*. Although she is often referred to as 'Lady Bertilak', I refer to her simply as 'the lady'.

tries to be faithful. These narratives therefore explore slightly different issues, revealing the variety possible within the motif of rejecting adultery, while also opening up possibilities for incorporating male victimhood and vulnerability in discussions of medieval coercion and rape.

Most of the romances discussed in this chapter date from the late fourteenth century, with Malory's *Morte Darthur* a later outlier (though one based upon earlier French sources). By this time, the romance genre was well established, enabling the works I discuss to create a dialogue with romances that include adultery as well as those that portray different forms of resistance to love. These connections illuminate the workings of rape culture but can also pave the way for challenging the punitive depiction of romantic a(nti)pathy. The motif of rejecting adultery therefore offers the opportunity to cast new light upon the arguments advanced in this book so far.

Exemplary Wives and Counter-Narratives: *Syr Tryamowre*, *The Erle of Tolous*, and *The Franklin's Tale*

Syr Tryamowre, *The Erle of Tolous*, and *The Franklin's Tale* all depict a woman propositioned by a knight or squire during her husband's absence; this man claims to love her but seems more specifically to want to have sex with her. In each case, she tries to reject his unwanted advances, but for Queen Margaret in *Syr Tryamowre* and Empress Beulybon in *The Erle of Toulous*, this leads to them being accused of treachery and exiled or imprisoned when the knights who propositioned them turn against them. In Dorigen's case, her imposition of an impossible condition backfires when Aurelius achieves this, though she is ultimately not forced to keep her word. These episodes hold different significance within the broader trajectory of each work. In *Syr Tryamowre*, it is vital that Margaret is exiled in order for her son, Tryamowre (the romance's hero), to grow up away from his father's influence and prove his merit in his own right – though the extreme violence planned by the steward, Marrok, who propositions Margaret, exceeds the plot's necessities and prompts reflection on the coercive structures it exposes. In *The Erle of Toulous*, Beulybon's rejection of adultery with the two knights who proposition her is complicated though not contradicted by her subsequent relationship with the Earl, offering a different perspective on desire and morality. And in *The Franklin's Tale*, Dorigen's condition initiates a debate about *gentillesse* and its role in romance, while also inviting comparison with other kinds of resistance to love. In their focus on attempts to reject adultery, these romances draw attention to the possibility for romances to function as 'a form of courtesy text' for married people as well as the unmarried, but the effects of rejection in each case also highlight and ultimately question medieval rape culture.[15] The moral valence of rejecting adultery combines with the portrayal of coercion to create particularly empathetic portrayals of how difficult and dangerous it can be to reject a man's advances as a woman living in a heteropatriarchal society.[16]

Syr Tryamowre's opening section presents Queen Margaret as a flawless wife. The narrative establishes a framework of transparent morality: the good and evil protagonists of the first section, Margaret and Marrok, are antonyms, she 'trewe as stele' and he 'false and fekyll'.[17] We are warned from the start that Margaret will be 'falsely [...] broght in blame' (18) and that Marrok will harm her 'for scho wolde not to hym assente' (23). This romance is clear and explicit about where the blame lies, leaving no space for doubt in the reader. In the scene where she is propositioned, including with assurances of secrecy, Margaret remains 'stedfaste of wylle' (73) and rejects Marrok in definite terms. She displays no temptation to assent to his advances, which further establishes her as an exemplary wife. Her exemplary role positions her as a figure with whom the reader is invited to empathise, if their morals align with those Margaret represents – those of a monogamous Christian society like medieval England.

But while there is no space for the reader to doubt Margaret's intentions, doubt is precisely what Margaret's husband, King Ardus, does. To lend credence to his false accusation of adultery, Marrok draws upon contemporary fears about illegitimacy, appealing to the King by claiming

> hyt were not feyre
> A horcop to be yowre heyre,
> But he ware of yowre kynne. (223–5)

This strategy is also deployed by an accuser in another calumniated queen romance included in CUL Ff.2.38, the mother-in-law in *Octavian*, who falsely laments 'that Rome schall wrong heyred bee'.[18] However, *Octavian* does

---

[15] Felicity Riddy, 'Middle English romance: family, marriage, intimacy', in *The Cambridge Companion to Medieval Romance*, ed. by Roberta L. Krueger (Cambridge: Cambridge University Press, 2000), pp. 235–52 (p. 242).

[16] 'Heteropatriarchy refers to the social, political, and economic system in which heterosexual men are the dominant group in a society or culture'; in this social system, heterosexual relationships are celebrated and enforced in ways that uphold patriarchal hierarchies. I use the term here because the pressures of expected heterosexual relationships and patriarchal dominance combine to make rejecting men's romantic advances particularly difficult. See Jacob Kelley and Andrea Arce-Trigatti, 'Heteropatriarchy', in *Encyclopedia of Queer Studies in Education*, ed. by Kamden K. Strunk and Stephanie Anne Shelton (Leiden: Brill, 2022), pp. 256–9 (p. 256).

[17] 'Syr Tryamowre', in *Of Love and Chivalry*, ed. by Jennifer Fellows, pp. 147–98. 'Trewe as stele' is repeated twice, lines 17 and 27; 'false and fekyll' comes at line 20.

[18] *Octovian*, ed. by Frances McSparran, EETS, o. s., 289 (London: Oxford University Press, 1986), Cambridge University Library, MS Ff.2.38, line 107.

not believe her as instantly as Ardus does Marrok, perhaps suggesting the importance of gender in whose accusations are given credence. Both accusers follow similar strategies, drawing upon powerful contemporary anxieties about female adultery and the ultimate unknowability of a child's paternity to turn the men against their wives by capitalising on their inner fears.[19] The concern about female adultery was exacerbated within royal marriages, as

> the queen's conception of an illegitimate child threatens the proper succession of the throne in a way that the birth of a king's bastard does not. The queen's child is born into the royal family, whether or not her husband is the father.[20]

Marrok is further aided in his accusation by the King's initial belief that he and his wife cannot conceive a child together, which prompts his absence as he leaves on crusade in an attempt to gain God's favour. This lends credibility to the claim that Margaret's pregnancy on his return is evidence of adultery, particularly if he is inclined to think himself potentially infertile. The romance does, therefore, indicate that there are some good reasons for the King to believe Marrok's false accusation, which he adroitly manipulates. However, the gap between the reader's certainty and Ardus's belief also opens up a counter-narrative in which the cultural assumption of women's fickleness and guilt can be critiqued.[21] I term this a counter-narrative even though it is overt within *Syr Tryamowre* because it works against the dominant cultural perception of women as unfaithful and the prominent French romance tradition of adultery. It thus aligns with the function of counter-narratives as 'resist[ing] another narrative', which is, or is 'perceived as being, more powerful', offering 'a vital tool for contesting canonicity, and ideological dominance, in fiction'.[22] While Marrok draws upon precisely this dominant narrative to make his accusations more believable, the reader's knowledge of its falsity not only highlights Margaret's innocence but exposes misogynistic perceptions as harmful and untrue.

Indeed, *Syr Tryamowre* critiques assumptions of women's fickleness overtly and implicitly. The narrator labels Ardus's refusal to speak to Margaret before exiling her, thus providing no opportunity for her to convey her side of the story, 'grete synne!' (234). But Ardus's actions may be critiqued in a more

---

[19] See further Caroline Dunn, *Stolen Women in Medieval England: Rape, Abduction, and Adultery, 1100–1500* (Cambridge: Cambridge University Press, 2012), p. 120.

[20] Peggy McCracken, *The Romance of Adultery: Queenship and Sexual Transgression in Old French Literature* (Philadelphia: University of Pennsylvania Press, 1998), p. 18.

[21] Alcuin Blamires sets out the classical and medical foundations of this belief in women's instability in *The Case for Women*, pp. 126–9.

[22] Klarissa Lueg, Ann Starbæk Bager, and Marianne Wolff Lundholt, 'Introduction: What counter-narratives are', in *Routledge Handbook of Counter-Narratives*, ed. by Klarissa Lueg and Marianne Wolff Lundholt (Abingdon: Routledge, 2021), pp. 1–14 (pp. 4, 11).

subtle and satirical light as well, through the episode involving Sir Roger's dog. When this dog, who helped Roger defend Margaret against Marrok's violent attack, in which Roger was killed, reappears at the King's court and kills Marrok, Ardus asks 'what may thys be to meene' (558)? Without pausing, he immediately fills in the gaps:

> Y trowe Syr Marrok, be Goddes payne,
> Have slayne Syr Roger be some trayne,
> And falsely flemyd my quene.
> The hound had not Syr Marrok slayne,
> Had not some treson byn,
> Be dereworth God, as y wene! (559–64)

While he initially took Marrok's word at face value, the actions of the dog are apparently sufficient to disprove Marrok's version of events, suggesting that the dog is a more reliable witness than either Marrok or Margaret.[23] I am being slightly facetious here: this episode is necessary to convey Margaret's innocence to Ardus in her absence and we are not supposed to read it in the light of psychological realism. And yet it builds on the gap between the reader's and Ardus's perceptions earlier in the romance, offering an opportunity for a resistant reader to advance the counter-narrative against his credulity. It exposes the power of voice and action in the male-dominated court of romance as a privilege at times granted to men and animals before women.

There is, however, one crucial area in which Margaret's voice and actions do count: in her rejection of Marrok. He responds to this violently and punitively, conspiring to have her exiled and in addition

> To do the quene a velanye,
> Hys luste for to fulfylle. (272–3)

That is, he plots to rape her. This violent response indicates that he understands Margaret's rejection to be absolute, as he sees no other means to preserve himself from the King's anger or gain his will than by turning Ardus against her and in doing so creating an opportunity to rape her (this also retrospectively adds to the impression that he is seeking sex, not love, when he propositions her). Margaret's fidelity is such that Marrok recognises the futility of persistence, and yet her exemplary response does not effect a positive outcome for her. The threat of rape in particular far exceeds the necessities of the plot at this point. It may offer a means of cementing Marrok's negative portrayal, aligning with the romance's self-identification as a 'gode ensaumpull' (10) by ensuring that adulterous desires are associated with a negative figure rather than being an understandable temptation. However, its excessive nature may

---

[23] The value of dogs compared to women as witnesses is also a feature of the *canis* legend that circulated as part of *The Seven Sages of Rome* tradition.

also cause the reader to pause and question the violence Marrok displays here. His vindictive response to Margaret's fidelity reflects a cultural perception of rejection as potentially dangerous for women, creating an environment in which rejection must be carefully framed in order not to cause offence. This is mentioned as a concern elsewhere in romance literature, albeit hyperbolically: in *Chaitivel*, Marie claims that

> Tutes les dames de une tere
> Vendreit il meuz d'amer requere
> Quë un fol de sun pan tolir;
> Kar cil volt an eire ferir.[24]

While this is a dramatic rather than a realistic claim, it may reflect an extreme version of reality. Punitive responses to resistance to love are relatively common in the works discussed in this book, and knowledge of the real danger of violent responses to rejection shapes women's responses to sexual advances in the modern and – it is probably safe to assume – the medieval world.[25] This is the operation of rape culture, forming part of the means by which it dominates women by 'keeping all women in fear of harm' and creates an atmosphere of fear in which 'no' is not safe or sufficient as a response to sexual pursuit.[26] By associating violent responses to rejection with the villain-ous Marrok, *Syr Tryamowre* goes beyond Marie's acknowledgement of this pattern to foreground it as a problem, opening it up to critique and protest.

An analogous pattern is followed by *The Erle of Tolous* and *The Frank-lin's Tale*, which configure resistance, empathy, and critique along similar lines. However, while Margaret is steadfast in her faithfulness to her husband throughout, these works shift the focus on exemplarity. When the Empress Beulybon rejects the two knights who proposition her during her husband's absence (a doubled role that heightens the link with 'Susanna and the Elders', as Jonathan Stavsky notes), she too behaves in an exemplary manner, her response in many ways closely echoing Margaret's.[27] Both question adulter-ous desires, describe the would-be lover as presumptuous, directly reject his adulterous advances, refer to the role he plays in the service of her husband,

---

[24] Marie de France, 'Chaitivel', in *Marie de France: Lais*, ed. by Alfred Ewert (London: Bristol Classical Press, 1995), pp. 116–22 (lines 19–22). 'It would be less dangerous for a man to court every lady in an entire land than for a lady to remove a single besotted lover from her skirts, for he will immediately attempt to strike back': Marie de France, 'Chaitivel', in *The Lais of Marie de France*, ed. & trans. by Glyn S. Burgess and Keith Busby, 2nd edn (London: Penguin, 2003), pp. 105–8 (p. 105).

[25] Violent responses to rejection are associated with modern 'incel' ideology: see Amia Srinivasan, 'The Right to Sex', in *The Right to Sex* (London: Bloomsbury, 2021), pp. 73–91; Laura Bates, 'Men Who Hate Women', in *Men Who Hate Women* (London: Simon & Schuster, 2020), pp. 11–62.

[26] Harris, *Obscene Pedagogies*, p. 10.

[27] Stavsky, 'Gode in all thynge', p. 550.

label his advances treachery, and threaten him with punitive consequences.[28] While some of these shared features remind the knight (and the reader) of the power balance between these figures and prompt the knight's attempt to prevent the lady revealing his advances to her husband, the women's questioning of adulterous desires and presumption also inscribe an emotional script for the innocent rejection of adultery. Questions like 'traytur, what ys thy thoght?' (*Syr Tryamowre*, 76), 'ys that youre wylle? / Yf hyt were myne, then dyd y ylle!' (*Erle of Tolous*, 646–7), 'how darste thou be so bolde?' (*Syr Tryamowre*, 84), and 'what woman holdyst thou me?' (*Erle of Tolous*, 648) express shock and anger at the knights' advances, emotional responses that effectively highlight the women's innocence.

However, while Beulybon's rejection of the two knights is exemplary, this is complicated by her relationship with Barnard, the Earl of Toulous, who falls in love with her and whom she eventually marries at the end of the romance, after her first husband's death. This relationship does not undermine Beulybon's resistance to adultery but enables a more nuanced portrayal of adulterous desire and exemplary conduct compared to *Syr Tryamowre*. The ambiguity of Beulybon's relationship with Barnard has been somewhat understated in critical approaches to *The Erle of Tolous*: Victoria Weiss suggests that 'the Earl of Tolouse and the Empress of Almayne [...] fall in love and suffer a series of misfortunes, before they are able to marry after the evil Emperor has died', while James Wade argues that the Empress is 'apparently mutually smitten (she gives him a ring)'.[29] As Wade's parenthetical explanation hints, the romance is quite ambiguous about Beulybon's feelings for Barnard. Although she gives him a ring, she does so when he asks for 'almes' (377), which was previously connected with Beulybon's virtue when she is described as being 'gode in all thynge, / Of almesdede and gode berynge' (40–1). While rings can be love-tokens in medieval romance,[30] they can also function in other ways: in the *Lai du Cor*, the Queen explains that the horn has labelled her adulterous because she once gave a ring to a boy in gratitude, although doubt may be cast on her explanation because she anticipates that the horn will shame her.[31] Operating as a dual token of apparent adultery and perhaps of innocence,

[28] See 'Syr Tryamowre', lines 76–108; 'The Erle of Tolous', lines 563–73, 646–57.
[29] Victoria L. Weiss, 'Blurring the Lines between the Play World and the Real World in "The Earl of Toulouse"', *Chaucer Review*, 31.1 (1996), 87–98 (p. 89); James Wade, 'Ungallant Knights', in *Heroes and Anti-Heroes in Medieval Romance*, ed. by Neil Cartlidge (Cambridge: D. S. Brewer, 2012), pp. 201–18 (p. 205).
[30] Rings appear as love-tokens in *King Horn, Guy of Warwick, Sir Isumbras, Sir Eglamour of Artois, Generydes, Sir Torrent of Portingale*, and *Amoryus and Cleopes*. The lady tries to give Gawain a ring in *Sir Gawain and the Green Knight*, but he refuses it. Rings can also appear as recognition tokens, for example in *Sir Tristrem, Lay le Freine*, and *Ipomadon*.
[31] See Robert Biket, *The Anglo-Norman Text of Le Lai du Cor*, ed. by C. T. Erickson, Anglo-Norman Texts, 24 (Oxford: Blackwell, 1973), lines 334–62; trans. in Robert Biket,

this ring provides a suggestive analogy to the ring in *The Erle of Tolous*.[32] But *The Erle of Tolous* is more emphatic about Beulybon's innocence than *Cor*, as Beulybon's confession of her gift to the Earl effectively expresses her innocence by revealing the relatively insignificant things she deems necessary to confess. In addition to the ring, we are also told that the Empress 'schewed opynly hur face, / For love of that knyght' (335–6), but even if we assume that love refers to romantic love here, this is a very brief reference that is counterbalanced by the more ambivalent representation of Beulybon's feelings for Barnard elsewhere.[33] There is no climactic, emotionally or sexually charged reunion between them after he has fought for her, as the romance instead highlights the peace established between the Earl and the Emperor. This focus may be heightened when reading the romance in Oxford, Bodleian Library, MS Ashmole 61, where its emphasis on friendship after a feud recalls the *exemplum* that immediately precedes *The Erle of Tolous*, *The Knight Who Forgave His Father's Slayer*. In addition, even Beulybon's will in her subsequent marriage to the Earl is elided, as it is 'be alexcion of the lordys free' (1202) that the Earl is made emperor and 'weddyd that lady to hys wyfe' (1207). Beulybon and Barnard's marriage is certainly a happy one, as they live 'wyth yoye and myrthe' (1208) and have fifteen children, a sign of sexual fulfilment that contrasts with the original Emperor's lack of heirs.[34] However, Beulybon is never actually said to want to marry the Earl. The romance 'work[s] hard to deflect the potentially illicit nature of the contact between Barnard and Beulybon' and in doing so takes a different approach to the relationship between rejections of adultery and exemplarity.[35]

Within the generic framework of romance, resistance to adultery is more likely than other kinds of resistance to love to be separated from the influence of desire and motivated instead by moral considerations. Although rejections

---

'Cor', in *Twenty-Four Lays from the French Middle Ages*, trans. by Glyn S. Burgess and Leslie C. Brook (Liverpool: Liverpool University Press, 2016), pp. 121–9 (p. 127).

[32] On the ring in *The Erle of Tolous*, see further Nicholas Perkins, 'Introduction: The Materiality of Medieval Romance and *The Erle of Tolous*', in *Medieval Romance and Material Culture*, ed. by Perkins (Cambridge: D. S. Brewer, 2015), pp. 1–22 (pp. 15–17).

[33] Blamires notes that the syntax here enables the possibility that this refers to Barnard's love of Beulybon, not hers of him: *The Case for Women*, p. 163. On the possibility of love meaning 'friendship' rather than romantic love, see definition 1a., 'Lǒve, n.(1)', *Middle English Dictionary*, ed. by Frances McSparran et al., Middle English Compendium (Ann Arbor: University of Michigan Library, 2000–18) <https://quod.lib.umich.edu/m/middle-english-dictionary/dictionary/MED26245> [accessed 19 July 2023].

[34] The Galenic idea that conception required female 'seed' (produced through orgasm) circulated widely, which would associate Beulybon's many pregnancies with sexual pleasure: see Corinne Saunders, *Rape and Ravishment in the Literature of Medieval England* (Cambridge: D. S. Brewer, 2001), p. 29; Cooper, *The English Romance in Time*, p. 222.

[35] Perkins, 'Introduction: The Materiality of Medieval Romance', pp. 13–14.

of love and marriage for the purpose of retaining virginity are common in saints' lives, in romance the generic expectation is that love between two worthy, equal, and single people will eventually be fulfilled in marriage (and sex). Fidelity to one's true love is important, but virginity is not usually preserved for its own sake. Resistance to adultery thus offers different insights into the operations of desire and morality since adulterous propositions can place them in a position of tension. The ambivalence of Beulybon's desire for the Earl encompasses the possibility that she does desire him but remains reluctant to commit adultery because of her loyalty to her husband. This need not 'radically revis[e] the conception of goodness underlying most narratives of righteous women on trial', as Stavsky argues; it may make Beulybon all the more praiseworthy to contemporary readers if she upholds her fidelity to her husband despite real temptation.[36] Unlike *Syr Tryamowre*, *The Erle of Tolous* does not necessarily condemn adulterous desire itself, but acting on such desires.[37]

The difference between desire and intention indeed differentiates the Earl's interactions with Beulybon from the knights'.[38] Barnard's speeches are marked by conditional and subjunctive expressions, as he wishes

> Y were so worthy a knyght
> That y myght be hur fere!
> And that sche no husbonde hadd. (365–7)

Likewise, when he receives the ring, he reflects

> Yf evyr y gete grace of the quene,
> That any love betwene us bene,
> Thys may be oure tokenyng. (403–5)

The knights' speeches, on the other hand, are characterised by warnings and imperatives, instructing Beulybon to 'graunt me youre love, / For the love of God' (643–4) and insisting

> But ye do aftur my rede,
> Certenly, y am but dede. (559–60)

To a modern reader this illuminates their sense of entitlement compared to the Earl's, but in their medieval context there is a parallel with scholastic views of

---

[36] Stavsky, 'Gode in all thynge', pp. 539–40.

[37] See further Arlyn Diamond, '*The Erle of Tolous*: The Price of Virtue', in *Medieval Insular Romance: Translation and Innovation*, ed. by Judith Weiss, Jennifer Fellows, and Morgan Dickson (Cambridge: D. S. Brewer, 2000), pp. 83–92 (p. 92).

[38] See also Myra Seaman's discussion of other differences in their approaches: *Objects of affection: The book and the household in late medieval England* (Manchester: Manchester University Press, 2021), pp. 103–4.

sin, which held that while feelings could not be helped, intent could be controlled to avoid sin.[39] This may be exactly what *The Erle of Tolous* portrays: although it avoids any direct reference to adulterous desire on the part of Beulybon, its narrative trajectory may tacitly admit the real possibility of desiring someone other than your marital partner. Acknowledging this possibility while avoiding committing adultery may have offered an important model for medieval readers, and perhaps particularly for the middle and upper classes. In these social circles, marriages were more likely to have been made on the basis of a short acquaintance or for family priorities rather than individual choice, which might have made people more prone to experience adulterous desires.[40] In addition, as men of these classes travelled for business, diplomacy, or war, their wives would be left alone for significant periods; as Katherine Harvey notes, wives and merchants were often asked about marital fidelity in confession, suggesting an association between travel and the potential for adultery.[41] In addition, 'while husbands were away, their wives were expected to keep friendship networks going for the practical advantages they could provide', engaging with 'respectable neighbour[s]', and 'cultivat[ing] [...] a network of social and business contacts'.[42] These situations may have opened up both the potential for and anxiety about adulterous desire, a dual perspective integrated into *The Erle of Tolous*. This romance seems to negotiate the line between friendship and adulterous desire carefully, ensuring that Beulybon earns the Earl's respect and affection without giving him anything more than the chance to admire her beauty and the gift of a ring. In this respect, it may distinguish gradations of affection that are more usually glossed over in romance representations of relationships between hero and heroine, but it also draws attention to the difficulties of making such distinctions.[43] *The Erle of Tolous* neither denies nor affirms Beulybon's desire for the Earl but does make

[39] See Holly A. Crocker, *The Matter of Virtue: Women's Ethical Action from Chaucer to Shakespeare* (Philadelphia: University of Pennsylvania Press, 2019), p. 10; Joan Cadden, *Nothing Natural Is Shameful: Sodomy and Science in Late Medieval Europe* (Philadelphia: University of Pennsylvania Press, 2014), p. 1.

[40] See Sara Butler, 'Runaway Wives: Husband Desertion in Medieval England', *Journal of Social History*, 40.2 (2006), 337–59 (p. 337).

[41] Katherine Harvey, *The Fires of Lust: Sex in the Middle Ages* (London: Reaktion, 2021), p. 27.

[42] Cathy Hume, *Chaucer and the Cultures of Love and Marriage* (Cambridge: D. S. Brewer, 2012), pp. 37–8; see also Cathy Hume, '"The name of soveraynetee": The Private and Public Faces of Marriage in *The Franklin's Tale*', *Studies in Philology*, 105.3 (2008), 284–303 (p. 292).

[43] This resonates with Brown's discussion of the relationship between Launcelot and the Maid of Astolat in the *Stanzaic Morte Arthur*: A. E. Brown, 'Lancelot in the Friend Zone: Strategies for Offering and Limiting Affection in the *Stanzaic Morte Arthur*', in *Emotion and Medieval Textual Media*, ed. by Mary C. Flannery (Turnhout: Brepols, 2018), pp. 75–97.

clear that whatever she feels, the important thing is her actions, in which she remains innocent of adultery.

Exemplary readings of *Syr Tryamowre* and *The Erle of Tolous* may have been encouraged and complicated by the manuscript contexts in which they survive. CUL Ff.2.38, in which both romances appear together, includes many religious and didactic texts alongside nine romances, some of which are themselves didactic in tone, such as *Robert of Cisyle* and *Le Bone Florence of Rome*.[44] The explicitly didactic works include two texts about adultery, *The Adulterous Falmouth Squire* and *How a Merchant did his Wife Betray*, placed shortly before the beginning of the romance section of the codex (at folios 56r–59r; the romances start at 63r).[45] The presence of *The Adulterous Falmouth Squire*, an afterlife vision in which a squire explains how he is being tortured in hell for committing adultery, seems likely to prompt the reader to attend to how *Syr Tryamowre* and *The Erle of Tolous* negotiate the issue of adultery. While this may draw attention to the exemplary portrayal of Margaret, the more nuanced approach of *The Erle of Tolous* is in tension with the extreme moral universe of the didactic work. Similarly, an exemplary reading of *The Erle of Tolous* may be both supported and questioned by its place in MS Ashmole 61. Lynne Blanchfield suggests 'it provides a complementary tale to the subsequent two exempla (items 22 and 23)', *The Jealous Wife* and *The Incestuous Daughter*, which are separated from *The Erle of Tolous* by *Lybeaus Desconus* and *Sir Corneus*.[46] In *The Jealous Wife*, suspicions of adultery are proven wrong, which may support Beulybon's innocence; *The Incestuous Daughter*, too, may highlight Beulybon's virtue in comparison with the daughter's extreme sexual sins. Rather than necessarily 'troubl[ing] the ethical preconditions of the other works', *The Erle of Tolous*'s moral yet nuanced approach to adultery seems to me to align precisely with Rory Critten's argument that medieval readers 'could conceive of good conduct as a shifting idea whose correct manifestation might change from one situation

---

[44] *Syr Tryamowre* is also preserved in the Percy Folio (as discussed later in this chapter), as well as in two fragments: Oxford, Bodleian Library, MS Eng. poet. d. 208 and Oxford, Bodleian Library, Rawlinson fragment. Their partial survival means they do not offer many insights into reading contexts. See 'MS. Eng. poet. d. 208', Medieval Manuscripts in Oxford Libraries (Bodleian Library, University of Oxford, 2017) <https://medieval.bodleian.ox.ac.uk/catalog/manuscript_4823> [accessed 5 February 2021]; Nicola McDonald et al., 'Sir Tryamour', *Database of Middle English Romance* (University of York, 2012) <https://www.middleenglishromance.org.uk/mer/65> [accessed 14 January 2021]. I discuss the manuscript contexts of *The Erle of Tolous* later in this chapter.

[45] Michael Johnston gives the folio numbers: *Romance and the Gentry in Late Medieval England* (Oxford: Oxford University Press, 2014), pp. 120–1.

[46] Lynne S. Blanchfield, 'The romances in MS Ashmole 61: an idiosyncratic scribe', in *Romance in Medieval England*, ed. by Maldwyn Mills, Jennifer Fellows, and Carol M. Meale (Cambridge: D. S. Brewer, 1991), pp. 65–87 (p. 66).

to the next'.[47] *The Erle of Tolous* acknowledges the possibility that desire can be in tension with morality but insists it need not triumph over willed fidelity, positioning it broadly in accord with the exemplary material that it circulated alongside.[48]

However, as with *Syr Tryamowre*, Beulybon's actions in *The Erle of Tolous* do not preserve her from danger, and it is all the more striking that this should be so in her interactions with the knights but not the Earl, given her potentially more morally dubious feelings for him (from the perspective of medieval Christian readers). While reasons of plot and characterisation underlie this, since Barnard as the romance hero is required to rescue the Empress rather than place her in danger for rejecting adultery, it also notably apportions blame for coercion to the men. That is, the romance indicates that it is not in any sense a victim's behaviour that provokes coercion or retribution but the violence and entitlement of those who coerce them. *The Erle of Tolous* thus approaches an acknowledgement of violence as a structural rather than personal issue. The knights seek to preserve their own lives and prevent Beulybon revealing their attempts at seduction, but they frame this as a vow to 'qwyte hur hur mede' (690), later admitting that they 'thoght hur to spylle / For sche wolde not do oure wylle' (1126–7). They had also previously plotted for one of them to coerce Beulybon into sex by catching her in the act with the other, again indicating the extent to which their pleas for love are actually sexual propositions – though this plan of course backfires. The knights then plot revenge for Beulybon's rejection, contributing to a cultural perception of rejection as dangerous and thus again making evident the dynamics of rape culture. The negative characterisation of these knights, who are ultimately punished for their treason by being burnt to death (again recalling 'Susanna and the Elders'), opens medieval rape culture up to critique.

The nuances of exemplary conduct and the dangers of rejecting men's advances in *The Erle of Tolous* offer models through which we might fruitfully reconsider *The Franklin's Tale*. Like Beulybon, we could understand Dorigen to inhabit an ambiguous moral position in her conduct towards Aurelius. While Susan Crane has pointed to the way Dorigen's 'impossible condition' introduces ambiguity into her rejection yet has suggested that this reflects the impossibility of saying no itself in romance, *Syr Tryamowre* and *The Erle of Tolous* illustrate that it is possible to say no and for that no to be taken seriously in romance literature – at least when what is being rejected is adulterous

---

[47] Rory G. Critten, 'Bourgeois Ethics Again: The Conduct Texts and the Romances in Oxford, Bodleian Library MS Ashmole 61', *Chaucer Review*, 50.1–2 (2015), 108–33 (pp. 132, 124).

[48] See further Seaman's discussion of the ethical slippage of *The Erle of Tolous*: *Objects of affection*, pp. 106–8.

sex.[49] Dorigen does clearly reject Aurelius, but her addition of the 'impossible condition' means he does not entirely give up on obtaining her love – although he does at first despair, indicating that he recognises an element of outright rejection in Dorigen's speech. The impossible condition is presented specifically as an addition through the structure of her response. She uses the vocabulary of outright rejection up to her affirmation of her 'fynal answere' (987), which marks out the point at which her response, if it is to accord with the accused queens' refusal of adultery, should, but does not, end. The intervening narratorial comment, 'but after that in pley thus seyde she' (988), also brackets off her shift to conditionality as a new and different direction. While some scholars have argued that what comes after Dorigen's 'fynal answere' should not be considered a true part of her response, I suggest instead that these speech markers indicate Dorigen's combination of different kinds of romance vocabulary.[50] The start and end of her answer align with the unambiguous rejections of adultery in accused queen romances, while the middle section diverts to the conditional vocabulary used by single characters like Felice or Horn when rejecting love. I am not suggesting that Dorigen should be blamed by the reader for this: although Aurelius's injunction 'every wyf be war of hire biheeste!' (1541) may attribute blame to Dorigen, the Franklin's earlier reflection on the ease of misspeaking (779–84) seems to pre-emptively absolve her. She could be read as turning to a condition in an attempt to avoid the dangers of rejection, which Beulybon's and Margaret's experiences make evident.[51] That Dorigen instead finds herself in a different kind of danger – in danger of committing adultery – testifies to the difficulty of finding a safe way to reject sexual advances within heteropatriarchal societies.

Turning from the vocabulary of rejecting adultery to that of a single person deferring love opens up a productive space of ambiguity within romance

---

[49] Susan Crane, *Gender and Romance in Chaucer's 'Canterbury Tales'* (Princeton: Princeton University Press, 1994), pp. 62–3, 65.

[50] For example, see John A. Pitcher, *Chaucer's Feminine Subjects: Figures of Desire in the 'Canterbury Tales'* (New York: Palgrave Macmillan, 2012), p. 68; Alison Ganze, '"My Trouth for to Holde – Allas, Allas!": Dorigen and Honor in the *Franklin's Tale*', *Chaucer Review*, 42.3 (2008), 312–29 (pp. 317–18); Carol A. Pulham, 'Promises, Promises: Dorigen's Dilemma Revisited', *Chaucer Review*, 31.1 (1996), 76–86 (p. 83). For a discussion of this and a rebuttal of the idea that a promise made 'in pley' compromises the legal validity of Dorigen's vow, see Neil Cartlidge, '"Nat that I chalange any thyng of right": Love, Loyalty, and Legality in the *Franklin's Tale*', in *Writings on Love in the English Middle Ages*, ed. by Helen Cooney (New York: Palgrave Macmillan, 2006), pp. 115–30 (p. 121).

[51] In this respect, Dorigen may also offer a parallel with Margery in *Dame Sirith*, who Alice Raw has recently argued may attempt to 'convey non-consent less directly in a situation where she is under threat': Alice Raw, 'Readers Then and Now: Coerced Consent in *Dame Sirith*', *Studies in the Age of Chaucer*, 44 (2022), 'Colloquium: Historicizing Consent: Bodies, Wills, Desires', ed. by Carissa M. Harris and Fiona Somerset, 307–14 (p. 311).

writing. While the accused queen romances tend to portray adultery in a negative light, other romances (particularly works written in or translated from French) use adultery to indicate desirability, deploying it to celebrate chivalric prowess and romantic love outside of marriage. *The Franklin's Tale* seems poised between these two traditions, its place highlighting the significance of Cooper's question: 'romances in part feed their audiences' appetite for fantasy; but that statement invites the question, whose fantasy?'.[52] Rather than focusing on the audience's relation to fantasy, I want to explore this question with regard to the fantasies associated with particular characters.[53] *The Franklin's Tale* incorporates elements that, in different circumstances, could provide a fantasy for Dorigen, with an attentive extra-marital lover who highlights her desirability and fulfils an impossible challenge for her love. But instead, what might seem like a fantasy is exposed as 'a trappe' (1341), a cause of 'feere' (1347) and 'compleynt' (1354). The Franklin does not seem to direct us to this reading of the tale, instead urging his audience to consider the *gentillesse* of Arveragus, Aurelius, and the Clerk in his concluding question. I therefore attribute this focus to Chaucer: in turning the adulterous fantasies of other romances into a nightmare, Chaucer seems to probe the moral lacunae of romance, exposing the limits of its exemplary functions. Aurelius behaves as if he is in a romance of adultery, while Dorigen adopts the wrong model of behaviour from romance, suggesting the misunderstandings that can occur when the genre is taken as exemplary. Chaucer seems to have felt some ambivalence towards romance as a genre:

> Chaucer uses the word 'romaunz' only rarely, and never to describe any of his own works. The sole occurrence of the term in the *Canterbury Tales*, although they certainly include works that we would consider romances, is in the tale of *Sir Thopas*, which [...] satirizes the popular romance tradition.[54]

While *Syr Tryamowre* and *The Erle of Tolous* hold firm to the notion that romance can offer a 'gode ensaumpull' (10), *The Franklin's Tale* undermines this, instead pointing to the ways in which romance intersects with fabliaux in its portrayal of adulterous sex and emphasis on exchange.[55] Overlaps between romance and fabliaux portrayals of desire or lust are also presented in

---

[52] Cooper, *The English Romance in Time*, p. 225.

[53] Pitcher explores the fantasy elements for Aurelius: *Chaucer's Feminine Subjects*, p. 65.

[54] Corinne Saunders, 'Chaucer's Romances', in *A Companion to Romance from Classical to Contemporary*, ed. by Corinne Saunders (Malden, MA: Blackwell, 2004), pp. 85–103 (p. 85).

[55] See further Ben Parsons, 'No Laughing Matter: Fraud, the Fabliau and Chaucer's Franklin's Tale', *Neophilologus*, 96.1 (2012), 121–36; and the broader discussion in Louise M. Sylvester, 'Romance Debased', in *Medieval Romance and the Construction of Heterosexuality* (New York: Palgrave Macmillan, 2008), pp. 129–60.

Chaucer's *Merchant's Tale*, perhaps again indicating a focus on deconstructing whose interests romance and its claims of exemplarity serves.

Like the accused queen romances, *The Franklin's Tale* also incorporates issues of coercion, which it seems to portray negatively. Dorigen is clearly unwilling to commit adultery with Aurelius: she is 'astoned' (1339) when he meets her condition, her bloodless face recalling that of Custance in scenes of her distress, where her paleness seems to function as an affective marker inviting empathy with her situation. Dorigen further displays her sorrow and confusion when she is sent to Aurelius by Arveragus, appearing 'half as she were mad' (1511) and crying 'allas, allas' (1513). This, and the Franklin's pre-emptive assertion that we should not judge Arveragus before we have heard the tale's end (1493–8), suggests that Dorigen being sent to Aurelius against her will is supposed to make us uncomfortable. Both Aurelius's attempt to hold Dorigen to her word and Arveragus sending her to Aurelius seem to be framed negatively, recalling the association of coercion and violence with the much more extremely negative characters in *Syr Tryamowre* and *The Erle of Tolous*. But I have also suggested that *The Franklin's Tale* opens up connections with other kinds of romances, including through Dorigen's use of the type of vocabulary the proud ladies might deploy to defer love. How might the portrayal of coercion in romances where adultery is rejected relate to the operation of coercion as a means of enforcing normative desire in the other romances discussed in this book?

In the context of resisting adultery, coercion and violence function as strategies of the desperate and vengeful – or in Aurelius's case, the desperately mistaken – not as an acceptable means to begin a romantic relationship. Might reading these romances therefore change the way we understand works in which those who are apathetic or hostile to love are punished? Addressing the diversity of gendered roles in medieval popular romance, Joanne Charbonneau and Désirée Cromwell argue that

> Even in the absence of a direct juxtaposition between good and evil archetypes, the distinctive construction of female identity depicted in any given romance stands in stark contrast to their opposing roles in other romance texts. The good daughter or faithful wife thus acts as antidote to the unfaithful and adulterous wife of other romances.[56]

Wade also reminds us that fruitful comparisons can be made not only in a broad generic context but on a smaller level between works that appear in the same manuscript. He suggests

---

[56] Joanne Charbonneau and Désirée Cromwell, 'Gender and Identity in the Popular Romance', in *A Companion to Medieval Popular Romance*, ed. by Raluca L. Radulescu and Cory James Rushton (Cambridge: D. S. Brewer, 2009), pp. 96–110 (p. 101).

the manuscript contexts of these romances can have a significant effect on how they might have been read for the moral, or rather on how early audiences might have used these miscellaneous combinations of texts to calibrate their understanding of the moral implications of particular romance heroes.[57]

In sketching a few possibilities for how vengeful responses to the rejection of adultery might interact with the positive or neutral depiction of punitive responses to single people who reject love, then, I begin by examining the manuscript contexts in which such works appear.

Taking *Syr Tryamowre* as an example, this work appears in CUL Ff.2.38 with *The Erle of Tolous* and *Guy of Warwick*, and in the Percy Folio (London, British Library, MS Additional 27879) alongside fourteen other romances, including *Eger and Grime* – a romance where romantic a(nti)pathy is treated punitively. Might reading *Syr Tryamowre*, which proclaims its heroine's innocence and the wrongful nature of her accusation and punishment, affect responses to Winglayne in *Eger and Grime*? While such an inquiry remains speculative, two main possibilities suggest themselves. The first is that reading *Syr Tryamowre*'s narrative of an innocent woman wrongfully accused and punished might not have affected a reading of *Eger and Grime*, because the difference between rejecting adulterous sex and rejecting love as a single person may have prohibited intersecting responses. This was an important distinction for medieval readers: Sara Torres notes that in *La querelle de la Belle Dame sans mercy*, one of the works that defends the *belle dame*, the *Dame Loyale en Amour*, recasts her not as a haughty figure who rejects love but as a faithful lover who resists seduction in order to remain true to her prior lover.[58] The *Dame Loyale en Amour* thus does not protest the idea that women owe men love (or sex), but indicates that fidelity to a pre-established relationship is an acceptable reason to refuse love, highlighting the extent to which these scenarios were differentiated. However, this division might not be so absolute as to prevent any transfer of meaning between the two kinds of episode. A reader who noted Margaret's innocence and the way in which assumptions of male trustworthiness conspire to allow her to be wrongfully punished might pause to consider whether Winglayne of *Eger and Grime* really merits so negative a depiction as she receives, without undermining the difference between rejecting adultery and rejecting a potential marital partner. In this case, then, these two episodes might facilitate resistant readings by those primed to respond in such a way.

---

[57] Wade, 'Ungallant Knights', p. 203.
[58] Sara V. Torres, '*Sans merci*: Affect, Resistance, and Sociality in Courtly Lyric', *Studies in the Age of Chaucer*, 44 (2022), 'Colloquium: Historicizing Consent', ed. by Harris and Somerset, 325–34 (pp. 332–3).

The Erle of Tolous opens up different areas of inquiry: as well as Ff.2.38 and MS Ashmole 61, this romance appears in Lincoln Cathedral Library, MS 91 (the Lincoln Thornton manuscript), alongside *Sir Degrevant*. In Chapter 2, I argued that *Sir Degrevant* offers us an emotional lacuna in Melidor's transition to loving Degrevant, attending with much greater precision and insight to Degrevant's own emotions. This pattern is reflected in *The Erle of Tolous*, potentially casting a different light upon its ambivalent representation of Beulybon's feelings for Barnard. I argued above that this ambiguity might reflect a reluctance to acknowledge adulterous desires openly, but comparison with *Sir Degrevant* may instead suggest that the romance is simply not that interested in Beulybon's emotions. The important trajectory here may be the establishment of the Earl's goodness, which eventually leads to him marrying the Empress, and the development of her love for him may not be important to this emphasis. We could also read these two narratives' connections in the opposite direction, however: while not a romance that particularly emphasises the use of coercion, *Sir Degrevant* does contain the scene in which Degrevant surprises Melidor and her maid within her castle gardens. In comparison with the knights' intrusive propositions in Beulybon's chamber, Degrevant's pursuit of Melidor may appear more or less threatening. The relative privacy of the garden offers an opportunity for sexual coercion, as it does in *Amis and Amiloun*, working in tension with its role as a *locus amoenus* in which love can be freely exchanged, but Degrevant behaves with more courtesy and less violence than the two knights in *The Erle of Tolous*.

Looking beyond the confines of individual codices, the accused queen romances and *The Franklin's Tale* may act as counter-narratives to the prevailing norms of gender and sexuality elsewhere in romance literature, challenging perceptions of women as fickle, coercive assertions of love as an obligation, and the glamorisation of adultery. Adultery is perceived negatively in each of these works, endowing them with an exemplary function, although they also gesture to the limits of exemplarity by acknowledging that even a perfect response to a sexual proposition does not guarantee safety. In doing so, they implicitly recognise that the conduct of the victim is irrelevant to the perpetrator of coercion, challenging medieval (and modern) rape culture's reliance upon victim-blaming. These romances, read in combination with works depicting romantic a(nti)pathy, may therefore encourage a reader to question the way unwilling lovers are punished or manipulated for their resistance to love. For example, comparative reading of this kind may invite us to notice that Blanchardyn forcibly kissing Eglantine reflects male chivalric entitlement rather than a reasonable response to her pride, or that the Fere does not deserve to be repeatedly abandoned by Ipomadon simply because she did not at first think he could accord with her vow. Challenging these perspectives may be seen as a modern way of looking at these works, but the different insights offered by the role of coercion in narratives where adultery is rejected reveal that medieval rape culture was not a monolith either, and some diversity of views – some counter-narratives – existed for those enabled to pursue them.

Locating Desire and Power in *Sir Gawain and the Green Knight*

The anonymous late fourteenth-century romance *Sir Gawain and the Green Knight* directly draws the reader's attention to the workings of medieval rape culture, as the lady tells Gawain

> Ȝe ar stif innoghe to constrayne wyth strenkþe, ȝif yow lykez,
> Ȝif any were so vilanous þat yow devaye wolde.[59]

Assuring Gawain that he could take with force anything that is denied him, the lady conjures the spectre of the Gawain who commits rape or coercive sexual encounters in other romances, such as the Old French *First Continuation* and *Fourth Continuation* of *Perceval*, *Lybeaus Desconus*, or the *Jeaste of Sir Gawain*.[60] That this is a Gawain she seems to admire supports the rape myth of women as secretly desiring rape. But the lady's words also draw attention to the class dynamics of medieval rape culture, since, as Monica Brzezinski Potkay argues, she effectively suggests that 'ladies will submit to him and he can rape any woman who's not a lady'.[61] Gawain responds in terms that do not disagree with her but that do try to turn away from the potential for violence:

[59] *Sir Gawain and the Green Knight*, ed. by J. R. R. Tolkien and E. V. Gordon, 2nd edn, rev. by Norman Davis (Oxford: Clarendon Press, 1967), lines 1496–7.

[60] For discussion of Gauvain and rape in the *First Continuation* of *Perceval*, see Amy N. Vines, 'Invisible Woman: Rape as a Chivalric Necessity in Medieval Romance', in *Sexual Culture in the Literature of Medieval Britain*, ed. by Amanda Hopkins, Robert Allen Rouse, and Cory James Rushton (Cambridge: D. S. Brewer, 2014), pp. 161–80 (pp. 167–74). For the *Fourth Continuation*, see Cory James Rushton, 'Gawain as Lover in Middle English Literature', in *The Erotic in the Literature of Medieval Britain*, ed. by Amanda Hopkins and Cory James Rushton (Cambridge: D. S. Brewer, 2007), pp. 27–37 (p. 30). In *Lybeaus Desconus*, the description of Gyngeleyn as 'getyn [...] of Sir Gawyne / By a forest syde' recalls the location of rape in the *pastourelle*, *The Wife of Bath's Tale*, and some real-life examples, suggesting a coercive sexual encounter: 'Lybeaus Desconus', in *Codex Ashmole 61: A Compilation of Popular Middle English Verse*, ed. by George Shuffelton, TEAMS (Kalamazoo: Medieval Institute Publications, 2008), pp. 111–64 (lines 8–9). On the *Jeaste*, in which Gawain may or may not actually rape the lady, see Sarah Lindsay, 'Chivalric Failure in *The Jeaste of Sir Gawain*', *Arthuriana*, 21.4 (2011), 23–41 (pp. 27, 32, 34).

[61] Monica Brzezinski Potkay, 'The Violence of Courtly Exegesis in *Sir Gawain and the Green Knight*', in *Representing Rape in Medieval and Early Modern Literature*, ed. by Elizabeth Robertson and Christine M. Rose (New York: Palgrave, 2001), pp. 97–124 (p. 105). See also David Mills, 'An Analysis of the Temptation Scenes in *Sir Gawain and the Green Knight*', *Journal of English and Germanic Philology*, 67.4 (1968), 612–30 (pp. 623–4); J. A. Burrow, *A Reading of 'Sir Gawain and the Green Knight'* (London: Routledge & Kegan Paul, 1965), p. 91.

Ʒe, be God [...] good is your speche,
Bot þrete is vnþryuande in þede þer I lende. (1498–9)

In affirming the truth of her words, Gawain acknowledges that he could rape the lady,[62] but insists that in the Arthurian court rape is considered improper, indicating a different framework for sexual ethics while not altogether erasing the violence to which the lady refers. These lines offer a characteristic glimpse of how *Sir Gawain and the Green Knight* both integrates and turns away from the narrative and ethical traditions of other Gawain romances. This work problematises and expands upon the focus on rape and force, taking a capacious approach to medieval power dynamics by revealing how they can operate through precise, contextually dependent categories.

Like *The Erle of Tolous*, *Sir Gawain* provides a nuanced perspective on adulterous desire, as it implies that Gawain desires the lady but still resists her adulterous propositions.[63] These works therefore implicitly challenge the idea that non-consent occurs 'only when there is no ambiguity in the words or actions of the victim'.[64] Gawain is clearly keen to make the lady's acquaintance when he first sees her: after a description of her beauty, in which we are told she is 'wener þen Wenore, as þe wyʒe þoʒt' (945), Gawain greets the two ladies, and 'þe loueloker he lappez a lyttel in armez', then 'askez / To be her seruaunt' (973–6). They also enjoy each other's company at the feast:

> Such comfort of her compaynye caʒten togeder
> Þurʒ her dere dalyaunce of her derne wordez,
> Wyth clene cortays carp closed fro fylþe,
> Þat hor play watz passande vche prynce gomen. (1011–14)

Of course, even here the *Gawain*-poet is careful to distinguish between enjoyment of each other's company and adulterous desire: their conversation is 'clene cortays carp closed fro fylþe'. But Gawain's admiration of the lady's beauty and enjoyment of her company suggest he does feel desire for her, if desire that is moderated by restraint, as with Beulybon and Barnard in *The Erle of Tolous*.[65] *Sir Gawain* invites empathy for Gawain in part by positioning his struggle to avoid the lady's temptation as one to which the reader is

---

[62] I therefore do not see him as straightforwardly rebuking her, as Heng argues: Geraldine Heng, 'A Woman Wants: The Lady, *Gawain*, and the Forms of Seduction', *Yale Journal of Criticism*, 5.3 (1992), 101–34 (p. 107).

[63] My interpretation here departs from those who see Gawain as entirely uninterested in the lady's advances: see, for example, Brzezinski Potkay, 'The Violence of Courtly Exegesis', p. 102; Mills, 'An Analysis of the Temptation Scenes', p. 621.

[64] Leah Schwebel, 'Chaucer and the Fantasy of Retroactive Consent', *Studies in the Age of Chaucer*, 44 (2022), 'Colloquium: Historicizing Consent', ed. by Harris and Somerset, 337–45 (p. 344).

[65] Mann similarly argues for the focus on Gawain controlling his desires: Jill Mann, 'Courtly Aesthetics and Courtly Ethics in *Sir Gawain and the Green Knight*', in *Life in*

given intimate access, in contrast to our lack of access to the lady's thoughts. This focus on Gawain as an exemplary though imperfect figure who experiences temptation aligns with his role in the poem's much-debated ending as a knight who accepts his flaws yet is still deemed 'on þe fautlest freke þat euer on fote 3ede' (2363).

This careful balance between desire and restraint is developed by the shift in their relationship that seems to occur when they move from the hall to the chamber. Gawain seems particularly concerned about their relationship in the chamber scenes, drawing attention to the difference between their joyful conversation in the hall, where they are watched by others, and the tension of the scenes that take place (apparently) without others watching. When the lady enters Gawain's chamber, Gawain 'schamed' (1189), and he pretends to sleep while he

> Compast in his concience to quat þat cace my3t
> Meue oþer amount – to meruayle hym þo3t.[66]

Gawain's response indicates the unusual and improper nature of the lady's actions: her intrusion into the chamber marks a stage of their relationship with which Gawain is less comfortable, indicating his unwillingness to overstep the boundary of adulterous desire, and revealing the way in which a relationship might differ (or appear to differ) depending on its physical location in particular spaces.[67] Although the public/private dichotomy is a post-medieval way of thinking, relative senses of public and private still existed in the Middle Ages, particularly in terms of how a space was used.[68] While the late medieval chamber was not necessarily a 'private' place, Hollie Morgan notes that 'the chamber in literary texts is almost always private, and for the sole use of the protagonists', however different this was from the everyday reality for most medieval people.[69] Gawain's concern about spending time with the lady in a relatively private place reveals the ways in which desire and control are differently inflected according to their

Words: Essays on Chaucer, the Gawain-Poet, and Malory, ed. by Mark David Rasmussen (Toronto: University of Toronto Press, 2014), pp. 187–220 (p. 217).

[66] *Sir Gawain and the Green Knight*, lines 1196–7. For discussion of the ethical importance of this pretence at sleep, see Megan G. Leitch, *Sleep and its spaces in Middle English literature: Emotions, ethics, dreams* (Manchester: Manchester University Press, 2021), pp. 131–4.

[67] See further Megan G. Leitch, 'Enter the Bedroom: Managing Space for the Erotic in Middle English Romance', in *Sexual Culture in the Literature of Medieval Britain*, pp. 39–53 (pp. 45, 47).

[68] See Shannon McSheffrey, 'Place, Space, and Situation: Public and Private in the Making of Marriage in Late-Medieval London', *Speculum*, 79.4 (2004), 960–90 (pp. 961, 977).

[69] Hollie L. S. Morgan, *Beds and Chambers in Late Medieval England: Readings, Representations and Realities* (York: York Medieval Press, 2017), p. 41.

precise context, perhaps reflecting back on the coercive dynamics of the chamber scenes in the accused queen romances.

The power balance between Gawain and the lady is also affected by the social dynamics of the space they inhabit, in which Gawain is a guest and the lady a host or hostess, adding to her 'implicit right to be dominant within the chamber'.[70] While Ad Putter discusses the importance of hospitality in this poem and earlier French romances, he concentrates primarily on why the audiences for these works might have been interested in the behaviours and dangers associated with hospitality; here, I address how this affects our interpretation of the seduction scenes.[71] The role of a female host is a complex and ambiguous one, as Judith Still notes, observing that women operate more often as hostesses, who 'impl[y] hospitality offered by the master of the house', acting only as 'an intermediary'.[72] In this romance, part of the problem Gawain faces is the ambiguity as to whether the lady acts as an extension of her husband's hospitality or whether she becomes a host in her own right within the confines of the chamber, a problem that further makes use of the ambiguous space of the chamber as both 'belong[ing] to the head of the household' and as a location in which women were able to exert particular agency.[73] Gawain's sense of tension between his loyalty to Bertilak and reluctance to offend the lady seems to suggest that he reads her as his host within the chamber, but Bertilak's climactic revelation reimposes the role of hostess rather than host upon his wife by suggesting that she was acting on his orders after all. Regardless of this precise role, as a host or hostess the lady holds a certain power over Gawain, which may be aligned or in tension with her husband's influence. Still argues that it is an 'imbalance of power that creates the need for hospitality in the first place', while Jacques Derrida notes that 'hospitality' derives from a combination of *hostis* (stranger/enemy) and *potis* (to have mastery or power), indicating that the potential for violence is inherent within hospitality.[74] Gawain's dependency upon Bertilak and his wife is emphasised by the circumstances in which he arrives at the castle, 'ner slayn wyth þe slete' (729) and praying for 'sum herber þer heȝly I myȝt here

---

[70] *Ibid.*, p. 219.

[71] Ad Putter, *Sir Gawain and the Green Knight and French Arthurian Romance* (Oxford: Clarendon Press, 1995), pp. 51–99.

[72] Judith Still, *Derrida and Hospitality: Theory and Practice* (Edinburgh: Edinburgh University Press, 2010), p. 21.

[73] Morgan, *Beds and Chambers*, p. 219.

[74] Still, *Derrida and Hospitality*, p. 13; Jacques Derrida, 'Hostipitality', in *Acts of Religion*, ed. & trans. by Gil Anidjar (London: Routledge, 2001), pp. 356–420 (pp. 401–2, 361–2). See also Emile Benveniste, 'Hospitality', in *Indo-European Language and Society*, trans. by Elizabeth Palmer (London: Faber & Faber, 1973), pp. 71–83, whose etymology Derrida is following. For a discussion of these aspects of hospitality in *Sir Gawain*, see Putter, *Sir Gawain and the Green Knight and French Arthurian Romance*, pp. 52–3, 76–99.

masse' (755). The balance of knowledge and power between these figures is also unequal: Gawain relies on Bertilak's assistance to find the Green Chapel, and while he does not even know his host's name, Bertilak and his court know Gawain's identity and purpose.[75] The roles of stranger and host are almost reversed, as Bertilak and his wife seem the strange and unknown figures to the reader and potentially to Gawain, while Gawain is all too well known to them and, of course, is the focal point of the reader's knowledge.[76] In keeping with this imbalance of knowledge, Bertilak controls and directs their relationship, suggesting the exchange of winnings and their respective roles within it: this seems to approach the need to 'act with "excess," make an absolute gift of his property' seen as characteristic of the impossibility of unconditional hospitality in modern philosophy.[77] But this imbalance of power also highlights Gawain's dependency on and vulnerability to Bertilak and his wife. His situation as the guest of Bertilak and his wife in some ways recalls that of Horn, Amis, and Bevis, who depend on the hospitality of another court, providing a suggestive resonance that hints at Gawain's potential vulnerability in these scenes.

Gawain's desire neither to 'lach þer hir luf, oþer lodly refuse' (1772) may recall the accused queen narratives and *The Franklin's Tale* with its emphasis on not causing offence. However, Gawain's concern seems to differ from the women's, as while the outcome of the queens' refusal highlights the dangers of any rejection whatsoever, Gawain's wish not to appear 'lodly' seems to reflect a concern with how the lady might perceive him. Although Putter suggests 'the face Gawain is trying to save […] is not his own, but the Lady's', it is 'his cortaysye' for which Gawain 'cared' (1773), and he is preoccupied with whether or not he is living up to his reputation as Gawain throughout these scenes and in the poem more widely.[78] There remains, then, an element of gendered power structuring the scene and its anxieties: Gawain is not so concerned as to truly fear retribution if he rejects the lady, and his wish not to offend her is perhaps an act of generosity rather than self-preservation. Yet this is not the only power dynamic shaping the scene, as the lady's role as host/hostess enables her to exert pressure and coercion upon Gawain; that her

---

[75] See lines 901–9. Derrida addresses the significance of names in hospitality: Anne Dufourmantelle and Jacques Derrida, *Of Hospitality*, trans. by Rachel Bowlby (Stanford: Stanford University Press, 2000), pp. 27–9.

[76] However, their knowledge of Gawain may be somewhat misleading. See Carolyne Larrington, 'English Chivalry and Sir Gawain and the Green Knight', in *A Companion to Arthurian Literature*, ed. by Helen Fulton (Chichester: Wiley-Blackwell, 2009), pp. 264–76 (pp. 269–70).

[77] *Deconstruction in a Nutshell: A Conversation with Jacques Derrida*, ed. by John D. Caputo (New York: Fordham University Press, 2021), p. 111.

[78] Putter, *Sir Gawain and the Green Knight and French Arthurian Romance*, p. 120.

213

hospitable role is crucial to this is borne out by the parallels Putter identifies in other romances where a knight is propositioned by a host or hostess figure.[79]

It is not difficult to identify elements of coercion in the lady's advances: although she tells Gawain that he could rape her if he wanted to and insists 'me behouez of fyne force / Your seruaunt be', it is she who jokingly threatens to 'bynde yow in your bedde' and claims to have 'kaȝt' him.[80] Moreover, that she enters his chamber while he is sleeping in the first and third seduction scenes may obliquely echo perhaps the most famous classical narrative that intertwines rape and hospitality, the rape of Lucretia, in which Tarquin is entertained by her as a guest and enters her chamber at night to rape her.[81] I do not want to conflate Lucretia's experience with Gawain's: the violence to which Lucretia is subjected is very different to the flirtation and potential sin that Gawain must negotiate (sin being the frame of reference Gawain brings, and medieval Christian readers probably would have brought, to this episode). I do not agree with Brzezinski Potkay that 'seduction slides into rape'; rather, my more moderate proposition is that we should recognise that Gawain is in a situation in which the lady is capable of coercing him.[82] There has tended to be a perception of the lady's actions as comic amongst critics who have focused primarily on the gender dynamics of their exchange, reflecting a broader, enduring stereotype that 'sexual violence against men is funny'.[83] Judith Weiss, for example, refers to Gawain's unease with the lady entering his chamber as 'a delightful moment of comic surprise', noting that 'for hundreds of years romances and novels have [...] portrayed women who take the initiative in courtship comically and critically'.[84] Yet the first scene in which the lady enters the chamber may carry something of horror in it, as well as the shift to social comedy in Gawain's awkward response to her unexpected entry. The half-heard sound of 'a littel dyn at his dor' (1183) that awakens

---

[79] *Ibid.*, pp. 117–18, 123–6.

[80] *Sir Gawain and the Green Knight*, lines 1239–40, 1211, 1225. See Brzezinski Potkay on the connection of 'force' with terms for rape: 'The Violence of Courtly Exegesis', pp. 106–7.

[81] See the discussion of Lucretia in Saunders, *Rape and Ravishment*, pp. 152–77.

[82] Brzezinski Potkay, 'The Violence of Courtly Exegesis', p. 108.

[83] Tanaka Mhishi, *Sons and Others: On Loving Male Survivors* (n.p.: 404 Ink, 2022), p. 2.

[84] Judith Weiss, 'The wooing woman in Anglo-Norman romance', in *Romance in Medieval England*, pp. 149–61 (p. 149). See also Susan Signe Morrison, 'The Body: Unstable, Gendered, Theorized', in *A Cultural History of Comedy in the Middle Ages*, ed. by Martha Bayless (London: Bloomsbury Academic, 2020), pp. 99–119 (pp. 111–13); Joseph E. Gallagher, '"Trawþe" and "luf-talkyng" in *Sir Gawain and the Green Knight*', *Neuphilologische Mitteilungen*, 78.4 (1977), 362–76 (pp. 369–72); Mills, 'An Analysis of the Temptation Scenes', pp. 612–13; Burrow, *A Reading of 'Sir Gawain and the Green Knight'*, p. 78. Mann offers a view of humour coupled with seriousness more similar to my own: 'Sir Gawain and the Romance Hero', in *Life in Words*, pp. 221–34 (p. 228).

Gawain and the instinctive urge to see what the noise might be, as 'a corner of þe cortyn he caȝt vp a lyttel' (1185), are a recognisably alarming situation in which to wake up.[85] While the lady's entrance is a comic anti-climax, the subtle predatory undertones of her entry may be reflected in the interlaced hunting scenes, which seem to position Gawain as hunted and the lady as a hunter.[86] There are elements of comedy in the seduction scenes, to be sure, but they may seem less comic and more threatening when we take into account the vulnerable position of Gawain as a guest in this household. The attendant potential for violence that accompanies hospitality is already a theme of the poem through the beheading game and the description of the hunt, and the lady's actions may work with these threads to suggest a more dangerous aspect to her seduction. This is compounded by Bertilak's later reinterpretation of the power dynamics behind the scenes in the chamber, when he claims that it was he who 'wroȝt' his wife's wooing (2361), suggesting a conspiracy between wife and husband, hostess and host, which reveals the extent of their control over the situation. Regardless of how we interpret the ending, Bertilak's final revelations do seem to return to and compound the imbalance of power between host and guest, indicating the issues of volition, consent, and will at play in this dynamic. In this light, *Sir Gawain* may further illustrate the range of people who are the targets of sexual coercion in medieval romance. This romance draws attention to the specific contexts in which gendered power dynamics can be reconfigured through alternative systems of power such as hospitality, providing a more capacious view of who was affected by medieval rape culture, as victim-survivors or perpetrators.

'That I ded was ayenste my wylle':
Sexual Violence and the Vulnerability of Malory's Launcelot

In Malory's *Morte Darthur*, Launcelot's resistance to infidelity is complicated by the fact that the relationship to which he tries to be faithful is itself adulterous, and is a relationship about which Malory is notably and deliberately ambiguous.[87] At the start of 'Sir Launcelot du Lake', Malory tells us that 'Quene Gwenyvere had [Launcelot] in grete favoure aboven all other knyghtis,

---

[85] See further Jordi Sánchez-Martí on this sonic moment and its 'reality effect': 'Noise, Sound and Silence in *Sir Gawain and the Green Knight*', in *Medieval Romance, Arthurian Literature: Essays in Honour of Elizabeth Archibald*, ed. by A. S. G. Edwards (Cambridge: D. S. Brewer, 2021), pp. 111–26 (pp. 123–6).

[86] See, for example, the discussion of this parallel (and its limits) in Burrow, *A Reading of 'Sir Gawain and the Green Knight'*, pp. 86–7, 98–9; Henry L. Savage, 'The Significance of the Hunting Scenes in Sir Gawain and the Green Knight', *Journal of English and Germanic Philology*, 27.1 (1928), 1–15.

[87] Sir Thomas Malory, *Le Morte Darthur*, ed. by P. J. C. Field, 2 vols (Cambridge: D. S. Brewer, 2013), I, 631.

215

and so he loved the quene agayne aboven all other ladyes dayes of his lyff, and for hir he dud many dedys of armys and saved her frome the fyre thorow his noble chevalry' (p. 190). However, the kind of love this implies is unclear, and this brief description is indicative of the ambiguous way in which Malory describes their relationship. While Malory eschews detail, Beverly Kennedy's view that Launcelot and Guenevere only commit adultery once is extreme, misrepresenting Malory's uncertainty as an avowal of innocence and, as Karen Cherewatuk notes, 'ignor[ing] both Malory's tendencies as a traditional writer who has chosen to follow the adulterous plot of his French sources and his skill as a subtle artist, able to imply a sexual relationship through a deftly chosen verb'.[88] In addition to the specific examples Cherewatuk discusses, the episodes in which Launcelot has non-consensual sex with Elaine of Corbyn while believing that she is Guenevere are hard to explain if Launcelot and Guenevere's affair is not a physical one. As P. J. C. Field argues, 'Galahad is conceived by the act that tells us, almost with certainty, that the rumours of adultery are true'.[89] Of the women who seek sexual or romantic encounters with Launcelot, the four queens, Hallewes, Elaine of Corbyn, and the female jailor in 'The Knight of the Cart' all mention Guenevere as a known obstacle. The damsel who asks Launcelot why he will not take a lover in 'Sir Launcelot du Lake' also mentions the Queen, and although Elaine of Astolat does not mention Guenevere herself, the Queen plays a prominent role in the episodes surrounding Launcelot's relationship with Elaine. While Launcelot does not confirm their speculation and it is not always clear whether he rejects these women because of a prior commitment to Guenevere, this is consistently mentioned as a possibility, and by the time of his relationship with Elaine of Corbyn Launcelot does seem to be trying to reject infidelity to his (adulterous) relationship with Guenevere. It may be the ambiguous nature of this relationship that paves the way for him to be so frequently propositioned. Launcelot in some ways spans the gap between the romantic a(nti)pathy of single people and the rejections of adultery discussed in this chapter.[90] Because his relationship with Guenevere has not been sanctioned through marriage, he can be pursued by other women for sex, love, or marriage, opening up further

---

[88] Beverly Kennedy, 'Adultery in Malory's *Le Morte d'Arthur*', *Arthuriana*, 7.4 (1997), 63–91 (p. 79); Karen Cherewatuk, *Marriage, Adultery and Inheritance in Malory's 'Morte Darthur'* (Cambridge: D. S. Brewer, 2006), p. 46.

[89] P. J. C. Field, 'Sir Thomas Malory's *Le Morte Darthur*', in *The Arthur of the English: The Arthurian Legend in Medieval English Life and Literature*, ed. by W. R. J. Barron (Cardiff: University of Wales Press, 2001), pp. 225–45 (p. 237).

[90] See the discussion of singleness in Dorsey Armstrong, 'Gender, Marriage, and Knighthood: Single Ladies in Malory', in *The Single Woman in Medieval and Early Modern England: Her Life and Representation*, ed. by Laurel Amtower and Dorothea Kehler (Tempe: Arizona Center for Medieval and Renaissance Studies, 2003), pp. 41–61 (p. 57).

intersections between romance portrayals of resisting adultery and romantic a(nti)pathy, and provoking questions about the role of coercion in each.

If Launcelot is the closest comparison to single people who reject love, it is striking how often his experiences involve coercion and violence, both from negative characters like the four queens and Hallewes and from more neutral or positive characters like Elaine of Corbyn.[91] Hallewes and the four queens are directly associated with violent sexual threats and abuses of power: the queens tell Launcelot that he must love one of them 'other ellys to dye in this preson' (p. 194), while Hallewes wishes 'to have thy body dede. Than wolde I have bawmed hit and sered hit, and so to have kepte hit my lyve dayes' (p. 216). Hallewes's necrophilic desire is an addition of Malory's own, as Adam Bryant Marshall notes: in the *Perlesvaus*, Malory's source for this episode, the lady wishes to show Lancelot the tomb she has made for him, but she does not voice sexual desire for his dead body.[92] The threats posed by these women in Malory's *Morte* can be read as attempts to coerce Launcelot into a relationship with them and simultaneously as punishments for his refusal to love them. While the four queens ostensibly give Launcelot the choice of loving one of them, they also declare that because 'we know well there can no lady have thy love but one, and that is Quene Gwenyvere, now thou shalt hir love lose for ever, and she thyne' (p. 194), positioning the acceptance of their love more as a punishment than a choice. Hallewes's plot also arises because Launcelot's love for Guenevere means that 'I myght nat rejoyse the nother to have thy body on lyve' (p. 216). Both groups of women therefore acknowledge that Launcelot cannot love them of his free will, recognising his inevitable rejection while at the same time trying to punish him for this. The female jailor in 'The Knight of the Cart' also attempts to coerce Launcelot in the same breath as she acknowledges Guenevere, telling him 'ye may never oute of this preson but if ye have my helpe. And also youre lady Quene Gwenyvere shall be brente in youre defaute onles that ye be there' (p. 856). Malory makes this figure much more coercive than his sources: at this point in the prose *Lancelot* and Chrétien de Troyes's *Chevalier de la Charrete*,[93] Meleagant's sister frees

---

[91] Kristina Hildebrand also notes the frequency with which Launcelot is threatened with sexual violence: see '"I love nat to be constreyned to love": Launcelot and Coerced Sex', *Arthuriana* 37 (2022), 175–92.

[92] Adam Bryant Marshall, 'Sir Lancelot at the Chapel Perelus: Malory's Adaptation of the *Perlesvaus*', *Arthuriana*, 25.3 (2015), 33–48 (p. 42). See *Le Haut Livre du Graal: Perlesvaus*, ed. by William A. Nitze and T. Atkinson Jenkins, 2 vols (New York: Phaeton, 1932; repr. 1972), I, 344–5; trans. in *The High Book of the Grail: A translation of the thirteenth century romance of Perlesvaus*, trans. by Nigel Bryant (Cambridge: D. S. Brewer, 1978), pp. 221–2.

[93] P. J. C. Field argues that while it is not possible to be sure which of these sources Malory used, 'the prose *Lancelot* is the more likely candidate': *Le Morte Darthur: Apparatus, Commentary, Glossary, and Index of Names*, 2 vols (Cambridge: D. S. Brewer, 2013),

Lancelot without asking for anything in return.[94] Although Malory seems to be combining this episode with the immediately preceding narrative of the seneschal's wife who frees Lancelot to attend the tournament at Pomeglai, Lancelot agrees only to grant this lady his love and indeed only 'ce que je puis fere sans contredit' ['what I can without lying']; in Chrétien's version, she recognises that Lancelot effectively grants her nothing.[95] In contrast, the female jailor in Malory specifically propositions Launcelot for sex (as do other ladies elsewhere in the prose *Lancelot* and Chrétien's *Chevalier de la Charrete*), and the leverage she holds because Launcelot wishes to save Guenevere may also exacerbate her coercion of him. She does not position accepting her love as a punishment, however, as the four queens and Hallewes do. As with the stories of accused queens, punishment for rejecting love that would be unfaithful to a prior relationship is associated with the most negative characters in the *Morte*, in contrast to the more accepted punishment of romantic a(nti)pathy discussed in the first two chapters of this book.

In Malory's *Morte* these two variations upon the motif of resisting love occur side by side, albeit within different sections of this romance. The episodes involving Hallewes, the two Elaines, and Ettarde indeed share a common narrative trajectory, as they all end in the death of the female protagonist.[96] This common feature opens up further possibilities for comparison, indicating some suggestive similarities and differences between the representation of Hallewes and Ettarde in particular. Although Hallewes threatens Launcelot, ultimately she is the one who dies in this episode, as Ettarde does in her narrative, positioning death as a punishment for sexual transgression. As Tison Pugh argues, 'normative sexuality kills in medieval romance'; death

---

II, 687. See also Ralph Norris, *Malory's Library: The Sources of the 'Morte Darthur'* (Cambridge: D. S. Brewer, 2008), pp. 119–20, 131.

[94] See *Lancelot: Roman en prose du XIIIe siècle*, ed. by Alexandre Micha, Textes littéraires français, 249, 9 vols (Geneva: Droz, 1978–83), II (1978), 103–5 (42. 1–6); trans. in *Lancelot Parts III and IV*, trans. by Samuel N. Rosenberg and Roberta L. Krueger, Lancelot-Grail: The Old French Arthurian Vulgate and Post-Vulgate in Translation, 10 vols (Cambridge: D. S. Brewer, 2010), IV, 242–3. Chrétien de Troyes, *Les Romans de Chrétien de Troyes: III. Le Chevalier de la Charrete*, ed. by Mario Roques, Classiques français du moyen âge, 86 (Paris: Champion, 1983), lines 6374–6706; trans. in Chrétien de Troyes, 'The Knight of the Cart (Lancelot)', in *Chrétien de Troyes: Arthurian Romances*, ed. & trans. by William W. Kibler (London: Penguin, 1991), pp. 207–94 (pp. 285–9).

[95] See *Lancelot*, ed. by Micha, II, 95–6 (41. 1–4, quotation at p. 96, 41. 3); trans. by Rosenberg and Krueger, p. 239; *Le Chevalier de la Charrete*, lines 5439–94 (5485); trans. by Kibler, pp. 274–5.

[96] Catherine La Farge notes the similarity between Elaine of Astolat and Hallewes: La Farge, 'Launcelot in Compromising Positions: Fabliau in Malory's "Tale of Sir Launcelot du Lake"', in *Blood, Sex, Malory: Essays on the 'Morte Darthur'*, ed. by David Clark and Kate McClune (= *Arthurian Literature*, 28 (2011)), pp. 181–97 (p. 195).

'frequently codes characters as heroes and as villains'.[97] However, Hallewes's and Ettarde's sexual transgressions are strikingly different: Hallewes's death acts as a punishment for and refutation of her desire for Launcelot, while Ettarde is punished for refusing to love Pelleas. There are reasons for this difference: Hallewes's necrophilic murder plot portrays her very differently from Pelleas, and Launcelot's prior relationship with Guenevere contrasts with Ettarde's single status. However, these examples still depict one woman being punished for her unrequited desire, while the other is punished for *not* requiting desire, highlighting the wide spectrum of behaviour that could be seen as sexually transgressive in women. Yet the potential connections between these episodes, as well as with the much more sympathetic portrayal of Elaine of Astolat, also open them up to critical readings that pause to ask why the women are treated similarly, enabling divergent and resistant approaches to the punitive treatment of romantic a(nti)pathy.

Even more strikingly, while the four queens and Hallewes are resoundingly negative figures, coercion is also a prominent issue in Launcelot's relationship with Elaine of Corbyn, where their sexual encounters are framed to some extent as rape, as Catherine Batt, David Grubbs, and Kristina Hildebrand have noted.[98] Although Elaine of Corbyn is a more sympathetic figure in Malory than in his sources,[99] her role necessitates her coercion of Launcelot, so that they can conceive a son while not destroying the spirit of Launcelot's fidelity to Guenevere.[100] Malory and his sources do not shy away from the coercive aspects of this encounter but instead explore several different aspects of coercion at work in their relationship, which exceed and problematise medieval definitions of *raptus* to draw attention to extra-legal forms of coercion that may have impacted men as victim-survivors as well as perpetrators.

[97] Tison Pugh, *Sexuality and its Queer Discontents in Middle English Literature* (New York: Palgrave Macmillan, 2008), pp. 118–19. Although death also has other functions in romance, including, as Batt notes, as a common outcome for victims of rape in the *Morte*, the deaths of Hallewes and Ettarde do seem to align with the punishment of sexual transgression. See Catherine Batt, 'Malory and Rape', *Arthuriana*, 7.3 (1997), 78–99 (p. 89).

[98] Batt, 'Malory and Rape'; David Grubbs, 'The Knight Coerced: Two Cases of Raped Men in Chivalric Romance', in *Teaching Rape in the Medieval Literature Classroom: Approaches to Difficult Texts*, ed. by Alison Gulley (Leeds: Arc Humanities Press, 2018), pp. 164–82; Hildebrand, 'Launcelot and Coerced Sex'.

[99] Cherewatuk, *Marriage, Adultery, and Inheritance*, p. 69; Siobhán M. Wyatt, *Women of Words in 'Le Morte Darthur': The Autonomy of Speech in Malory's Female Characters* (New York: Palgrave Macmillan, 2016), pp. 117–18, 135.

[100] See Larrington, 'Gender/Queer Studies', in *Handbook of Arthurian Romance: King Arthur's Court in Medieval European Literature*, ed. by Leah Tether and Johnny McFadyen (Berlin: de Gruyter, 2017), pp. 259–72 (p. 260).

Elaine's coercion of Launcelot is acknowledged through the language Malory uses to describe their encounters. Launcelot insists to Guenevere 'that I ded was ayenste my wylle' (p. 631) and subsequently says to Elaine that he lay with her 'magry myne hede' (p. 651). These phrases are associated with the rape and violation of women in Middle English romance: *Havelok* condemns those who 'dide maydne shame', '*bute it were by hire wille*' (my emphasis); the fairy knight who rapes the Princess in *Sir Degaré* 'dide his wille, what he wolde'; Heurodis in *Sir Orfeo* says that the Fairy King abducts her (performing *raptus*) 'wold ich, nold ich'; the demon disguised as the Duchess's husband in *Sir Gowther* 'with hur is wyll he wroghtth', revealing himself as a demon 'when he had is wylle all don'.[101] Launcelot's insistence 'that I ded was ayenste my wylle' (p. 631) may imply, then, a link with the violated women who are raped in accordance with men's wills in other Middle English romances. This phrase is used in the prose *Lancelot*, the ultimate source behind Malory's work here, but rather than in a direct exchange with Guinevere, Lancelot tells Bors 'en nule manniere [...] je ne voldroie que ma dame seust ceste chose, car ele ne cuideroit mie que je l'eusse fet outre mon gré' ['on no account do I want my lady to know of this [...] for she wouldn't believe I did it against my will'].[102] In contrast, Malory invokes no such disbelief and thus places greater emphasis on Launcelot's direct perception of what he has experienced as 'ayenste my wylle', expressing this simply as his truth.

The phrase 'magry myne hede' (p. 651), which so far as I have been able to find does not occur in Malory's source, the *Tristan en prose*, or its source, the prose *Lancelot*, also develops this connection between Launcelot and victim-survivors of rape in medieval romance.[103] Within the *Morte*, it is used to refer to *raptus* in the form of abduction, when Meliot de Logrus says that he

---

[101] *Havelok*, ed. by G. V. Smithers (Oxford: Clarendon Press, 1987), lines 83–5; 'Sir Degaré', in *The Middle English Breton Lays*, ed. by Anne Laskaya and Eve Salisbury, TEAMS (Kalamazoo: Medieval Institute Publications, 1995), pp. 101–29 (line 112); 'Sir Orfeo', in *The Middle English Breton Lays*, pp. 26–41 (line 154); 'Sir Gowther', in *The Middle English Breton Lays*, pp. 274–95 (lines 72–3).

[102] *Lancelot*, ed. by Micha, VI (1980), 59 (101. 13); *Lancelot Parts V and VI*, trans. by William W. Kibler and Carleton W. Carroll, Lancelot-Grail: The Old French Arthurian Vulgate and Post-Vulgate in Translation, 10 vols (Cambridge: D. S. Brewer, 2010), V, 348. This phrase does not appear in the *Tristan en prose*, Malory's immediate source, so far as I have been able to find, but I cannot rule out the possibility that it occurs in some manuscript versions.

[103] In the prose *Tristan* and *Lancelot*, Lancelot tells Pelles' daughter that 'vous m'avés tolu tous les biens et toutes les joies que je soloie avoir el roiaume de Logres' [you have deprived me of all the goods and all the pleasures that I once enjoyed in the kingdom of Logres], but does not specifically refer to how 'ye and Dame Brusen made me to lye be you magry myne hede', as he does in Malory (p. 651). *Le Roman de Tristan en prose*, ed. by Emmanuèle Baumgartner and Michèle Szkilnik, 9 vols (Geneva: Droz, 1993), VI, 205 (10. 75). My translation. The *Lancelot* expresses this very similarly to the *Tristan*: *Lancelot*, ed. by Micha, VI, 231 (107. 43); trans. by Kibler and Carroll, p. 430.

heard Nyneve 'complayne that she was with [Outelake] magré hir hede' (p. 93). Elsewhere, in *The Wife of Bath's Tale,* for instance, it refers specifically to rape, when the knight 'maugree hir heed […] rafte hire maydenhed'.[104] Malory uses language associated with the rape and *raptus* of women to construct Launcelot's encounter with Elaine as comparable to these experiences.[105] I am not suggesting that Malory intends us to read Launcelot as a rape victim here: as discussed in the Introduction, *raptus* was considered a gender-specific crime in the Middle Ages (and rape still is to some extent in the modern world). However, the vocabulary Malory uses for Launcelot – to a greater extent than that of his sources – creates a conceptual link between the coercion of men and the violation of women, opening up the definitions of *raptus* and coercion to include male victim-survivors and female perpetrators and engaging with issues outside the framework of *raptus* law.

The episodes involving Launcelot and Elaine indeed portray a constellation of issues pertinent to medieval and modern understandings of rape and coercion. They seem to encompass what would now be referred to as deceptive sex or rape by fraud, 'an action whereby a person obtains sexual consent and has sexual intercourse of any type by fraud, deception, misrepresentation, or impersonation', as Launcelot is deceived into thinking that Elaine is Guenevere.[106] This is a plot necessity rather than explicitly an issue of consent, but the focus on deception is clear in Malory and his sources: in the *Morte,* Launcelot 'wente that mayden Elayne had bene Quene Gwenyvere' (p. 623), and asks Elaine in the morning 'what arte thou' (p. 624)? During their second non-consensual encounter he is said to have 'wende that he had had another in hys armys' (p. 632). Launcelot therefore focuses upon the issue of her identity and his false impression of it, making this central to his anger and sense of violation. The issue of deceptive sex, mistaken identity, and *raptus* occurs prominently elsewhere in Arthurian literature, including in the conception of Arthur by Uther and Igrayne and, to some extent, in the conception of Mordred by Arthur and Morgause. But deception for sex also features as a prominent device in the fabliaux, a contrasting context that

---

[104] Geoffrey Chaucer, 'The Wife of Bath's Tale', in *The Riverside Chaucer*, pp. 116–22 (lines 887–8). Grubbs and Batt also quote the line 'magry my hede', but Grubbs emphasises its translation as 'against my will' rather than its association with rape, while Batt mentions it in general terms: Grubbs, 'The Knight Coerced', p. 173; Batt, 'Malory and Rape', p. 92.

[105] See further Batt, 'Malory and Rape', p. 84.

[106] Michael Mullen, 'Rape by Fraud: Eluding Washington Rape Statutes', *Seattle University Law Review*, 41.3 (2018), 1035–52 (p. 1035). I use this article because, unlike other approaches, it does not include transphobic arguments about rape by deception. For a direct argument against these transphobic appropriations of the law see Joseph J. Fischel, *Screw Consent: A Better Politics of Sexual Justice* (Oakland: University of California Press, 2019), pp. 94–116.

illuminates the much more serious and sobering reflections upon deception facilitated by romance's focus on love and fidelity.

In addition to deception, the Elaine of Corbyn episode encompasses a concern with intoxication and consent, as Brusen gives Launcelot a cup of wine in his first encounter with Elaine, which makes him 'asoted and madde' (p. 623). In Malory, the effects of the wine are causally connected to his mistaken impression that he is in bed with Guenevere: '*And so* he wente that mayden Elayne had bene Quene Gwenyvere' (p. 623, my italics). The correlation is less direct in his sources, but they indicate that the potion means 'il porra legierement estre deceüs' [he could easily be deceived].[107] In all three accounts, the drink makes Launcelot vulnerable to deception and violation, but it does not seem to 'function as preemptive consent' in the manner Harris argues alcohol does in *The Reeve's Tale*.[108] This may support the 'misogynist double standards governing drinking' that Harris identifies, insofar as a man is not blamed for consuming alcohol but this is not explicitly used to question perceptions of women drinking.[109] However, the episode does separate the consumption of an intoxicant from culpability for sexual assault, perhaps enabling women to query any such treatment of their own experiences. All three accounts of this scene make clear that Launcelot is tricked because of the drink, but none of them suggest that he is to blame for consuming it in the first place. Malory focuses entirely on Brusen, who 'brought Sir Launcelot a kuppe full of wyne' (p. 623). In the French prose accounts, Launcelot asks for some wine, but they do not attribute culpability to him for this. Another small shift in Malory's account also portrays inebriation slightly differently: here, we are not told what the drink contains, whether it is a kind of spell that prevents Launcelot from recognising that Elaine is not Guenevere, an aphrodisiac, or a strong cup of wine to make Launcelot drunk, whereas in the prose *Tristan* and *Launcelot* it is a 'puison' [potion].[110] The greater ambiguity in Malory may point to (or allow a reader to perceive) the irrelevance of such details in situations of assault. All three accounts, however, offer important testimonies to the complexity and sensitivity with which coercive experiences, including those involving inebriation, could be treated in the Middle Ages.

If Launcelot's consumption of the wine/potion does not reduce the extent to which he is seen as a victim of assault, neither is he described as granting

---

[107] *Tristan en prose*, ed. by Baumgartner and Szkilnik, VI, 122 (3. 34), my translation. It is described very similarly in the prose *Lancelot*, ed. Micha, IV, 209 (78. 56); trans. by Kibler and Carroll, p. 103.

[108] Harris, *Obscene Pedagogies*, p. 57. Grubbs discusses inebriation in Elaine's deception of Launcelot: 'The Knight Coerced', pp. 170–1.

[109] Harris, *Obscene Pedagogies*, p. 56.

[110] Both refer to it at first as a 'boire' [drink], but then as 'le puison': *Tristan en prose*, ed. by Baumgartner and Szkilnik, VI, 121 (3. 33), 121 (3. 34); see also *Lancelot*, ed. by Micha, IV, 207 (78. 53), 209 (78. 55).

'retroactive consent' through his treatment of Elaine the following morning.[111]
Retroactive consent was built into medieval English *raptus* law: in the Second
Statute of Westminster (1285), *raptus* is defined as a crime where a woman 'ne
se est assentue ne avaunt ne apres' ['did not consent neither before nor after']
or where she 'se assente apres […] si il seit ateint a la suite le Rei' ['consent[s]
after […] if he be convicted at the king's suit'].[112] Retroactive consent was
thus clearly considered a possibility within medieval English law, but this is
not a framework invoked for Launcelot. Initially furious with Elaine, Malory's Launcelot forgives her when he knows who she is, Malory commenting
'for she was as fayre a lady, and therto lusty and yonge and wyse, as ony was
that tyme lyvynge' (p. 624).[113] Lancelot's fury is more extensive in the prose
Tristan and *Lancelot*, and Lancelot and Pelles' daughter part on worse terms
here, Lancelot asserting 'je m'en irai si vaincu et si recreans' [I leave you as
a man vanquished and defeated].[114] Yet Launcelot's forgiveness of Elaine, in
Malory and his sources, is not seen as retroactive consent, as he continues to
assert that what occurred was against his will. Accounts of Launcelot's experiences with Elaine do not shy away from the complexities of non-consensual
sex, again challenging the perception that rape occurs 'only when there is no
ambiguity in the words or actions of the victim'; instead, they acknowledge
nuance while insisting on Launcelot's non-consent.[115] The care with which
Launcelot's experiences are recounted may reflect how the medieval privileging of men's experiences allows Launcelot greater empathy than female victim-survivors – though this in itself is noteworthy, given the *lack* of empathy
with which male victim-survivors are often confronted in the modern world
– but Launcelot's gender is also important in reframing our understanding of
who might experience sexual and romantic coercion in medieval romance.[116]

While Launcelot is coerced by Elaine of Corbyn, his experiences with
Elaine of Astolat reflect on and challenge the logic of love as an obligation
in representations of romantic a(nti)pathy. Cherewatuk observes that the
Morte expresses an 'incredible sense of waste in Elaine's death, not only to
Sir Barnarde and his sons, but to the larger society: as both Gawain and Bors
recognize, Elaine *could* have served Launcelot as a fine wife', indicating that

---

[111] On retroactive consent and problematic readings of it in medieval literature, see Schwebel, 'Retroactive Consent', 337–45.

[112] Dunn, *Stolen Women*, p. 197.

[113] Hildebrand argues Launcelot forgives Elaine in part because he considers her less cul-
pable than her father and Brusen: 'Launcelot and Coerced Sex', p. 185.

[114] *Tristan en prose*, ed. by Baumgartner and Szkilnik, VI, 127 (4. 36), my translation. See
also *Lancelot*, ed. by Micha, IV, 213 (79. 3); trans. by Kibler and Carroll, p. 105.

[115] Schwebel, 'Retroactive Consent', p. 344.

[116] On this lack of empathy see, for example, Mhishi, *Sons and Others*, pp. 2, 4–5, 33–8.
For a discussion of the problematic gender stereotypes associated with rape in the modern world, see Mithu Sanyal, *Rape: From Lucretia to #MeToo* (London: Verso, 2019),
pp. 4–8.

Launcelot is encouraged to love Elaine.[117] But Launcelot maintains that 'I love nat to be constrayned to love, for love muste only aryse of the harte selff, and nat by none constraynte' (p. 830), upholding his fidelity to Guenevere but also challenging the dominant assumption within romance that there is an obligation to return the love of a worthy partner. Launcelot's defence is unique to Malory: in *La Mort la roi Artu* and the stanzaic *Morte Arthur*, Malory's sources for this section, Launcelot is not present to voice his response to the discovery of the maid's body and indeed is blamed for his role in her death by Arthur and Gawain, whereas the King and many knights affirm his response in Malory's account.[118] Malory's Launcelot puts forward a strikingly different perspective, and one that directly contrasts with the earlier episode of Pelleas and Ettarde, where Ettarde is ultimately 'constrayned to love' and even this is not sufficient to redeem her from a death that seems to function as punishment for her rejection of Pelleas. I suggested in relation to Ettarde that the issue was her refusal to love a worthy knight, but this scenario seems closely mirrored in that of Elaine and Launcelot, in which Elaine could be a worthy wife. Launcelot's commitment to Guenevere does differentiate his resistance to Elaine from a rejection of the logic of love as obligatory, but his affirmation that love cannot be constrained operates in tension with romances in which romantic a(nti)pathy is resolved through constraint and coercion. That Launcelot rejects a socially acceptable relationship to uphold his commitment to the Queen may reflect his gendered and personal privileges, as one of the highest-ranking knights in the Arthurian court. But this episode may also enable us to question any gendered division, as the tendency to depoliticise love and treat it as some kind of universal ideal, after all, seems to position Launcelot's maxim as a truth for everyone: love should only ever arise from the heart itself.

Conclusion

Rejecting adulterous sex serves an exemplary function in the romances discussed in this chapter, aligning with prohibitions of adultery in monogamous Christian culture and often offering models of behaviour for medieval readers to reflect upon and emulate. These works indicate some of the appeal romances may have held for married readers: while this genre is often thought to hold special appeal for the young and unmarried, the works explored in this chapter

---

[117] Cherewatuk, *Marriage, Adultery, and Inheritance*, p. 66.

[118] See *Mort Artu: An Old French Prose Romance of the XIIIth Century*, ed. by J. Douglas Bruce (Halle: Niemeyer, 1910), pp. 75–7. I use this edition because Norris argues that the manuscript on which it is based is 'occasionally closer to Malory's manuscript': *Malory's Library*, p. 119 n. 1. See also 'Stanzaic Morte Arthur', in *King Arthur's Death: The Middle English 'Stanzaic Morte Arthur' and 'Alliterative Morte Arthure'*, ed. by Larry D. Benson (Exeter: University of Exeter Press, 1986), pp. 1–111 (lines 984–1127). Names are taken from the 'Stanzaic Morte'.

reveal how romances attended to the desires, concerns, and fears of married readers.[119] Although romance 'audiences [...] resist generalisation and easy classification', married couples certainly owned romances, and Felicity Riddy argues that they were 'read within the family'.[120] *The Erle of Tolous* is preserved in a manuscript that may have been a wedding or engagement gift from a groom to his bride: as Wade argues, despite the ambiguous representation of the Empress's relationship with the Earl, attending to the nuanced virtues associated with the Empress in this work reveals 'why a young man in the 1520s might think it appropriate reading matter for his bride-to-be'.[121] The exemplary nature of the characters who reject adultery functions, for those invested in the virtues they represent, to invite empathy with them, including through their experiences of coercion, false accusation, and violence. Yet this empathy can function in more unexpected ways. Rather than simply exhorting readers to avoid adultery, the portrayals explored here also shed light upon, question, and at times explicitly critique the ideas upon which medieval rape culture depends. While they all support the idea of the perfect victim, they expose other beliefs entrenched within rape culture as false. In contrast to the assumption that women will be unfaithful and the accusation of 'asking for it' that may accompany this stereotype, they present women who are 'trewe as stele' no matter the temptations they are offered.[122] They show that coercion and violence are caused solely by the perpetrator but also acknowledge that perpetrators are structurally enabled by dominant cultural narratives of misogyny, victim-blaming, and even the illegibility of male victim-survivors of sexual violence. They also do not perceive prior sexual history to negate non-consent: where Alice Raw notes that scholars have traditionally treated *Dame Sirith*'s Margery differently from other comparable figures because she is not a virgin, sexual experience is not seen to undermine non-consent in the works I have discussed, perhaps reflecting the extent to which romance values fidelity over virginity *per se*.[123] The works explored in this chapter thus exist in productive tension with the other romances analysed in this book, exposing

---

[119] See Cooper, *The English Romance in Time*, p. 225; Riddy, 'Family, marriage, intimacy', pp. 239–45.
[120] Carol M. Meale, '"gode men / Wiues maydnes and alle men": Romance and Its Audiences', in *Readings in Medieval English Romance*, ed. by Meale (Cambridge: D. S. Brewer, 1994), pp. 209–25 (p. 225); Riddy, 'Family, marriage, intimacy', p. 237.
[121] James Wade, 'Confession, Inquisition and Exemplarity in *The Erle of Tolous* and Other Middle English Romances', in *The Culture of Inquisition in Medieval England*, ed. by Mary C. Flannery and Katie L. Walter (Cambridge: D. S. Brewer, 2013), pp. 112–29 (p. 129). For a discussion of this copy of *The Erle of Tolous* (Oxford, Bodleian Library, MS Ashmole 45), see Meale, 'An Early Sixteenth-Century Presentation Copy of *The Erle of Tolous*'; Perkins, 'Introduction: The Materiality of Medieval Romance', pp. 1–3, 10–18.
[122] 'Syr Tryamowre', lines 17, 27.
[123] Raw, 'Coerced Consent in *Dame Sirith*', pp. 313–14.

their coercive practices and assertions that love is obligatory as ideological structures that can be challenged. But they also align with the ways in which the other romances discussed complicate gendered ideas about sexual violence, offering a more capacious consideration of violence and power, as well as one attuned to the precise nuances of individual situations. If the works centred in previous chapters overall present a view of romance as an ideological structure that seeks to impose love, desire, and sexuality where it is not freely given, those explored here draw out some of the possibilities for resistance that exist within this varied and capacious mode of writing.

Conclusion: The Ends of Romance

The first big ruse of romance is that it is ubiquitous because it is natural, and it is natural because it is ubiquitous.[1]

What are we consenting to, if or when we consent to happiness?[2]

Whom and what we desire are perennial human concerns that play a central role in fiction through the ages. As *the* genre of secular fiction in medieval England, and one particularly focused upon the concerns and wishes of the individual, romance offered a crucial space for medieval readers to encounter, think through, and negotiate these issues. Some romances suggest that love and desire are overpowering forces that operate outside and sometimes in violation of societal norms and expectations, but the works discussed here show that romances also construct desire within and in service of these norms, organising it 'into legible and socially acceptable forms'.[3] Middle English romance celebrates love and marriage, and desire and sexuality within them, endorsing these as normal and natural things to want. In itself, this is not surprising. What is more unexpected, though, is the lengths to which the genre goes to achieve this. The repeated reliance on coercion to resolve resistance to love and the integration of coercive practices into romanticised relationships point to the need to construct love and marriage as natural and thereby reveal that they are *not* natural. They are always shaped by and contingent upon societal, cultural, political, and literary perspectives.

The first half of this book highlighted that romances celebrate (heterosexual) love itself as normative, exploring how the genre anticipates the resolution of romantic a(nti)pathy and mandates this for women in particular. Women's resistance, consent, and desire are perceived as more problematic than men's,

---

[1] yingchen and yingtong, *An Aromantic Manifesto* (Calaméo, 2018), p. 7 <https://en.calameo.com/read/0056336139d7e661d8f3c> [accessed 21 February 2021].

[2] Sara Ahmed, *The Promise of Happiness* (Durham, NC: Duke University Press, 2010), p. 1.

[3] Nicola McDonald, 'Desire Out of Order and *Undo Your Door*', *Studies in the Age of Chaucer*, 34 (2012), 247–75 (p. 247).

both in works where two mutually unwilling protagonists are directly contrasted and in the broader development of the proud lady in love as a specific motif, compared to the more sporadic representation of men's resistance. This gendered difference – which also constructs ideas of appropriate gendered behaviour – highlights the political, economic, and dynastic implications of women's desires in this period. While resistance to love marks dissent from normative expectations, and some romances allow more space for alternative desires and protest, even these tend to adopt strategies to (re-)assimilate queer alternatives to normative models, from the association of Guigemar's asexuality with adolescence in Marie's *lai* to Dynadan's performance of a comic role in Malory's *Morte Darthur*. These strategies are not always effective, but they do illustrate how romance tries to contain queer desires within its dominant structures. Taken together, the first two chapters of this book highlight the ways in which romance adopts and endorses a 'horizon of feeling' that approximates heteronormative expectations.[4] While some characteristic features of medieval sexualities are different to those of modern heteronormativity, recognising the restrictive aspects they share may offer an important way of advancing our understanding of all sexualities, including queer desires, in the medieval period.[5]

Chapters 3, 4, and 5 drew attention to the ways in which romances do not just celebrate (heterosexual) desire itself but define whom their readers *ought* to desire in accordance with dominant cultural perceptions of social status, race and/or faith, and morality. The romances discussed in Chapter 3 suggest that interclass relationships are undesirable and dangerous, implicitly cautioning readers against *mésalliance*, while also offering guidance on how, when, and by whom such relationships might be pursued. Chapter 4 demonstrated that desirability is bound up in political perceptions of race and religion in romance writing: the tendency to view love and sexuality as purely personal matters, which remains dominant in the modern world, obscures the fact that racism and prejudice infiltrate every aspect of our lives, including whom we desire. Chapter 5 showed that rather than endorsing adulterous desire as demonstrating the power of love to overcome social constraints, Middle English romances often reject infidelity, asserting the importance

---

[4]   See Sif Ríkharðsdóttir, *Emotion in Old Norse Literature: Translations, Voices, Contexts* (Cambridge: D. S. Brewer, 2017), pp. 18–19.

[5]   I am influenced here by Lucy M. Allen-Goss on the importance of confronting 'ugly emotions' and pejorative views, in *Female Desire in Chaucer's 'Legend of Good Women' and Middle English Romance* (Cambridge: D. S. Brewer, 2020), pp. viii–ix; Tess Wingard, *Unclean Beasts: Sex, Animality, and the Invention of Heteronormativity, 1200–1550* (forthcoming); and the turn in medieval trans studies to examine transmisogyny, transphobia, and pessimism, discussed in 'Revisiting Romances from Trans and Genderqueer Perspectives' (organised by A. E. Brown at the 57th International Congress on Medieval Studies, Kalamazoo, 2022).

of loyalty to marriage even in the face of temptation. The romances I have explored thus shape their readers' desires in accordance with contemporary norms, constructing desirability in terms of status, race, religion, and morality. Romance's celebration of 'desirable desire' might well often be a positive motif that endows women in particular with agency over their own lives, but its definition of what is desirable can also act as a restrictive force, limiting what desires are possible.[6]

The types of ending typical of romance also serve this restrictive function, closing off the possibility of other endings and thereby delimiting the kinds of desires that are (and are not) deemed worthy of reward in this genre. While romance's drive towards happy resolution may seem an innocuous means of wish fulfilment or fantasy, positive reinforcement of this kind can play an important role in endorsing particular kinds of wants as acceptable and achievable. As Sara Ahmed writes in her interrogation of happiness, 'there is no doubt about the power of the "no words"', but 'it might be harder to hear the "yes words" [...] because the words seem to "go along" with or affirm what we are already doing'.[7] Yet 'to encourage can also be forceful'; it 'can be a way of being directed toward somebody else's wants. The generosity of encouragement can hide the force of being directed somewhere'.[8] Romance's endorsement of particular kinds of happy endings may be both more effective and more difficult to observe as a means of control because of its positive focus. The narrative trajectory romance shares in common with the *bildungsroman*, the growth of a protagonist into a new identity, highlights the aspirational qualities of the genre – its focus on possible identities, discovering new skills and new inheritances, its celebration of what people can become. But romance aspirations also fix particular *kinds* of becoming as desirable. The predictability of romance plots – including the frequent, though not inevitable, transformation of resistance to love into willed commitment – further contributes to this effect. In thinking about the role 'the happy family' plays in shaping desire, Ahmed writes that 'happiness involves here the comfort of repetition, of following lines that have already been given in advance'.[9] The same is true of romance's happy endings, which offer both their protagonists and their readers the 'comfort of repetition'. In doing so, they etch in more deeply those 'lines that have already been given in advance'. The many examples of resistance to love being transformed into romantic commitment discussed in this book therefore have a cumulative effect. Chapter 1 explored how pairing together two people who resist love not only anticipates their

6   Helen Cooper, 'Desirable desire: "I am wholly given over unto thee"', in *The English Romance in Time: Transforming motifs from Geoffrey of Monmouth to the death of Shakespeare* (Oxford: Oxford University Press, 2004), pp. 218–68.
7   Ahmed, *The Promise of Happiness*, p. 48.
8   *Ibid.*, pp. 47–8.
9   *Ibid.*, p. 48.

eventual coupling from the start but sets out a normative trajectory for the other protagonist to follow when one partner is shown transforming from resistance to willingness to love. This pattern is echoed more widely across different works within this genre: for each instance where resistance is transformed into acceptance, the drive towards love becomes a stronger generic expectation and is thereby further normalised and made to seem inevitable. As aromanticism theorists yingchen and yingtong argue in the epigraph to this chapter (though they are writing about romantic relationships, not romance as a literary genre), 'the first big ruse of romance is that it is ubiquitous because it is natural, and it is natural because it is ubiquitous'.[10]

Yet romance, as I have argued repeatedly throughout this book, is not and never can be solely a restrictive force. Its projection of happy fantasies shapes its readers' desires in particular ways, but the very strategy by which it does so also holds the means of escape. While Nicola McDonald has argued that desire itself is 'inherently disruptive' and romance's capacity to contain it 'never assured', Ahmed (writing specifically about the 'feminist killjoy') suggests more broadly that 'imagination is what allows women to be liberated from happiness and the narrowness of its horizons', 'what allows girls to question the wisdom they have received and to ask whether what is good for all is necessarily good for them'.[11] Imaginative fiction plays a crucial role in shaping horizons of desire and possibility; as I have argued, the fantastical nature of romance should not lead us to overlook its power in this respect. But in inviting its readers to imagine, to fantasise, romance also opens up the potential for new horizons, new desires, new possibilities that cannot be contained. The motif of resisting love both reveals the socio-political shaping of love and desire and at times offers opportunities to challenge it, opening out onto alternative and sometimes queer possibilities. Romance may have lessons to teach us that its writers might not have anticipated or desired.

This book has argued that the motif of resistance to love permeates medieval English romance writing, but in doing so I have tried not to homogenise it. It takes varied forms and serves diverse functions in different works, sometimes operating more conventionally and at other times raising more subversive questions about the representation of gender, consent, and desire in romance literature. While I have brought together the questions it raises and the ideologies it upholds within one framework, I hope to have preserved a sense of the generic diversity to be found within Middle English romance. Romance – and its discourses of love, marriage, and sexuality – is not a monolith, and resistance to love opens up dissenting perspectives and alternative possibilities. Such possibilities are often closed off or reintegrated into a normative

---

[10] yingchen and yingtong, *An Aromantic Manifesto*, p. 7.
[11] McDonald, 'Desire Out of Order', pp. 253, 273; Ahmed, *The Promise of Happiness*, p. 62.

ending, offering valuable evidence for how dominant perspectives co-opt or silence queer and dissenting voices, including the repression of asexuality into normative sexual scripts for desire and marriage. However, normative endings do not and cannot entirely close off earlier expressions of resistance and dissent. Romance protagonists' resistance may fail, but perhaps by looking more closely at their resistance, ours may not. By attending to dissenting voices and acknowledging attempts to negotiate romance expectations, we are better placed to critique the ideologies romance endorses, to express our own resistance to the coercive fictions of heteronormativity, and to construct better futures to the past and the fictions it leaves behind.

Bibliography

Primary Sources

'The Adulterous Falmouth Squire', in *Codex Ashmole 61: A Compilation of Popular Middle English Verse*, ed. by George Shuffelton, TEAMS (Kalamazoo: Medieval Institute Publications, 2008), pp. 351–6

Amadas and Ydoine, ed. & trans. by Ross G. Arthur, Garland Library of Medieval Literature, Series B, 95 (New York: Garland, 1993)

Amadas et Ydoine: roman du XIIIe siècle, ed. by John R. Reinhard, Classiques français du moyen âge, 51 (Paris: Champion, 1926)

Ami and Amile: A Medieval Tale of Friendship, trans. by Samuel N. Rosenberg and Samuel Danon (Ann Arbor: University of Michigan Press, 1996; first publ. York, SC: French Literature Publications Company, 1981)

Ami et Amile: Chanson de Geste, ed. by Peter F. Dembowski, Classiques français du moyen âge, 97 (Paris: Champion, 1969)

Amis and Amiloun, ed. by MacEdward Leach, EETS, o. s., 203 (London: Oxford University Press, 1937)

'Amis and Amilun', in *The Birth of Romance in England: 'The Romance of Horn', The 'Folie Tristan', The 'Lai of Haveloc', and 'Amis and Amilun'*, ed. & trans. by Judith Weiss, FRETS, 4 (Tempe: Arizona Center for Medieval and Renaissance Studies, 2009), pp. 171–88

Amys e Amillyoun, ed. by Hideka Fukui, Plain Texts Series, 7 (London: Anglo-Norman Text Society, 1990)

Ancrene Wisse, ed. by Robert Hasenfratz, TEAMS (Kalamazoo: Medieval Institute Publications, 2000)

Andreas Capellanus on Love, ed. & trans. by P. G. Walsh (London: Duckworth, 1982)

Anglo-Norman 'Amys e Amilioun': The Text of Karlsruhe, Badische Landesbibliothek, MS 345 (olim Codex Durlac 38) in parallel with London, British Library, MS Royal 12 C. XII, ed. by John Ford, Medium Ævum Monographs, 27 (Oxford: Society for the Study of Medieval Languages and Literature, 2011)

The Anglo-Norman Lay of 'Haveloc': Text and Translation, ed. & trans. by Glyn S. Burgess and Leslie C. Brook (Cambridge: D. S. Brewer, 2015)

Der Anglonormannische Boeve de Haumtone, ed. by Albert Stimming, Bibliotheca Normannica, 7 (Halle: Niemeyer, 1899)

Augustine, *De civitate Dei. The City of God*, trans. by George E. McCracken, Loeb Classical Library, 411, 7 vols (Cambridge, MA: Harvard University Press, 1957), I

———, *De libero arbitrio*, ed. by William Green, Corpus christianorum series latina, 29 (Turnhout: Brepols, 1970)

Biket, Robert, *The Anglo-Norman Text of Le Lai du Cor*, ed. by C. T. Erickson, Anglo-Norman Texts, 24 (Oxford: Blackwell, 1973)

——, 'Cor', in *Twenty-Four Lays from the French Middle Ages*, trans. by Glyn S. Burgess and Leslie C. Brook (Liverpool: Liverpool University Press, 2016), pp. 121–9

Blancandin et l'Orgueilleuse d'amour: Roman d'aventures, ed. by H. Michelant (Paris: Librairie Tross, 1867)

Blancandin et l'Orgueilleuse d'amours: Versioni in prosa del XV secolo, ed. by Rosa Anna Greco, Bibliotheca Romanica: Studi e Testi, 3 (Alessandria: Edizioni dell'Orso, 2002)

Boccaccio, Giovanni, *The Filostrato of Giovanni Boccaccio: A Translation with Parallel Text*, trans. by Nathaniel Edward Griffin and Arthur Beckwith Myrick (Philadelphia: University of Pennsylvania Press, 1929; repr. 2016)

'Boeve de Haumtone', in *'Boeve de Haumtone' and 'Gui de Warewic': Two Anglo-Norman Romances*, ed. & trans. by Judith Weiss, FRETS, 3 (Tempe: Arizona Center for Medieval and Renaissance Studies, 2008), pp. 25–95

Caulier, Achilles, 'The Cruel Woman in Love', in *Alain Chartier, The Quarrel of the Belle dame sans mercy*, ed. & trans. by Joan E. McRae (London: Routledge, 2014; first publ. Taylor & Francis, 2004), pp. 229–93

Caxton, William, *Blanchardyn and Eglantine, c. 1489*, ed. by Leon Kellner, EETS, e. s., 58 (Oxford: Oxford University Press, 1890)

Chartier, Alain, 'La belle dame sans mercy', trans. by Joan E. McRae with Demas Boudreaux, Henrik Rasmussen, and Dale Cornett, in *Alain Chartier, The Quarrel of the Belle dame sans mercy*, ed. by Joan E. McRae (London: Routledge, 2014; first publ. Taylor & Francis, 2004), pp. 43–95

Chaucer, Geoffrey, 'The Franklin's Tale', in *The Riverside Chaucer*, ed. by Larry D. Benson, 3rd edn (Oxford: Oxford University Press, 2008), pp. 178–89

——, 'The Man of Law's Tale', in *The Riverside Chaucer*, ed. by Larry D. Benson, 3rd edn (Oxford: Oxford University Press, 2008), pp. 87–104

——, 'The Prioress's Tale', in *The Riverside Chaucer*, ed. by Larry D. Benson, 3rd edn (Oxford: Oxford University Press, 2008), pp. 209–12

——, 'Troilus and Criseyde', in *The Riverside Chaucer*, ed. by Larry D. Benson, 3rd edn (Oxford: Oxford University Press, 2008), pp. 471–585

——, 'The Wife of Bath's Tale', in *The Riverside Chaucer*, ed. by Larry D. Benson, 3rd edn (Oxford: Oxford University Press, 2008), pp. 116–22

Chrétien de Troyes, 'The Knight of the Cart (Lancelot)', in *Chrétien de Troyes: Arthurian Romances*, ed. & trans. by William W. Kibler (London: Penguin, 1991), pp. 207–94

——, *Le Roman de Perceval ou Le Conte du Graal*, ed. by Keith Busby (Tübingen: Niemeyer, 1993)

——, *Les Romans de Chrétien de Troyes: III. Le Chevalier de la Charrete*, ed. by Mario Roques, Classiques français du moyen âge, 86 (Paris: Champion, 1983)

——, 'The Story of the Grail (Perceval)', in *Chrétien de Troyes: Arthurian Romances*, ed. & trans. by William W. Kibler (London: Penguin, 1991), pp. 381–494

'Doon', in *French Arthurian Literature IV: Eleven Old French Narrative Lays*, ed. & trans. by Glyn S. Burgess and Leslie C. Brook, Arthurian Archives, 14 (Cambridge: D. S. Brewer, 2007), pp. 259–73

Eger and Grime: A parallel-text edition of the Percy and the Huntington-Laing Versions of the Romance, ed. by James Ralston Caldwell (Cambridge, MA: Harvard University Press, 1933)

'The Erle of Tolous', in *Of Love and Chivalry: An Anthology of Middle English Romance*, ed. by Jennifer Fellows (London: Dent, 1993), pp. 231–65

Fierabras: Chanson de geste du XIIe siècle, ed. by Marc Le Person, Classiques français du moyen âge, 142 (Paris: Champion, 2003)

Fierabras: roman en prose de la fin du XIVe siècle, ed. by Jean Miquet, Publications médiévales de l'Université d'Ottawa, 9 (Ottawa: Éditions de l'Université d'Ottawa, 1983)

Firumbras and Otuel and Roland, ed. by Mary Isabelle O'Sullivan, EETS, o. s., 198 (London: Oxford University Press, 1935)

Gaimar, Geffrei, *Estoire des Engleis | History of the English*, ed. & trans. by Ian Short (Oxford: Oxford University Press, 2009)

Gower, John, 'Tale of Constance', in *Confessio Amantis*, ed. by Russell A. Peck, TEAMS, 2nd edn, 3 vols (Kalamazoo: Medieval Institute Publications, 2003), II, II. 588–1613

——, 'Tale of Florent', in *Confessio Amantis*, ed. by Russell A. Peck, TEAMS, 2nd edn, 3 vols (Kalamazoo: Medieval Institute Publications, 2006), I, I. 1407–1882

——, 'Tale of Narcissus', in *Confessio Amantis*, ed. by Russell A. Peck, TEAMS, 2nd edn, 3 vols (Kalamazoo: Medieval Institute Publications, 2006), I, I. 2275–2398

'Graelent', in *French Arthurian Literature IV: Eleven Old French Narrative Lays*, ed. & trans. by Glyn S. Burgess and Leslie C. Brook, Arthurian Archives, 14 (Cambridge: D. S. Brewer, 2007), pp. 375–412

'Gui de Warewic', in *'Boeve de Haumtone' and 'Gui de Warewic': Two Anglo-Norman Romances*, ed. & trans. by Judith Weiss, FRETS, 3 (Tempe: Arizona Center for Medieval and Renaissance Studies, 2008), pp. 97–243

Gui de Warewic: roman du XIIIe siècle, ed. by Alfred Ewert, Classiques français du moyen âge, 74–5, 2 vols (Paris: Champion, 1933)

Guillaume de Lorris and Jean de Meun, *Le Roman de la Rose*, ed. by Félix Lecoy, Classiques français du moyen âge, 92, 3 vols (Paris: Champion, 1965), I

——, *The Romance of the Rose*, ed. & trans. by Frances Horgan (Oxford: Oxford University Press, 1994)

'Hali Meithhad', in *The Katherine Group (MS Bodley 34)*, ed. & trans. by Emily Rebekah Huber and Elizabeth Robertson, TEAMS (Kalamazoo: Medieval Institute Publications, 2016), pp. 189–219

Harvey, Ruth, and Linda Paterson, eds, *The Troubadour 'Tensos' and 'Partimens': A Critical Edition*, 3 vols (Cambridge: D. S. Brewer, 2010), I

Le Haut Livre du Graal: Perlesvaus, ed. by William A. Nitze and T. Atkinson Jenkins, 2 vols (New York: Phaeton, 1932; repr. 1972), I

Havelok, ed. by G. V. Smithers (Oxford: Clarendon Press, 1987)

Herenc, Baudet, 'Accusations against the Belle dame sans mercy', in *Alain Chartier, The Quarrel of the Belle dame sans mercy*, ed. & trans. by Joan E.

McRae (London: Routledge, 2014; first publ. Taylor & Francis, 2004), pp. 127–68

The High Book of the Grail: A translation of the thirteenth century romance of Perlesvaus, trans. by Nigel Bryant (Cambridge: D. S. Brewer, 1978)

'Horn Childe and Maiden Rimnild', in *King Horn: A Middle-English Romance*, ed. by Joseph Hall (Oxford: Clarendon Press, 1901), pp. 179–92

Hue de Rotelande, *Ipomedon: poème de Hue de Rotelande (fin du XIIe siècle)*, ed. by A. J. Holden, Bibliothèque française et romane, série B, éditions critiques de textes, 17 (Paris: Éditions Klincksieck, 1979)

Ipomadon, ed. by Rhiannon Purdie, EETS, o. s., 316 (Oxford: Oxford University Press, 2001)

Kempe, Margery, *The Book of Margery Kempe*, ed. by Barry Windeatt (Harlow: Pearson, 2000)

King Horn: A Middle-English Romance, ed. by Joseph Hall (Oxford: Clarendon Press, 1901)

The King of Tars, ed. from the Auchinleck MS, Advocates 19.2.1, ed. by Judith Perryman, Middle English Texts, 12 (Heidelberg: Winter, 1980)

Lancelot Parts III and IV, trans. by Samuel N. Rosenberg and Roberta L. Krueger, Lancelot-Grail: The Old French Arthurian Vulgate and Post-Vulgate in Translation, 10 vols (Cambridge: D. S. Brewer, 2010), IV

Lancelot Parts V and VI, trans. by William W. Kibler and Carleton W. Carroll, Lancelot-Grail: The Old French Arthurian Vulgate and Post-Vulgate in Translation, 10 vols (Cambridge: D. S. Brewer, 2010), V

Lancelot: Roman en prose du XIIIe siècle, ed. by Alexandre Micha, Textes littéraires français, 9 vols (Geneva: Droz, 1978–83)

'Lybeaus Desconus', in *Codex Ashmole 61: A Compilation of Popular Middle English Verse*, ed. by George Shuffelton, TEAMS (Kalamazoo: Medieval Institute Publications, 2008), pp. 111–64

Malory, Thomas, *Le Morte Darthur*, ed. by P. J. C. Field, 2 vols (Cambridge: D. S. Brewer, 2013), I

Marie de France, 'Chaitivel', in *The Lais of Marie de France*, ed. & trans. by Glyn S. Burgess and Keith Busby, 2nd edn (London: Penguin, 2003), pp. 105–8

——, 'Chaitivel', in *Marie de France: Lais*, ed. by Alfred Ewert (London: Bristol Classical Press, 1995), pp. 116–22

——, 'Guigemar', in *The Lais of Marie de France*, ed. & trans. by Glyn S. Burgess and Keith Busby, 2nd edn (London: Penguin, 2003), pp. 43–55

——, 'Guigemar', in *Marie de France: Lais*, ed. by Alfred Ewert (London: Bristol Classical Press, 1995), pp. 3–25

'The Marriage of Sir Gawain', in *Sir Gawain: Eleven Romances and Tales*, ed. by Thomas Hahn, TEAMS (Kalamazoo: Medieval Institute Publications, 1995), pp. 362–9

The Middle English Versions of Partonope of Blois, ed. by A. Trampe Bödtker, EETS, e. s., 109 (London: Paul, Trench, and Trübner, 1912; repr. New York: Kraus, 1981)

Mort Artu: An Old French Prose Romance of the XIIIth Century, ed. by J. Douglas Bruce (Halle: Niemeyer, 1910)

Narcisus et Dané, ed. & trans. by Penny Eley, Liverpool Online Series, Critical Editions of French Texts, 6 (Liverpool: University of Liverpool, 2002)

Octovian, ed. by Frances McSparran, EETS, o. s., 289 (London: Oxford University Press, 1986)

Ovid, *The Art of Love and Other Poems*, trans. by J. H. Mozley, rev. by G. P. Goold, Loeb Classical Library, 232 (Cambridge, MA: Harvard University Press, 1929)

————, *Heroides. Amores*, trans. by Grant Showerman, Loeb Classical Library, 41, 2nd edn (Cambridge, MA: Harvard University Press, 1977)

————, *Metamorphoses, Books 1–8*, trans. by Frank Justus Miller, rev. by G. P. Goold, Loeb Classical Library, 42, 2 vols (Cambridge, MA: Harvard University Press, 1916), I

Paston Letters and Papers of the Fifteenth Century, ed. by Norman Davis, EETS, s. s., 20, 3 vols (Oxford: Oxford University Press, 2004; first publ. Oxford: Clarendon Press, 1971), I

The Post-Vulgate Cycle: The Merlin Continuation, trans. by Martha Asher, Lancelot-Grail: The Old French Arthurian Vulgate and Post-Vulgate in Translation, 10 vols (Cambridge: D. S. Brewer, 2010), VIII

Renart, Jehan, *Le Lai de l'Ombre*, ed. by Alan Hindley and Brian J. Levy, trans. by Adrian P. Tudor, Liverpool Online Series, Critical Editions of French Texts, 8 (Liverpool: University of Liverpool, 2004)

Le Roman de Tristan en prose, ed. by Emmanuèle Baumgartner and Michèle Szkilnik, 9 vols (Geneva: Droz, 1993), VI

Le Roman de Tristan en prose: Version du manuscrit fr. 757 de la Bibliothèque nationale de Paris, ed. by Joël Blanchard and Michel Quéreuil, Classiques français du moyen âge, 123, 5 vols (Paris: Champion, 1997), I

The Romance of Guy of Warwick: The First or Fourteenth-Century Version, ed. by Julius Zupitza, EETS, e. s., 42, 49, 59 (London: Paul, Trench, and Trübner, 1883)

The Romance of Guy of Warwick: The Second or Fifteenth-Century Version, ed. by Julius Zupitza, EETS, e. s., 25–6 (London: Trübner, 1875)

The Romance of Sir Degrevant, ed. by L. F. Casson, EETS, o. s., 221 (London: Oxford University Press, 1949; repr. 1970)

Sir Bevis of Hampton, ed. by Jennifer Fellows, EETS, o. s., 349–50, 2 vols (Oxford: Oxford University Press, 2017)

'Sir Degaré', in *The Middle English Breton Lays*, ed. by Anne Laskaya and Eve Salisbury, TEAMS (Kalamazoo: Medieval Institute Publications, 1995), pp. 101–29

Sir Ferumbras, ed. by Sidney J. Herrtage, EETS, e. s., 34 (London: Paul, Trench, and Trübner, 1879)

Sir Gawain and the Green Knight, ed. by J. R. R. Tolkien and E. V. Gordon, 2nd edn, rev. by Norman Davis (Oxford: Clarendon Press, 1967)

'Sir Gowther', in *The Middle English Breton Lays*, ed. by Anne Laskaya and Eve Salisbury, TEAMS (Kalamazoo: Medieval Institute Publications, 1995), pp. 274–95

'Sir Orfeo', in *The Middle English Breton Lays*, ed. by Anne Laskaya and Eve Salisbury, TEAMS (Kalamazoo: Medieval Institute Publications, 1995), pp. 26–41

The Sowdone of Babylone, ed. by Emil Hausknecht, EETS, e. s., 38 (London: Paul, Trench, and Trübner, 1881)

'Stanzaic Morte Arthur', in *King Arthur's Death: The Middle English 'Stanzaic Morte Arthur' and 'Alliterative Morte Arthure'*, ed. by Larry D. Benson (Exeter: University of Exeter Press, 1986), pp. 1–111

La Suite du Roman de Merlin, ed. by Gilles Roussineau, Textes littéraires français, 472, 2 vols (Geneva: Droz, 1996), II

'Syr Tryamowre', in *Of Love and Chivalry: An Anthology of Middle English Romance*, ed. by Jennifer Fellows (London: Dent, 1993), pp. 147–98

Thomas, *The Romance of Horn*, ed. by Mildred K. Pope, Anglo-Norman Texts, 9–10, 2 vols (Oxford: Blackwell, 1955), I

———, 'The Romance of Horn', in *The Birth of Romance in England: 'The Romance of Horn', The 'Folie Tristan', The 'Lai of Haveloc', and 'Amis and Amilun'*, ed. & trans. by Judith Weiss, FRETS, 4 (Tempe: Arizona Center for Medieval and Renaissance Studies, 2009), pp. 45–137

Trevet, Nicholas, 'De la noble femme Constance', in *Sources and Analogues of the Canterbury Tales*, ed. by Robert M. Correale with Mary Hamel, 2 vols (Cambridge: D. S. Brewer, 2005), II, 297–329

'Trot', in *Three Old French Narrative Lays: Trot, Lecheor, Nabaret*, ed. & trans. by Glyn S. Burgess and Leslie C. Brook, Liverpool Online Series, Critical Editions of French Texts, 1 (Liverpool: University of Liverpool, 1999), pp. 13–43

'The Wedding of Sir Gawain and Dame Ragnelle', in *Sir Gawain: Eleven Romances and Tales*, ed. by Thomas Hahn, TEAMS (Kalamazoo: Medieval Institute Publications, 1995), pp. 47–70

Secondary Sources

Adams, Tracy, '"Arte Regendus Amor": Suffering and Sexuality in Marie de France's *Lai de Guigemar*', *Exemplaria*, 17.2 (2005), 285–315

Aertsen, Henk, '*Havelok the Dane*: A Non-Courtly Romance', in *Companion to Early Middle English Literature*, ed. by N. H. G. E. Veldhoen and Henk Aertsen, 2nd edn (Amsterdam: VU University Press, 1995), pp. 29–50

Ahmed, Sara, *The Promise of Happiness* (Durham, NC: Duke University Press, 2010)

———, *Willful Subjects* (Durham, NC: Duke University Press, 2014)

Ailes, Marianne, '*Gui de Warewic* in its Manuscript Context', in *Guy of Warwick: Icon and Ancestor*, ed. by Alison Wiggins and Rosalind Field (Cambridge: D. S. Brewer, 2007), pp. 12–26

Ailes, Marianne, and Phillipa Hardman, *The Legend of Charlemagne in Medieval England: The Matter of France in Middle English and Anglo-Norman Literature* (Cambridge: D. S. Brewer, 2017)

Akard, Lucia, 'Unequal Power and Sexual Consent: The Case of Cassotte la Joye', *Studies in the Age of Chaucer*, 44 (2022), 'Colloquium: Historicizing Consent: Bodies, Wills, Desires', ed. by Carissa M. Harris and Fiona Somerset, 285–92

Akard, Lucia, and Alice Raw, 'Global Response: Futures of Medieval Consent', *Studies in the Age of Chaucer*, 44 (2022), 'Colloquium: Historicizing Consent: Bodies, Wills, Desires', ed. by Carissa M. Harris and Fiona Somerset, 363–7

Bibliography

Akbari, Suzanne Conklin, *Idols in the East: European Representations of Islam and the Orient, 1100–1450* (Ithaca: Cornell University Press, 2009)

Alberghini, Jennifer, "'A kysse onely": The Problem of Female Socialization in William Caxton's *Blanchardyn and Eglantine*', *Studies in the Age of Chaucer*, 44 (2022), 'Colloquium: Historicizing Consent: Bodies, Wills, Desires', ed. by Carissa M. Harris and Fiona Somerset, 347–57

Allen, Rosamund, 'The Date and Provenance of *King Horn*: Some Interim Reassessments', in *Medieval English Studies Presented to George Kane*, ed. by Edward Donald Kennedy, Ronald Waldron, and Joseph S. Wittig (Cambridge: D. S. Brewer, 1988), pp. 99–125

Allen-Goss, Lucy M., *Female Desire in Chaucer's 'Legend of Good Women' and Middle English Romance* (Cambridge: D. S. Brewer, 2020)

Andersen-Wyman, Kathleen, *Andreas Capellanus on Love?: Desire, Seduction, and Subversion in a Twelfth-Century Latin Text* (Basingstoke: Palgrave Macmillan, 2007)

Anderson, Michelle J., 'Negotiating Sex', *Southern California Law Review*, 78.6 (2005), 1401–38

Angel, Katherine, *Tomorrow Sex Will Be Good Again: Women and Desire in the Age of Consent* (London: Verso, 2021)

Arkenberg, Megan, "'A Mayde, and Last of Youre Blood": Galahad's Asexuality and its Significance in *Le Morte Darthur*', *Arthuriana*, 24.3 (2014), 3–22

Armstrong, Dorsey, *Gender and the Chivalric Community in Malory's 'Morte d'Arthur'* (Gainesville: University Press of Florida, 2003)

——, 'Gender, Marriage, and Knighthood: Single Ladies in Malory', in *The Single Woman in Medieval and Early Modern England: Her Life and Representation*, ed. by Laurel Amtower and Dorothea Kehler (Tempe: Arizona Center for Medieval and Renaissance Studies, 2003), pp. 41–61

Arthur, Ross G., 'Introduction', in *Amadas and Ydoine*, ed. & trans. by Ross G. Arthur, Garland Library of Medieval Literature, Series B, 95 (New York: Garland, 1993), pp. 9–16

Baechle, Sarah, 'Speaking Survival: Chaucer Studies and the Discourses of Sexual Assault', *Chaucer Review*, 57.4 (2022), 463–74

Baechle, Sarah, Carissa M. Harris, and Elizaveta Strakhov, 'Introduction: Recovering the Pastourelle', in *Rape Culture and Female Resistance in Late Medieval Literature*, ed. by Sarah Baechle, Carissa M. Harris, and Elizaveta Strakhov (University Park: Pennsylvania State University Press, 2022), pp. 1–14

——, eds, *Rape Culture and Female Resistance in Late Medieval Literature* (University Park: Pennsylvania State University Press, 2022)

——, 'Reassessing the Pastourelle: Rape Culture, #MeToo, and the Literature of Survival', in *Rape Culture and Female Resistance in Late Medieval Literature*, ed. by Sarah Baechle, Carissa M. Harris, and Elizaveta Strakhov (University Park: Pennsylvania State University Press, 2022), pp. 17–28

Barnes, Geraldine, *Counsel and Strategy in Middle English Romance* (Cambridge: D. S. Brewer, 1993)

Baron, Salo Wittmayer, *A Social and Religious History of the Jews*, 20 vols (New York: Columbia University Press, 1952), XI

Bates, Laura, *Men Who Hate Women* (London: Simon & Schuster, 2020)

Batt, Catherine, 'Malory and Rape', *Arthuriana*, 7.3 (1997), 78–99

Baugh, A. C., 'Documenting Sir Thomas Malory', *Speculum*, 8.1 (1933), 3–29

Bell, Kimberly K., 'Resituating Romance: The Dialectics of Sanctity in MS Laud Misc. 108's *Havelok the Dane* and Royal *Vitae*', *Parergon*, 25.1 (2008), 27–51

Bell, Kimberly K., and Julie Nelson Couch, 'Introduction: Reading Oxford, Bodleian Library, MS Laud Misc. 108 as a "Whole Book"', in *The Texts and Contexts of Oxford, Bodleian Library, MS Laud Misc. 108: The Shaping of English Vernacular Narrative*, ed. by Kimberly K. Bell and Julie Nelson Couch (Leiden: Brill, 2011), pp. 1–18

———, eds, *The Texts and Contexts of Oxford, Bodleian Library, MS Laud Misc. 108: The Shaping of English Vernacular Narrative* (Leiden: Brill, 2011)

Bennett, Judith M., and Ruth Mazo Karras, 'Women, Gender, and Medieval Historians', in *The Oxford Handbook of Women and Gender in Medieval Europe*, ed. by Judith M. Bennett and Ruth Mazo Karras (Oxford: Oxford University Press, 2013), pp. 1–18

Benson, Larry D., 'Explanatory Notes', in *The Riverside Chaucer*, ed. by Larry D. Benson, 3rd edn (Oxford: Oxford University Press, 2008), pp. 795–1116

Benveniste, Emile, *Indo-European Language and Society*, trans. by Elizabeth Palmer (London: Faber & Faber, 1973)

Bérat, Emma O'Loughlin, 'Constructions of Queenship: Envisioning Women's Sovereignty in *Havelok*', *Journal of English and Germanic Philology*, 118.2 (2019), 234–51

Besamusca, Bart, 'Readership and Audience', in *Handbook of Arthurian Romance: King Arthur's Court in Medieval European Literature*, ed. by Leah Tether and Johnny McFadyen (Berlin: de Gruyter, 2017), pp. 117–32

Best, Debra E., '"A lowed laghtur that lady logh": Laughter, Snark, and Sarcasm in Middle English Romance', in *Words that Tear the Flesh: Essays on Sarcasm in Medieval and Early Modern Literature and Cultures*, ed. by Stephen Alan Baragona and Elizabeth Louise Rambo (Berlin: de Gruyter, 2018), pp. 143–64

Birkholz, Daniel, *Harley manuscript geographies: Literary history and the medieval miscellany* (Manchester: Manchester University Press, 2020)

Black, Daisy, 'Broken Shells' (performed at 'Gender and Aliens', the annual Gender and Medieval Studies Conference, Durham University, 2019) <https://daisyblack.uk/storytelling/> [accessed 30 September 2022]

———, '"Diverse women said diverse things…": Storytelling, Research, and Shipping Custance and Hermengyld' (presented at Leeds International Medieval Congress, Leeds, 2021)

———, *Play time: Gender, anti-Semitism and temporality in medieval biblical drama* (Manchester: Manchester University Press, 2020)

Blake, N. F., 'Vernon Manuscript: Contents and Organisation', in *Studies in the Vernon Manuscript*, ed. by Derek Pearsall (Cambridge: D. S. Brewer, 1990), pp. 45–59

Blamires, Alcuin, *The Case for Women in Medieval Culture* (Oxford: Clarendon Press, 1997)

Blanchfield, Lynne S., 'The romances in MS Ashmole 61: an idiosyncratic scribe', in *Romance in Medieval England*, ed. by Maldwyn Mills, Jennifer Fellows, and Carol M. Meale (Cambridge: D. S. Brewer, 1991), pp. 65–87

Blatt, Heather, '"Whiteness seeps through": Resisting colorblind racism in Man-deville's *Travels*', *postmedieval*, 11.4 (2020), 484–92

Bloch, R. Howard, 'The Medieval Text – "Guigemar" – as a Provocation to the Discipline of Medieval Studies', *Romanic Review*, 79.1 (1988), 63–73

Blud, Victoria, *The Unspeakable, Gender and Sexuality in Medieval Literature 1000–1400* (Cambridge: D. S. Brewer, 2017)

Bly Calkin, Siobhain, 'Marking Religion on the Body: Saracens, Categorization, and *The King of Tars*', *Journal of English and Germanic Philology*, 104.2 (2005), 219–38

———, 'Saracens', in *Heroes and Anti-Heroes in Medieval Romance*, ed. by Neil Cartlidge (Cambridge: D. S. Brewer, 2012), pp. 185–200

———, *Saracens and the Making of English Identity: The Auchinleck Manu-script* (London: Routledge, 2005)

———, 'The Anxieties of Encounter and Exchange: Saracens and Christian Her-oism in *Sir Beves of Hamtoun*', *Florilegium*, 21 (2004), 135–58

Brewer, Derek, 'Chivalry', in *A Companion to Chaucer*, ed. by Peter Brown (Ox-ford: Blackwell, 2000), pp. 58–74

Brown, A. E., 'Lancelot in the Friend Zone: Strategies for Offering and Limiting Affection in the *Stanzaic Morte Arthur*', in *Emotion and Medieval Textual Me-dia*, ed. by Mary C. Flannery (Turnhout: Brepols, 2018), pp. 75–97

Brown-Grant, Rosalind, *French Romance of the Later Middle Ages: Gender, Mo-rality, and Desire* (Oxford: Oxford University Press, 2008)

Brundage, James A., *Law, Sex, and Christian Society in Medieval Europe* (Chica-go: University of Chicago Press, 1987)

———, 'Sex and Canon Law', in *Handbook of Medieval Sexuality*, ed. by Vern L. Bullough and James A. Brundage (New York: Routledge, 1996), pp. 33–50

———, *Sex, Law and Marriage in the Middle Ages* (Aldershot: Variorum, 1993)

Brzezinski Potkay, Monica, 'The Violence of Courtly Exegesis in *Sir Gawain and the Green Knight*', in *Representing Rape in Medieval and Early Modern Liter-ature*, ed. by Elizabeth Robertson and Christine M. Rose (New York: Palgrave, 2001), pp. 97–124

Buchwald, Emilie, Pamela R. Fletcher, and Martha Roth, 'Preamble', in *Trans-forming a Rape Culture*, ed. by Emilie Buchwald, Pamela R. Fletcher, and Martha Roth, rev. edn (Minneapolis: Milkweed Editions, 2005), pp. i–xii

Burge, Amy, *Representing Difference in the Medieval and Modern Orientalist Romance* (New York: Palgrave Macmillan, 2016)

Burger, Glenn D., *Conduct Becoming: Good Wives and Husbands in the Later Middle Ages* (Philadelphia: University of Pennsylvania Press, 2018)

Burgess, Glyn S., 'Marie de France and the Anonymous Lays', in *A Companion to Marie de France*, ed. by Logan E. Whalen (Leiden: Brill, 2011), pp. 117–56

Burgwinkle, William E., *Sodomy, Masculinity, and Law in Medieval Literature: France and England, 1050–1230* (Cambridge: Cambridge University Press, 2004)

Burrow, J. A., *A Reading of 'Sir Gawain and the Green Knight'* (London: Rout-ledge & Kegan Paul, 1965)

Busby, Keith, 'The Likes of Dinadan: The Rôle of the Misfit in Arthurian Litera-ture', *Neophilologus*, 67.2 (1983), 161–74

————, 'The Manuscripts of Chrétien's Romances', in *A Companion to Chrétien de Troyes*, ed. by Norris J. Lacy and Joan Tasker Grimbert (Cambridge: D. S. Brewer, 2005), pp. 64–75

————, 'The Manuscripts of Marie de France', in *A Companion to Marie de France*, ed. by Logan E. Whalen (Leiden: Brill, 2011), pp. 303–17

Butler, Judith, *Gender Trouble: Feminism and the Subversion of Identity* (New York: Routledge, 2002; first publ. 1990)

Butler, Sara, 'Runaway Wives: Husband Desertion in Medieval England', *Journal of Social History*, 40.2 (2006), 337–59

Byrne, Aisling, and Victoria Flood, 'The Romance of the Stanleys: Regional and National Imaginings in the Percy Folio', *Viator*, 46.1 (2015), 327–51

Cadden, Joan, *Nothing Natural Is Shameful: Sodomy and Science in Late Medieval Europe* (Philadelphia: University of Pennsylvania Press, 2014)

Caldwell, James Ralston, 'Introduction', in *Eger and Grime: A parallel-text edition of the Percy and the Huntington-Laing Versions of the Romance*, ed. by James Ralston Caldwell (Cambridge, MA: Harvard University Press, 1933), pp. 3–176

Calin, William, *The Lily and the Thistle: The French Tradition and the Older Literature of Scotland – Essays in Criticism* (Toronto: University of Toronto Press, 2014)

Cannon, Christopher, 'Chaucer and Rape: Uncertainty's Certainties', in *Representing Rape in Medieval and Early Modern Literature*, ed. by Elizabeth Robertson and Christine M. Rose (New York: Palgrave, 2001), pp. 255–79 (first publ. in *Studies in the Age of Chaucer*, 22 (2000), 67–92)

Caputo, John D., ed., *Deconstruction in a Nutshell: A Conversation with Jacques Derrida* (New York: Fordham University Press, 2021)

Carpenter, Christine, 'Sir Thomas Malory and Fifteenth-Century Local Politics', *Bulletin of the Institute of Historical Research*, 53.127 (1980), 31–43

Cartlidge, Neil, *Medieval Marriage: Literary Approaches, 1100–1300* (Cambridge: D. S. Brewer, 1997)

————, '"Nat that I chalange any thyng of right": Love, Loyalty, and Legality in the *Franklin's Tale*', in *Writings on Love in the English Middle Ages*, ed. by Helen Cooney (New York: Palgrave Macmillan, 2006), pp. 115–30

————, '"Vinegar upon Nitre"? Walter Map's Romance of "Sadius and Galo"', in *Cultural Translations in Medieval Romance*, ed. by Victoria Flood and Megan G. Leitch (Cambridge: D. S. Brewer, 2022), pp. 117–33

Casson, L. F., 'Introduction', in *The Romance of Sir Degrevant*, ed. by L. F. Casson, EETS, o. s., 221 (London: Oxford University Press, 1949; repr. 1970), pp. ix–lxxv

Cawsey, Kathy, 'Disorienting Orientalism: Finding Saracens in Strange Places in Late Medieval English Manuscripts', *Exemplaria*, 21.4 (2009), 380–97

Charbonneau, Joanne, and Désirée Cromwell, 'Gender and Identity in the Popular Romance', in *A Companion to Medieval Popular Romance*, ed. by Raluca L. Radulescu and Cory James Rushton (Cambridge: D. S. Brewer, 2009), pp. 96–110

Chen, Angela, *Ace: What Asexuality Reveals About Desire, Society, and the Meaning of Sex* (Boston: Beacon, 2020)

Cherewatuk, Karen, *Marriage, Adultery and Inheritance in Malory's 'Morte Darthur'* (Cambridge: D. S. Brewer, 2006)

Chess, Simone, 'Asexuality, Queer Chastity, and Adolescence in Early Modern Literature', in *Queering Childhood in Early Modern English Drama and Culture*, ed. by Jennifer Higginbotham and Mark Albert Johnston (Cham: Palgrave Macmillan, 2018), pp. 31–55

Childress, Diana T., 'Between Romance and Legend: "Secular Hagiography" in Middle English Literature', *Philological Quarterly*, 57.3 (1978), 311–22

Cichon, Michael, '"As ye have brewd, so shal ye drink": The Proverbial Context of *Eger and Grime*', in *Medieval Romance, Medieval Contexts*, ed. by Rhiannon Purdie and Michael Cichon (Cambridge: D. S. Brewer, 2011), pp. 35–46

Cixous, Hélène, 'Fiction and Its Phantoms: A Reading of Freud's *Das Unheimliche* (The "uncanny")', trans. by Robert Dennomé, *New Literary History*, 7.3 (1976), 525–48

Cleto, Fabio, 'Introduction: Queering the Camp', in *Camp: Queer Aesthetics and the Performing Subject*, ed. by Fabio Cleto (Edinburgh: Edinburgh University Press, 1999), pp. 1–42

Clifton, Nicole, 'The Seven Sages of Rome, Children's Literature, and the Auchinleck Manuscript', in *Childhood in the Middle Ages and the Renaissance*, ed. by Albrecht Classen (Berlin: de Gruyter, 2005), pp. 185–201

Cohen, Jeffrey Jerome, *Medieval Identity Machines* (Minneapolis: University of Minnesota Press, 2003)

———, 'Race', in *A Handbook of Middle English Studies*, ed. by Marion Turner (Chichester: Wiley-Blackwell, 2013), pp. 109–22

Coope, Jessica, *The Martyrs of Córdoba: Community and Family Conflict in an Age of Mass Conversion* (Lincoln: University of Nebraska Press, 1995)

Cooper, Helen, *The English Romance in Time: Transforming motifs from Geoffrey of Monmouth to the death of Shakespeare* (Oxford: Oxford University Press, 2004)

———, 'Passionate, eloquent and determined: Heroines' tales and feminine poetics', *Journal of the British Academy*, 4 (2016), 221–44

Correale, Robert M., with Mary Hamel, eds, *Sources and Analogues of The Canterbury Tales*, 2 vols (Cambridge: D. S. Brewer, 2005), II

Cowen, Janet M., 'The English Charlemagne Romances', in *Roland and Charlemagne in Europe: Essays on the Reception and Transformation of a Legend*, ed. by Karen Pratt (London: King's College London, Centre for Late Antique and Medieval Studies, 1996), pp. 149–68

Crane, Susan, *Gender and Romance in Chaucer's 'Canterbury Tales'* (Princeton: Princeton University Press, 1994)

———, *Insular Romance: Politics, Faith, and Culture in Anglo-Norman and Middle English Literature* (Berkeley: University of California Press, 1986)

Crenshaw, Kimberlé, 'Mapping the Margins: Intersectionality, Identity Politics, and Violence against Women of Color', *Stanford Law Review*, 43.6 (1991), 1241–99

Critten, Rory G., 'Bourgeois Ethics Again: The Conduct Texts and the Romances in Oxford, Bodleian Library MS Ashmole 61', *Chaucer Review*, 50.1–2 (2015), 108–33

Crocker, Holly A., *The Matter of Virtue: Women's Ethical Action from Chaucer to Shakespeare* (Philadelphia: University of Pennsylvania Press, 2019)

Daniel, Norman, *Heroes and Saracens: An Interpretation of the 'Chansons de Geste'* (Edinburgh: Edinburgh University Press, 1984)

Dannenbaum [Crane], Susan, 'Insular Tradition in the Story of Amis and Amiloun', *Neophilologus*, 67.4 (1983), 611–22

Davidson, Roberta, 'Reading Like a Woman in Malory's "Morte Darthur"', *Arthuriana*, 16.1 (2006), 21–33

Decker, Julie Sondra, *The Invisible Orientation: An Introduction to Asexuality* (New York: Skyhorse, 2014)

Delany, Sheila, 'A, A and B: Coding same-sex union in *Amis and Amiloun*', in *Pulp Fictions of Medieval England: Essays in Popular Romance*, ed. by Nicola McDonald (Manchester: Manchester University Press, 2004), pp. 63–81

Delany, Sheila, and Vahan Ishkanian, 'Theocratic and Contractual Kingship in *Havelok the Dane*', *Zeitschrift für Anglistik und Amerikanistik*, 22 (1974), 290–302

Dell, Helen, *Desire by Gender and Genre in Trouvère Song* (Cambridge: D. S. Brewer, 2008)

Derrida, Jacques, *Acts of Religion*, ed. & trans. by Gil Anidjar (London: Routledge, 2001)

Desmond, Marilynn, *Ovid's Art and the Wife of Bath: The Ethics of Erotic Violence* (Ithaca: Cornell University Press, 2006)

Diamond, Arlyn, '*Sir Degrevant*: what lovers want', in *Pulp Fictions of Medieval England: Essays in Popular Romance*, ed. by Nicola McDonald (Manchester: Manchester University Press, 2004), pp. 82–101

———, '*The Erle of Tolous*: The Price of Virtue', in *Medieval Insular Romance: Translation and Innovation*, ed. by Judith Weiss, Jennifer Fellows, and Morgan Dickson (Cambridge: D. S. Brewer, 2000), pp. 83–92

Dinshaw, Carolyn, *Chaucer's Sexual Poetics* (Madison: University of Wisconsin Press, 1989)

———, 'Pale Faces: Race, Religion, and Affect in Chaucer's Texts and Their Readers', *Studies in the Age of Chaucer*, 23 (2001), 19–41

Djordjević, Ivana, '*Guy of Warwick* as a Translation', in *Guy of Warwick: Icon and Ancestor*, ed. by Alison Wiggins and Rosalind Field (Cambridge: D. S. Brewer, 2007), pp. 27–43

Doggett, Laine E., *Love Cures: Healing and Love Magic in Old French Romance* (University Park: Penn State University Press, 2009)

Dolmans, Emily, *Writing Regional Identities in Medieval England: From the 'Gesta Herwardi' to 'Richard Coer de Lyon'* (Cambridge: D. S. Brewer, 2020)

Driver, Martha W., '"In her owne persone semly and bewteus": Representing Women in Stories of Guy of Warwick', in *Guy of Warwick: Icon and Ancestor*, ed. by Alison Wiggins and Rosalind Field (Cambridge: D. S. Brewer, 2007), pp. 133–53

Dufourmantelle, Anne, and Jacques Derrida, *Of Hospitality*, trans. by Rachel Bowlby (Stanford: Stanford University Press, 2000)

Dunn, Caroline, *Stolen Women in Medieval England: Rape, Abduction, and Adultery, 1100–1500* (Cambridge: Cambridge University Press, 2012)

Edwards, A. S. G., 'Codicology and Translation in the Early Sections of the Auchinleck Manuscript', in *The Auchinleck Manuscript: New Perspectives*, ed. by Susanna Fein (York: York Medieval Press, 2016), pp. 26–35

——, 'The Contexts of the Vernon Romances', in *Studies in the Vernon Manuscript*, ed. by Derek Pearsall (Cambridge: D. S. Brewer, 1990), pp. 159–70

——, 'The Reception of Malory's *Morte Darthur*', in *A Companion to Malory*, ed. by Elizabeth Archibald and A. S. G. Edwards (Cambridge: D. S. Brewer, 1996), pp. 241–52

——, 'The *Speculum Guy de Warwick* and Lydgate's *Guy of Warwick*: The Non-Romance Middle English Tradition', in *Guy of Warwick: Icon and Ancestor*, ed. by Alison Wiggins and Rosalind Field (Cambridge: D. S. Brewer, 2007), pp. 81–93

Edwards, Suzanne M., *The Afterlives of Rape in Medieval English Literature* (Basingstoke: Palgrave Macmillan, 2016)

——, 'Medieval Saints and Misogynist Times: Transhistorical Perspectives on Sexual Violence in the Undergraduate Classroom', in *Teaching Rape in the Medieval Literature Classroom: Approaches to Difficult Texts*, ed. by Alison Gulley (Leeds: Arc Humanities Press, 2018), pp. 12–28

Eley, Penny, 'Introduction', in *Narcisus et Dané*, ed. & trans. by Penny Eley, Liverpool Online Series, Critical Editions of French Texts, 6 (Liverpool: University of Liverpool, 2002), pp. 7–30

Elias, Marcel, 'Interfaith Empathy and the Formation of Romance', in *Emotion and Medieval Textual Media*, ed. by Mary C. Flannery (Turnhout: Brepols, 2018), pp. 99–124

Evans, Deanna Delmar, 'Scott's *Redgauntlet* and the Late Medieval Romance of Friendship, *Eger and Grime*', *Studies in Scottish Literature*, 31.1 (1999), 31–45

Faris, David E., 'The Art of Adventure in the Middle English Romance: *Ywain and Gawain, Eger and Grime*', *Studia Neophilologica*, 53.1 (1981), 91–100

Fein, Susanna [Greer], 'Compilation and Purpose in MS Harley 2253', in *Essays in Manuscript Geography: Vernacular Manuscripts of the English West Midlands from the Conquest to the Sixteenth Century*, ed. by Wendy Scase (Turnhout: Brepols, 2007), pp. 67–94

——, 'The Complete Harley 2253 Manuscript, Volume 2: Introduction', in *The Complete Harley 2253 Manuscript*, ed. by Susanna Greer Fein, trans. by Susanna Greer Fein, David Raybin, and Jan Ziolkowski, TEAMS, 3 vols (Kalamazoo: Medieval Institute Publications, 2014), ii, 1–13

——, 'The Contents of Robert Thornton's Manuscripts', in *Robert Thornton and His Books: Essays on the Lincoln and London Thornton Manuscripts*, ed. by Susanna Fein and Michael Johnston (York: York Medieval Press, 2014), pp. 13–65

——, 'Explanatory Notes', in *The Complete Harley 2253 Manuscript*, ed. by Susanna Greer Fein, trans. by Susanna Greer Fein, David Raybin, and Jan Ziolkowski, TEAMS, 3 vols (Kalamazoo: Medieval Institute Publications, 2014), ii, 371–454

Fellows, Jennifer, 'Introduction', in *Sir Bevis of Hampton*, ed. by Jennifer

Fellows, EETS, o. s., 349, 2 vols (Oxford: Oxford University Press, 2017), I, pp. xv–lxxviii

Fetterley, Judith, *The Resisting Reader: A Feminist Approach to American Fiction* (Bloomington: Indiana University Press, 1978)

Field, P. J. C., *The Life and Times of Sir Thomas Malory* (Cambridge: D. S. Brewer, 1993)

——, ed., *Le Morte Darthur: Apparatus, Commentary, Glossary, and Index of Names*, 2 vols (Cambridge: D. S. Brewer, 2013), II

——, 'Sir Thomas Malory's *Le Morte Darthur*', in *The Arthur of the English: The Arthurian Legend in Medieval English Life and Literature*, ed. by W. R. J. Barron (Cardiff: University of Wales Press, 2001), pp. 225–45

Field, Rosalind, 'Children of Anarchy: Anglo-Norman Romance in the Twelfth Century', in *Writers of the Reign of Henry II: Twelve Essays*, ed. by Ruth Kennedy and Simon Meecham-Jones (New York: Palgrave Macmillan, 2006), pp. 249–62

——, 'The King Over the Water: Exile-and-Return Revisited', in *Cultural Encounters in the Romance of Medieval England*, ed. by Corinne Saunders (Cambridge: D. S. Brewer, 2005), pp. 41–53

Fischel, Joseph J., *Screw Consent: A Better Politics of Sexual Justice* (Oakland: University of California Press, 2019)

Flannery, Mary C., *Practising shame: Female honour in later medieval England* (Manchester: Manchester University Press, 2020)

Fradenburg, Louise O., '"Our owen wo to drynke": Loss, Gender and Chivalry in *Troilus and Criseyde*', in *Chaucer's Troilus and Criseyde: 'Subgit to Alle Poesye': Essays in Criticism*, ed. by R. A. Shoaf (Binghamton, NY: Medieval and Renaissance Texts and Studies, 1992), pp. 88–106

Frankis, John, 'Taste and Patronage in Late Medieval England as Reflected in Versions of *Guy of Warwick*', *Medium Ævum*, 66.1 (1997), 80–93

Freidenreich, David M., 'Muslims in Eastern canon law, 1000–1500', in *Christian-Muslim Relations: A Bibliographical History, Volume 4 (1200–1350)*, ed. by David Thomas et al., 7 vols (Leiden: Brill, 2012), IV, 45–57

——, 'Muslims in Western canon law, 1000–1500', in *Christian-Muslim Relations: A Bibliographical History, Volume 3 (1050–1200)*, ed. by David Thomas and Alexander Mallett, 7 vols (Leiden: Brill, 2009), III, 41–68

Friðriksdóttir, Jóhanna Katrín, 'From Heroic Legend to "Medieval Screwball Comedy"? The Origins, Development and Interpretation of the Maiden-King Narrative', in *The Legendary Sagas: Origins and Development*, ed. by Annette Lassen, Agneta Ney, and Ármann Jakobsson (Reykjavík: University of Iceland Press, 2012), pp. 229–49

——, *Women in Old Norse Literature: Bodies, Words, and Power* (New York: Palgrave Macmillan, 2013)

Friedman, Jamie, 'Making whiteness matter: *The King of Tars*', in *Making Race Matter in the Middle Ages*, ed. by Cord J. Whitaker (= *postmedieval*, 6.1 (2015)), pp. 52–63

Friedrichs, Rhoda L., 'The Remarriage of Elite Widows in the Later Middle Ages', *Florilegium*, 23.1 (2006), 69–83

Fumo, Jamie C., 'Ovid: Artistic Identity and Intertextuality', in *The Oxford*

Handbook of Chaucer, ed. by Suzanne Conklin Akbari and James Simpson (Oxford: Oxford University Press, 2020), pp. 219–37

Furnish, Shearle, 'The Modernity of *The Erle of Tolous* and the Decay of the Breton Lai', *Medieval Perspectives*, 8 (1993), 69–77

Furrow, Melissa, *Expectations of Romance: The Reception of a Genre in Medieval England* (Cambridge: D. S. Brewer, 2009)

Gallagher, Joseph E., '"Trawþe" and "luf-talkyng" in *Sir Gawain and the Green Knight*', *Neuphilologische Mitteilungen*, 78.4 (1977), 362–76

Ganze, Alison, '"My Trouth for to Holde – Allas, Allas!": Dorigen and Honor in the *Franklin's Tale*', *Chaucer Review*, 42.3 (2008), 312–29

Gassman, Jürg, 'Mounted Combat in Transition: The Transformation of the Eleventh Century: Early Medieval Cavalry Battlefield Tactics', in *The Horse in Premodern European Culture*, ed. by Anastasija Ropa and Timothy Dawson (Berlin: de Gruyter, 2019), pp. 71–86

Gaunt, Simon, 'The Châtelain de Couci', in *The Cambridge Companion to Medieval French Literature*, ed. by Simon Gaunt and Sarah Kay (Cambridge: Cambridge University Press, 2008), pp. 95–108

———, *Gender and Genre in Medieval French Literature* (Cambridge: Cambridge University Press, 1995)

Gertz, SunHee Kim, 'Transforming Lovers and Memorials in Ovid and Marie de France', *Florilegium*, 14 (1995), 99–122

Gilbert, Jane, 'Putting the pulp into fiction: the lump-child and its parents in *The King of Tars*', in *Pulp Fictions of Medieval England: Essays in Popular Romance*, ed. by Nicola McDonald (Manchester: Manchester University Press, 2004), pp. 102–23

Gillingham, John, 'Love, Marriage, and Politics in the Twelfth Century', *Forum for Modern Language Studies*, 25.4 (1989), 292–303

Glasser, Marc, '"He nedes moste hire wedde": The Forced Marriage in the "Wife of Bath's Tale" and Its Middle English Analogues', *Neuphilologische Mitteilungen*, 85.2 (1984), 239–41

Goodison, Natalie, Deborah J. G. Mackay, and Karen Temple, 'Genetics, Molar Pregnancies and Medieval Ideas of Monstrous Births: The Lump of Flesh in *The King of Tars*', *Medical Humanities*, 45.1 (2019), 2–9

Gravdal, Kathryn, *Ravishing Maidens: Writing Rape in Medieval French Literature and Law* (Philadelphia: University of Pennsylvania Press, 1991)

Green, Richard Firth, 'Troilus and the Game of Love', *Chaucer Review*, 13.3 (1979), 201–20

Grubbs, David, 'The Knight Coerced: Two Cases of Raped Men in Chivalric Romance', in *Teaching Rape in the Medieval Literature Classroom: Approaches to Difficult Texts*, ed. by Alison Gulley (Leeds: Arc Humanities Press, 2018), pp. 164–82

Gulley, Alison, '"How do we know he really raped her?": Using the BBC *Canterbury Tales* to Confront Student Skepticism towards the Wife of Bath', in *Teaching Rape in the Medieval Literature Classroom: Approaches to Difficult Texts*, ed. by Alison Gulley (Leeds: Arc Humanities Press, 2018), pp. 113–27

———, ed., *Teaching Rape in the Medieval Literature Classroom: Approaches to Difficult Texts* (Leeds: Arc Humanities Press, 2018)

Gunn, Cate, and Liz Herbert McAvoy, 'Introduction: "No Such Thing as Socie-ty"? Solitude in Community', in *Medieval Anchorites in their Communities*, ed. by Cate Gunn and Liz Herbert McAvoy (Cambridge: D. S. Brewer, 2017), pp. 1–12

Guynn, Noah D., *Allegory and Sexual Ethics in the High Middle Ages* (Basing-stoke: Palgrave Macmillan, 2007)

Hall, Joseph, 'Introduction', in *King Horn: A Middle-English Romance*, ed. by Joseph Hall (Oxford: Clarendon Press, 1901), pp. vii–xv

——, 'The Story', in *King Horn: A Middle-English Romance*, ed. by Joseph Hall (Oxford: Clarendon Press, 1901), pp. li–lvi

Hall, Kim F., '"These bastard signs of fair": Literary whiteness in Shakespeare's sonnets', in *Post-Colonial Shakespeares*, ed. by Ania Loomba and Martin Or-kin (London: Routledge, 1998), pp. 64–83

——, *Things of Darkness: Economies of Race and Gender in Early Modern England* (Ithaca: Cornell University Press, 1995)

Hamad, Ruby, *White Tears/Brown Scars: How White Feminism Betrays Women of Color* (New York: Catapult, 2020)

Hames-García, Michael, 'How Real Is Race?', in *Material Feminisms*, ed. by Stacy Alaimo and Susan Hekman (Bloomington: Indiana University Press, 2008), pp. 308–39

Hanks, Jr., D. Thomas, 'Characterization or Jumble? Sir Dinadan in Malory', *Medieval Perspectives*, 2.1 (1987), 167–76

——, 'Foil and Forecast: Dinadan in *The Book of Sir Tristram*', *Arthurian Yearbook*, 1 (1991), 149–63

Hanning, R. W., 'Courtly Contexts for Urban *Cultus*: Responses to Ovid in Chré-tien's *Cligès* and Marie's *Guigemar*', *Symposium*, 35.1 (1981), 34–56

Hardman, Phillipa, 'Popular Romances and Young Readers', in *A Companion to Medieval Popular Romance*, ed. by Raluca L. Radulescu and Cory James Rushton (Cambridge: D. S. Brewer, 2009), pp. 150–64

Hardwick, C., et al., eds, *A Catalogue of the Manuscripts Preserved in the Library of the University of Cambridge*, 5 vols (Cambridge: Cambridge University Press, 1858), III

Harper, Elizabeth, 'Teaching the Potiphar's Wife Motif in Marie de France's *Lan-val*', in *Teaching Rape in the Medieval Literature Classroom: Approaches to Difficult Texts*, ed. by Alison Gulley (Leeds: Arc Humanities Press, 2018), pp. 128–37

Harris, Barbara J., *English Aristocratic Women, 1450–1550: Marriage and Fami-ly, Property and Careers* (Oxford: Oxford University Press, 2002)

Harris, Carissa M., *Obscene Pedagogies: Transgressive Talk and Sexual Educa-tion in Late Medieval Britain* (Ithaca: Cornell University Press, 2018)

——, 'On Servant Women, Rape Culture, and Endurance', *Chaucer Review*, 57.4 (2022), 475–83

Harris, Carissa M., and Fiona Somerset, eds, 'Colloquium: Historicizing Consent: Bodies, Wills, Desires', *Studies in the Age of Chaucer*, 44 (2022), 267–367

Harvey, Katherine, *The Fires of Lust: Sex in the Middle Ages* (London: Reakton, 2021)

Harwood, Sophie, *Medieval Women and War: Female Roles in the Old French Tradition* (London: Bloomsbury Academic, 2020)

Hasler, Antony J., 'Romance and Its Discontents in *Eger and Grime*', in *The Spirit of Medieval English Popular Romance*, ed. by Ad Putter and Jane Gilbert (London: Routledge, 2013; first publ. 2000), pp. 200–18

Hausknecht, Emil, 'Notes', in *The Sowdone of Babylone*, ed. by Emil Hausknecht, EETS, e. s., 38 (London: Paul, Trench, and Trübner, 1881), pp. 95–132

Heng, Geraldine, *Empire of Magic: Medieval Romance and the Politics of Cultural Fantasy* (New York: Columbia University Press, 2003)

———, *The Invention of Race in the European Middle Ages* (Cambridge: Cambridge University Press, 2018)

———, 'A Woman Wants: The Lady, *Gawain*, and the Forms of Seduction', *Yale Journal of Criticism*, 5.3 (1992), 101–34

Herbert McAvoy, Liz, 'Textual Phantoms and Spectral Presences: The Coming to Rest of Mechthild of Hackeborn's Writing in the Late Middle Ages', in *Women's Literary Cultures in the Global Middle Ages: Speaking Internationally*, ed. by Kathryn Loveridge, Liz Herbert McAvoy, Sue Niebrzydowski, and Vicki Kay Price (Cambridge: D. S. Brewer, 2023), pp. 209–24

Hibbard, Laura A., *Mediæval Romance in England: A Study of the Sources and Analogues of the Non-Cyclic Metrical Romances* (New York: Franklin, 1924; repr. 1969)

Hicks, Edward, *Sir Thomas Malory: His Turbulent Career* (Cambridge, MA: Harvard University Press, 1928; repr. 2014)

Hildebrand, Kristina, '"I love nat to be constreyned to love": Launcelot and Coerced Sex', *Arthuriana*, 37 (2022), 175–92

Hochman, Adam, 'Is "Race" Modern? Disambiguating the Question', *Du Bois Review*, 16.2 (2020), 647–65

Hoffman, Donald L., 'Dinadan: The Excluded Middle', *Tristania*, 10.1–2 (1984–85), 3–16

Holford, Matthew, 'History and Politics in *Horn Child and Maiden Rimnild*', *Review of English Studies*, 57.229 (2006), 149–68

Hordis, Sandra M., 'Gender Anxiety and Dialogic Laughter in Malory's *Morte Darthur*', in *Medieval English Comedy*, ed. by Sandra M. Hordis and Paul Hardwick (Turnhout: Brepols, 2007), pp. 145–70

Hosington, Brenda, 'The Englishing of the Comic Technique in Hue de Rotelande's *Ipomedon*', in *Medieval Translators and Their Craft*, ed. by Jeanette Beer (Kalamazoo: Medieval Institute Publications, 1989), pp. 247–63

van Houts, Elisabeth, *Married Life in the Middle Ages, 900–1300* (Oxford: Oxford University Press, 2019)

Hsy, Jonathan, *Antiracist Medievalisms: From 'Yellow Peril' to Black Lives Matter* (Leeds: Arc Humanities Press, 2021)

Hsy, Jonathan, and Julie Orlemanski, 'Race and Medieval Studies: A Partial Bibliography', *postmedieval*, 8 (2017), 500–31

Hume, Cathy, 'The Auchinleck *Adam and Eve*: An Exemplary Family Story', in *The Auchinleck Manuscript: New Perspectives*, ed. by Susanna Fein (York: York Medieval Press, 2016), pp. 36–51

————, *Chaucer and the Cultures of Love and Marriage* (Cambridge: D. S. Brewer, 2012)

————, '"The name of soveraynetee": The Private and Public Faces of Marriage in *The Franklin's Tale*', *Studies in Philology*, 105.3 (2008), 284–303

Hume, Kathryn, 'Structure and Perspective: Romance and Hagiographic Features in the Amicus and Amelius Story', *Journal of English and Germanic Philology*, 69.1 (1970), 89–107

Huot, Sylvia, *From Song to Book: The Poetics of Writing in Old French Lyric and Lyrical Narrative Poetry* (Ithaca: Cornell University Press, 1987)

Huppé, Bernard F., 'Rape and Woman's Sovereignty in the *Wife of Bath's Tale*', *Modern Language Notes*, 63.6 (1948), 378–81

Jauss, Hans Robert, *Toward an Aesthetic of Reception*, trans. by Timothy Bahti (Minneapolis: University of Minnesota Press, 1982)

Johnson, David F., '"A grete bourder and a passynge good knyght": Sir Dinadan: "Gareth with a Twist"', *Arthurian Literature*, 37 (2022), pp. 49–65

Johnston, Michael, 'New Evidence for the Social Reach of "Popular Romance": The Books of Household Servants', *Viator*, 43.2 (2012), 303–31

————, *Romance and the Gentry in Late Medieval England* (Oxford: Oxford University Press, 2014)

————, 'Two Leicestershire Romance Codices: Cambridge, University Library MS Ff.2.38 and Oxford, Bodleian Library MS Ashmole 61', *Journal of the Early Book Society*, 15 (2012), 85–100

Johnstone, Boyda, '"Far semed her hart from obeysaunce": Strategies of Resistance in *The Isle of Ladies*', *Studies in the Age of Chaucer*, 41 (2019), 301–24

Jost, Jean E., 'Hearing the Female Voice: Transgression in *Amis and Amiloun*', *Medieval Perspectives*, 10 (1995), 116–32

————, 'Intersecting the Ideal and the Real, Chivalry and Rape, Respect and Dishonor: The Problematics of Sexual Relationships in *Troilus and Criseyde, Athelston*, and *Sir Tristrem*', in *Sexuality in the Middle Ages and Early Modern Times*, ed. by Albrecht Classen (Berlin: de Gruyter, 2008), pp. 599–632

Kahf, Mohja, *Western Representations of the Muslim Woman: From Termagant to Odalisque* (Austin: University of Texas Press, 1999)

Kalinke, Marianne E., *Bridal-Quest Romance in Medieval Iceland* (Ithaca: Cornell University Press, 1990)

Karras, Ruth Mazo, *From Boys to Men: Formations of Masculinity in Late Medieval Europe* (Philadelphia: University of Pennsylvania Press, 2003)

————, *Sexuality in Medieval Europe: Doing Unto Others*, 2nd edn (London: Routledge, 2012)

Kato, Tomomi, *A Concordance to the Works of Sir Thomas Malory* (Tokyo: University of Tokyo Press, 1974)

Kaufman, Amy S., 'The Law of the Lake: Malory's Sovereign Lady', *Arthuriana*, 17.3 (2007), 56–73

————, 'Malory and Gender', in *A New Companion to Malory*, ed. by Megan G. Leitch and Cory James Rushton (Cambridge: D. S. Brewer, 2019), pp. 164–76

Kay, Sarah, *Subjectivity in Troubadour Poetry* (Cambridge: Cambridge University Press, 1990)

Kelley, Jacob, and Andrea Arce-Trigatti, 'Heteropatriarchy', in *Encyclopedia of*

Queer Studies in Education, ed. by Kamden K. Strunk and Stephanie Anne Shelton (Leiden: Brill, 2022), 256–9

Kellner, Leon, 'Introduction', in *Blanchardyn and Eglantine, c. 1489*, ed. by Leon Kellner, EETS, e. s., 58 (Oxford: Oxford University Press, 1890), pp. v–cxxvi

Kennedy, Beverly, 'Adultery in Malory's *Le Morte d'Arthur*', *Arthuriana*, 7.4 (1997), 63–91

Kim, Dorothy, and M. W. Bychowski, eds, *Visions of Medieval Trans Feminism* (= *Medieval Feminist Forum*, 55.1 (2019))

Kinoshita, Sharon, *Medieval Boundaries: Rethinking Difference in Old French Literature* (Philadelphia: University of Pennsylvania Press, 2006)

Kinoshita, Sharon, and Peggy McCracken, *Marie de France: A Critical Companion* (Cambridge: D. S. Brewer, 2012)

Knapp, Peggy, *Time-Bound Words: Semantic and Social Economies from Chaucer's England to Shakespeare's* (Basingstoke: Macmillan, 2000)

Knox, Philip, *The 'Romance of the Rose' and the Making of Fourteenth-Century English Literature* (Oxford: Oxford University Press, 2022)

Kratins, Ojars, 'The Middle English *Amis and Amiloun*: Chivalric Romance or Secular Hagiography?', *PMLA*, 81.5 (1966), 347–54

Krueger, Roberta L., 'Misogyny, Manipulation, and the Female Reader in Hue de Rotelande's *Ipomedon*', in *Courtly Literature: Culture and Context*, ed. by Keith Busby and Erik Kooper (Amsterdam: Benjamins, 1990), pp. 395–409

———, *Women Readers and the Ideology of Gender in Old French Verse Romance* (Cambridge: Cambridge University Press, 1993)

Kruger, Steven F., 'Conversion and Medieval Sexual, Religious, and Racial Categories', in *Constructing Medieval Sexuality*, ed. by Karma Lochrie, Peggy McCracken, and James A. Schultz (Minneapolis: University of Minnesota Press, 1997), pp. 158–79

Kukla, Quill R., 'A Nonideal Theory of Sexual Consent', *Ethics*, 131.2 (2021), 270–92

Kukla, Rebecca, 'That's What She Said: The Language of Sexual Negotiation', *Ethics*, 129.1 (2018), 70–97 [cited as per author's preference]

La Farge, Catherine, 'Launcelot in Compromising Positions: Fabliau in Malory's "Tale of Sir Launcelot du Lake"', in *Blood, Sex, Malory: Essays on the 'Morte Darthur'*, ed. by David Clark and Kate McClune (= *Arthurian Literature*, 28 (2011)), pp. 181–97

LaFleur, Greta, Masha Raskolnikov, and Anna Kłosowska, eds, *Trans Historical: Gender Plurality before the Modern* (Ithaca: Cornell University Press, 2021)

Larrington, Carolyne, 'English Chivalry and Sir Gawain and the Green Knight', in *A Companion to Arthurian Literature*, ed. by Helen Fulton (Chichester: Wiley-Blackwell, 2009), pp. 264–76

———, 'Gender/Queer Studies', in *Handbook of Arthurian Romance: King Arthur's Court in Medieval European Literature*, ed. by Leah Tether and Johnny McFadyen (Berlin: de Gruyter, 2017), pp. 259–72

———, *King Arthur's Enchantresses: Morgan and Her Sisters in Arthurian Tradition* (London: Tauris, 2006)

———, '"This was a sodeyn love": Ladies Fall in Love in Medieval Romance', in *Medieval Romance, Arthurian Literature: Essays in Honour of Elizabeth*

Archibald, ed. by A. S. G. Edwards (Cambridge: D. S. Brewer, 2021), pp. 93–110

Le Saux, Françoise, 'From *Ami* to *Amys*: Translation and Adaptation in the Middle English *Amys and Amylion*', in *The Formation of Culture in Medieval Britain: Celtic, Latin, and Norman Influences on English Music, Literature, History, and Art*, ed. by Françoise Le Saux (Lewiston: Mellen, 1995), pp. 111–27

Lee, Christina, 'Healing Words: St Guthlac and the Trauma of War', in *Trauma in Medieval Society*, ed. by Wendy J. Turner and Christina Lee (Leiden: Brill, 2018), pp. 259–73

Leicester, Jr., H. Marshall, 'The Voice of the Hind: The Emergence of Feminine Discontent in the *Lais* of Marie de France', in *Reading Medieval Culture: Essays in Honor of Robert W. Hanning*, ed. by Robert M. Stein and Sandra Pierson Prior (Notre Dame: University of Notre Dame Press, 2005), pp. 132–69

Leitch, Megan G., 'Enter the Bedroom: Managing Space for the Erotic in Middle English Romance', in *Sexual Culture in the Literature of Medieval Britain*, ed. by Amanda Hopkins, Robert Allen Rouse, and Cory James Rushton (Cambridge: D. S. Brewer, 2014), pp. 39–53

———, 'Introduction, Middle English Romance: The Motifs and the Critics', in *Romance Rewritten: The Evolution of Middle English Romance, A Tribute to Helen Cooper*, ed. by Elizabeth Archibald, Megan G. Leitch, and Corinne Saunders (Cambridge: D. S. Brewer, 2018), pp. 1–24

———, *Sleep and its spaces in Middle English literature: Emotions, ethics, dreams* (Manchester: Manchester University Press, 2021)

Leitch, Megan G., and Cory James Rushton, 'Introduction', in *A New Companion to Malory*, ed. by Megan G. Leitch and Cory James Rushton (Cambridge: D. S. Brewer, 2019), pp. 1–10

Lewis, Katherine J., '"…doo as this noble prynce Godeffroy of boloyne dyde": Chivalry, masculinity, and crusading in late medieval England', in *Crusading and Masculinities*, ed. by Natasha R. Hodgson, Katherine J. Lewis, and Matthew M. Mesley (Abingdon: Routledge, 2019), pp. 311–28

Lewis, Molly, '"Blob Child" Revisited: Conflations of Monstrosity, Disability, and Race in *King of Tars*', in *Monstrosity, Disability, and the Posthuman in the Medieval and Early Modern World*, ed. by Richard H. Godden and Asa Simon Mittman (Cham: Palgrave Macmillan, 2019), pp. 147–62

Lindsay, Sarah, 'Chivalric Failure in *The Jeaste of Sir Gawain*', *Arthuriana*, 21.4 (2011), 23–41

Little, Katherine C., and Nicola McDonald, 'Introduction', in *Thinking Medieval Romance*, ed. by Katherine C. Little and Nicola McDonald (Oxford: Oxford University Press, 2018), pp. 1–10

Liuzza, Roy Michael, 'Representation and Readership in the Middle English *Havelok*', *Journal of English and Germanic Philology*, 93.4 (1994), 504–19

Livingston, Sally A., *Marriage, Property, and Women's Narratives* (New York: Palgrave Macmillan, 2012)

Lochrie, Karma, 'Between women', in *The Cambridge Companion to Medieval Women's Writing*, ed. by Carolyn Dinshaw and David Wallace (Cambridge: Cambridge University Press, 2003), pp. 70–88

———, *Heterosyncrasies: Female Sexuality When Normal Wasn't* (Minneapolis: University of Minnesota Press, 2005)

Lomuto, Sierra, 'The Mongol Princess of Tars: Global Relations and Racial Formation in *The King of Tars* (c. 1330)', *Exemplaria*, 31.3 (2019), 171–92

Lueg, Klarissa, Ann Starbæk Bager, and Marianne Wolff Lundholt, 'Introduction: What counter-narratives are', in *Routledge Handbook of Counter-Narratives*, ed. by Klarissa Lueg and Marianne Wolff Lundholt (Abingdon: Routledge, 2021), pp. 1–14

Maddox, Donald, *Fictions of Identity in Medieval France* (Cambridge: Cambridge University Press, 2000)

Mahoney, Dhira, '"Ar ye a knyght and ar no lovear?": The Chivalry Topos in Malory's *Book of Sir Tristram*', in *Conjunctures: Medieval Studies in Honor of Douglas Kelly*, ed. by Keith Busby and Norris J. Lacy (Amsterdam: Rodopi, 1994), pp. 311–24

Mainer, Sergi, '*Eger and Grime* and the Boundaries of Courtly Romance', in *Joyous Sweit Imaginatioun: Essays on Scottish Literature in Honour of R. D. S. Jack*, ed. by Sarah Carpenter and Sarah M. Dunnigan (Amsterdam: Rodopi, 2007), pp. 77–95

Manion, Lee, *Narrating the Crusades: Loss and Recovery in Medieval and Early Modern English Literature* (Cambridge: Cambridge University Press, 2014)

Mann, Jill, *Life in Words: Essays on Chaucer, the Gawain-Poet, and Malory*, ed. by Mark David Rasmussen (Toronto: University of Toronto Press, 2014)

Marshall, Adam Bryant, 'Sir Lancelot at the Chapel Perelus: Malory's Adaptation of the *Perlesvaus*', *Arthuriana*, 25.3 (2015), 33–48

Martin, Molly, *Vision and Gender in Malory's 'Morte Darthur'* (Cambridge: D. S. Brewer, 2010)

Matyushina, Inna, 'Treacherous Women at King Arthur's Court: Punishment and Shame', in *Treason: Medieval and Early Modern Adultery, Betrayal, and Shame*, ed. by Larissa Tracy (Leiden: Brill, 2019), pp. 288–319

McCarthy, Conor, *Marriage in Medieval England: Law, Literature and Practice* (Woodbridge: Boydell Press, 2004)

McCracken, Peggy, 'Chaste Subjects: Gender, Heroism, and Desire in the Grail Quest', in *Queering the Middle Ages*, ed. by Glenn Burger and Steven F. Kruger (Minneapolis: University of Minnesota Press, 2001), pp. 123–42

———, *The Romance of Adultery: Queenship and Sexual Transgression in Old French Literature* (Philadelphia: University of Pennsylvania Press, 1998)

McDonald, Nicola, 'Desire Out of Order and *Undo Your Door*', *Studies in the Age of Chaucer*, 34 (2012), 247–75

McKinley, Kathryn L., 'The Silenced Knight: Questions of Power and Reciprocity in the *Wife of Bath's Tale*', *Chaucer Review*, 30.4 (1996), 359–78

McSheffrey, Shannon, *Marriage, Sex, and Civic Culture in Late Medieval London* (Philadelphia: University of Pennsylvania Press, 2006)

———, 'Place, Space, and Situation: Public and Private in the Making of Marriage in Late-Medieval London', *Speculum*, 79.4 (2004), 960–90

McSheffrey, Shannon, and Julia Pope, 'Ravishment, Legal Narratives, and Chivalric Culture in Fifteenth-Century England', *Journal of British Studies*, 48.4 (2009), 818–36

Meale, Carol M., '"gode men / Wiues maydnes and alle men": Romance and Its Audiences', in *Readings in Medieval English Romance*, ed. by Carol M. Meale (Cambridge: D. S. Brewer, 1994), pp. 209–25

——, 'Patrons, Buyers and Owners: Book Production and Social Status', in *Book Production and Publishing in Britain, 1375–1475*, ed. by Jeremy Griffiths and Derek Pearsall (Cambridge: Cambridge University Press, 1989), pp. 201–38

——, '"Prenes: engre": an early sixteenth-century presentation copy of *The Erle of Tolous*', in *Romance reading on the book: Essays on Medieval Narrative presented to Maldwyn Mills*, ed. by Jennifer Fellows, Rosalind Field, Gillian Rogers, and Judith Weiss (Cardiff: University of Wales Press, 1996), pp. 221–36

Menuge, Noël James, 'Female Wards and Marriage in Romance and Law: A Question of Consent', in *Young Medieval Women*, ed. by Katherine J. Lewis, Noël James Menuge, and Kim M. Phillips (Stroud: Sutton, 1999), pp. 153–71

——, *Medieval English Wardship in Romance and Law* (Cambridge: D. S. Brewer, 2001)

——, 'The Wardship Romance: A New Methodology', in *Tradition and Transformation in Medieval Romance*, ed. by Rosalind Field (Cambridge: D. S. Brewer, 1999), pp. 29–43

Metlitzki, Dorothee, *The Matter of Araby in Medieval England* (New Haven: Yale University Press, 1977)

Mhishi, Tanaka, *Sons and Others: On Loving Male Survivors* (n.p.: 404 Ink, 2022)

Mieszkowski, Gretchen, *Medieval Go-Betweens and Chaucer's Pandarus* (New York: Palgrave Macmillan, 2006)

Miller, Mark, *Philosophical Chaucer: Love, Sex, and Agency in the 'Canterbury Tales'* (Cambridge: Cambridge University Press, 2004)

Mills, David, 'An Analysis of the Temptation Scenes in *Sir Gawain and the Green Knight*', *Journal of English and Germanic Philology*, 67.4 (1968), 612–30

Minnis, Alastair, 'The Wisdom of Old Women: Alisoun of Bath as *Auctrice*', in *Writings on Love in the English Middle Ages*, ed. by Helen Cooney (New York: Palgrave Macmillan, 2006), pp. 99–114

Morgan, Hollie L. S., *Beds and Chambers in Late Medieval England: Readings, Representations and Realities* (York: York Medieval Press, 2017)

Moss, Rachel E., *Fatherhood and its Representations in Middle English Texts* (Cambridge: D. S. Brewer, 2013)

Mula, Stefano, 'Dinadan Abroad: Tradition and Innovation for a Counter-Hero', in *The European Dimensions of Arthurian Literature*, ed. by Bart Besamusca, Frank Brandsma, and Keith Busby (= *Arthurian Literature*, 24 (2007)), pp. 50–64

Mullen, Michael, 'Rape by Fraud: Eluding Washington Rape Statutes', *Seattle University Law Review*, 41.3 (2018), 1035–52

Nagy, Gergely, 'A Fool of a Knight, a Knight of a Fool: Malory's Comic Knights', *Arthuriana*, 14.4 (2004), 59–74

Neal, Derek G., *The Masculine Self in Late Medieval England* (Chicago: University of Chicago Press, 2008)

Nelson Couch, Julie, 'Defiant Devotion in MS Laud Misc. 108: The Narrator of *Havelok the Dane* and Affective Piety', *Parergon*, 25.1 (2008), 53–79

Newby, Rebecca, 'The Three Barriers to Closure in Hue de Rotelande's *Ipomedon* and the Middle English Translations', in *Cultural Translations in Medieval Romance*, ed. by Victoria Flood and Megan G. Leitch (Cambridge: D. S. Brewer, 2022), pp. 135–52

Newton, Esther, *Mother Camp: Female Impersonators in America* (Chicago: University of Chicago Press, 1972)

Nicholson, Peter, 'The *Man of Law's Tale*: What Chaucer Really Owed to Gower', *Chaucer Review*, 26.2 (1991), 153–74

Norris, Ralph, *Malory's Library: The Sources of the 'Morte Darthur'* (Cambridge: D. S. Brewer, 2008)

Orme, Nicholas, 'Children and Literature in Medieval England', *Medium Ævum*, 68.2 (1999), 218–46

———, *From Childhood to Chivalry: The Education of the English Kings and Aristocracy 1066–1530* (London: Methuen, 1984)

Osterwald, Gwendolyn, 'Contradictions in the Representation of Asexuality: Fiction and Reality', *IAFOR Journal of Arts & Humanities*, 4.1 (2017), 36–44

Parsons, Ben, 'No Laughing Matter: Fraud, the Fabliau and Chaucer's Franklin's Tale', *Neophilologus*, 96.1 (2012), 121–36

Pastoureau, Michel, *Red: The History of a Color*, trans. by Jody Gladding (Princeton: Princeton University Press, 2017)

Pearsall, Derek, 'The Auchinleck Manuscript Forty Years On', in *The Auchinleck Manuscript: New Perspectives*, ed. by Susanna Fein (York: York Medieval Press, 2016), pp. 11–25

Pellegrini, Ann, 'After Sontag: Future Notes on Camp', in *A Companion to Lesbian, Gay, Bisexual, Transgender, and Queer Studies*, ed. by George E. Haggerty and Molly McGarry (Oxford: Blackwell, 2007), pp. 168–93

Peraino, Judith A., *Giving Voice to Love: Song and Self-Expression from the Troubadours to Guillaume de Machaut* (Oxford: Oxford University Press, 2011)

Perkins, Nicholas, *The gift of narrative in medieval England* (Manchester: Manchester University Press, 2021)

———, 'Introduction: The Materiality of Medieval Romance and *The Erle of Tolous*', in *Medieval Romance and Material Culture*, ed. by Nicholas Perkins (Cambridge: D. S. Brewer, 2015), pp. 1–22

Perry, John H., 'Opening the Secret: Marriage, Narration, and Nascent Subjectivity in Middle English Romance', *Philological Quarterly*, 76.2 (1997), 133–57

Perryman, Judith, 'Introduction', in *The King of Tars*, ed. by Judith Perryman, Middle English Texts, 12 (Heidelberg: Winter, 1980), pp. 7–72

Phipps, Alison, 'White Tears, White Rage: Victimhood and (as) Violence in Mainstream Feminism', in *The Politics of Victimhood*, ed. by Sarah Banet-Weiser and Lilie Chouliaraki (= *European Journal of Cultural Studies*, 24.1 (2021)), pp. 1–13

Pickens, Rupert T., '*En bien parler* and *mesparler*: Fecundity and Sterility in the Works of Marie de France', *Le Cygne*, n. s., 3 (2005), 7–22

———, 'Thematic Structure in Marie de France's *Guigemar*', *Romania*, 95.2–3 (1974), 328–41

Pickering, O. S., 'The *South English Legendary*: Teaching or Preaching?', *Poetica*, 45 (1996), 1–14

Piercy, Hannah, 'Desire, Consent and Misogyny in Post-medieval Adaptations of the Pelleas and Ettarde Story', *Arthurian Medievalism*, ed. by Andrew B. R. Elliott and Renée Ward (= *JIAS*, 10.1 (2022)), pp. 5–28

———, 'The Ethics of Community in the *Lai d'Haveloc*', *Le Cygne: Journal of the International Marie de France Society*, 3rd ser., 8 (2022), 53–71

Pitcher, John A., *Chaucer's Feminine Subjects: Figures of Desire in the 'Canterbury Tales'* (New York: Palgrave Macmillan, 2012)

Price, Paul, 'Confessions of a Godless Killer: Guy of Warwick and Comprehensive Entertainment', in *Medieval Insular Romance: Translation and Innovation*, ed. by Judith Weiss, Jennifer Fellows, and Morgan Dickson (Cambridge: D. S. Brewer, 2000), pp. 93–110

Pugh, Tison, *Sexuality and its Queer Discontents in Middle English Literature* (New York: Palgrave Macmillan, 2008)

Pulham, Carol A., 'Promises, Promises: Dorigen's Dilemma Revisited', *Chaucer Review*, 31.1 (1996), 76–86

Purdie, Rhiannon, 'General Introduction: *Ipomedon* in Middle English', in *Ipomadon*, ed. by Rhiannon Purdie, EETS, o. s., 316 (Oxford: Oxford University Press, 2001), pp. xiii–xvi

Putter, Ad, 'A Historical Introduction', in *The Spirit of Medieval English Popular Romance*, ed. by Ad Putter and Jane Gilbert (London: Routledge, 2013; first publ. 2000), pp. 1–15

———, 'Middle English Romances and the Oral Tradition', in *Medieval Oral Literature*, ed. by Karl Reichl (Berlin: de Gruyter, 2012), pp. 335–51

———, *Sir Gawain and the Green Knight and French Arthurian Romance* (Oxford: Clarendon Press, 1995)

Radulescu, Raluca L., 'Genre and Classification', in *A Companion to Medieval Popular Romance*, ed. by Raluca L. Radulescu and Cory James Rushton (Cambridge: D. S. Brewer, 2009), pp. 31–48

Ramey, Lynn T., *Black Legacies: Race and the European Middle Ages* (Gainesville: University Press of Florida, 2014)

Raw, Alice, 'Readers Then and Now: Coerced Consent in *Dame Sirith*', *Studies in the Age of Chaucer*, 44 (2022), 'Colloquium: Historicizing Consent: Bodies, Wills, Desires', ed. by Carissa M. Harris and Fiona Somerset, 307–14

Reddy, William M., *The Navigation of Feeling: A Framework for the History of Emotions* (Cambridge: Cambridge University Press, 2001)

Reichl, Karl, 'Orality and Performance', in *A Companion to Medieval Popular Romance*, ed. by Raluca L. Radulescu and Cory James Rushton (Cambridge: D. S. Brewer, 2009), pp. 132–49

Revard, Carter, 'Oppositional Thematics and Metanarrative in MS Harley 2253, Quires 1–6', in *Essays in Manuscript Geography: Vernacular Manuscripts of the English West Midlands from the Conquest to the Sixteenth Century*, ed. by Wendy Scase (Turnhout: Brepols, 2007), pp. 95–112

Richman, Gerald, 'Rape and Desire in *The Wife of Bath's Tale*', *Studia Neophilologica*, 61.2 (1989), 161–5

Riddy, Felicity, 'Middle English romance: family, marriage, intimacy', in *The

Cambridge Companion to Medieval Romance, ed. by Roberta L. Krueger (Cambridge: Cambridge University Press, 2000), pp. 235–52

Rider, Jeff, 'The Inner Life of Women in Medieval Romance Literature', in *The Inner Life of Women in Medieval Romance Literature: Grief, Guilt, and Hypocrisy*, ed. by Jeff Rider and Jamie Friedman (New York: Palgrave Macmillan, 2011), pp. 1–25

Ríkharðsdóttir, Sif, *Emotion in Old Norse Literature: Translations, Voices, Contexts* (Cambridge: D. S. Brewer, 2017)

——, 'Hybridity', in *A Critical Companion to Old Norse Literary Genre*, ed. by Massimiliano Bampi, Carolyne Larrington, and Sif Ríkharðsdóttir (Cambridge: D. S. Brewer, 2020), pp. 31–45

——, *Medieval Translations and Cultural Discourse: The Movement of Texts in England, France and Scandinavia* (Cambridge: D. S. Brewer, 2012)

Robertson, Elizabeth, 'Apprehending the Divine and Choosing To Believe: Voluntarist Free Will in Chaucer's *Second Nun's Tale*', *Chaucer Review*, 46.1–2 (2011), 111–30

——, 'Public Bodies and Psychic Domains: Rape, Consent, and Female Subjectivity in Geoffrey Chaucer's *Troilus and Criseyde*', in *Representing Rape in Medieval and Early Modern Literature*, ed. by Elizabeth Robertson and Christine M. Rose (New York: Palgrave, 2001), pp. 281–310

——, 'Response: A Telling Difference – Sexual Violence, Consent, and Literary Form', in *Rape Culture and Female Resistance in Late Medieval Literature*, ed. by Sarah Baechle, Carissa M. Harris, and Elizaveta Strakhov (University Park: Pennsylvania State University Press, 2022), pp. 167–80

Robertson, Elizabeth, and Christine M. Rose, eds, *Representing Rape in Medieval and Early Modern Literature* (New York: Palgrave, 2001)

Roger, Euan, 'Appendix 2. Transcriptions and Translations', *Chaucer Review*, 57.4 (2022), 440–9

Roger, Euan, and Sebastian Sobecki, 'Geoffrey Chaucer, Cecily Chaumpaigne, and the Statute of Laborers: New Records and Old Evidence Reconsidered', *Chaucer Review*, 57.4 (2022), 407–37

Rose, Christine M., 'Reading Chaucer Reading Rape', in *Representing Rape in Medieval and Early Modern Literature*, ed. by Elizabeth Robertson and Christine M. Rose (New York: Palgrave, 2001), pp. 21–60

Rouse, Robert [Allen], 'Crusaders', in *Heroes and Anti-Heroes in Medieval Romance*, ed. by Neil Cartlidge (Cambridge: D. S. Brewer, 2012), pp. 173–83

——, 'English Identity and the Law in *Havelok the Dane*, *Horn Childe and Maiden Rimnild* and *Beues of Hamtoun*', in *Cultural Encounters in the Romance of Medieval England*, ed. by Corinne Saunders (Cambridge: D. S. Brewer, 2005), pp. 69–83

——, 'An Exemplary Life: Guy of Warwick as Medieval Culture-Hero', in *Guy of Warwick: Icon and Ancestor*, ed. by Alison Wiggins and Rosalind Field (Cambridge: D. S. Brewer, 2007), pp. 94–109

——, 'Romance and Crusade in Late Medieval England', in *The Cambridge Companion to the Literature of the Crusades*, ed. by Anthony Bale (Cambridge: Cambridge University Press, 2019), pp. 217–31

Royle, Nicholas, *The Uncanny* (Manchester: Manchester University Press, 2008)

Rushton, Cory James, 'The Awful Passion of Pandarus', in *Sexual Culture in the Literature of Medieval Britain*, ed. by Amanda Hopkins, Robert Allen Rouse, and Cory James Rushton (Cambridge: D. S. Brewer, 2014), pp. 147–60

———, 'Gawain as Lover in Middle English Literature', in *The Erotic in the Literature of Medieval Britain*, ed. by Amanda Hopkins and Cory James Rushton (Cambridge: D. S. Brewer, 2007), pp. 27–37

Salih, Sarah, *Versions of Virginity in Late Medieval England* (Cambridge: D. S. Brewer, 2001)

Samson, Annie, 'The South English Legendary: Constructing a Context', *Thirteenth Century England*, 1 (1986), 185–95

Sánchez-Martí, Jordi, 'Noise, Sound and Silence in *Sir Gawain and the Green Knight*', in *Medieval Romance, Arthurian Literature: Essays in Honour of Elizabeth Archibald*, ed. by A. S. G. Edwards (Cambridge: D. S. Brewer, 2021), pp. 111–26

———, 'Reading Romance in Late Medieval England: The Case of the Middle English *Ipomedon*', *Philological Quarterly*, 83.1 (2005), 13–39

Sanyal, Mithu, *Rape: From Lucretia to #MeToo* (London: Verso, 2019)

Saunders, Corinne, 'Affective Reading: Chaucer, Women, and Romance', in *Women's Literary Culture and Late Medieval English Writing*, ed. by Liz Herbert McAvoy and Diane Watt (= *Chaucer Review*, 51.1 (2016)), pp. 11–30

———, 'Chaucer's Romances', in *A Companion to Romance from Classical to Contemporary*, ed. by Corinne Saunders (Malden, MA: Blackwell, 2004), pp. 85–103

———, 'Gender, Virtue and Wisdom in *Sir Bevis of Hampton*', in *'Sir Bevis of Hampton' in Literary Tradition*, ed. by Jennifer Fellows and Ivana Djordjević (Cambridge: D. S. Brewer, 2008), pp. 161–75

———, '"Greater love hath no man": Friendship in Medieval English Romance', in *Traditions and Innovations in the Study of Medieval English Literature: The Influence of Derek Brewer*, ed. by Charlotte Brewer and Barry Windeatt (Cambridge: D. S. Brewer, 2013), pp. 128–43

———, 'Love and the Making of the Self: *Troilus and Criseyde*', in *A Concise Companion to Chaucer*, ed. by Corinne Saunders (Oxford: Blackwell, 2006), pp. 134–55

———, 'A Matter of Consent: Middle English Romance and the Law of *Raptus*', in *Medieval Women and the Law*, ed. by Noël James Menuge (Woodbridge: Boydell Press, 2000), pp. 105–24

———, *Rape and Ravishment in the Literature of Medieval England* (Cambridge: D. S. Brewer, 2001)

Savage, Henry L., 'The Significance of the Hunting Scenes in Sir Gawain and the Green Knight', *Journal of English and Germanic Philology*, 27.1 (1928), 1–15

Schibanoff, Susan, 'Worlds Apart: Orientalism, Antifeminism, and Heresy in Chaucer's Man of Law's Tale', in *Chaucer's Cultural Geography*, ed. by Kathryn L. Lynch (New York: Routledge, 2002), pp. 248–80 (first publ. in *Exemplaria*, 8 (1996), 59–96)

Schultz, James A., 'Heterosexuality as a Threat to Medieval Studies', *Journal of the History of Sexuality*, 15.1 (2006), 14–29

Schwebel, Leah, 'Chaucer and the Fantasy of Retroactive Consent', *Studies in the Age of Chaucer*, 44 (2022), 'Colloquium: Historicizing Consent: Bodies, Wills, Desires', ed. by Carissa M. Harris and Fiona Somerset, 337–45

Seal, Samantha Katz, 'Chasing the Consent of Alice Chaucer', *Studies in the Age of Chaucer*, 44 (2022), 'Colloquium: Historicizing Consent: Bodies, Wills, Desires', ed. by Carissa M. Harris and Fiona Somerset, 273–83

———, 'Whose Chaucer? On Cecily Chaumpaigne, Cancellation, and the English Literary Canon', *Chaucer Review*, 57.4 (2022), 484–97

Seaman, Myra, *Objects of affection: The book and the household in late medieval England* (Manchester: Manchester University Press, 2021)

Sedgwick, Eve Kosofsky, *Tendencies* (London: Routledge, 1994)

Short, Ian, 'Introduction', in *Estoire des Engleis | History of the English*, ed. & trans. by Ian Short (Oxford: Oxford University Press, 2009), pp. ix–liii

Signe Morrison, Susan, 'The Body: Unstable, Gendered, Theorized', in *A Cultural History of Comedy in the Middle Ages*, ed. by Martha Bayless (London: Bloomsbury Academic, 2020), pp. 99–119

Smith Marzec, Marcia, 'What Makes a Man? Troilus, Hector, and the Masculinities of Courtly Love', in *Men and Masculinities in Chaucer's 'Troilus and Criseyde'*, ed. by Tison Pugh and Marcia Smith Marzec (Cambridge: D. S. Brewer, 2008), pp. 58–72

Smithers, G. V., 'Introduction', in *Havelok*, ed. by G. V. Smithers (Oxford: Clarendon Press, 1987), pp. xi–xciii

Somerset, Fiona, 'Consent/Assent', in *A New Companion to Critical Thinking on Chaucer*, ed. by Stephanie L. Batkie, Matthew W. Irvin, and Lynn Shutters (Leeds: Arc Humanities Press, 2021), pp. 27–41

Spence, Sarah, *Rhetorics of Reason and Desire: Vergil, Augustine, and the Troubadours* (Ithaca: Cornell University Press, 1988)

———, *Texts and the Self in the Twelfth Century* (Cambridge: Cambridge University Press, 1996)

Spencer-Hall, Alicia, and Blake Gutt, eds, *Trans and Genderqueer Subjects in Medieval Hagiography* (Amsterdam: Amsterdam University Press, 2021)

Srinivasan, Amia, *The Right to Sex* (London: Bloomsbury, 2021)

Star, Sarah, '*Anima Carnis in Sanguine Est*: Blood, Life, and *The King of Tars*', *Journal of English and Germanic Philology*, 115.4 (2016), 442–62

Stavsky, Jonathan, '"Gode in all thynge": *The Erle of Tolous*, Susanna and the Elders, and Other Narratives of Righteous Women on Trial', *Anglia*, 131.4 (2013), 538–61

Still, Judith, *Derrida and Hospitality: Theory and Practice* (Edinburgh: Edinburgh University Press, 2010)

Strohm, Paul, *Social Chaucer* (Cambridge, MA: Harvard University Press, 1989)

Summit, Jennifer, 'William Caxton, Margaret Beaufort and the Romance of Female Patronage', in *Women, the Book, and the Worldly*, ed. by Lesley Smith and Jane H. M. Taylor (Cambridge: D. S. Brewer, 1995), pp. 151–65

Sylvester, Louise M., *Medieval Romance and the Construction of Heterosexuality* (New York: Palgrave Macmillan, 2008)

Szkilnik, Michelle, 'Medieval Translations and Adaptations of Chrétien's Works', in *A Companion to Chrétien de Troyes*, ed. by Norris J. Lacy and Joan Tasker Grimbert (Cambridge: D. S. Brewer, 2005), pp. 202–13

Tatlock, John S. P., and Arthur G. Kennedy, *A Concordance to the Complete Works of Geoffrey Chaucer and to the Romaunt of the Rose* (Gloucester, MA: Peter Smith, 1963; first publ. 1927)

Taylor, Andrew, "'Her Y Spelle": The Evocation of Minstrel Performance in a Hagiographical Context', in *The Texts and Contexts of Oxford, Bodleian Library, MS Laud Misc. 108: The Shaping of English Vernacular Narrative*, ed. by Kimberly K. Bell and Julie Nelson Couch (Leiden: Brill, 2011), pp. 71–86

———, *Textual Situations: Three Medieval Manuscripts and Their Readers* (Philadelphia: University of Pennsylvania Press, 2002)

Tobin, Prudence Mary O'Hara, ed., *Les Lais anonymes des XIIe et XIIIe siècles: édition critique de quelques lais bretons* (Geneva: Droz, 1976)

Torres, Sara V., '*Sans merci*: Affect, Resistance, and Sociality in Courtly Lyric', *Studies in the Age of Chaucer*, 44 (2022), 'Colloquium: Historicizing Consent: Bodies, Wills, Desires', ed. by Carissa M. Harris and Fiona Somerset, 325–34

Torres, Sara V., and Rebecca F. McNamara, 'Female Consent and Affective Resistance in Romance: Medieval Pedagogy and #MeToo', *New Chaucer Studies: Pedagogy and Profession*, 2.1 (2021), 34–49

Trigg, Stephanie, 'Cloudy Thoughts: Cognition and Affect in *Troilus and Criseyde*', in *Gender, Poetry, and the Form of Thought in Later Medieval Literature: Essays in Honor of Elizabeth A. Robertson*, ed. by Jennifer Jahner and Ingrid Nelson (Bethlehem: Lehigh University Press, 2022), pp. 25–46

———, '"Laughe and pleye so womanly": Feeling Happy' (presented at the 22nd Biennial New Chaucer Society Congress, Durham, 2022)

Turner, Marion, *Chaucer: A European Life* (Princeton: Princeton University Press, 2019)

Turner, Wendy J., and Christina Lee, 'Conceptualizing Trauma for the Middle Ages', in *Trauma in Medieval Society*, ed. by Wendy J. Turner and Christina Lee (Leiden: Brill, 2018), pp. 3–12

Van Duzee, Mabel, *A Medieval Romance of Friendship: Eger and Grime* (New York: Franklin, 1963)

Vinaver, Eugène, *The Works of Sir Thomas Malory*, ed. by Eugène Vinaver, 2nd edn, 3 vols (Oxford: Clarendon, 1967), III

Vines, Amy N., 'Invisible Woman: Rape as a Chivalric Necessity in Medieval Romance', in *Sexual Culture in the Literature of Medieval Britain*, ed. by Amanda Hopkins, Robert Allen Rouse, and Cory James Rushton (Cambridge: D. S. Brewer, 2014), pp. 161–80

———, 'The Many Wives of Potiphar: Rape Culture in Medieval Romance', in *Rape Culture and Female Resistance in Late Medieval Literature*, ed. by Sarah Baechle, Carissa M. Harris, and Elizaveta Strakhov (University Park: Penn State University Press, 2022), pp. 97–113

———, *Women's Power in Late Medieval Romance* (Cambridge: D. S. Brewer, 2011)

Wade, Erik, '*Ower Felaws Blake*: Blackface, Race, and Muslim Conversion in the Digby *Mary Magdalene*', *Exemplaria*, 31.1 (2019), 22–45

Wade, James, 'Confession, Inquisition and Exemplarity in *The Erle of Tolous* and Other Middle English Romances', in *The Culture of Inquisition in Medieval*

England, ed. by Mary C. Flannery and Katie L. Walter (Cambridge: D. S. Brewer, 2013), pp. 112–29

———, *Fairies in Medieval Romance* (Basingstoke: Palgrave Macmillan, 2011)

———, 'Ungallant Knights', in *Heroes and Anti-Heroes in Medieval Romance*, ed. by Neil Cartlidge (Cambridge: D. S. Brewer, 2012), pp. 201–18

Walsh, P. G., 'Introduction', in *Andreas Capellanus on Love*, ed. & trans. by P. G. Walsh (London: Duckworth, 1982), pp. 1–26

Wang, Yu-Chiao, 'Caxton's Romances and Their Early Tudor Readers', *Huntington Library Quarterly*, 67.2 (2004), 173–88

Ward, Jennifer, ed. & trans., *Women of the English Nobility and Gentry, 1066–1500* (Manchester: Manchester University Press, 1995)

de Weever, Jacqueline, *Sheba's Daughters: Whitening and Demonizing the Saracen Woman in Medieval French Epic* (New York: Garland, 1998)

Weiss, Judith, 'Introduction', in *The Birth of Romance in England: The 'Romance of Horn', The 'Folie Tristan', The 'Lai of Haveloc', and 'Amis and Amilun'*, ed. & trans. by Judith Weiss, FRETS, 4 (Tempe: Arizona Center for Medieval and Renaissance Studies, 2009), pp. 1–43

———, 'Introduction', in *'Boeve de Haumtone' and 'Gui de Warewic': Two Anglo-Norman Romances*, ed. & trans. by Judith Weiss, FRETS, 3 (Tempe: Arizona Center for Medieval and Renaissance Studies, 2008), pp. 1–24

———, 'The wooing woman in Anglo-Norman romance', in *Romance in Medieval England*, ed. by Maldwyn Mills, Jennifer Fellows, and Carol M. Meale (Cambridge: D. S. Brewer, 1991), pp. 149–61

Weiss, Victoria L., 'Blurring the Lines between the Play World and the Real World in "The Earl of Toulouse"', *Chaucer Review*, 31.1 (1996), 87–98

Whalen, Logan E., 'A Matter of Life and Death: Fecundity and Sterility in Marie de France's *Guigemar*', in *Shaping Courtliness in Medieval France: Essays in Honor of Matilda Tomaryn Bruckner*, ed. by Daniel E. O'Sullivan and Laurie Shepard (Cambridge: D. S. Brewer, 2013), pp. 139–50

Whetter, K. S., '*Gest* and *Vita*, Folktale and Romance in *Havelok*', *Parergon*, 20.2 (2003), 21–46

———, *Understanding Genre and Medieval Romance* (Abingdon: Routledge, 2016; first publ. Aldershot: Ashgate, 2008)

Whitaker, Cord J., *Black Metaphors: How Modern Racism Emerged from Medieval Race-Thinking* (Philadelphia: University of Pennsylvania Press, 2019)

———, 'Race-ing the dragon: the Middle Ages, race and trippin' into the future', in *Making Race Matter in the Middle Ages*, ed. by Cord J. Whitaker (= *postmedieval*, 6.1 (2015)), pp. 3–11

Wiggins, Alison, 'Imagining the Compiler: *Guy of Warwick* and the Compilation of the Auchinleck Manuscript', in *Imagining the Book*, ed. by Stephen Kelly and John J. Thompson (Turnhout: Brepols, 2005), pp. 61–73

———, 'The Manuscripts and Texts of the Middle English *Guy of Warwick*', in *Guy of Warwick: Icon and Ancestor*, ed. by Alison Wiggins and Rosalind Field (Cambridge: D. S. Brewer, 2007), pp. 61–80

———, 'Middle English Romance and the West Midlands', in *Essays in Manuscript Geography: Vernacular Manuscripts of the English West Midlands from the Conquest to the Sixteenth Century*, ed. by Wendy Scase (Turnhout: Brepols, 2007), pp. 239–55

Windeatt, Barry, '"Love that oughte ben secree" in Chaucer's *Troilus*', *Chaucer Review*, 14.2 (1979), 116–31

——, *Troilus and Criseyde*, Oxford Guides to Chaucer (Oxford: Clarendon, 1992)

——, '*Troilus and Criseyde*: Love in a Manner of Speaking', in *Writings on Love in the English Middle Ages*, ed. by Helen Cooney (New York: Palgrave Macmillan, 2006), pp. 81–97

——, 'Troilus and the Disenchantment of Romance', in *Studies in Medieval English Romances: Some New Approaches*, ed. by Derek Brewer (Cambridge: D. S. Brewer, 1988), pp. 129–47

Wingard, Tess, *Unclean Beasts: Sex, Animality, and the Invention of Heteronormativity, 1200–1550* (forthcoming)

Witalisz, Władysław, 'A (Crooked) Mirror for Knights – The Case of Dinadan', *Studia Anglica Posnaniensia*, 44 (2008), 457–62

Wogan-Browne, Jocelyn, 'Recovery and Loss: Women's Writing around Marie de France', in *Women Intellectuals and Leaders in the Middle Ages*, ed. by Kathryn Kerby-Fulton, Katie Ann-Marie Bugyis, and John Van Engen (Cambridge: D. S. Brewer, 2020), pp. 169–89

Wogan-Browne, Jocelyn, Thelma Fenster, and Delbert W. Russell, eds and trans., *Vernacular Literary Theory from the French of Medieval England: Texts and Translations, c.1120–c.1450* (Cambridge: D. S. Brewer, 2016)

Wyatt, Siobhán M., *Women of Words in 'Le Morte Darthur': The Autonomy of Speech in Malory's Female Characters* (New York: Palgrave Macmillan, 2016)

Unpublished Theses

Ailes, Marianne, 'A Comparative Study of the Medieval French and Middle English Verse Texts of the Fierabras Legend' (unpublished PhD thesis, University of Reading, 1989)

Ford, John, 'From *Poésie* to Poetry: *Remaniement* and Mediaeval Techniques of French-to-English Translation of Verse Romance' (unpublished PhD thesis, University of Glasgow, 2000) <http://theses.gla.ac.uk/2690/> [accessed 20 January 2021]

Wahlgren, Erik, 'The Maiden King in Iceland' (unpublished PhD thesis, University of Chicago, 1938)

Web-based Sources

Bychowski, Gabrielle, 'Were there Transgender People in the Middle Ages?', *The Public Medievalist* (1 November 2018) <https://www.publicmedievalist.com/transgender-middle-ages/> [accessed 17 September 2022]

'Controlling or Coercive Behaviour in an Intimate or Family Relationship', The Crown Prosecution Service (2017) <https://www.cps.gov.uk/legal-guidance/controlling-or-coercive-behaviour-intimate-or-family-relationship> [accessed 27 July 2022]

De Wilde, Geert, et al., eds, *Anglo-Norman Dictionary (AND2 Online Edition)* (Aberystwyth University, 2021) <https://anglo-norman.net> [accessed 18 October 2021]

Bibliography

Halsall, Paul, ed, 'Medieval Sourcebook: Twelfth Ecumenical Council: Lateran IV 1215', *Medieval Sourcebook* (1996) <https://sourcebooks.fordham.edu/basis/lateran4.asp> [accessed 28 September 2022]

Harris, Carissa M., 'Rape and Justice in the *Wife of Bath's Tale*', in *The Open Access Companion to the Canterbury Tales*, ed. by Candace Barrington, Brantley L. Bryant, Richard H. Godden, Daniel T. Kline, and Myra Seaman (2015–17) <https://opencanterburytales.dsl.lsu.edu/wobt1/> [accessed 1 February 2021]

Kim, Dorothy, 'Introduction to Literature Compass Special Cluster: Critical Race and the Middle Ages', *Literature Compass*, 16.9–10 (2019) <https://doi.org/10.1111/lic3.12549>

Kim, Dorothy, 'The Unbearable Whiteness of Medieval Studies', *In the Middle* (10 November 2016) <https://www.inthemedievalmiddle.com/2016/11/the-unbearable-whiteness-of-medieval.html> [accessed 22 April 2023]

McDonald, Nicola, et al., eds, *Database of Middle English Romance* (University of York, 2012) <https://www.middleenglishromance.org.uk> [accessed 28 September 2022]

McSparran, Frances, et al., eds, *Middle English Dictionary*, Middle English Compendium (Ann Arbor: University of Michigan Library, 2000–18) <https://quod.lib.umich.edu/m/middle-english-dictionary/dictionary/> [accessed 28 September 2022]

Medieval Manuscripts in Oxford Libraries (Bodleian Library, University of Oxford, 2017–18) <https://medieval.bodleian.ox.ac.uk> [accessed 28 September 2022]

Proffitt, Michael, et al., eds, *Oxford English Dictionary* (Oxford: Oxford University Press, 2020) <https://www.oed.com> [accessed 1 October 2022]

'RaceB4Race', Arizona Center for Medieval and Renaissance Studies <https://acmrs.asu.edu/RaceB4Race> [accessed 20 September 2022]

Rajabzadeh, Shokoofeh, 'The depoliticized Saracen and Muslim erasure', *Literature Compass*, 16.9–10 (2019) <https://doi.org/10.1111/lic3.12548>

Rambaran-Olm, Mary, and Erik Wade, 'Race 101 for Early Medieval Studies (Selected Readings)', Medium (2020) <https://mrambaranolm.medium.com/race-101-for-early-medieval-studies-selected-readings-77be815f8d0f> [accessed 26 August 2022]

Rose, Steve, 'A deadly ideology: how the "great replacement theory" went mainstream', *Guardian* (8 June 2022) <https://www.theguardian.com/world/2022/jun/08/a-deadly-ideology-how-the-great-replacement-theory-went-mainstream> [accessed 18 August 2022]

'Sexual Offences Act 2003' (2003) <https://www.legislation.gov.uk/ukpga/2003/42/section/1> [accessed 6 January 2023]

Whitaker, Cord J., 'Race and Racism in the *Man of Law's Tale*', in *The Open Access Companion to the Canterbury Tales*, ed. by Candace Barrington, Brantley L. Bryant, Richard H. Godden, Daniel T. Kline, and Myra Seaman (2017) <https://opencanterburytales.dsl.lsu.edu/mlt1/> [accessed 26 August 2022]

yingchen and yingtong, *An Aromantic Manifesto* (Calaméo, 2018) <https://en.calameo.com/read/0056336139d7e661d8f3c> [accessed 21 February 2021]

Index

Volumes Already Published

Printed and bound by CPI Group (UK) Ltd, Croydon, CR0 4YY

09/06/2025

14685698-0003